Leading in Turbulent Times

Leading in Turbulent Times
Managing in the New World of Work

Edited by

RONALD J. BURKE
CARY L. COOPER

Blackwell
Publishing

350 Main Street, Malden, MA 02148-5020, USA
108 Cowley Road, Oxford OX4 1JF, UK
550 Swanston Street, Carlton, Victoria 3053, Australia

First published 2004 by Blackwell Publishing Ltd

Library of Congress Cataloging-in-Publication Data

Leading in turbulent times / edited by Ronald J. Burke, Cary L. Cooper.
    p. cm. — (Manchester business and management series)
    Includes bibliographical references and index.
    ISBN 1-4051-1522-X (hardcover : alk. paper)
    1. Executive ability.   2. Executives—Conduct of life.   3. Leadership.
    4. Organizational change.   5. Crisis management.   6. Work environment.
    7. Personnel management.   I. Burke, Ronald J.   II. Cooper, Cary L.
        III. Series: Manchester business and management.
HD38.2.L422 2004
658.4′092—dc21

                                                            2003001711

A catalogue record for this title is available from the British Library.

Set in 10/12½pt Bembo
by Graphicraft Limited, Hong Kong
Printed and bound in the United Kingdom
by TJ International, Padstow, Cornwall

For further information on
Blackwell Publishing, visit our website:
http://www.blackwellpublishing.com

Contents

List of Figures

List of Tables

List of Contributors

Nancy J. Adler, Professor of International Management, McGill University, Montreal

Ronald J. Burke, Professor of Organizational Behavior, School of Business, York University, Toronto

Philippe Byosiere, Associate Professor of Organization Management and International Business, School of Management, University of Michigan at Flint

David Carnegie, Head of Education Americas, UBS Warburg, Stamford

Catherine E. Connelly, PhD candidate, School of Business, Queen's University, Kingston, Ontario

Cary L. Cooper, BUPA Professor of Organizational Psychology, Manchester School of Management, University of Manchester Institute of Science and Technology

Daniel G. Gallager, Professor of Management, College of Business, James Madison University

Paulette R. Gerkovich, Director of Research, Catalyst, New York

Alvin L. Gibson, Assistant Professor of Business Administration, School of Business, Mount Ida College, Massachusetts

Rachel Gonzalez, Senior Associate, Research, Catalyst, New York City

Jerry Goodstein, Professor of Management and Decision Sciences, Washington State University, Vancouver

Douglas T. Hall, Professor of Organizational Behavior, School of Management, Boston University

Mary A. Hamilton, Assistant Professor of Management, Darden School of Business, University of Virginia

Nicole H. Johnsen, Senior Associate, Research, Catalyst, New York City

Robert B. Kaiser, Director of Research and Development, Kaplan-Devries Inc., Greensboro

Robert E. Kaplan, Co-president, Kaplan-Devries Inc., Greensboro

Ayse Karaevli, Doctoral Candidate, Organizational Behavior Department, School of Management, Boston University

Mary P. Kosarzycki, Doctoral student, Institute for Simulation and Training, University of Central Florida

Suzan Lewis, Professor of Organizational and Work Life Psychology, Department of Psychology, Manchester Metropolitan University

Denise J. Luethge, Associate Professor of Corporate Strategy and International Business, School of Management, University of Michigan at Flint

Mitchell Lee Marks, Independent consultant, San Francisco

Mary C. Mattis, Associate Director and Senior Research Faculty, Center for Gender in Organizations, Simmons College School of Management

Philip H. Mirvis, Organizational Psychologist, private practice

James Campbell Quick, Professor of Organizational Behavior, Center for Research on Organizational and Managerial Excellence, University of Texas at Arlington

Eduardo Salas, Department of Psychology, University of Central Florida

Scott I. Tannenbaum, President, The Group for Organizational Effectiveness, and Consulting Professor, State University of New York at Albany

David Wheeler, Erivan K. Haub Professor of Business and Sustainability, Schulich School of Business, York University, Toronto

Gary Yukl, Professor, Management and Decision Sciences, State University of New York at Albany

Acknowledgments

Most writing starts with a rough first draft. I have been fortunate in having support staff over the years who can take material that I can't even read and make sense out of it, most recently Louise Coutu and Sandra Osti. Their eyesight however is fading. Thanks.

I am grateful to Cary Cooper for over 20 years of friendship. Most of our collaborations begin informally; this collection took shape around the swimming pool at the Sheraton Hotel in Toronto at the 2001 Academy of Management Meeting. I am indebted to our international contributors. We have worked with editorial and production staff at Blackwell for the past five years and have been impressed with their support and professionalism.

Ronald J. Burke

Introduction

RONALD J. BURKE AND CARY L. COOPER

This edited collection is the third in a series published by Blackwell. All were prompted by our concerns about the challenges faced by organizations, organizational responses to these challenges, and the effects of these responses on a number of different stakeholders.

The first, *The Organization in Crisis* (Burke and Cooper 2000), examined organizational restructuring that swept through the industrialized world and downsizing and efforts to revitalize an anxious and cynical workforce. Our contributors came from a number of countries (Australia, Canada, Finland, Israel, Portugal, the UK, and the US) reflecting the worldwide nature of these events. The second, *The New World of Work* (Cooper and Burke 2002), took a more detailed look at the organizational reality that was emerging in the new millennium. The *New World of Work* reflected both the forces that were placing some organizations in crisis as well as adaptive and maladaptive responses to these new challenges.

The 1980s and 1990s saw considerable organizational restructuring, mergers and acquisitions, downsizing, and closures. These events first hit blue-collar workers in the manufacturing sector and later affected white-collar managers and professionals in all sectors. Organizations in both public and private sectors have similarly experienced these transitions.

Millions of workers have lost their jobs through no fault of their own; millions of families have been directly or indirectly affected by these dislocations. Tens of millions of workers who survived these wrenching changes have had to cope with increased job insecurity, heightened levels of stress and increased feelings of anger, cynicism, and aliena-tion. There is evidence that levels of cynicism have increased in the broader society in both North America and UK. The irony is that at least half of these organizational structurings and downsizings failed to realize the financial results that motivated them in the first place. Many were poorly planned and badly implemented, almost always produc-ing emotional turmoil in staff.

The new technology has also served to intensify the work experiences of an increasing number of employees. This technology has quickened the pace at which individuals receive and can respond to others as well as increased the number of hours in the day that an individual can work and the places in which an individual can work. Related to these experiences is the myth that increasing use of technology will produce productivity increases. As a consequence, more attention has been paid to technology at the expense of attention to people. A major reason for the failure of process reengineering efforts in organizations has been the neglect of employees. When anticipated gains in productivity do not materialize, employee morale drops.

Recent events in Seattle, Washington, host city for the World Trade Organization meetings, and events surrounding other such meetings, highlight other international concerns. On the one hand, demonstrators *outside* the WTO meetings were protesting – sometimes destructively – against what they perceived to be the exploitation of workers, the devastation of the physical environment and the undemocratic nature of the WTO, which behind closed doors develops policies that affect millions of people who have no voice in the debate. On the other hand, have-not countries *inside* the WTO refused to support policies advocated by the have countries, which they believed would place their countries at an economic disadvantage.

Concerns were expressed several decades ago about the undue influence that the US, or the West more broadly, was having on the developing world. Fears of US imperialism and domination were commonplace. Such concerns are still being expressed today, often in a narrower sense to refer to the bottom line focus and intense work commitment seen in the US. Colleagues in some EU countries use the phrase the "Americanization" of their industries to capture this notion. The French government attempted to pass legislation reducing the work week but this legislation has been attacked by both employers and groups of workers.

There have also been worldwide efforts to apply a corporate or business model to the organization and management of both government and not-for-profit organizations. This has taken the form of privatization in most of the developed world. While there is some evidence that particular services may be delivered to tax payers with lower cost for a period of time, it is too early to tell whether there are costs related to privatization that are then borne by other publicly funded efforts.

The last decade has also seen increasing interest in developing the high-involvement work organization. While a potentially positive initiative for individuals and organizations, at least as far as work experiences and job performance are concerned, there may be longer term individual well-being and family consequences. And when individuals choose to be at work rather than at home who will take care of the children?

The new employment contract is an exciting concept to some employees. Taking responsibility for one's own career, engaging in self-management of one's career, optimizing one's employability as a free agent in an open market with potential employers bending over backwards to appeal to those high potential employees sounds idyllic. There is also a "dark" side to the new employment contract. Not all individuals are young, educated, computer literate, interpersonally skilled, flexible, adaptable and eager to learn. What about them?

There is also increasing tension on the work–family front. As women increase their participation in the workforce, and as more women move into more demanding managerial roles, women, men and families are increasingly challenged by these demands.

Technological advances have made it possible to work more hours per day, in more locations and at greater distances from home or office. Recent Canadian data have shown that increasing levels of employee absenteeism is costing firms billions of dollars per year in lost productivity as employees take time off work to take care of home and family needs.

The income disparity between the top and bottom organizational levels likewise continues to grow. Real income of most workers in the industrialized world has basically remained flat, or decreased in some cases, over the past decade. Although some organizations are doing better, many of their employees are not. It was recently reported that the richest individual in Mexico has as much wealth as the bottom 15 million Mexicans.

There is no doubt that developed countries have generally raised the standard of living of many of their citizens. Individuals are more likely to report greater income and more creature comforts now than 20 years ago. But has the increase in individual and social wealth brought about corresponding increases in happiness and well-being? The best available incidence suggests that the answer is no. "Doing better but feeling the same" summarizes much of the research findings.

Some of the dramatic changes affecting work and organizations include increased global competition, the impact of information technology, the reengineering of business processes, smaller companies that employ fewer people, the shift from making a product to providing a service, and the increasing disappearance of the job as a fixed collection of tasks. These forces have produced wrenching changes in all industrialized economies. These changes have impacted most profoundly in terms of job losses.

The increasing globalization of business has exposed many organizations to more competition than they have ever experienced before. Differential wage rates between developed and developing countries have added to these pressures. One implication of these forces is that companies are increasingly concerned about managing their costs. Levels of management have been removed; cost cutting has taken place.

Now concepts of management, organization and work have been introduced. Management has become more informational, based on knowledge workers, knowledge, management, and learning organization concepts. Organizational structures have also changed dramatically from hierarchical command and control structures to flatter, network structures. Organizations are increasingly becoming flexible, more people centered, and fluid.

The pattern of employees' daily working lives has also changed dramatically. Career structures have been most heavily impacted. More employees are insecure; motivation and commitment have been reduced and loyalty may be dead. There is also a sense that many employing organizations have handled these transitions in the employment relationship badly.

The new world of work is also characterized by inceasing diversity among employees. Dimensions among which employees may differ include gender, age, marital status, parental status, race, ethnicity, education, sexual orientation, job tenure and experience, and physical disability. There is a sense that diversity has both potential benefits as well as disadvantages. The benefits include a more inclusive and representative workforce, a workforce that mirrors prospective customers and clients resulting in better products and services, and more innovation as a consequence of the existence of multiple perspectives.

Disadvantages are thought to include heightened tensions between various subgroups and more flexibility in meeting these needs.

Organizations are also facing greater challenges in motivating and managing a workforce whose members include several generations of employees, each having unique attitudes and values, many of which are significantly different across these generations.

Family structures have also changed. Historically as organizations emerged and grew in the early 1900s the typical employee was a married man with a partner who was employed as a homemaker and who shouldered almost all of the family responsibilities. Today this pattern represents about 15 percent of family structures. This raises huge needs for flexibility on the part of organizations and adaptability or resilience on the part of individuals and families.

There is also a belief that teamwork and the use of teams will be a major factor in the way work is carried out. Project teams and project management will be more common. This focus places a much higher emphasis on the "softer" skills, interpersonal competencies such as listening, communication, conflict management, negotiation and coaching without reducing the technical and competitive requirements necessary to perform successfully in newly evolving jobs.

This collection, *Leading in Turbulent Times*, is a natural extension of our two earlier collections. It highlights the crucial role of organizational leadership in responding in innovative ways to even more demanding local and global challenges in an environment that is becoming increasingly turbulent. Emery and Trist (1973) first called attention to increasing environmental turbulence almost 30 years ago. Turbulent times are reflected by change, speed, complexity, uncertainty, ambiguity, unpredictability, interdependence, and chaos. The events of September 11, followed shortly thereafter by the collapse of Enron and the Arthur Andersen scandal, are illustrative of turbulent times.

These events are only a sample of the global challenges facing those entrusted with leading private and public sector organizations. Our international contributors examine the type of leading that is needed to address these challenges, the kinds of organizations likely to be up to this task, initiatives that have proven successful in contributing to high performance in these turbulent times, and how those leading organizations maintain their own balance and focus.

Many of the readers of this collection will be researchers and educators associated with schools of business administration and management. Those of us teaching and managing in schools of business and management have a special role to play by virtue of our responsibilities in educating men and women for leading in turbulent times.

North American confidence in our largest corporations is at an all time low. Stories in the popular press highlight the lack of ethics and the lack of standards, ironic since ethical issues have been the topic of increased discussion and education in both university business management programs and corporations.

While not all those implicated in recent scandals had business education, many did and those that did not were advised by them. What kinds of ethics were Jeffrey Skilling of Enron and the Wall Street analysts who encouraged investors to buy stocks they knew to be junk taught in their business management programs? We believe that schools of business management need to take some responsibility for what they teach their students.

Business schools did not create the current scandals and crises in North American corporations. But the climate that produces and tolerates such actions likely starts and is perpetuated in schools of business. As Mintzberg, Simons, and Basu (2002) suggest, ethics in business must be part of a way of life, selflessness must replace selfishness and being responsible to the larger community needs to come before self. Business school educators can be central to reforming the profession of management and the essence of leading in increasingly turbulent times.

The Great Divide

We have written previously about the gap between research and practice. And although concerns about this gap have also been raised by others, there is little evidence that it is being closed.

Rynes, Bartunek, and Daft (2001) conclude that academic research has become less useful in solving the practical problems of managers. The gulf between the science and practice of management is widening. There is increasing concern that findings from academic and consulting studies are not useful for managers and do not get implemented (Beer 2001).

The basic challenge for academics in business schools is to contribute to both the science and the practice of management. Academics need to address questions and anomalies arising in management practice, conduct rigorous research that examines these questions but also translate research findings to both contribute knowledge to our scientific discipline and advance the practice of management (Van de Ven 2002).

In this collection we have invited contributions by researchers who have reputations for attempting to bridge the gap. Some are consultants to organizations; all have done applied research. We hope our efforts to provide guidance to both researchers and managers can be seen in the chapters that follow.

The fifteen chapters in this collection have been grouped into four sections: Leading Self, Leading Others, Leading on Issues, and Leading Change. We think this grouping addresses areas that are critical for leading in turbulent times.

Part I puts the spotlight on those men and women leading in turbulent times. In the first chapter, we set the stage for much of what follows in the rest of the collection. One only needs to look back at events of the past year to understand the meaning of the word turbulent. The next two chapters emphasize self-development, renewal, and balance. The final chapter in this section proposes models of leading likely to be relevant in the current business and organizational environment.

Part II focuses on the difficult task of managing others. There is increasing use of a variety of team structures to unleash human potential and contribution. These efforts involve not only new breeds of employees with somewhat unique experiences and needs but also a variety of employment arrangements.

The four chapters in Part III tackle issues that have been critical for peak performing organizations. These include corporate governance, business and the environment, work–family integration and employee health and well-being.

The final section, Part IV, highlights the necessity of bringing about constructive change by those entrusted with leading in turbulent times. Four areas of ongoing change are considered: enhancing knowledge and learning, creating workplaces where employee differences can be harnessed in support of company objectives, managing a range of organizational transitions and supporting women's advancement to more senior leadership roles.

NOTES

Preparation of this introduction was supported in part by the School of Business, York University and the Manchester School of Management, University of Manchester Institute of Science and technology. Louise Coutu prepared the manuscript.

REFERENCES

Beer, M. 2001. Why management research findings are unimplementable: An action science perspective. *Reflections* 2:58–65.

Burke, R. J., and Cooper, C. L. 2000. *The Organization in Crisis*. Oxford: Blackwell.

Cooper, C. L., and Burke, R. J. 2002. *The New World of Work*. Oxford: Blackwell.

Emery, F. E., and Trist, E. L. 1973. *Toward a Social Ecology*. London: Tavistock.

Mintzberg, H., Simons, R., and Basu, K. 2002. Beyond selfishness <http://p:// www.henrymintzberg.com>.

Rynes, S. L., Bartunek, J. M., and Daft, R. L. 2001. Across the great divide: Knowledge creation and transfer between practitioners and academics. *Academy of Management Journal* 44:340–55.

Van de Ven, A. H. 2002. Presidential address: Strategic directions for the Academy of Management. This Academy is for you! *Academy of Management Review* 27:171–84.

Part I

Leading Self

1

Leading in Turbulent Times: Issues and Challenges

RONALD J. BURKE AND CARY L. COOPER

As Yogi Berra was reported to have said, "The future ain't what it used to be." We have previously chronicled the many changes and challenges that managers in organizations throughout the world are having to address (Burke and Cooper 2000; Cooper and Burke 2002). These include the globalization of business, heightened competition, increased use of technology, a premium on speed often reflected in shorter product lifecycles, a more educated and demanding workforce, a more racially and ethnically diverse workforce, more sophisticated consumers and greater demands for efficiency, effectiveness, and innovation (Capelli 1999).

These changes are obviously reflected in the managerial job and the shape of organizations themselves. The managerial job has become more demanding on many fronts (Hammer 2001). More managers today live in a fishbowl subject to greater scrutiny from multiple stakeholders. Managers are facing greater pressures to achieve both short-term and long-term results. The challenges managers are now facing are also increasingly complex. Managers are encouraged to employ the latest approaches to their jobs: empowerment, teamwork, delegation, benchmarking, total quality management, leveraging diversity, and change-readiness among them (Lawler 2002). In addition managers need time to reflect on their own experiences and learn from them, to take care of their personal needs for replenishment and development, and to maintain high levels of focus, energy, and health (Loehr and Schwartz 2001). Among the consequences of these requirements are the increased terminations of managers, increases in the voluntary departures of managers, and decreases in the length of time CEOs are remaining in their jobs. CEOs worldwide are more likely to be forced from office than to die while in office or leave on their own accord. In 1995, 72 percent either died or left voluntarily; in 2001, only 47 percent died or left voluntarily. CEOs continue only as long as they perform at exceptional levels.

Organizational forms have also changed dramatically during the past decade (Lawler 1996). More organizations have restructured, merged, acquired, downsized, outsourced, and divested and this has been accompanied by reductions in levels of hierarchy, the realization of network organizations and the emergence of virtual organizations (Burke 2002; Cascio 2002). These new forms of organizations, and changes to older organization forms, have also impacted those responsible for leading in significant ways. New competencies are required such as leading from a distance, influencing colleagues through personal rather than coercive approaches, and being responsive to unanticipated changes.

Leading in turbulent times is a tall order. This chapter presents an overview of the new landscape as well as setting the stage for the remainder of the collection. It identifies the challenges that face managers in increasingly turbulent times and suggests skills and actions for managers wanting to better understand how to proactively respond to them. The chapter addresses the following:

- leading
- a turbulent environment
- new and unexpected challenges
- ongoing challenges

Leading

The irony is that while students increasingly flock to and graduate from business schools, there is a shortage of leaders (Grove 1999). There are tens of thousands of articles on leading and it is not possible to review and integrate this vast body of work here. However, we have found the writings of John Kotter to be particularly relevant to the challenges at hand as we see them.

Kotter (1999) states that most organizations today lack the leadership they need and that this leadership deficit is large. Interestingly, this lack of leadership is not a function of a shortage of talent or effort. Rather, few individuals are providing the leadership now needed. And as the environment becomes more turbulent, leadership becomes even more critical. Effective leadership can impact on factors both inside and outside the organization. With inadequate leadership, firms fail or underperform. Leaders must bring about change. Leaders must function in a complex array of relationships. Leaders must anticipate and respond to changes in the contexts in which they work that are being driven by technology, the globalization of competition and markets, and changing workforce characteristics. Leadership style is not the issue; leadership substance is. These changes result in greater speed and less stability that demands more from managers, particularly in terms of bringing about change (reengineering, restructuring, restrategizing, quality management, culture change, mergers, and acquisitions).

Leading is different from managing. Leading is "the development of vision and strategies, the alignment of relevant people behind these strategies, and the empowerment of individuals to make the vision happen, despite obstacles" (Kotter 1999, 10). Managing involves "keeping the current system operating through planning budgeting, organizing, staffing, controlling, and problem solving" (Kotter 1999, 10). Leading and managing serve different purposes in organizations. Leading produces change; managing keeps the current systems operating. Management is about coping with complexity; leadership is about coping with change. Organizations need both. Managers must combine leading and managing, maintenance and change, and the use of hierarchy as well as personal networks. Kotter believes that most organizations are overmanaged and underled.

However, it is not good enough to identify what successful managers and effective organizations are doing *now*. It is also important to anticipate some of the changes that are likely to occur and to proactively address these new challenges. Increasing environmental turbulence has created an atmosphere of change and uncertainty that requires new abilities to be successfully addressed. Managers and their organizations are facing wave after wave of change, posing both challenges and opportunities. Leaders must be proactive and future oriented. In addition, leading relates not only to business activities but also to how individuals manage their lives and the balance between self, family, work, health, and social activities.

Leading also includes representing your organization to the outside world. Dowling (2001) believes that strengthening a company's corporate image and reputation builds a strategic advantage over one's competitors. Leaders play a key role in establishing an organization's reputation. Important contributions to a corporate reputation include vision and mission statements in implementing company policies and the important role played by organizational culture and company communications in conveying an organization's goals and values to stakeholders. Employees must be treated as first-class citizens: many groups of stakeholders must be addressed, and time and money must be spent to implement a company's vision.

Watkins, Edwards, and Thakrar (2001) make the point that as a consequence of 9–11, business leaders and the public are placing new demands on government to act in several market areas. Governments are being asked to increase airline security, provide emergency financing for airlines, help airline workers who lost jobs, rebuild damaged areas of New York City, deal with the anthrax scare, and pass anti-terrorism legislation. All of these efforts will increase the role of governments in markets and society. Business leaders more than ever need to understand the importance of building relationships with the government agencies that affect their organziations.

Business leaders have both a right and an obligation to help governments shape their decisions and rules. This involves the development of relationships with elected and appointed government officials, regulators, suppliers, buyers, public interest organizations, and other stakeholders.

A Turbulent Environment

Being a manager 50 years ago was simple. Competitors were few and local, suppliers were local, and employees were relatively homogeneous (white males). When the manager went to bed at night and when he (yes, he) awoke the next morning, the world he entered was identical to the world he had left the night before. That is not the reality in the twenty-first century. A challenge we offer to our MBA students when they wake up each day is to examine media coverage of business and world events and identify those events that occurred overnight that were unanticipated. Welcome to a turbulent environment.

The notion of an increasingly turbulent environment first emerged in the late 1960s. Somewhat surprisingly, writing on this subject since then has been limited. Some writers make reference to increasing environmental turbulence, raising potential implications of this for managing, but do not go much further (Aldrich 1979).

Organizational environments are becoming increasingly turbulent as a result of more rapid change, more complex problems, more interconnections among these events or problems, greater uncertainty about the consequences of one's actions, and an increasing unpredictability of what will happen in the future and when it will happen (Courtney 2001).

Environmental turbulence refers to the extent to which environments are being disturbed by increasing environmental *interconnection* and an increasing rate of interconnection (Emery and Trist 1965; Terreberry 1968). Increasing interconnections lead to externally induced changes due to forces that are hard to identify and therefore difficult to predict and plan for. These factors imply a decrease in organizational autonomy and an increasing inability to plan for the future. Turbulence also includes increases in potential as well as actual linkages between these events.

Turbulence does not imply chaos, but to an increasing causal interconnection that makes it more difficult for managers to understand (read) their environments. The causal links between external events become incomprehensible to executives lacking first-hand knowledge (understanding) of the distant forces at work.

Morgan (1988) uses the term "fracture lines" to refer to "points of change and transformation that have the potential to alter the nature of whole industries, services, and their constituent organizations" (Morgan 1988, xii). Leaders need to identify fracture lines and then specify the competencies necessary to deal with their consequences as they emerge over time. In an increasingly turbulent environment, the pace and complexity of change also accelerates. Many changes are unanticipated, placing a greater need to read and anticipate trends in the environment – to identify fracture lines. Leaders must take a more proactive and entrepreneurial approach to their environment. They must look ahead, seeking to identify problems and opportunities. They must respond to both problems and opportunities, reframing problems as opportunities. Leaders need to unleash the talents and knowledge of staff. This increasingly turbulent environment places more emphasis on learning and innovation (Weick and Sutcliffe 2002). To achieve peak performance, leaders must coordinate and align people through shared values (Katzenbach 2000).

Managerial competencies vary along with the nature of changes in the business environment. Different times demand different skills. Increased environmental turbulence, accompanied by change and uncertainty, demands new abilities in the face of new challenges. Managers must be proactive and future oriented (Morgan 1988) to grapple with the opportunities posed by this new reality. Many of the problems facing an organization reside in the broader socioeconomic contexts in which they operate; global competition, economic growth patterns, government regulations, and social attitudes and values. This is what this book is about.

New and Unexpected Challenges

Events of 9–11

Terrorism is the process of inducing fear in a civil population through violent acts that undercut trust and confidence, while creating a sense of personal vulnerability to random acts of evil.

Zimbardo 2002

The events of 9–11 have had significant short-term effects on some parts of the world. These include a loss of innocence, a heightened sense of vulnerability, the exploitation of freedom, grieving with the families of the deceased, compassion for those who suffered losses, confirming the centrality of the human condition, revitalizing bonds of social connection, recognizing the fragility of life and chance events, and highlighting the need to work less, play more, connect more closely with family and friends, nourish one's roots, and seek meaning and spiritual values in one's daily transactions.

There have been serious economic costs as well. The stock market has not yet recovered. The September 11 attacks on the US will cost property insurers over US$20 billion for claims on the World Trade Center and the Pentagon. The insurance industry will likely pay out over US$40 billion when other costs of property damage and related charges such as business-interruption insurance liability insurance, workers compensation, and life and health insurance losses are included.

The American public did not respond with panic but instead with effective and adaptive action. Panic was prevented by providing timely and accurate information and instructions so the public could make timely decisions. New heroes emerged, ordinary people, volunteers who made sacrifices for the well-being of others.

Aon Consulting conducts research on employee attitudes in the US on a regular basis. Their surveys have two broad objectives: examining the commitment of employees to their current employer and identifying what employers are doing to heighten commitment. They undertook a planned survey in February 2001, but following the events of 9–11 decided to collect new data in October 2001 (Aon Consulting 2001). This time period (2001) also coincided with a slowing American economy. They found that employee responses had generally not changed significantly. Some exceptions were observed however. First, employees indicated a shift in work–life balance priorities with more employees wanting to spend more time with their families. Second, employee commitment to their employers had increased. Third, employees had generally favorable views on how their employers had responded to events of 9–11 as well as on the state of the economy. Fourth, employees expressed less confidence, however, about the future of their own employers.

Employees gave their employers their highest evaluation in terms of managing business issues, lower evaluations in providing for employee safety and effective leadership in helping their workforce deal with the attacks of 9–11 and their aftermaths, and the lowest evaluations in helping employees cope with stress and anxiety arising from the terrorist attacks of 9–11 and future threats. Organizations directly affected by the 9–11 attacks were likely to provide crisis counseling to their employees; employers less directly affected did less or nothing. Employees, following 9–11, had more positive perceptions of their organization's recognition of the importance of personal and family life.

Six months following 9–11, Americans seem to be getting back to "normal," the way things were on September 10. In the months following 9–11, the US was a wounded nation, having suffered the largest attack ever on its soil. In response, the US developed a common project and a higher cause. But the US is also a target. The citizens have generally rallied around President Bush and he has performed in ways that have exceeded the modest expectations many people had for him.

But some things have changed. Americans have a higher opinion of how government can help than they had in previous decades. An increasing number of Americans have invested in family, neighbors and community. Many Americans are now more tolerant of other cultures and religions. More Americans expressed interest in international politics and news. But these increases may only be short lived.

The Anthrax Scare

The anthrax infections of a few letters sent to US politicians and a news anchor following 9–11 have had various effects on the workplace and organizations. A few organizations had to shut down for days or weeks to permit testing and cleaning. A few deaths had also been attributed to anthrax infected letters. Mail is now more closely scrutinized, some hoaxes have been identified with culprits apprehended and punished. Individuals have been encouraged to report potential perpetrators (scientists in particular have taken part in this search). Potential perpetrators have been identified by government officials and anonymous letters have named other potential bioterrorists. This has led to heightened anxiety, paranoia, and bioterrorist conspiracy theories.

Enron

> *Why Enron went bust. Start with arrogance. Add greed, deceit and financial chicanery. What do you get? A company that wasn't what it was cracked up to be.*
>
> **McLean 2001**

The bankruptcy of Enron in the fall of 2001 has given renewed interest to issues that were previously identified but ignored. These include poor quality financial reporting by firms making it difficult for investors to make informed decisions, the separation (prohibition) of providing consulting services to firms that accounting firms audit, concerns about corporate governance, and the roles and responsibilities of corporate directors.

In Enron, as many as 3,000 off-book partnerships were created, at least in part to hide massive debts and inflate profits. A scathing report undertaken by a special committee of

Enron board members blames greed, a corporate culture of "pushing the limits" and manipulation of the financial records as leading to the company's demise.

Enron's board, particularly the six person executive committee, had both Kenneth Lay and Jeffrey Skilling as members; the four other directors had been on the board since the mid–80s and were lacking in financial expertise. The same was true of its audit committee. Of its six members, only two had an accounting background and none had expertise in derivatives. The Board of Directors of Enron either was fooled by senior executives, or went along with shady deals as Enron failed.

Most Enron executives called to testify at Congressional hearings into the company's collapse took the Fifth Amendment (not to testify on the grounds that my testimony may incriminate me). Two key Enron employees were trying to make deals with federal investigators in the US to avoid prosecution or lessen possible criminal liability in exchange for providing testimony (David Duncan, chief auditor; Ben Glison, Enron's former treasurer).

Enron executives were paid huge one-time bonuses of about US$320 million as a reward for hitting stock price targets in 2000 at the same time that executives were improperly inflating the company's profits by a billion dollars. A total of US $55 million in bonus payments were paid to top executives immediately prior to the company's collapse. Kenneth Lay sold around US $100 million of Enron stock in 2001.

Enron filed for bankruptcy court protection in December 2001 wiping out large sums of employee retirement savings and shareholder investment. Both Duncan and Glison were fired by Enron: Duncan for disposal of documents (shredding); Glison was centrally involved in partnerships used to inflate Enron's earnings and hide its debt, also profiting personally from these transactions. Enron admitted overstating its net income for 1997 to 2000 by nearly $400 million or more than 10 percent.

Enron Corp. paid out more than $744 million in cash and stock to its 140 top executives as it was rapidly moving toward collapse in 2001 ($310 million in salaries and bonuses; $435 million in stocks). Kenneth Lay, former chairman and CEO, received $153 million, Andrew Fastow, former CFO, $4.2 million, Jeffrey Skilling, former CEO $35 million, and Mark Trevert, former vice-chairman, received $32 million. Former Enron employees who were laid off stood to collect a maximum severance of $13,500.

The lawyers representing Enron Corp. in its defense submitted a bill for $26.1 million (US) for four months' work. This included $23.8 million in legal fees for 66,276 hours of work performed by 360 lawyers and staff. A charge of $2.3 million covered expenses: $67,000 for taxis, $129,000 for meals, $612,000 for photocopying, and a $40 charge for "professional development." The top three lawyers charged $700 an hour: 56 other lawyers charging between $500 and $605 an hour. Dollars spent on these fees are not available to pay creditors or former employees.

Arthur Andersen

No one would have predicted the demise of Arthur Andersen LLP as recently as one year ago. Although Andersen had been sanctioned and fined for its conduct of audits during the 1990s, it appeared to be no different from the other Big Five accounting firms. Enron changed everything. Andersen was Enron's auditor.

As the investigation of what happened at Enron was launched, Andersen employees in Houston (the headquarters of Enron) and other cities took steps to hinder this investigation by shredding documents. Andersen now faced criminal indictment from the US Department of Justice (criminal obstruction of justice) and the trial began in Houston on May 6, 2002.

Andersen had 55,000 employees in 84 countries in 2001. Since this scandal arose, hundreds of Andersen clients have dropped the accounting firm. Defections are a who's who of worldwide businesses: North East Utilities, Polaris Industries, Brunswick Corp., Valero Energy, FedEx Corp., National Bank of Canada, Abbott Laboratories, Liz Claiborne, Merck, Delta Airlines, Freddie Mac, Sara Lee, Kerr-McGee Corp., and Introgen Therapeutics Inc.

Morale within Andersen offices has plummeted. Employees are afraid they will lose their jobs, and thousands have. KPMG and Andersen have had talks on ways of possibly combining operations outside the US. Andersen units in Switzerland, Spain, China, and Chile have independently announced plans to leave Andersen's global network. Andersen affiliates in other countries (Canada, Spain, Chile) explored breaking away from the international network of partnerships. As this chapter was being written signed arrangements had been undertaken to acquire the operations of Andersen by other Big Five firms in a number of countries worldwide. This raises the daunting task of merging two very different firms such as Deloitte and Touche and Andersen in Canada, for example.

Andersen advised Global Crossing Ltd and Qwest Communications International Inc., as well as other telecommunications clients, on how to structure the controversial "swaps" of network capacity. The swaps may have been used to inflate earnings.

Andersen's insurer has been rendered insolvent. Andersen is now unable to pay settlements it had previously agreed to (including Enron's employees) or future lawsuits. The collapse of Enron and the probable collapse of Arthur Anderson may shift the risk of billions of dollars of liability from Enron to the banks that were financially involved with Enron. A US $25 billion dollar lawsuit has been filed against Enron by former shareholders. CIBC, along with eight US banks, was seen as complicit in the Enron affair because of their knowledge of the questionable partnerships and other transactions, thus knowing Enron's true financial situation as they sold Enron securities to investors.

Should Andersen fail, however, this would create a problem for over 2,000 Andersen clients who would now have to find another auditor. It is unlikely that, because of limited resources, the other Big Five accounting firms would be able to pick up this work.

The US Securities and Exchange Commission (SEC) indicated (March 18, 2002) how clients of Arthur Andersen LLP should handle their regulatory filing requirements following the indictment against Andersen. Clients ending their relationship with Anderson will be permitted to file unaudited financial statements on a temporary basis. Andersen will continue to provide auditing services following GAAP.

A Houston jury found Andersen guilty of obstruction of justice on June 15, 2002 sounding the death knoll of the company.

Ongoing Challenges

How do you know when management is lying? Their lips are moving.

Business Week (May 13, 2002) had as its cover story "Wall Street: How corrupt is it?" Concerns about the workings of the financial system are not new. What is highlighted now is how many stakeholders in the financial system are being implicated in shady or incompetent activities. The *New York Daily News* renamed Wall Street "Crook Street." On June 26, 2002, US President Bush deplored the lack of corporate ethics in America and called on company leaders to clean up their acts or face prosecution. Trust in the financial system itself is at stake.

Trustworthiness of Financial Analysts and Brokers

Financial analysts who research and recommend stock are supposed to be independent and objective in their work. So too are the brokers who market this stock. In light of their recommendations and marketing of Enron stock, however, the trustworthiness of these professionals has been tainted. As former SEC Chairman Arthur Levitt has been quoted as saying, "It is not merely the accounting firm that was to blame for this [Enron] tragedy. It was the Board of Directors that was seduced. It was the security analysts that simply weren't doing their job and had their own levels of conflict. It was the rating agencies, which dropped the ball." He also noted that in early December 2001, at which time Enron stock was trading at roughly 75 cents per share, 12 of the 17 analysts who covered the company rated the stock either a hold or buy. Conflicts of interest are rampant. Sell ratings made up less than 2 percent of analysts' recommendations.

The US SEC has begun an investigation of conflict of interest on Wall Street focusing on the role of research analysts. The New York Stock Exchange and the National Association of Securities Dealers have proposed rules to reduce analysts' conflicts but it is also possible that national standards will be imposed. Analysts touted stocks they believed to be "junk" and "crap" solely to generate investment banking fees.

But despite the flurry of activities over the past year, not much of a tangible nature has happened. No one has gone to jail. Only one individual (David Duncan, partner with Andersen) has been charged. Enron was a problem of greed and opportunity. If no one goes to jail there will be no deterrent effect. If the flaws in the system aren't corrected there will be more Enrons. So far only millions of investors have lost.

Investors are alleging that analysts at brokerage firms were fraudulently promoting stocks of companies with which their firms had investment banking relationships. Several levels and departments of government have begun investigations of at least ten firms. Concerns were voiced about Wall Street's initial public offering (IPO) allocation practices, its selling of partnerships involved in the Enron collapse, the huge fees Wall Street insiders made by advising clients to hold stock in Enron until it went bankrupt. The very integrity of financial markets is being questioned.

Canadian business leaders want tough actions taken against brokerage houses to prevent conflicts of interest. Seventy percent of CEOs and business leaders were concerned about brokerage house conflicts, about the same percentage worried about accounting firms in an earlier poll. About 70 percent of those surveyed supported barring brokerage houses from providing both investment banking to corporations and investment counseling to individual investors to protect counseling independence. Fifty-nine percent indicated that efforts by the New York attorney general were long overdue, and an additional 25 percent said these efforts were somewhat overdue. Seventy percent stated it should be easier to sue brokerage houses whose analysts provide bad advice grounded in conflict of interest. There was, not surprisingly, lower support for the creation of a government agency to supervise and discipline brokerage firms.

Trustworthiness of Securities Firms

Related to the trustworthiness of research analysts and brokers is the trustworthiness of securities firms, under whose auspices these professionals work. Specifically, securities firms have been found accountable for pressuring analysts and brokers to behave nonindependently and nonobjectively in their work. These pressures created conflicts of interest for analysts and brokers, which paralyzed them from behaving according to their professional ethical standards. As President and CEO of the Association for Investment Management and Research (AIMR), Thomas A. Bowman, testified at the Senate Governmental Affairs Committee hearing, "Wall Street analysts [and brokers] are sometimes pressured to be positive about the prospects of the companies they follow." As such the trustworthiness of securities firms has been tainted. Included in Bowman's five key recommendations to reduce and eliminate this pressure are for securities firms to "foster a corporate culture that protects analysts [and brokers] from undue pressure to be positive from the companies they follow" and to "not link analyst [and broker] compensation directly to the success of investment-banking activities."

Trustworthiness of Banks

The trustworthiness of banks has also been tainted. For example, since 1992 Oveseas Private Investment Corporation loaned $544 million to support various Enron projects abroad. The Export-Import Bank of the United States loaned $675 million to companies affiliated with Enron. The biggest lenders to Enron were J. P. Morgan Chase and Citigroup. J. P. Morgan Chase helped to finance the merger that created Enron in 1985, and Citigroup helped Kenneth Lay "pay off" a corporate raider a year later. Citigroup disclosed that its exposure from Enron exceeded $1 billion, and it and J. P. Morgan Chase wrote off more than $680 million against their 2001 fourth-quarter earnings to cover anticipated losses. The immensity of these loans, and their subsequent defaultings – especially to such prestigious and reputable banks – raises the question of whether the capability of banks in general to assess the creditworthiness of potential creditors can be trusted. Furthermore, it has also been speculated that Enron's lenders were strong-armed (by Enron's sheer power and size) into lending the company money. This raises the perhaps more serious question of whether the immunity of banks in general to the duress of large institutional creditors can be trusted.

Swiss and US banks that financed South Africa's apartheid regime are facing a US $50 billion obstruction lawsuit brought on behalf of the victims of apartheid. Finance ministers of G7 countries raised the prospect of sanctions against countries that they experience as uncooperative in their campaigns against tax evasion and money laundering. Although not mentioned by name, Switzerland defended its actions in this regard.

Trustworthiness of Financial Statements

The trustworthiness of publicly issued financial statements has also been tainted. A major source of this has been Enron's perverted use of "special purpose entities" (SPEs). SPEs are suborganizations that parent organizations may create, in order to, among other things, move assets and debts off their statements. The financials of SPEs do not appear on the financials of the parent. Enron created such entities under the guise of them having research and development missions. Since the nature of R&D is to incur years of heavy upfront losses before beginning to turn a profit "no one was the wiser." Specifically, Enron funneled the capital raised by its SPEs back into its (parent) financial statements, while retaining the debt associated with raising this capital in its SPEs. Enron's 2000 annual report lists more than 300 such entities. As a result of this, the trustworthiness of public companies' financial statements in general has been jeopardized. General Electric is a popular cited example of this; of its $500 billion in assets, approximately $55 billion are in SPEs. As a result of the attention drawn to public companies' use of SPEs, many have chosen to incur the penalty of filing their taxes late, in order to get their SPEs "in order."

Xerox Corp. admitted on June 28, 2002, that it had inflated revenue by $1.9 billion and profit by $1.4 billion over a five year period.

Trustworthiness of Auditors

Related to the trustworthiness of public companies' financial statements is the trustworthiness of the auditors who authorize these statements. While their trustworthiness has no doubt been tainted, comments by former SEC Chairman David Ruder, in *Business Week* (January 15, 2002), put this in perspective:

> I think the auditing function is still being handled extremely well. We're not talking about any high percentage of audits. We have 4,000 to 5,000 companies filing audited financial statements every year with the SEC, and the number of poor audits is remarkably small . . . I happen to think that the auditors overwhelmingly are honest and are trying to do the right job, and what we're seeing are the occasional aberrations in their performance. And we need

to be very concerned about it and try to prevent it in the future. But I don't think we can say the system is broken.

While Ruder's comments suggest that the public might take the allegations against Andersen with respect to Enron in stride, their behavior clearly indicates the opposite. Specifically, as at April 30, Andersen is reported to have already lost at least 10 percent of its auditing clients (2,300 to 2,062).

USA Today and the Gallup Poll undertook a survey of 1,001 adults on February 8–10, 2002, on how the public views accountants. Here are some of their results. Only 32 percent rated the honesty and ethical standards of accountants very high or high. Only 56 percent were confident that the audits by major accounting firms provide an accurate assessment of a corporation's financial situation. Fifty-six percent believed that the way that large corporations are audited needs a complete overhaul or major reform. There was also a decrease in percent of respondents who gave accountants very high or high ratings for honesty and integrity: 32 percent in 2002, 41 percent in 2001, and 38 percent in 2000.

Trustworthiness of Regulators and CEOs

Concerns have been raised about the behaviors of regulators and those being regulated. There were "gifts" between Enron officials and regulators/CEOs – conflict of interest (e.g., even President Bush). Why didn't the SEC do a better job to enforce insider-trading rules – with so many already existing rules, how did former Enron CEOs squeak by without having to disclose their exercise of options and large dumps of shares prior to leaving the company? Why were so many CEOs allowed to jump ship when times are tough or when forced to face the heat.

The June 24, 2002, issue of *Business Week* had as its Special Report cover story "Restoring trust in Corporate America." The first page of the story (30) had 16 color pictures of CEOs who have been indicted, arrested, resigned their jobs or were under pressure to resign. CEOs must speak up; business must lead the way to real change. Instead too many CEOs are silent and some have protested against any change.

Trustworthiness of Board of Directors

When it comes to corporate acquisitions, do managers act in the best interest of share-holders or themselves? This question was addressed by Paul Gompers and Joy Ishii of Harvard and Andrew Metrick of The Wharton School. They created a Governance Index for 1,500 US firms between 1990 and 1999. They looked at twenty-four provisions, including poison pills, golden parachutes and super-majority requirements for approval of mergers. Firms with at least 14 of these provisions were grouped in a Management Portfolio, indicating high management power, while firms with 5 or fewer were grouped into a Shareholder Portfolio. For example, in 1990, Kmart Corp. was included in the Shareholder Portfolio.

After adjusting for several factors such as market performance and firm size, the Shareholder Portfolio outperformed the market, while the Management Portfolio underperformed. Firms with weaker shareholder rights tended to have lower profits, lower sales growth and higher capital expenditures.

Byrne (2002) quotes an incoming CEO of a troubled company describing his boardroom "like an aquarium filled with dead fish." Boards should be independent of management and have no special arrangements or interlocking contracts (consulting). Their major role is to hire, oversee and – if necessary – fire the CEO. The CEO should focus on managing the business, not on external relationships: compensation should reflect a "pay for performance" philosophy. The role of board chair and CEO should be split.

In Canada 12 institutional investors with combined assets of $500 billion have joined forces (The Canadian Coalition for Good Governance) to pressure Canadian companies into better corporate governance.

Trustworthiness of Consulting/Accounting Firms

The trustworthiness of consulting/accounting firms has also been tainted. From an economy-of-scale perspective it makes sense for those firms who audit a company's financial statements, and are thus deeply familiar with it, to then provide the company with other consulting services. However, as Andersen's "kick at the can" has suggested, firms may have difficulty separating out their auditing and consulting services so that "one hand does not wash the other." Major companies such as Apple, Borland Software, Freddie Mac, and Walt Disney have already announced that they will no longer use the same firm for both auditing and technology-consulting services. Shareholders of least 30 other companies, including Johnson & Johnson, Motorola, and PG&E, have proposed similar measures. The remaining four of the Big Five have followed suit. Specifically, Deloitte & Touche, Ernst & Young, and PricewaterhouseCoopers have announced plans to separate out their accounting and consulting services, just as Arthur Andersen did roughly two years ago when it separated out its consulting services to Accenture.

Greed

Time magazine (June 17, 2002, vol. 159, 36–9) in a story on Dennis Kozlowski, just resigned CEO of Tyco, wrote that he was fond of saying that "Money is the only way to keep score."

Capitalism has, as an economic system, been shown to produce benefits such as a higher living standard for many people. Unfortunately, some individuals get so caught up pursuing the economic benefits of capitalism that they engage in self-destructive behaviors. Enron has been described as a story of greed. A number of executives ending up in prison for a variety of criminal offenses (fraud, insider trading, embezzlement) have

enjoyed lavish lifestyles funded by their ill-gotten gains. A number of behavioral patholo-
gies (workaholism, coronary prone behavior) have, as an antecedent, the need to prove
oneself, the need to be valued by one's colleagues because of one's possessions (homes,
cars, lifestyles).

There is increasing evidence that working hard, making lots of money or having a con-
spicuously consumptive lifestyle per se are not harmful; rather, the motives for embarking
on these paths are potentially harmful. Srivastava, Locke, and Bartol (2001) found, in
samples of MBA students and entrepreneurs, an association between motives for money
and psychological health. Ten motives for money were considered. MBA students and
entrepreneurs more strongly endorsing motives of social comparison and overcoming self-
doubt also indicated greater psychological distress. There are negative and positive motives
for money.

Ethics and ethical issues are now more commonly discussed in the popular media as
well as in the training of managers in MBA programs. Can you teach ethical behavior?
This is debatable. Courses in ethics certainly highlight the complex role ethics plays in
leading. Managers-to-be are more aware of how ethics is relevant to several areas of
organizational functioning (marketing, finance, accounting, etc.). Individuals who feel a
need to prove themselves by engaging in shady activities so others will esteem them so
they can value themselves are likely to cut corners. Police officers in North America have
been charged and convicted of robbing banks, selling drugs, and stealing money from their
police forces. It is almost certain that these police officers were aware that robbing banks
was unethical.

Cynicism

69 percent say Government corrupt

National Post headline, April 22, 2002

A recent poll of 1,500 Canadians showed that 69 percent believed their federal and
provincial politicians were corrupt. Eighty percent of Canadians wanted major reforms of
rules and regulating the awarding of government contracts.

And also consider that the CEOs of Canada's largest companies saw their compensation
increase 54 percent in 2001 despite an average earnings fall of 13 percent. This trend is a
betrayal of shareholders who have seen their investments diminish severely. This lack of
pay as an incentive encourages mediocrity, neither rewarding CEOs for good performance
nor punishing them for poor performance.

Kanter and Mirvis (1989), in a national survey of American employees, conclude that
cynicism has become widespread in the workplace. Confidence in business leaders fell
from about 70 percent in the late 1960s to about 15 percent in 1988. Causes of cynicism
include a lack of meaningful and challenging work, limited opportunity for advancement and negative managerial styles that lead to disillusionment and disappointment.
Heightened expectations also feed into increased disillusionment. There is a growing gap

between what people want from their jobs and what they get, and the gap between the search for excellence and most company realities has also widened.

Is it any wonder that people are cynical? The mass media over the years has been full of stories showing the widespread hypocrisy between words and deeds.

- President Clinton's statement that it all depends on the meaning of the word.
- Executives get paid huge salaries yet pay almost no taxes.
- Enron paid no taxes and even got a tax rebate.
- Corporate leaders take the Fifth Amendment or if they speak (Jeffery Skilling) they stonewall or remember little.
- Catholic Church sex scandal, hundreds of priests molesting little boys with few punished. The Vatican stonewalls.
- Everybody is doing it (insider trading).
- Doping scandals at the Olympics; fixed judging at the Olympics.
- Greed of athletes, drug use by athletes, and crime committed by athletes.
- Free agents – sell talents to the highest bidder. Loyalty is dead.
- The rise of "paper entrepreneurialism," the dot coms. The widespread shuffling of corporate assets, the millions lost or gained in paper transactions, the massive hirings, firings, and layoffs that continue today. Successful companies still downsize.
- Short-term focus on profits.
- Greed over ideals.
- Buy companies and sell-off assets (asset stripping).
- Golden parachutes; stock options.
- Shoddy goods and services. Deceptive advertising.

Globalization

Globalization is an international system with its own rules and logic that directly or indirectly influences the politics, environment, geopolitics, and economics in almost every country in the world (Friedman 1999). Globalization is the spread of free-market capitalism to almost every country of the world, involving the increasing integration of markets, countries, and technologies. Under globalization you have both the clash of civilizations and the homogenization of cultures, the triumph of free market capitalism and a backlash against it. Countries throughout the world are increasingly being tied together into a single globalized marketplace and village. More countries are now tied together through economics and information (telecommunications). Countries can reach farther, faster, cheaper, and deeper around the world than ever before. The world has been increasingly dominated by the American dollar, the American military, American power, and American culture.

Globalization is creating a backlash from those hurt or left behind by this new system (Friedman 1999). One byproduct of globalization is a winner-take-all ethos. This shows up in greater income inequalities within countries. For example, the incomes of the poorest fifth of working families in the US dropped by 21 percent between 1979 and

1995, adjusted for inflation, while the incomes of the richest fifth jumped by 30 percent during this same period (cited in Friedman 1999). The US had 170 billionaires in 1998 compared with 13 in 1982.

According to a 1999 UN Report, the 20 percent of the world's people living in the highest income countries have 86 percent of the world's GDP, 82 percent of the world export market, 68 percent of foreign direct investments, and 74 percent of the world's telephone lines. The bottom fifth in the poorest countries was about 1 percent in each of these areas. In 1990, 20 percent of the world's people living in the richest countries had 30 times the income of the poorest 20 percent; by 1995, the richest 20 percent had 52 times as much income.

A backlash to globalization began to emerge in the early 1990s, culminating at the 1999 WTO meetings in Seattle. Rapid changes brought about by globalization were producing disruptions to traditional business practices, social structures, cultural traditions, and environments (Stiglitz 2002). Plant closings, downsizings, moving plants to Mexico (and other low-wage paying countries), nonunion workplaces, the need for more education and skills, and increasing numbers of people under threat or who have lost ground were some of the symptoms targeted. Some people have developed a negative reaction to the Americanization of the world. There is both admiration and envy and resentment toward the US.

Others, however, embrace globalization. They realize that if they are to have a better life, an improved standard of living, they must get into the capitalist system (prosperity, freedom, choices). How do we use globalization to benefit more people and countries, the 1.3 billion people in the world still living on one dollar a day? You need better and more accountable governments. The US still is the best example we have of a country well prepared to use globalization for benefit.

As the World Economic Forum concluded in New York in early February 2002, some of the euphoria of globalism appeared to diminish. The developed world was challenged to address high levels of poverty. A parallel forum was held in Porto Alegri, Brazil, by opponents of globalization and free trade (The World Social Forum).

The financial crisis in Argentina threatens to become an equally significant social crisis. The unemployment rate in 2003 is 20 percent. The peso has lost half its value against the US dollar since January 1, 2002. The banking system is insolvent. The recession is in its forty-sixth consecutive month. Inflation is climbing. As the poor become more desperate and disillusioned, Argentina may see a massive social explosion. Compounding this is the likelihood that the recovery plan put together by the current president (the fourth in three months) may be unrealistic and unworkable. Instead more major reforms are needed. The International Monetary Fund would require Argentina to reduce spending dramatically, including large-scale job cuts. The IMF is called the International Misery Fund in Argentina. With unemployment running at over 20 percent, the IMF is making efforts to prevent Argentina's continuing economic troubles from spreading to Brazil, Uruguay, and the Caribbean region.

A coup in Venezuela (April 1, 2002) forced President Hugo Chavez to resign. At least 14 people were killed in street demonstrations with more than 200 people wounded. Venezuela is the world's fourth largest oil exporter but has extreme levels of poverty. A leading Venezuelan businessman had been nominated to replace the duly elected Chavez, but Chavez regained the presidency a few days later. At the time of writing, street demonstrations continue in Venezuela on an almost daily basis.

Is Capitalism Working?

The World Bank *World Development Report: Attacking Poverty*, 2000/2001, classified country economies by estimates of 1999 GNP per capita:

- High-income countries, averaging $25,730 GNP/capita (with individuals earning $9,266 or more), represent 15 percent of the world's population. These include Europe (Switzerland [$38,350], Norway [$32,880], Japan [$32,230]), the United States ($306,000), Singapore ($29,610), Australia ($20,050), Canada ($19,320), and New Zealand ($12,780).
- Upper middle-income countries, averaging $4,900 GNP/capita (ranging from $2,966 to $9,265), represent 10 percent of the world's population. These include Argentina ($7,600), Brazil ($4,420), and Mexico ($4,400).
- Lower-middle income countries, averaging $1,200 GNP/capita (ranging from $755 to $2,995), include 36 percent of the world's population. This includes China, with $780 GNP/capita and 1.3 billion people – the world's most populated country.
- Low-income countries, averaging $410 GNP/capita (with individuals earning $755 or less) are inhabited by 45 percent of the world's population. This includes India, with $450 GNP/capita and nearly 1 billion people – the world's second most populated country.

These are country averages; obviously, great variations exist within countries. There are tremendous social and technical disparities that go with this economic stratification among the countries of this world. For example:

- The adult illiteracy rate varies from 30 percent of males and nearly half of all females in low-income countries to only 1 percent or 2 percent for men and women in high-income countries. In fact, nearly one-third of all women and 18 percent of all men in the world are illiterate.
- The secondary school enrollment ratio – the percent of high school age kids enrolled in secondary school – varies from 51 percent in low-income to 96 percent in high-income countries. As expected, enrollment in higher education drops precipitously below these ratios. One in one hundred people in the world today have a college education.
- And if you think that distance learning and e-commerce over the web can address these disparities, think again. People in low-income countries have only 3 personal computers per 1,000 people, and people in lower- and upper-middle income countries have only 13 and 53, respectively, whereas people in high-income countries have 311 computers per 1,000. Fewer than 1 in 100 people in the world today own a computer.

The citizens and nations of the world are becoming increasingly polarized into the haves versus the have-nots, the rich versus the poor. While the business elites and political elites were in New York City attending the World Economic Forum at the Waldorf Hotel, an antiglobalization conference was being held in Brazil. There is increasing concern that the elites are out of touch with the plight of billions of the world's inhabitants. Pro and anti-globalization forces have fought pitched battles in Vancouver, Seattle, Genoa, Quebec City, Munich, and New York City over the past few years. In the absence of dialogue and part-nerships, it is certain that the backlash and violence these forums have produced will increase.

The magnitude of the economic gap between rich and poor in the US has widened. Shapiro, Greenstein, and Primus (2001) reported that between .1979 and 1997 the after tax income of the poorest fifth of US households fell from $10,900 to $10,800 while that of the top 1 percent of households increased from $263,700 to $677,900. Figures for childhood poverty were roughly the same in 1979 and 1997: of over 12 million children, one-sixth live in poverty. The poverty rate among single working mothers was 19.4 percent, the same level in 1995 and 1999 (Single mothers 2001). The US, along with the other developed countries, is not a classless society.

In 1981, America's ten most highly paid CEOs were paid an average of US $3.5 million; in 1988, the average was $19.3 million; by 2000, the average was $154 million. The wages of top US executives rose 1,300 percent between 1981 and 2000; the wages of ordinary workers doubled. A number of apologies have been offered for these wages. First, these CEOs were rewarded for huge achievements. Most of the top ten made money by selling stock options before their firms experienced financial downturns. Second, nothing can be done to limit the accumulation of wealth. The biggest fears posed by capitalism are not economic but political. The great imbalance of wealth and democracy will be increasingly difficult to maintain in the years to come.

Mintzberg, Simons, and Basu (2002) recently took issue with the short-term focus on shareholder value. Too many companies look good in the short term by reducing staff while increasing job demands and exhaustion of staff. They describe a model of selfishness building on what they term "half-truths": a narrow view of actors as economic men, organizations focusing on shareholder value, leaders as heroes, organizations becoming lean and mean, and a view of society best represented by rising tides of prosperity that improves the lives of everyone. In the 1990s self-interest was on the rise, reaching perhaps unprecedented levels. Greed became an important but unexpressed priority, companies focused more narrowly on shareholder value over the short term, and it seemed as though CEOs alone made organizations successful. They argue that if capitalism only stands for individualism, it too will collapse.

Individuals are more than economic men (and women). A focus on short-term share-holder value pits the interests of those who create the economic performance and those that benefit from it.

Heroic leaders create a gulf between themselves and everyone else. Effective organ-izations can be lean and mean; such organizations can also produce exhausted, angry employees, poor quality products, and unhappy customers. Finally, the evidence indicates that increased economic prosperity has not trickled down proportionately to those at the bottom levels of society.

Mintzberg and his colleagues propose engagement as a concept to balance selfishness. They note the increase in selfless behaviors such as helping, becoming engaged and sensing a collective need in one's larger community. There needs to be a balance between self-interest and selflessness. They challenge directly the glorification of greed. The best way to do this, they argue, is to promote values of trust, judgment, and commitment to promote socially responsible behavior. Engagement is possible.

Rich countries, members of the G7 in particular, have an obligation to help the poorest countries. One initiative that has already been implemented calls for the forgiving of the debts of the world's poorest countries. The World Bank and the IMF have been slow to respond however. To qualify for debt forgiveness countries had to prove they had policies and programs in place to make their economies stable. Few countries have demonstrated this however.

Few wealthy nations attended the UN food summit meetings held in Rome on June 10, 2002. Kofi Annan, UN secretary-general, opened the conference by calling for cutting the number of hungry in the world to 400 million by 2015, a target that looks increasingly unrealistic. World hunger appears to have a low international political priority. The Italian prime minister ended the four day conference early to accommodate a World Cup soccer game featuring Italy. Country delegates seemed to spend as much time shopping and sightseeing as they did grappling with hunger among 805 million starving people world-wide. Some sessions were sparsely attended.

Kim et al. (2000) examine how and why poverty, vulnerability, and social suffering flourish as wealth and technological power increase. Large numbers of people remain poor at a time when much of the world shows growth and material gains from economic prosperity. The structure and current rules of market-led economic globalization widens the gap between rich and poor. These growth-oriented policies have not improved living standards of the poor and have added more suffering.

Conclusions

CEOs are becoming increasingly visible, in some cases achieving celebrity status (Jack Welch, Mathew Barrett, Carly Fiorina). This living in a fishbowl, working under heightened scrutiny, adds to the demands of an inherently difficult job. It has been reported that 45 CEOs of the top 200 US firms left their jobs in 2000, either voluntarily or involuntarily. These departures are increasingly played out in the pages of the business press.

The current recession, compounded by events of 9–11, have heightened performance pressures. An increasing number of firms worldwide have reported below expected returns, in some cases huge losses. Air Canada was expected to announce losses of $1 billion in 2001, an increase over the $200 million loss in 2000.

Organizations today are searching for the best available talent. Demographic realities indicate that this talent is increasingly found in nontraditional employees (i.e., women, people of color). It has been reported that three-quarters of new workforce entrants in this decade will be nontraditional. North American organizations have attempted to leverage this resource over the past ten years with some, but mixed success. It has proven difficult to create new mindsets placing diversity as a central competitive advantage, in a strategic sense, rather than as short-term tactical initiatives. Cross-generational differences in values among traditional employees (white males) also raise significant management challenges (Zemke, Raines, and Filipczak 2000).

The Enron debacle has raised ethical concerns to a central place on the corporate radar screen. This is not a new circumstance. Ethical concerns become a topic of concern whenever a major scandal captures national attention (Watergate, the Savings and Loan scandal, Monica Lewinsky). But when the dust settles it seems to be back to business as usual.

The US treasury secretary Paul O'Neill has called for CEOs to come out publicly against corporate abuses (June 18, 2002). A few other CEOs in North America have also come forward and expressed the same sentiments. In addition, the US Senate Banking Committee and the SEC have proposed accounting committees to review corporate audits.

The scandals of Corporate America are hurting US moral authority. The US has criticized Japan in the past for many of the same events that have recently damaged the US financial system. The US business model and accompanying ideology is now being questioned.

Given a demanding job in turbulent times, how do women and men in senior management maintain their own emotional and physical well-being? How do they achieve an integration of their work and personal lives (Rapaport et al. 2002)? How do they recuperate in times of duress and revitalize their spirits and souls?

Organization leaders today are more than ever required to be abreast of events in their competitive environment both locally and internationally. Cross-culturally, sensitivities have achieved a new status. In addition, more expatriate managers now function in executive positions in other countries.

Organizations continue to restructure, reorganize, merge, and downsize. These transitions are complex and difficult to undertake successfully. It has been reported that perhaps half of these transitions fail to achieved the financial objectives that were anticipated.

There are movements toward a common currency and a common trading block (the Euro, the EEU). NAFTA ties together Canada, the USA, and Mexico. There is some discussion in Canada about whether it should have a common currency with the US. Business–government relationships take on a new importance in these initiatives.

Changes are occurring in the nature of the employee–employer relationship (Hall 1996). Loyalty may in fact be dead! Greater use is now being made of part-time, contract (temporary workers) and outsourced functions. Managing contingent workers poses a different set of challenges.

Too many corporate boards have traditionally underperformed. Conger, Lawler, and Finegold (2001) document this concern and offer new suggestions for adding value at the top. They offer guidance on board functions, board member recruitment selection and evaluation, and group process dynamics.

The career landscape is also in flux. Employees and employers are now more likely to develop a contractual relationship, rather than a long-term relationship. Employees are more likely to change places of employment, voluntarily or involuntarily. It is now clear that employees will have a number of careers during their working life. How does one build a career under these circumstances? How does one develop the competencies, knowledge and relationships necessary for continued success? What competencies or metacompetencies contribute to continued success?

Organizational restructuring and downsizing continues. Recently, Nortel has cut another 4,000 employees to bring layoffs to 55 percent of their staff; 44,000 remain following the latest cuts, having reduced by 50,500 employees since the start of 2001. Ericsson planned to cut 20,000 jobs, Lucent Technologies another 6,000 jobs, and Telecom companies have cut 517,229 jobs since the start of 2001 (Nortel, 51,000; Lucent, 51,000; Motorola, 43,000). Mergers show no sign of slowing, now involving larger units and moving across borders. In the UK, electricity and gas networks announced plans to merge (April 22, 2002) to create a US $34 billion group, National Grid Group PLC and Transco UK.

There is "no quick fix," no "magic bullet" to equip leaders for managing in turbulent times. Managers, particularly in North America, have jumped on the bandwagon of the latest fad only to be disappointed. Such fads have included one minute managing, process reengineering, total quality mangement (TQM,) just-in-time (JIT), and executive coaching. The evaluative evidence on these and other initiatives indicates that they fail to achieve results as often as they contribute to results. Instead, a much longer-term investment is needed if success is to be realized.

NOTES

Preparation of this chapter was supported in part by the School of Business, York University and the Manchester School of Management, University of Manchester Institute of Science and technology. Joe Krasman helped identify relevant literature; Louise Coutu prepared the manuscript.

REFERENCES

Aldrich, H. E. 1979. *Organizations and Environments*. Englewood Cliffs, NJ: Prentice Hall.

Aon Consulting. 2001. *United States back @ work^{TM}*.

Burke, R. J. 2002. Organizational transitions. In C. L. Cooper and R. J. Burke (eds.), *The New World of Work*. Oxford: Blackwell.

Burke, R. J., and Cooper, C. L. 2000. *The Organization in Crisis*. Oxford: Blackwell.

Business Week. 2002. Wall Street: How corrupt is it? 13 May, 36–46.

Byrne, J. 2002. What went wrong? *Fortune*, 144, 64–79.

Capelli, P. 1999. *The New Deal at Work: Managing the Market-Driven Workforce*. Boston: Harvard Business School Press.

Cascio, W. F. 2002. The virtual organization. In C. L. Cooper and R. J. Burke (eds.), *The New World of Work*. Oxford: Blackwell.

Conger, J. A., Lawler, F. E., and Finegold, D. L. 2001. *Corporate Boards: New Strategies for Adding Value at the Top*. San Francisco: Jossey-Bass.

Cooper, C. L., and Burke, R. J. (eds.) 2002. *The New World of Work: Challenges and Opportunities*. Oxford: Blackwell.

Courtney, H. 2001. *20/20 Foresight: Crafting Strategy in an Uncertain World*. Boston: Harvard Business School Press.

Dowling, G. 2001. *Creating Corporate Reputations: Identity, Image and Performance*. Oxford: Oxford University Press.

Emery, F. E., and Trist, E. L. 1965. The causal texture of organizational environments. *Human Relations* 18:21–32.

Friedman, T. L. 1999. *The Lexus and the Olive Tree*. New York: Farrar, Straus, and Giroux.

Grove, A. 1999. *Only the Paranoid Survive: How to Exploit the Crisis Points that Challenge Every Company*. New York: Bantham.

Hall, D. T. 1996. *The Career Is Dead – Long Live the Career*. San Francisco: Jossey-Bass.

Hammer, M. 2001. *The Agenda: What Every Business Must Do to Dominate the Decade*. New York: Crown Business.

Kanter, D. L., and Mirvis, P. H. 1989. *The Cynical Americans: Living and Working in an Age of Discontent and Disillusion*. San Francisco: Jossey-Bass.

Katzenbach, J. R. 2000. *Peak Performance*. Boston: Harvard Business School Press.

Kim, J. Y., Millen, J. V., Irwin, A., and Gershman, J. 2000. *Dying for Growth: Global Inequality and the Health of the Poor*. Monroe: Common Courage.

Kotter, J. P. 1999. *John P. Kotter on what Leaders Really Do*. Cambridge, MA: Harvard Business Review.

Lawler, E. E. 1996. *From the Ground up*. San Francisco: Jossey-Bass.

Lawler, E. E. 2002. Designing change-capable organizations. In C. L. Cooper and R. J. Burke (eds.), *The New World of Work*. Oxford: Blackwell.

Loehr, J., and Schwartz, T. 2001. The making of a corporate athlete. *Harvard Business Review* 120:122–8.

Massey, D. S. 1996. The age of extremes: Concentrated affluence and poverty in the twenty-first century. *Demography* 33:395–412.

McLean, B. 2001. The Enron disaster: Lies, arrogance, betrayal. *Fortune* 144:58–62, 66, 68.

Mintzberg, H., Simons, R., and Basu, K. 2002. Beyond selfishness. Working draft. Montreal: Faculty of Management, McGill University.

Morgan, G. 1988. *Riding the Waves of Change: Developing Managerial Competencies for a Turbulent World*. San Francisco: Jossey-Bass.

Providence Journal. 2001. Single mothers off welfare are no better off, study finds (17 August): A.8.

Rapaport, R., Bailyn, L., Fletcher, J. K., and Pruitt, B. H. 2002. *Beyond Work–Family Balance*. San Francisco: Jossey-Bass.

Schwartz, N. D. 2001. Enron fallout: Wide, but not deep. *Fortune* 145:65–72.

Shapiro, I., Greenstein, R., and Primus, W. 2001. *Pathbreaking CBO Study Shows Dramatic Increase in Income Disparities in 1980s and 1990s: An Analysis of CBO Data*. Center on Budget and Policy Priorities.

Srivastava, A., Locke, E. A., and Bartol, K. M. 2001. Money and subjective well-being: It's not the money; it's the motives. *Journal of Personality and Social Psychology* 80:959–97.

Stiglitz, J. E. 2002. *Globalization and its Discontents*. New York: W. W. Norton.

Terreberry, S. 1968. The evolution of organizational environments. *Administrative Science Quarterly* 12:590–613.

Watkins, M., Edwards, M., and Thakrar, U. 2000. *Winning the Influence Game: What Every Business Leader Should Know about Government*. New York: John Wiley.

Weick, K. E., and Sutcliffe, K. 2002. *Managing the Unexpected*. San Francisco: Jossey-Bass.

World Bank. 2000/2001. *World Development Report: Attacking Poverty*. New York: Oxford University Press.

Zemke, R., Raines, C., and Filipczak, B. 2000. *Generations at Work*. New York: AMACOM.

Zimbardo, P. G. 2002. Ground zero: Looking up and beyond. *Monitor on Psychology* 33:5.

2

The Turbulence Within: How Sensitivities Throw off Performance in Executives

ROBERT E. KAPLAN AND ROBERT B. KAISER

How leaders contend with the turbulence in the outside world is in part a function of how they deal with the turbulence within – within themselves as individuals. Of the many factors that bear on leadership in turbulent times, this is one: how, inside their skin, senior people respond to the press of events. Is the executive unsettled by any of the demands of the job, however self-assured he or she may appear to others? The root of "turbulence" is stirred up, thrown into disorder or confusion. Inner turbulence of this kind can cloud the individual's judgment on key strategic decisions. Is the executive shaken up, as they say, by any part of the job? Does he or she overreact and in so doing respond less than optimally? Arguably, turbulent times require senior leaders' form to be at its best and yet it is when we are under stress that their form is more likely to deteriorate.

When executives react more strongly than a situation objectively calls for, it is usually because of what they bring to the situation. "Baggage" is the popular word for it. We think of it as sensitivities and the associated distorted beliefs that come into play. Unwarranted fears do many a leader in. There is a lot at stake here, not just the clarity of an executive's thought process and the quality of his or her decision making but also the individual's use of scarce resources like time, energy, and people.

To illustrate the point, here are two brief cases. Both are composites and both are based on four executives, two men and two women. The first executive, whom we'll call Lane, is reactive with people. Lane has knee-jerk reactions when anything goes wrong that she interprets as reflecting badly on her. This is her inner turbulence: she gets stirred up emotionally and strikes back at the other people involved when her view of herself as an effective executive is threatened. The stimulus elicits an instantaneous response with no mediating thought. Except for those secure individuals who learn not to take Lane's reactions personally, the effect on others is not good. One co-worker described her this way: "She's impatient and sharp-tongued and her emotions get the better of her in meetings. She'll launch at someone or give the person a withering look that says, you're an idiot." Growing up, she came in for more than her share of harsh criticism, from her mother in particular, that left her sensitive to this day to being found wanting in any way. About her mother she said, "I could hardly do anything right. And I got practically no emotional support from her – or my father." As a result, she is given to having these brief episodes of angry emotion – flare-ups – that get expressed as put-downs or otherwise punitive treatment of others.

A male executive we'll call Gene is a different case of the effects of inner turbulence. Not episodic, the effect is an enduring off-kilter perspective on his role as a leader. Exceptionally bright and technically gifted, Gene has defined his role as "knowing things and getting things done." Noticeably absent from his conception is having effective relationships. He didn't realize that the road to success also ran through that aspect of leadership. This innocent oversight has translated into, for one thing, overlooking the importance of networking with peers. Reacting to this feedback, he said, "This is a big aha – networking, getting buy-in. Because I didn't realize it was important. I thought I was doing enough of it." Notice that even this insight misses part of the value of strong bonds in leadership. Here he is only recognizing the *instrumental* role of connecting with people. His incomplete definition of the job went beyond not fully appreciating the importance of relationships to actively disparaging them in his own mind. A self-honest person, he admitted, "The soft side! I've had disdain for that side. I've had that prejudice for a long time. Part of me knows I'm no good at it so it's easy to say, 'that's crap, it doesn't matter.'" In saying that he's no good at relationships, he touches on the underlying sensitivity, the fearful expectation of proving inadequate socially. Although you would never know it from how self-assured with people he seems, he actually feels very unsure of himself in relationships, more so with peers than his own staff. Gene reports that growing up he found himself in a one-down position with peers. His family moved several times and each time that left him fighting an uphill struggle for acceptance by peers. On top of repeatedly being the new kid on the block he was unathletic and somewhat overweight and therefore came in for quite a bit of teasing, if not outright hazing. He adapted by opting, instinctively, for the solitary pursuit of academic success as a pathway to self-esteem. But now his concerns about rejection and his sense of himself as ill equipped interpersonally hamper him in his upper-level job. Unlike Lane, he does not flare up. His inner turbulence has instead led him to shy away from the interpersonal part of his job. It has brought into play a vector of fear that has thrown his idea of the job chronically out of whack.

Introduction to Off-Kilter Leadership

Most executives are very capable people. They know a great deal about how the world works; they follow the trends that have an impact on their organizations; they can make decisions on complex issues full of trade-offs; they assume the burden of being public figures; they work with a wide range of people in many different settings, often under trying circumstances; and they have the stamina to keep it up for months and years at a time. Yet, despite how much capacity they bring to their exquisitely demanding jobs, executives regularly have trouble with their form. (Just as athletes have form, good or bad, so do managers.)

How is their form off? When executives don't perform well in some respect, their form is off in one of two ways. They either overdo it or they underdo it.

We are all familiar with the tendency for intense, driven people to go overboard. So the advice they offer each other often is "tone it down. Temper your intense devotion to that principle." To be forceful is necessary but executives often make the mistake of being overly forceful. Just ask the people who work for them. To empower is good, but individuals inclined in that direction tend to empower to a fault. To be strategic is indispensable to anyone holding a senior line job, but visionary leaders often place too much weight on the strategic part of their jobs. To be operationally adept is highly desirable, yet it is so easy for executives with this gift to get bogged down in operational detail.

If it is fairly commonly recognized that senior people are capable of overdoing it, it may not be as evident that they are just as susceptible to underdoing it – despite their typically aggressive personalities. Top people have to make tough calls but many can't quite manage it or it takes too long for them to muster the courage. Also, it helps in creating followership to treat other people well, but some executives are so concerned with being nice people that they have trouble taking stands or confronting performance problems. Some executives unaccountably give short shrift to the strategic part of their jobs, while others stay at a high level and neglect the blocking and tackling needed for their organization to execute.

To point out these distortions in others is one thing. For the executives to recognize it in themselves is quite another. They tend to justify their behavior, even see it as necessary. What makes these patterns difficult to break is that they are predicated on assumptions that the individuals may take to be axiomatic.

Insiders can tell when an executive's form is off. What we can't see as easily is why. What throws an executive's form off? As with any athlete, it can be something as simple as fatigue or illness. Low on energy, it is harder to be sharp, one's threshold for frustration is lower, one is more likely to overreact. But, in addition to circumstantial factors like these, we have found, from years of experience consulting to top executives on leadership, that an individual's "baggage" comes into play. Although it may seem out of character for successful, seemingly self-assured people to be threatened, many executives are. They carry with them sensitivities that predispose them to be threatened. (See figure 2.1 for a diagram of the link between personal functioning and managerial performance.)

Vulnerable to feelings of inadequacy, they first of all react more strongly than they need to when things go wrong. And, second, they are, often unconsciously, threatened by the situations that confront them. They do everything in their power to measure up – and try too hard. Or they err in the other direction: they don't try hard enough. They make a half-hearted attempt or bail out completely.

This is not as simple as being especially sensitive to failure. Wrapped up in this insidious, yet ever so human, dynamic are distorted beliefs that feed into the problem. Like the rest of us, executives who are unduly threatened by inadequacy subscribe to beliefs that set them up to feel inadequate in the first place. One, they tend to have unrealistically high

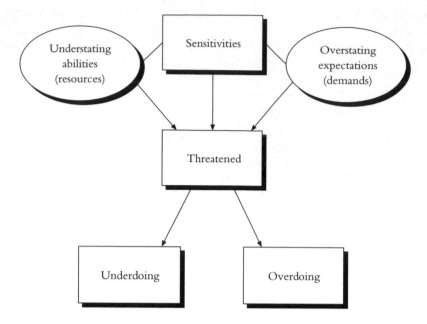

Figure 2.1: How sensitivities throw off performance in executives

expectations of what constitutes good performance, and, two, they tend to have unrealistically low estimates of their ability to perform, in general or in a particular respect.

Our point, though, is not that executives are susceptible to feelings of inadequacy. The point is that many performance problems can be traced to sensitivities that predispose them to be threatened when they don't have to be. This chapter explores that dynamic and identifies strategies that executives can use to contend with it.

Sensitivities

Sensitivities are much of what creates the turbulence within. Underneath it all, many executives are sensitive one way or another – sensitive in the sense of being quick to react to perceived inadequacy. If you subscribe to the popular idea of senior people as super-capable and supremely confident, then the idea that many of them are saddled with sensitivities may be incongruous. The fact that sensitivities are not visible to the naked eye, however, doesn't mean they don't exist.

Sensitivities are part of everyone's original human equipment. Built into a human being's natural survival system, they are the sensors that pick up threats to the individual's self-interests. Sensitivities also develop from life experience – bad experiences, that is. Overlaid onto the innate tendency to react to danger, the lesson learned makes for a heightened sensitivity.

A sensitivity is a mechanism that individuals adopt instinctively after experiencing considerable pain, physical or psychological. The sensitivity is a little complex of expectations, beliefs, incipient emotion, and reflex reactions that are designed to protect the individual from repetition of an earlier painful experience. The sensitivity puts the individual on alert for cues that would indicate this painful event might occur and equips the individual with a repertoire of fast reactions to remove him or her from harm's way. These cognitive-emotional mechanisms usually operate outside of the person's awareness and get triggered instantaneously.

When an executive carries around an incipient fear of proving inadequate, that feeling almost always has its roots in bad experiences in the individual's past. These are experiences from which the individual came away feeling inferior or inept or unworthy or hurt. Although experiences that leave lasting negative effects classically occur in childhood, they can also happen to adults, such as when a marriage fails or a career runs aground. The effect can be to instill a sensitivity to inadequacy in the individual.

Seymour Epstein, who has done extensive research on adaptive and maladaptive modes of coping, defined a sensitivity as a conclusion one draws "that certain kinds of situations or events are dangerous" (1990, 172). One comes to this conclusion because one was greatly threatened by that kind of situation or event. According to Epstein, "the hallmark of a sensitivity is that whenever certain stimuli or situations arise, the individual becomes excessively distressed" (Epstein 1990, 172).

In effect, one's sense of self has a hurt place, one that hasn't healed. It remains sensitive to the touch. This is a little like bruising part of your body, your right arm for example. If you happen to bump your other arm against the wall you might not notice. But if you so much as graze the bruised arm against a hard surface, it hurts. When it is a bad bruise, you might unconsciously go out of your way to avoid contact. No one, executives included, wants a repetition of a painful experience. No one with a bad sunburn wants to be out in the sun. To be sensitive then is also to be vigilant. A sensitivity is a vulnerability. Derived from the Latin word *vulnus*, meaning wound, to be vulnerable is to feel at risk of being wounded.

A prime example of a sensitivity in executives is a concern about their intellectual adequacy. It can be a feeling of inferiority from not graduating college or from attending a lesser school. It often has to do with not having been a good student in elementary school or high school, but it also occurs in people who were excellent students. Those individuals who didn't excel academically as young people may have gotten off on the wrong foot and never recovered. Often the root of the problem turns out to have been *not* a lack of ability but a lack of effort. Once the idea of themselves as poor students formed, it became a self-fulfilling prophecy. Children avoid the thing they don't think they're good at and thereby make it so. (This dynamic is not confined to children.) Believing that they are not smart, children don't apply themselves at school, their grades suffer, and the poor grades provide evidence of intellectual inferiority. This twisted logic can have a long shelf life. We have seen it in 50- or 60-year-old executives. Smart as they are now, they have trouble seeing that the poor grades that led them to conclude they aren't smart resulted from the fact that they didn't try. Yet their injured sense of their intellectual ability makes it hard for them to be objective about this important bit of history. The sensitivity lives on.

What toll does this sensitivity take? We have seen executives, on the one hand, who shy away from subjects containing what they take to be intellectual content – information technology or R&D projects or even strategy. On the other hand, we have encountered individuals who attempt to compensate for their perceived intellectual deficiency by working excessively hard, by having to master every detail, or by having to be "the one with the answer."

Sensitivities come into play in two ways. One is prospectively, as senior managers come up against a problem. Two is retrospectively, as they react to having not done a good job of solving a problem. The prospect of not proving adequate threatens them, as does the reality, as they perceive it, of not having done well.

Because of the pain wrapped up in a sensitivity, executives are typically either not conscious of it or not inclined to acknowledge it. Since we almost never hear executives talk this way, we were startled one time when one of our clients said to us, "I get threatened," to explain why she was prone to overreact. Likewise we were impressed when another executive in our initial interview referred to his "interpersonal insecurities." But it is unusual for senior managers to talk openly about their fears. In fact, like all of us, they can be reluctant to acknowledge a sensitivity. In going over a personality profile, one executive was taken aback by how his results revealed a sensitivity to rejection: "I think it's a more accurate reading of the situation than I would like to admit. This all speaks to some fundamental social insecurity at a deep level. The scores are true but it bums me out. In a backdoor way that I wouldn't expect, it taps something that bothers me a lot. I'm getting touchy now. It's getting too close to home."

Note the use of the word "touchy." This is a variant of sensitive to the touch, a readiness to take offense at the least provocation.

Even after an executive has identified a tender spot, it can fade back out of his or her awareness. The light bulb goes on, but does it stay on?

A sensitivity can be global, a readiness to feel bad about oneself across the board. It can also be localized, confined to a particular characteristic like intelligence. Or it can have to do with any of a great range of specific tasks or job requirements like making speeches, setting long-term direction, having a working knowledge of IT, confronting someone about a performance problem, delegating and trusting others, presenting to Wall Street analysts.

How Sensitivities Come into Play

Every day senior managers find the gauntlet thrown down in front of them in the form of a steady stream of challenging tasks. Even minor incidents can constitute a small moment of truth. How well they cope or deal with these things is fundamental to their effectiveness as leaders. Coping is not, however, just a matter of how well individuals respond to an objectively difficult situation but also the stress they create for themselves – as a result of the way they construe the situation and how they react emotionally to that reading.

Every difficult situation that presents itself is a fork in the road. One alternative is to experience the situation as an unwelcome threat, and the other is to regard the situation as a welcome challenge. This is not binary but a matter of degree – the degree to which a given demand placed on individuals poses a threat to them.

As if to ratify the fact that one response is healthy and the other one not, the body experiences them differently (Tomaka et al. 1993). When people are threatened, their heart rate increases and so does vascular resistance, which, in turn, leads to a dramatic increase in blood pressure and tension. Yet when people experience challenge as welcome, their heart rate may increase but their vascular resistance actually *decreases*. The result is little or no increase in blood pressure. Because blood flows more freely, the body does a better job of activating itself to meet the challenge.

What do we mean by a good response to a challenge? The ideal response is to engage it fully and calmly – and to look upon it as a chance to be effective, a chance to have an impact, a chance to learn. If there is a recipe for happiness, this may be it: to lose oneself in the experience of meeting worthy challenges (Csikszentmihalyi 1990). Part of this definition of the ideal is having one's attention fully available for the situation at hand as opposed to being distracted by anxious self-concern. This is the court vision that great point guards have, the ability to take in the action on the entire basketball court as that action plays out. It is what Larry Wilson called "relaxed concentration." The leader is intently engaged and at the same time utterly relaxed. An executive we once worked with had this marvelous combination of opposites. A co-worker who knew him well offered this observation: "He pays attention to the signals – to what people are doing and to what is really going on in the room. It's that base self-confidence. He's not thinking, what are people thinking about me? He is tuned into the other."

This executive evidently had enough confidence that he could free himself virtually completely to grapple with the organization's challenges.

Another executive described this capacity as "mental toughness, being calm and confident no matter what comes at you." She reported her progress towards this ideal. "I look at my emotional evolution over the last ten years. There's always a huge potential for panic. Back then I worried a lot about things, day to day. I worried about how people reacted to the decisions I made. I realize now that you need empathy but you can't let others' negative emotion pull you down." She grew in her ability to make tough calls that her staff might not like and to not shy away out of fear of a backlash, and hand in hand her confidence grew.

Most of us, executives included, fall short of the ideal. What is it that throws us off? At its most basic it is the threat of proving inadequate – to a task, to an interpersonal situation, to the overall challenge posed by a job. To a surprising degree, this is what we find when we jointly dig into situations with our executive clients. It is a fear of failing to meet an expectation, along with the unpleasant if not painful feelings that accompany failing. Therefore, how well executives deal with the demands placed on them, more often than one might imagine, comes down to how threatened the individual is in the face of any of one of those demands.

The word adequate means "equal to." When executives feel inadequate, they don't feel equal to the task at hand. Adequate can connote barely sufficient. What we mean is fully capable of meeting the requirement.

The fact of inadequacy does not have to be threatening. If executives determine that a situation is beyond them, that does not have to throw them. If the individual is threatened at first, he or she can regard *that* as a challenge: how can I construe the situation so that it becomes manageable? How can I contain my anxiety? If the situation is beyond what I am personally able to do, how can I get help to deal with it? Or how can I turn this into an opportunity to learn? Whether executives feel threatened then is not so much a function of whether the situation exceeds their capacities as it is a function of how they react to the situation.

When inadequacy threatens the individual and he or she is not able to tamp down the experience of threat, the response is often instantaneous. In the manner of a reflex, the state of being threatened translates so quickly into a reaction that stimulus and response occur almost simultaneously. An executive hears from his direct report that a project won't be done on time, and he comes down on the person. Even though one thing followed the other in quick succession, there was time for the executive to have a lightning-quick response inside: "This person let me down, failed me really, and has made me a failure too."

The fact that executives often react reflexively to what they experience as a threat is another reason why they can easily be unaware that their behavior is a response to being threatened. A major pathway to development and performance improvement is for them to come to know these reflex reactions in themselves and to learn to interrupt the sequence.

Correlates of Sensitivities: Distorted Beliefs about Adequacy

Sensitivities go hand in hand with two types of distorted beliefs – about what it takes to be adequate to a given task and how adequate the individual is to perform the task. A distorted idea about adequacy in either sense sets the individual up to feel adequate, the very thing that is a sore point with the person!

We all have beliefs about how much is expected of us and how capable we are of meeting these expectations. Thanks to our experience, these beliefs can be biased in a way that predisposes us to feel inadequate when encountering a situation. The first bias: we have unrealistically high expectations. We read situations as requiring more or better work than necessary. The second bias: we have an unrealistically low assessment of our abilities to perform a given task. We see ourselves as less able to handle situations than we actually are.

When a difficult situation presents itself to us, we go through an instantaneous two–step appraisal (Lazarus and Folkman 1984). First, we quickly scan the situation for its relevance to us. If we deem it relevant – that is, if we have a stake in it – we proceed the next instant to an assessment of the demands it places on us and the resources we have at our disposal to meet those demands. When we determine, usually unconsciously, that the demands exceed the resources available to us, we feel inadequate. If our core beliefs are distorted about adequacy, they bias our reading of situations and predispose us to feel inadequate. What in theory could be an eminently rational process of taking stock of a situation becomes fraught with subjectivity.

We have found in our work with executives that many of them underestimate their ability. They rate themselves lower than co-workers do either overall or in specific areas like interpersonal skills or intellect. When confronted with the discrepancy, they do not immediately surrender their view. Perhaps because they are afraid of not being good enough, they have trouble believing that their fears are unwarranted.

We have also encountered many executives who subscribe to fear-tinged expectations that lead them to interpret demands as requiring better work or harder work than is necessary. As a result, they come to believe that others have loftier expectations than those others actually do, that they will be scrutinized closely or judged harshly – all hallmarks of perfectionism (Blatt 1995). Co-workers may know how unrealistic those assumptions are, but the individuals themselves are captive to them.

Both sensitivities and the distorted beliefs associated with them typically arise from bad experiences that the individuals went through earlier on. We all know how early experience can lead children to conclude that they are inadequate – not smart, not acceptable socially, not attractive. If the feeling sticks, it becomes a chronic sore point. We also know how early experience can lead children to internalize excessively high standards – from being burdened by their parents' high expectations or to compensate for being continually faulted or denigrated or even abused. Many times the legacy is a wounded feeling bound up with distorted ideas related to one's adequacy or worth.

It is common for executives to be subject to these sensitivities and distorted notions and not know it. It is common for executives to have their responses to work demands thrown off by these standing predispositions and not know it. To outgrow sensitivities, to learn how to manage their effect on performance, executives must discover these inner workings and recognize how they relate to performance.

Off the Mark: Impact on Performance

When executive performance misses the mark, it is almost always in one of two directions. Executives overdo a given function or they underdo it. This applies to any immediate task as well as a standing requirement like setting strategic direction. Threatened by the possibility of not doing well at something, they do their damnedest to prevail: they overdo it. Or make only a half-hearted attempt to deal with it or they avoid it altogether: they underdo it.

In either case their behavior is off. First, they overreact emotionally to the situation at hand, and that emotion may not be visible to others or even evident to the individuals themselves. Next what they do is wide of the mark, one way or the other. The extent to which they get involved in something is off, the importance they place on it is off.

A footnote: we should point out that not all behavior that misses the mark is a result of being threatened. Genes also come into play. Some human beings are born with innately strong personalities that tend to be overwhelming, just as others enter the world with innately mild personalities and tend to be "underwhelming." Based on his research on children 20 to 30 months of age, Jerome Kagan (1989) identified two types of temperament, which he called "inhibited" and "uninhibited". He found the patterns of behavior in these children when they were seven and a half.

We think of overdoing and underdoing as being driven by compulsions and inhibitions, respectively. Whereas compulsions are those things that individuals feel compelled to do to fight off threat, inhibitions are those things they feel compelled not to do to avoid

Table 2.1 Some types of overdoing and underdoing – stemming from fears of inadequacy

Overdoing	Underdoing
Pressing – trying too hard (e.g., out of a fear of not performing well)	**Indecisiveness** (e.g., out of a fear that one's decisions will be wrong)
Overpreparing (e.g., out of fear that one's output won't be good enough)	**Lack of engagement with others** (e.g., out of a fear of disapproval or rejection)
Being too hard on others (e.g., from being unduly threatened by others' mistakes)	**Avoiding strategy** (e.g., as a result of feelings of intellectual inadequacy)

exposure to threatening situations. Both compulsions and inhibitions are "convictions that certain types of behavior are effective ways to reduce threat" (Epstein 1990, 172).

It is important to keep in mind that by overdoing and underdoing we mean classes of behavior and not types of executives. The reason is that most every executive is both an overdoer and underdoer. Yes, some executives strike all of us as engaging in overkill and other executives create the general impression of holding back. But give us an executive who goes overboard and it will not be difficult to identify corresponding areas in which that individual is inhibited. Likewise, those restrained executives almost always can be found to take corresponding managerial functions to an extreme. Overdoing one behavior at least raises the question of whether the individual underdoes an opposing behavior.

Executives who avoid strategy tend to overdo operational involvement. Executives who overprepare also tend to be indecisive. Both behaviors stem from perfectionistic tendencies, which cause individuals like this to "loop" repeatedly in search of an airtight answer.

Consistent with how closely linked overdoing and underdoing can be, we find it useful to think of leadership in terms of dualities. Two basic dualities stand out in executive leadership: strategic versus operational leadership and forceful versus enabling leadership (Kaplan 1996; Kaplan and Kaiser, in press). In our work with executives we regularly find senior managers who are lopsided on one or both of these dualities. We might mention that some executives underdo both sides. They are disengaged – for example, neither bringing issues to a head nor containing conflict and fostering harmony.

Recognizing that overdoing and underdoing are often linked, we will delve into them one at a time to bring out their distinctive character. (See table 2.1 for a summary of this discussion.)

Overdoing

Going all out can be a way to prevail; under extraordinary circumstances, it may be the only way to prevail. The drawback, however, is that executives who chronically go to extremes may, ironically, undermine their performance or waste time and energy. Of the many ways that executives overdo it, we offer three.

Pressing

Like athletes, senior managers impede their performance when they press. Phil Simms, the former New York Giants quarterback who guided his team to two Super Bowl victories in 1987 (he was the MVP) and 1991 was quoted in the *New York Times* (Anderson 1996) as saying, "Overgripping is the most frequent mistake I see among quarterbacks at all levels, including the pros. I found the harder I'd squeeze, the less control I'd have. Your arm should move like a whip. It can't when the muscles are tense."

Desperate to perform well, quarterbacks throw off their form. Following the same principle that it helps to modulate intensity, golf pros advise players to hold the club like a bird. When intense becomes tense, executives, athletes in their own way, impair their performance.

Overpreparing

A common excess among executives is to overprepare. They deal with an important upcoming event, whether a key meeting with the CEO or a Board presentation or an earnings report to Wall Street analysts, by making doubly sure they are prepared. The threat is they will look foolish or be found wanting. It is of course functional to do one's homework and the extra effort can pay off if they perform exceptionally well. But even when the extra effort results in an excellent product, it isn't efficient. Executives can find it difficult to modify this pattern of behavior because in their minds they are being responsible.

About one such executive, who thinks through issues with great care, a colleague said the following: "His idea of being ready is to overprepare. He feels like he has to answer every question, think of every angle, and he doesn't." Sensing the underlying feeling of inadequacy that lay behind the behavior, another co-worker made the following observation: "He underestimates his capabilities. He's talented but he doesn't give himself enough credit. No one expects him to be perfect. He worries too much." Another insightful co-worker sensed a self-protective motivation: "He protects himself – he prepares himself for the worst case." This executive suffered from the double whammy of expecting too much of himself and underrating his abilities. Like other executives who operate this way, his concern about adequacy clouded his otherwise good judgment, leading him to attach too much importance to preparation. Thoroughness is a virtue. He took it to an extreme.

Too hard on others

Just as executives can put undue pressure on themselves, they can apply too much pressure to others. They may impose excessively high expectations on the front end or they overreact later when their people don't meet those expectations. Experienced as insensitive, their behavior actually springs from being sensitive – sensitive to not being good enough. Sensitivity begets insensitivity. Overdoing it in this way is self-defeating. Not only does it depress the performance of others; it can hurt an executive's chances for advancement. Abrasiveness is a leading cause of derailment (Leslie and Van Velsor 1996; McCall and Lombardo 1983).

An outburst is one form of being hard on other people. We might note that outbursts can occur simply because the individual is exhausted or sick – which itself can result from another form of overdoing, overwork. A talented executive had a habit of coming down on people in meetings when he wasn't satisfied with their grasp of the business. At the very instant an outburst occurred, he had what could be described as an anxiety attack, a shot of fear that his people would never know the business well enough. He was most susceptible to overreacting when he first took over a business and was desperately search-ing for solid ground. "Until I know what to focus on, I'm hopeless; all the destructive behavior centers on not knowing what the vital few aspects are and being deathly afraid I won't ever get there." Early on, before he established himself, he was liable to panic if a small crack in the knowledge base came to his attention. Fear would undo him – "fear that I'm not good enough or I'll never be good enough."

Executives who overreact to a fault in a direct report are in effect overgeneralizing. They jump from the specific failure or failing to a broad judgment about the person. Overreacting throws off their judgment about people.

In general, the problem with overdoing is that it can undermine the executive's effectiveness – which is ironic, since the individual is trying so hard to keep from being ineffective. The other problem with overdoing is that it is inefficient. No self-respecting executive concerned with paring back on bloated cost structures would tolerate the waste in the way many executives function personally. What perpetuates overdoing is that it is rewarded when the extra lengths that executives go to produce good results.

Overdoing is a difficult habit to break because it is hard for the individuals so habituated to see it that way. In their minds it is integral to the success they have enjoyed. Since their success has come after extreme exertion, they come to believe that success depends on extreme exertion and they don't make the distinction between necessary intensity and excess intensity.

Underdoing

In collecting data for an assessment of an executive, we ask co-workers, "Does this person shy away from or avoid anything related to her job?" To a surprising degree, the answer to the question is no – no, this is a hard-driving individual who steps up to what the job requires. Co-workers don't tend to interpret weaknesses in their colleagues as avoidance. Instead they take the behavior at face value, perhaps because they don't suspect the underlying vulnerability. Yet there is as much underdoing as overdoing out there.

Of the many performance problems that are cases of underdoing, we treat three here: lack of decisiveness, lack of engagement with others, and lack of attention to strategy.

Lack of decisiveness

One thing that breeds indecisiveness is fear of making a mistake, as the following com-ment by a top executive about a direct report shows: "He's allowed himself to slip into a mode where he almost sees ghosts in closets. He finds reasons not to make decisions. He finds reasons to do more analysis and he'll raise red herrings. It's lack of confidence in himself, lack of confidence in his organization."

To decide exposes the individual, and the threat of being wrong can lead executives to shy away from committing themselves. They overreact and therefore don't place enough importance on timeliness.

Lack of engagement with others

To a degree that would perhaps surprise their immediate co-workers, many senior managers lack confidence interpersonally. They are able to work with people on tasks but if the truth were known they are uncomfortable relating to people. When interaction is elective, at least in their minds, they have a tendency to opt out. You might find them spending too much time in their offices. You might find them leaving people out of the process. You might find them uncharacteristically shy in purely social settings.

Feeling inadequate in relationships inhibits them, as do the assumptions they make about what other people expect of them. One successful executive – let us call him Harry – possessed good interpersonal skills and, relatively rare among executives, a lovely ability to make a personal connection to people. Yet he hardly ever walked the halls. What held him back? As his HR manager said about him in his presence, "He doesn't know what will come up; he might feel inadequate."

Harry felt the same way: "I might not remember their name. Or I might not know what they are working on and so they would feel, 'he doesn't know the freaking project I'm working on!'"

We clarified, "So you think people expect you to know everything?"

Harry replied, "Yes. Otherwise I'd leave the person deflated. I say to myself, I should know because that is how I would want to be treated."

Us again: "How would it reflect on you?"

Harry: "Negatively. I'd come across as aloof, unaware, out of touch."

Us: "How bad would this be?"

Harry: "Unacceptable to me. Not okay. I would *avoid* the negative part (emphasis added)."

Avoidance is the key word. In protecting himself – keeping his guard up – he passes up a chance to use his excellent interpersonal skills to stay in touch with the organization. In cases like this, executives with otherwise good judgment turn out to have little pockets of poor judgment. Objectively, Harry did not have to worry about knowing the names and situations of lower-level people. Yet for years he had operated on this half-conscious assumption.

Neglecting strategy

We have run across a number of top executives who fail to do justice to the strategic side of the job, and we have a hypothesis as to why. Strategy, especially systematic industry analysis and long-term direction-setting, is intellectual work. In addition to any lack of skill, we suspect that some executives who avoid strategy do so for emotional reasons.

Whether coincidence or not, our small sample of top people who neglect strategy were not good students and have bad associations with school. Perhaps coincidentally, a number of these executives were younger brothers or sisters of obnoxiously high-achieving older siblings. As a result of an underlying feeling of intellectual inferiority, executives may not only shy away from strategy personally but also devalue the importance of strategy and therefore not see to it that others do that work.

Fear of inadequacy would seem to cloud the individual's judgment about the importance of strategic direction.

In general, underdoing is avoidance of something that the job requires. Different from a rational choice, the logic of which co-workers would support, underdoing is a reluctance to engage fully. There is wisdom in opting out of a task that is not a priority or for which one is not well suited. In contrast, underdoing is a self-protective reflex reaction that leaves an important task undone or poorly done. The avoidant reaction may extend to devaluing the function altogether. However they may rationalize their decision, executives who avoid something have given up on themselves in that respect. One individual told us about learning to play a new sport. "I give up too easily. I don't like being bad at anything. I tried golf. After two or three lessons that I took together with my son, he was better than me so I quit." Humans like to be competent and are prone to avoiding situations where they aren't. Underdoing has a tragic aspect: you are fated not to learn something you avoid doing.

Different Faces, Similar Functions

Underdoing and overdoing look like diametrical opposites. When executives overdo it, they pour themselves into something to the point where their involvement nearly knows no bounds. When executives underdo it, the flow of energy into a neglected part of their job slows down, sometimes to a trickle. They either make no effort at all or make only a halfhearted attempt. Where overdoing is a can-do attitude to a fault, underdoing is can't-do. Where one is overly expansive, the other is self-limiting. Where overdoing can be viewed as undersocialized or undercontrolled, underdoing can be viewed as oversocialized or overcontrolled (McClelland 1975). Where overdoing is fueled by a fear I won't do enough to get what I want, underdoing is driven by a fear that I will do too much and somehow overstep my bounds (Higgins 1997).

Underdoing is self-protective, which, following the literal meaning of the word "protect," is "to cover oneself." To protect oneself is, in a sense, to hide. Overdoing is defensive in an aggressive sense: the individual fends off or fights off the threat.

As different as they appear on the surface, though, overdoing and underdoing are both strategies for contending with perceived threat. Overdoing and underdoing are also both reflex reactions. The situation at hand acts as a stimulus and executives respond reflexively to it, usually without knowing that fear of inadequacy intervened between stimulus and response.

A classic case of how overdoing and underdoing are two sides of the same coin united by a common emotional need is overpreparing and lack of decisiveness, both driven by perfectionism. Individuals with these twin predilections study an issue to death and hesitate to decide for fear the decision won't turn out to be right. At the core of this brand of perfectionism is a sensitivity to proving inadequate coupled with an unrealistically low estimate of their problem-solving ability and unrealistically high standard for what constitutes good decision making.

Whether taken singly or in combination, both overdoing and underdoing have a life of their own. One reason is that they often occur outside the individual's awareness. Secondly, executives tend not to regard their behavior as off-target. To the contrary, they tend to look upon it as the right and proper response to the task at hand. In their minds what they are doing is appropriate, even if others don't think so. Because they place a high value on those things they overdo, they have a difficult time seeing how they could do too much of that thing. Because they place a low value on the things they underdo, they have trouble seeing how they could be neglecting that thing. It is no wonder that performance problems don't get corrected easily.

Corrective Measures, Long Term and Short Term

How can executives learn to operate more effectively in a personal sense so that they perform more effectively in a managerial sense – learn to experience challenges of all kinds less as threats and more as opportunities?

The developmental work for minimizing the disruptive effects of a sensitivity divides itself into two levels, both of which can go on at the same time. One level is deep work that gets at the sensitivities along with core beliefs that predispose executives to be threatened in the first place. The desired result is for executives over time to reduce the level of vulnerability itself, so that they are not as easily threatened, so they do not react as emotionally, so that there is less emotional perturbation to throw off their leadership. By whatever method, outgrowing vulnerability is a long-run proposition.

The second level of development work takes place closer to the surface and is aimed at directly altering behavior so it is closer to the mark. It amounts to helping executives adopt better coping mechanisms that allow them to interrupt the sequence that distorts their managerial behavior. While they wait to take the next step in their evolution as a person, they can understand better what about the way they deal with things doesn't work well. And they can gain insight into the feelings and operating assumptions that influence the way they handle things. Armed with better self-awareness, they can learn techniques for modifying their behavior as well as the thoughts and feelings behind the behavior.

Helping Executives Outgrow their Vulnerability

To reduce one's vulnerability at the core entails either doing deep personal work or persisting for years or both. This effort amounts to giving a boost to one's natural evolution as a person. What can executives actually do to help their personal development along, and how can consultants facilitate that? Executives can accumulate experience – ideally, by design, they can learn to recognize their fears, they can raise their unrealistically low estimates of themselves, and they can lower their unrealistically high expectations for themselves.

Accumulate experience

When people have had a significant wounding experience way back, the painful associations and the distorted ideas they form about themselves and about what it takes to be worthy have remarkable staying power. Evidently, the wound becomes lodged deep in the basic part of the brain, the limbic system, that humans have in common with all animals and proves very difficult to heal (Damasio 1999). In the worst case the individual's faith that he will be safe and secure in the world is shaken. What does it take to heal that wound?

One of the best chances that people have of reducing their essential vulnerability is to accumulate vast piles of experience that eventually proves to them they are adequate to those situations that threaten them. They build up experience doing what they are good at, their work, so that they become comfortable with the idea that they are as competent as others take them to be.

They can improve their chances of reducing their sensitivity to inadequacy, however, by not limiting themselves to those areas where they excel. It is easy to limit oneself to those things that come naturally. We see executives do it all the time, but to have the best chance to grow fundamentally, they are well advised to seek out experiences in other areas. If they are masterful at solving business problems but, truth be known, feel unsure of themselves in relationships, it behooves them to build up vast stores of successful experience in relationships. To start with, they need to come up with a larger idea for who they are and how they might develop – in other words, set a strategic direction for their development. This is where consultants come in. It is so easy for executives never to embark on the journey. They, like all of us, are given to saying, "That's not me." What they are really saying is they have given up on themselves in some respect. We have had highly placed male managers tell us, "I have no desire for close relationships." Feeling no need, they are poor prospects for having experiences of that kind. For executives to transcend basic feelings of inadequacy, we believe they must stop ruling out broad classes of experience, whether it is interpersonal or intellectual or technical. Their best chance of growing is to add dimensions to who they are, and in so doing become more versatile leaders.

Long-run evolution is the path out of stasis. It is the way to escape the patterns that we adopted long ago to deal with the original trying circumstances: "It becomes all too easy to settle down into the narrow boundaries of the self developed in adolescence" (Csikszentmihalyi 1990, 47). It is through a consistent practice of meeting a wide variety of challenges that people gain strength. Slowly, in a process of accretion akin to the gradual way a coral reef grows bit by organic bit, even managers with chronic feelings of inadequacy can build up their faith in themselves. Consultants who are lucky enough to have a long-run relationship with their clients can serve as a guide.

Recognize one's fears

For executives to recognize that they are afraid may be the hardest work of all. There is a reason why fear of inadequacy so often has its effect below the level of consciousness. To feel inadequate is itself threatening, all the more so for self-respecting males. But what we are talking about goes beyond feelings of inadequacy in the moment. These are the historic fears, the sensitivities that have their roots in earlier painful experiences. Given the reluctance of executives to acknowledge their fears, consultants can serve as a catalyst. Empathy is perhaps the most useful agent. To draw out the individual is often the greatest service. All it may take is the simple question, what keeps you from doing that, what holds you back?

One executive client, some considerable time after the feedback session, initiated a conversation with us about how easily threatened she was. She understood that under certain conditions she felt "unsafe." What impressed us was her ability to see how feeling threatened led directly to her counterproductive behavior. She described vividly how at those times her focus narrowed sharply and all her energies were directed at countering the perceived threat.

As much as executives may resist knowing that they are afraid, acknowledging their fears is liberating. It is a form of self-acceptance. "I may not want to be this way but this is who I am." To do so begins to dispel the sense of oneself as unworthy and to better accept those parts of oneself that have troubled the person. By a curious process of disidentification, one moves from a condition of "being" those things to "having" those things (Kegan 1982). As our colleague Bill Hodgetts pointed out, there is tremendous potential released from achieving deep self-acceptance.

Raise an unrealistically low estimate of oneself

Low self-evaluations prove to be durable. Of the specific ways that individuals can attempt to alter their estimate of their abilities, one that we have found to work is intensive assessment, which many executive coaches have in their repertoire. What they may not do is make strategic use of the positive feedback for this purpose. One way we have found to help executives correct self-evaluations that are pegged too low is to expose themselves to a heavy and concentrated dose of feedback on their *strengths* (Kaplan 1999).

We find that the majority of our clients underestimate their capability one way or another. They either underrate their overall effectiveness or they underestimate how effective they are in a particular respect, often interpersonal or intellectual. Suffused with emotion, these self-deprecating self-perceptions resist change.

When executives receive 360-degree feedback, the data on weaknesses exert a strong gravitational pull. For years we allowed ourselves to be pulled in the same direction. Like our clients, we took the data on weaknesses to be the meat of the assessment. Only recently did we in our consulting practice learn to exploit the power of positive feedback. We have found that a heavy dose of the good things that co-workers have to say can temper an executive's fearful, self-diminishing notion of himself or herself, and result in greater self-acceptance. Beware the careless assumption that the strengths that an executive's co-workers report are as obvious to him or her as they are to the those looking on. In our capacity as consultants, we have learned to carefully check out whether the individual takes exception to any of his or her co-workers' high opinions – always a telltale sign.

When executives allow themselves to be influenced by the data and revise their depressed self-estimate upward, they are then less likely to be threatened by problems and they are less inclined to overdo or underdo their response to demands placed on them. They bring their estimate of the resources at their disposal into alignment with the demands on them.

Lower excessively high expectations of oneself

We all have them, archaic beliefs about the way we must behave. These imperatives, things we feel we must do or must avoid doing, exert an extraordinary power over us. Tinged with an almost religious feeling, these potent "shoulds" and "should not's" acquire the status of unquestioned truths in our lives, absolutes. Some executives are driven by a sense of responsibility that dictates that they absolutely do their part, that they never fail to take accountability. Other executives, a smaller proportion, are possessed by an expectation that they respond to the needs of others, that they never fail to put other people's needs ahead of their own. Still others have internalized a stricture against arrogance to the point where they have become constitutionally unable to take credit for their contributions – a coercive modesty.

The consultant's role is to engineer a retooling of these unrealistic expectations – to help senior managers get a perspective on these standards that dictate how good their work must be and how much work they must do. The challenge for the individual is to stand outside the tightly wrapped system of thought. It helps to look upon these articles of faith *relative* to the conditions under which they originally arose, as conclusions reached at an earlier time about how to keep the self out of harm's way. If executives achieve this distance on their impossible expectations, they take some power out of them (Kegan 1982). Those executives who succeed in this effort are often those who at the same time have internalized their strengths. The result is to take some of the internal pressure off.

Helping Executives Take Short-Term Corrective Action

Apart from doing deep personal development and banking on long-term maturation, there are steps that executives can take that are managerial in character. They can go after the problems with their performance in the same way they go after any problem – understand what isn't working, understand why it isn't working, and take corrective action. This is the stock in trade of the vast majority of executive coaches. Here we inform the behavioral approach by redefining it somewhat in terms of our framework.

The object is first of all to help individuals recognize that their behavior is off. Then it is to help them become aware of the fast sequence of steps, starting with emotional overreactions as well as operating assumptions, that clandestinely throw off their reading of situations and then their actions as a leader, and finally to learn to interrupt the sequence.

Among the immediate corrective steps that can be made available to them, executives can modify their behavior directly, they can learn to know it when they are threatened, they can identify the operating assumptions that underlie the behavior in question, and they can learn to draw on other people's resources.

Attack the behavior

The most straightforward approach is to help the individual work out a plan for attacking the behavior in question directly. Simply put, what is required is that executives recognize that they are overdoing it or underdoing it in some respect that matters to them and that they resolve to change. This is simply put but not simply done, however, because efforts to show executives the error of their ways collide with their cherished beliefs in the value of what they are doing.

Fresh from having their eyes opened, executives frequently report "catching themselves" as they are about to fall into an old pattern of behaving. They narrowly avert doing the old thing. Many find it helpful to recognize the emotions that immediately precede the behavior. One individual, overcoming a tendency to hold back in meetings, reported, "I now notice when I'm uncomfortable; I notice when there's tension." He uses the feeling as an indication that he is at risk of hanging back and, recognizing that he has a choice, pushes himself to the fore. Since feelings are often accompanied by a physical sensation, it is helpful to pick up on physical cues, one of the best ways of recognizing that one is threatened. These cues can include increased heart rate, headache, perspiring, tension in one's neck or shoulders, stomach pain, a tic, and so on.

To catch oneself is to fight the gathering potential to engage in a habitual behavior and substitute a new one. This applies to efforts to correct both overdoing and underdoing. Executives who are resisting a habit of going overboard make themselves keep their commitment to themselves to tone it down. Executives struggling with a tendency to *avoid* doing something make themselves produce the behavior.

It is no small job to contain the urge that would throw off one's performance in either direction. If executives can succeed in catching themselves at the moment of truth, they free themselves to try new behavior. Should they fail to interrupt the sequence, it still helps to realize after the fact and at least clean up after oneself.

Behaving in new ways can contain an element of coercion in the sense that in the early stages it requires an act of will. Up against a tendency to overdo, senior managers have to battle it – and forcibly allay the anxiety that if they moderate their hard driving they will no longer get the same results. Others, up against their tendency to underdo, must push past their resistance if they are to demonstrate to themselves that they can engage in the feared behavior and not suffer ill-effects.

As long as the impulse to do what they have always done remains strong, executives can invent little outlets for it, and consultants can help them do it. Bursting at the seams to take on one's superior in a staff meeting, a senior manager can bleed off the tension by writing down one's views rather than voicing them. Fairly shuddering with apprehension about having a difficult conversation with a direct report, the individual can calm himself by applying some form of applied relaxation (e.g., Ost 1987).

Desensitization is a proven strategy for helping people overcome phobias like these (Lazarus 1971; Seligman 1993). By doing the thing that fear precluded – and doing it not just once but consistently – we gradually learn that our fears are unwarranted. "Phobias" become self-sealing by depriving the individual of the very experience that could disprove the fearful assumption, and therefore it is no small accomplishment to get over this barrier. The way to reduce one's fear is to do what one is afraid of, safely.

By producing the feared behavior, managers put themselves in a position to experience its benefits. An executive learning to be more potent informed us after a couple of months of trying out the new behavior, "I actually enjoy myself being more assertive." The rewards for him were not just having a greater impact but also the satisfaction of using his powers more fully: "This sort of flexing around these issues is a good thing to do."

Recognize being threatened

Beyond developing a vague sense of the discomfort that triggers one's actions, executives benefit from coming face to face with the not so pretty reality that they get threatened. To know that underneath it all one's fears are the culprit equips executives to exercise better control over their behavior. Assisting their clients in their attempt at self-honesty and self-acceptance is a vital role for consultants who are equipped to do it.

Earlier we mentioned an executive who would get upset if he found that a direct report didn't have a commanding knowledge of the business. Mistreating people gave him no pleasure and, in exploring its roots, he discovered that it was fear of inadequacy that prompted his outbursts. Once he identified the source, he had better luck in containing his overreactions. When he felt the panicky feeling coming on, he could "press the pause button," as we put it to him.

Another executive adopted the same mechanism for ameliorating a relationship problem with subordinates, who complained that he was not only inaccessible but also distant when they did manage to get time with him. In talking with us it came to light that he felt uncomfortable, unsafe, inadequate in relationships in general. To protect himself, he avoided interaction. Or if he began to feel uncomfortable in a conversation he would end it. We suggested to him that, at the point when he was ready to bolt, he interrupt the reflex reaction. The pause would give him a chance to ask himself whether it was the present situation that made him uneasy or the old sensitivity carried over from the past.

Knowing what threatens us gives us a distinct advantage in managing our fears and even helps us avert their disruptive effects. Executives so armed are in a much stronger position to catch themselves, as well as to contain their emotional reactions. Having made a study of the state of being threatened, they also become acquainted with the bodily sensations that accompany this state. They come to know when these feelings are about to waylay their ability to think rationally and be under control.

Call operating assumptions into question

In addition to fear of inadequacy, operating assumptions can throw off an executive's performance. In contrast to sweeping core beliefs about oneself, these are specific "truths" that translate directly into the tactics an individual employs. The first step towards improving one's effectiveness is to question what has been taken for granted. It is the consultant's job to enable the individual to make these tacit assumptions explicit.

Harry, the executive who avoided walking the halls because he assumed that people would be offended if he didn't know their names or what they were working on, proved able to see the assumption for what it was, faulty. It had survived intact for years, escaped scrutiny, and led him to give short shrift to an important part of his job as the head of a large organization – to keep his finger on the pulse and to be visible to people lower in the organization. The shame of it was that he had a singular ability with people – the personal touch – that he did not exploit. An otherwise smart, rational person, he came to see that his expectation of himself had been unrealistic: "I realize now that people will give me more slack than I think. So I don't have to be so fortified or guarded." Because being out and about no longer posed the same threat, he could stop using his office as a kind of fortress.

Another example: in working with an executive on the problem of imbalance between her work life and her private life, we ran across an inviolate operating assumption she made. Although she had two young children whose soccer games she wanted to see, she would not permit herself to leave work early during the week. Having the quality of a compulsion, this principle she followed gave her no choice. When she exposed the assumption to the light of day and acknowledged to herself her extraordinary dedication, which other people gave her credit for, she was able to consider making an exception to her ironclad rule. As she told us, it was not just the principle that dictated her behavior, it was the guilt she would feel if she departed from the principle.

Operating assumptions in another form come into play when executives contemplate a change in their behavior. These are assumptions as to what is more or less important for them to do – values. In executives who overdo a behavior, we find a high value placed on that behavior. They see it as important to their effectiveness. They prize it, place their faith in it. Because they depend so much on it, they continue to work at improving the capability. For executives to moderate a behavior taken to an extreme, they need to come to place somewhat less value on it. By the same token, they need to come to place somewhat greater value on the complementary behavior that they underplay – and, because they have underplayed it, that they have not developed fully. So in addition to the fear of proving inadequate at the neglected side, their prejudicial attitude toward the other side stands in the way of making better use of it and getting better at it. Consultants can provide a valuable service by helping executives be honest with themselves about their biases for or against the various functions they must perform.

Make better use of other people

According to the model pictured in figure 2.1, people are susceptible to feeling inadequate when they read the demand on them as exceeding their capacity to respond. It follows then that one way to respond to this imbalance is to draw on the resources of others. It doesn't have to fall entirely to the individual to meet the challenge. One can extend one's capabilities indirectly. The consultant is one such resource. In fact, at the risk of seeming self-serving, we have found that an individual's ability or inability to involve others in his or her development is one index of their prospects for growth.

Executives can call upon others for two types of help. One is to get assistance in performing the task that they experience as beyond them. The other is to get a hand in containing the anxiety triggered by not feeling adequate. Besides providing moral support, others can help correct a distorted reading of a situation. Consultants are responsible for helping their clients expand their capacity to draw on others in their lives.

The logic that other people can extend one's capabilities, however, can escape a person under stress. It may also fly in the face of an assumption an individual makes about what he or she should know or should do personally. Sensitive to feeling inadequate, executives may instinctively view asking for help as a sign of weakness. This particular inhibition can derive from a spotty record in relationships. It can also come from a compensatory need to be the "hero," someone who consistently does outstanding work. A ruggedly individualistic management culture can further militate against seeking help and moral support.

Conclusion

It would be easy to view the task of leading organizations in turbulent times as only the outward work of staying on top of relevant changes in the environment and positioning the organization accordingly. As if that were not enough, senior people have their own inner dynamics to deal with. Disturbances, if not on occasion outright turbulence, come from within as well. If not managed well, they interfere with the clear thinking needed to contend with external challenges and they impede the leader's ability to bring people along.

A feeling of inadequacy often lies at the root of executive performance problems, even if that is the last thing that onlookers suspect of seemingly confident senior leaders. The individuals themselves may have a better sense of what they are feeling than we might give them credit for, but we find that their grasp on that uncomfortable reality is typically weak. Their work is to come to grips with their sensitivities as much as it is to grapple with suboptimal behaviors. Ours is not an ideological position. This is practical: executives have a better chance of getting their behavior into line if they address the sensitivities that throw that behavior out of alignment.

Attaining this sort of self-awareness holds one important key to development and performance improvement, but it is difficult for adults to do, especially successful adults. And executives – the usually proud, masterful possessors of positions of power – can find it difficult to acknowledge weakness. To be threatened can be viewed as a form of weakness. It is likewise difficult for them to uncover past hurts that have not healed. Like a thorn in one's foot that the skin has grown over, it continues to bother them but they have learned to live with it. This is where guides like leadership consultants come in.

At a minimum, progress is climbing out of the closed system of our self-protective beliefs and rationalizations sufficiently to see the distortions in our performance for what they are and make modifications. A step beyond that is to make the explicit connection between the off behavior and feelings of inadequacy and begin to manage the dysfunction at the source. We learn to take our sensitivity into account and make allowances for it. In shifting from being utterly subject to it to attaining some degree of objectivity about it we take a step towards releasing ourselves from it (Kegan 1982). The best case is when, through a variety of means, we are actually able to outgrow the sensitivity and the associated outdated beliefs and attain a greater comfort with ourselves, one that simultaneously liberates us and takes the ragged edge off our intensity.

REFERENCES

Anderson, D. 1996. Required reading for Brown and O'Donnell. *New York Times*, September 29, D1, D3.

Blatt, S. J. 1990. The destructiveness of perfectionism: Implications for the treatment of depression. *American Psychologist* 50:1003–20.

Csikszentmihalyi, M. 1990. *Flow: The Psychology of Optimal Experience*. New York: Harper and Row.

Damasio, A. 1999. *The Feeling of what Happens: Body and Emotion in the Making of Consciousness*. New York: Harcourt Brace.

Epstein, S. 1990. Cognitive-experiential self-theory. In L. A. Pervin (Ed.) *Handbook of Personality: Theory and Research*. New York: Guilford.

Higgins, E. T. 1997. Beyond pleasure and pain. *American Psychologist* 52:1280–300.

Kagan, J. 1989. Temperamental contributions to social behavior. *American Psychologist* 44:668–74.

Kaplan, R. E. 1996. *Forceful Leadership and Enabling Leadership: You Can Do Both*. Greensboro, NC: Center for Creative Leadership.

Kaplan, R. E. 1999. *Getting the Strengths to Sink in: A Little Used Lever in Executive Development*. Greensboro, NC: Center for Creative Leadership.

Kaplan, R. E., and Kaiser, R. B. In press. Rethinking a classic distinction in leadership: Implications for the assessment and development of executives. *Consulting Psychology Journal: Practice and Research*.

Kegan, R. 1982. *The Evolving Self: Problem and Process in Human Development*. Cambridge, MA: Harvard University Press.

Lazarus, A. 1971. *Behavior Therapy and beyond*. New York: McGraw-Hill.

Lazarus, R. S., and Folkman, S. 1984. *Stress, Appraisal, and Coping*. New York: Springer.

Leslie, J. B., and Van Velsor, E. 1996. *A Look at Derailment Today: North America and Europe*. Greensboro, NC: Center for Creative Leadership.

McCall, M. W., and Lombardo, M. M. 1983. *Off the Track: Why and how Successful Executives Get Derailed*. Greensboro, NC: Center for Creative Leadership.

McClelland, D. C. 1975. *Power: The Inner Experience*. New York: Irvington.

Seligman, M. 1993. *What you Can Change and What you Can't*. New York: Knopf.

Tomaka, J., Blascovich, J., Kelsey, R. M., and Leitten, C. L. 1993. Subjective, physiological, and behavioral effects of threat and challenge appraisal. *Journal of Personality and Social Psychology* 65:248–60.

3

Career Variety and Executive Adaptability in Turbulent Environments

AYSE KARAEVLI AND DOUGLAS T. HALL

In light of the events of the fall of 2001, the ability of organizations to cope with new realities of the global, political, social, economic, and technical environment is more important than ever. It is clear from theory and research that the adaptation of the organization to changing environmental demands is mediated by the nature of its executive leadership (e.g., Tushman and Romanelli 1985). Since executives have boundary spanning roles between organizations and their environment, it is important to understand the true nature of executive adaptability, what it really is, whether it can be developed, and its implications for organizational adaptation and performance, particularly in turbulent environments.

The new age concept of a flexible or "protean career" is not measured by chronological age and life stages, but by continuous learning and adaptability (Hall 1996). However, we know little about *adaptability*, which requires continuous learning, employing learning tactics and reflecting. The main challenge for many organizations has been to create learning events for tomorrow's leaders that are as dynamic as the companies' business environment. In these turbulent times, much has been written about the need for organizations to become learning organizations, an idea that expresses the importance of continually expanding organizational capacity to shape the future. With the emergence of the idea of learning organizations, we have begun to think about the role of a manager or a leader as one who facilitates organizational learning both individually and collectively.

However, although a lot of good learning happens every day, we do not always know how to tap into and take advantage of that learning. Consequently, we repeat the same mistakes at both the individual and the organizational level. In other words, we do not always know how to *adapt* to changing circumstances by using our previous experiences. The question then is how we can develop skills for engaging in the learning challenge, choosing and employing learning tactics and using reflection in order to capture learning from experience.

Leveraging a new notion of "career variety," we argue that a variety of career experiences is necessary to optimize individual learning and adaptability; leaders must effectively, and more rapidly, develop adaptive capacities from their diverse experiences to build critical relational and organizational competencies. We focus on the importance of cumulative experience and learning, as an experiential network of multiple organizational contexts, on long-term career success and adaptability.

Adaptability

Hall (1996, 2002) proposed adaptability as a higher order quality that is called metacompetency – the capacity to master many more specific skills when you master this metacompetency. Morrison and Hall (2002, 206) define adaptability as follows:

> *Adaptability* is the predisposition and readiness to consciously and continuously scan and read external signals and develop or update a diverse set of role behaviors so that they maintain an effective response to constantly changing environmental requirements and influence the environment (response learning); strive for a more complete and accurate fund of knowledge about the self to develop the potential to modify or maintain one's identity (identity exploration); maintain congruence between one's personal identity and those behaviors that are timely and appropriate responses to the ever changing demands of the environment (integrative potential); be willing to develop adaptive competence and apply it to a given situation (adaptive motivation).

Therefore, in Morrison and Hall's (2002) model of adaptability, in order for a person to adapt to a change in the environment, the person must be *able* and *willing* to change. So *adaptive competence* and *motivation* are the main two elements of adaptability. However, as they acknowledge, definitions of adaptability involve multiple elements and are quite complicated.

The same problem has been identified by various scholars in diverse fields. Various studies define adaptability by using different names and definitions for the concept, such as role flexibility (Murphy and Jackson 1999), adaptive performance (Hesketh and Neal 1999; Pulakos et al. 2000), and competence to manage new learning experiences (London and Mone 1999). Thus adaptability and its closer concepts flexibility and versatility are "elusive concepts that have not been well defined in the literature, and therefore, difficult to measure, predict and teach effectively" (Pulakos et al. 2000). While Hall (1996) and Morrison and Hall (2002) treat adaptability as a higher order competence that predicts variety of cognitive, affective, and behavioral outcomes, Pulakos et al.'s (2000) treatment of the construct is mainly performance or behavioral oriented.

Managerial Expertise and Adaptability

Behavioral decision-making researchers treat expertise as the competence to use previous knowledge and skills when circumstances are different and the ability to generalize or "strategically conceptualize" from earlier experiences (Neale and Northcraft 1989). This is very similar to the definition of an adaptive individual as a person who can modify previously learned methods and use existing knowledge to generate new approaches (Smith, Ford, and Kozlowski 1997), and who can combine cognitive and affective dimensions in specifying learning, self-confidence, and coping abilities as keys to approaching new tasks (Hesketh and Neal 1999).

Therefore, the definitions of expertise can help us to determine the dimensions of adaptability. According to the cognitive-based view, the expertise is the "possession of an organized body of conceptual and procedural knowledge that can be readily accessed and used with superior monitoring and self-regulation skills" (Glaser and Chi 1988, 21). In order to be able to model managerial judgment and decision making as computer-based representations of management expertise, decision support systems researchers examined the nature of management expertise and how it is acquired or developed through managerial experience. Based on the findings of various empirical studies, Reuber (1997) argues that managerial experience does not lead to managerial expertise directly as it would in professional domains, since managerial and professional work are very different from each other. Therefore, since leadership work is most of the time not task-specific, and not decomposable to lower level tasks in nature (Reuber 1997), mastering the metacompetency of adaptability seems very critical for performing higher-level managerial jobs effectively.

Expert performance has been identified to develop as a consequence of a complex interaction between motivation, self-regulation, and multiple types of domain specific experiences (Glaser and Chi 1988). Similarly, the development of executive adaptability requires more than cognitive competencies. Based on our review of the literature on managerial expertise and effective leadership, we have identified some individual qualities that might constitute the core dimensions of adaptability. Although these are by no means an exhaustive list of adaptability dimensions, we feel that it is a good start for a better conceptualization and measurement of this very important construct.

Behavioral Aspect of Adaptability: Adaptive Performance

Pulakos et al. developed a taxonomy of adaptive job performance and examined the implications of this taxonomy for understanding, predicting, and training adaptive behavior in work settings. They identified the critical dimensions of adaptive performance as "handling emergencies, or crisis situations, handling work stress, solving problems creatively, dealing with uncertain and unpredictable work situations, learning work tasks, technologies, and procedures, demonstrating interpersonal adaptability, demonstrating cultural adaptability, demonstrating physically oriented adaptability" (2000, 617). The Job Adaptability Inventory, based on their study, attempts to measure the adaptive performance. However, the jobs they examined in developing the inventory may not have included the exhaustive adaptability behaviors or dimensions that could be relevant in other jobs. Most of all, it does not necessarily target the executive level jobs, although dimensions that emerged out of their study seem relevant to that category as well.

Morrison and Hall's (2002) review of literature in adaptive competence support the critical dimensions identified by Pulakos et al. (2000). Accordingly, in the first category of studies, adaptive abilities are defined in terms of developing appropriate *behavioral responses* to the environment, such as dealing with unique or stressful external demands (Baltes and Baltes 1990) and positive adaptations maximizing gains over losses in functioning (Featherman, Smith, and Peterson 1990).

Cognitive Aspects of Adaptability: Task and Self–Related

Learning Transfer

We believe that being able to show adaptive performance in the long term requires one to be able to *transfer previous learning to subsequent tasks*. Transfer of learning occurs whenever experience or performance in one learning task can influence and improve performance on subsequent learning tasks (Ellis 1965). What is learned from prior experience, and what inferences can be generated from the knowledge, are the two key questions that must be answered to predict transfer (Gick and Holyoak 1987).

Learning transfer involves knowledge content transfer and learning process transfer ("learning to learn": Ellis 1965, 32) (Schilling et al. 2002). Learning process transfer indicates how individuals become better over time at applying previous learning to how to assimilate or process particular types of information to new problems (Ellis 1965). This is especially important for the development of individual adaptability. However, traditional educational and training programs mostly emphasize the facilitation of knowledge content transfer. So our next challenge should be designing executive development programs that emphasiz "learning process understanding" skills. This requires encouraging people to be conscious of the learning process and to reflect on their learning. Furthermore, the learning process in each assignment or task execution should be clear to both manager and learner.

Identity

An individual's clarity of identity and understanding of developmental needs and values has been identified as important dimensions of personal learning and change (Kram 1996). Adaptive competence is involved with the internal changes an individual is capable of making, such as resilience, positivity, and flexibility in personal changes (Phillips 1997), and clarity of direction and persistence (Shepard 1984).

From the point of view of the individual, one's awareness of self, or identity,[1] is probably one of the most important aspects of adult and career development, going back to the pioneering work of Donald Super (1957), who described the work career as the implementation of one's conception of the self. It is the person's sense of identity that, by definition, helps her evaluate herself. It tells her how she fits into her social environment. And it tells her about her uniqueness as a human being.

Hall (2002) has defined identity as a complex, multifaceted construct that relates to the way individuals perceive themselves in relation to "others" in the environment. These "others" can be people, groups, organizations, the physical environment, or any other entities with which a person has a relationship.

Emotional and Social Dimensions of Adaptability: Emotional Competence

Closely related to the concept of identity is emotional intelligence, which can lead to more adaptive and productive behavior in the workplace (Goleman 1998). As opposed to a long-held belief that conceptual skills are most important at senior executive levels (Katz 1974), new research suggests that emotional competencies account for the effectiveness of 85 percent of leaders (Goleman 1998). However, our theories of individual and organizational change have mostly focused on microcognitive processes, at the expense of social and emotional bases of change (Huy 1999). At the individual level, emotional intelligence is defined as "the subset of social intelligence that involves *the ability to monitor one's own and others' feelings and emotions, to discriminate among them and to use this information to guide one's thinking and actions*" (Salovey and Mayer 1990, 189; emphasis in original). In other words, it is simply related to how we handle ourselves and others.

Although emotional intelligence is considered innate, emotional competencies can be developed with motivation, practice, feedback, and support. They enhance the potential emotional intelligence of a given individual. Goleman (1998) defines emotional intelligence as "the abilities to recognize and regulate emotions in ourselves and in others" and emotional competence as "a learned capability based on emotional intelligence that results in outstanding performance at work." By building on Gardner's (1983) work, Goleman (2001) places these four dimensions into two categories of emotional intelligence: intrapersonal intelligence (self-awareness, self-management) and interpersonal intelligence (social awareness and relationship management). "Although our emotional *intelligence* determines our potential for learning the practical skills that underlie the four emotional intelligence clusters, our emotional *competence* shows how much of that potential we have realized by learning and mastering skills and translating intelligence into on-the-job capabilities" (Goleman 2001, 28; emphasis in original). What makes up emotional intelligence? Daniel Goleman outlines four components of emotional intelligence for leadership development in our organizations (Goleman 2001; see also McCarthy 1999):

- *Self-awareness.* Self-awareness, which we see as synonymous with identity, is the ability to understand one's capabilities, and to accurately evaluate performance, as well as to correctly outline development areas. People who are self-aware recognize their own emotions and their effects, know their own strengths and limits, and have a strong sense of their own self worth and capabilities.
- *Self-management.* This is the ability to handle new circumstances and harness one's own emotional responses. A highly self-regulated person has qualities of self-control, trustworthiness, conscientiousness, adaptability, achievement, and initiative.

    (Our literature review also indicated that, although self-regulation has traditionally been viewed as a cognitive construct, there has been increasing awareness that managerial effectiveness requires the appropriate *affective* reactions to the task [Gist,

Schwoerer, and Rosen 1989; Kanfer and Ackerman 1989], which have an impact on the self-regulatory processes that influence subsequent performance [Bandura 1986; Kanfer and Ackerman 1989]. Since managerial work is complex and ambiguous [Katz and Kahn 1978], and it is very hard to completely regulate high-level managers, self-regulation has been identified as an important mechanism to achieve control and coordinated action [Ashford and Tsui 1991], as well as individual motivation and performance [Gist and Mitchell 1992]. A closer concept to self-regulation is self-reliance, which has been found to develop as a result of a variety of prior experiences [Norburn 1989], and "secure relationships at work" [Kahn 2001].)

- *Social awareness.* This dimension entails being aware of and understanding others inside and outside organizations. Social awareness attributes as outlined by Goleman (1998) are empathy, understanding others and taking interest in their concerns, organizational awareness, empathizing at the organizational level, and service orientation, recognizing and meeting customers' needs.

- *Relationship management (previously called social skills).* The final dimension of emotional intelligence involves finding ways to work effectively with others by creating foundational and resilient relationships. The attributes of social skills as outlined by Goleman (1998) include sensing others' development needs and bolstering their abilities, visionary leadership, having effective interpersonal influence tactics, sending clear and convincing messages, initiating or managing change, resolving disagreements, nurturing instrumental relationships, and creating a shared vision and synergy in teamwork toward shared goals.

There is growing evidence that emotional competence is learnable and can be grown (Goleman 1998). However, it takes a strong desire to change, unlearning old habits, and building a new behavioral repertoire, and a lot of practice. Once achieved, however, emotionally intelligent leaders will likely be effective change agents for their organizations in the times of organizational turbulence in today's global economy.

How Does Executive Adaptability Develop?
The Importance of Career Variety

Research has shown that learning from job experience is the most powerful source of learning (McCall, Lombardo, and Morrison 1988; Robinson and Wick 1992). Recently, it has been discussed that executives' work experiences help to form their skill sets and perspectives as well as their networks and professional ties (Carpenter, Sanders, and Gregersen 2001). The developments that have come with the knowledge-based economy, where there has been a shift from position-based power to individual-based learning, have highlighted the importance of having diverse experiences and adaptability (Arthur and Rousseau 1996a; Hall 1996). However, how managerial adaptability can develop from diverse experiences has not been understood very well.

Different streams of research have focused on different individual outcomes as results of job experiences and transitions. For example, career researchers have focused on personal identity change (Ashforth 2001; Hall 1971; Ibarra 1999; Louis 1980) and role development and innovation (Nicholson 1984; Van Maanen and Schein 1979). Mentoring research has focused on individual feedback and help-seeking behavior after career transitions (e.g., Callister, Kramer, and Turban 1999). Although this previous work is very important for managerial career success, it is still not clear how organizations can develop *adaptive leaders* who can solve complex problems in novel settings, who can bring fresh perspectives to the strategy making process, and who can relate to the people they are managing.

Learning how to deal with different people in different roles, such as different types of bosses, subordinates, and customers, learning how to manage high stress and high stake situations, and so on, brings the most profound managerial learning (McCall, Lombardo, and Morrison 1988). In other words, a diversity of experiences provides exposure to a wide variety of both positive and negative situations, and through surviving those novel situations managerial learning takes place (McCall, Lombardo, and Morrison 1988). The importance of this will be particularly pronounced in highly changing environments, such as in growth industries. Through a variety of experiences, a person develops the managerial ability to differentiate and integrate various components of the environment. For example, Bartunek, Gordon, and Weathersby argued almost two decades ago that effective managers develop "the ability to generate several interpretations and understanding of organizational events so that the 'variety' in their understanding is equivalent to the variety in the situation" (1983, 273).

Furthermore, the risks associated with becoming specialized, such as the risk of becoming trapped in "core rigidities" (Leonerad-Barton 1992) by overinvesting in the exploitation of the current competencies (Levinthal and March 1993) and loss of cognitive flexibility (Abernathy and Wayne 1974) has directed the attention toward the importance of variety of experiences in improving learning.

Therefore, at the heart of the model we are proposing here is the concept of "career variety": through variety of experiences, we believe that individuals will acquire certain conceptual organizational management capabilities as well as personal skills necessary for effective leadership. When they need to operate in different circumstances, or when the environment of businesses changes, those skills will help them to achieve adaptation to various environmental circumstances without lengthy training or socialization. Therefore, we argue that our career and executive development systems should offer sufficient alternative routes and experiences for accomplishing desired individual and organizational outcomes. Acquiring metacompetencies, such as adaptability at the individual level, will reduce the time necessary to promote to the upper levels of organizations, which currently takes on average 20–25 years.

Contingencies Affecting the Impact of Career Variety on Executive Adaptability

We have already discussed that the development of managerial adaptability requires a variety of career experiences. However, there are many individual, organizational, and environmental factors that might hinder or enhance the process. Those include personality differences, the magnitude of the change in job transitions, pacing of job experiences, career stage in which job transitions occur, subjective perceptions of change in job transitions, and the organizational context in which job experiences takes place. The following sections describe the major moderators that might effect the relationship between career variety and executive adaptability.

Career Transitions

In Louis' formulation of career transitions, a transition is the period during which an individual is either taking on a different objective role (inter-role transition), or changing his or her orientation to a role already held (intra-role transition) (1980, 329). Our focus here is career transitions, a concept closer to "macro role transitions" defined as the physical and psychological movement between *sequentially* held work roles (Ashforth 2001, 7). Within the framework of self-managed, or protean careers, role transitions have been identified as affecting an individual's behavior (i.e., work satisfaction, performance) more strongly than overall career cycle (Ashforth 2001).

Magnitude of Objective Change in Career Transitions

Under conditions of high novelty, since people are not able to practice routine behavioral patterns, some personal development and learning is inevitable (Hall 1986; Nicholson 1984). The stretch assignments, or out of comfort zone stretch targets, have been found to enhance motivation, performance, and creative decision making (Thompson, Hochwarter, and Mathys 1997). Most of those stretch assignments involve assigning managers to jobs unrelated to their previous learning.

Unrelated variety in career experiences may also improve learning by giving the individual the chance to take some time off from the core job and reflect on what he or she has learned. In psychology, this process is called "distributive practice," which may give the learner time to do deep and elaborate processing that is necessary to draw general principles underlying the task (Mumford et al. 1994; Schilling et al. 2002). The importance of reflection on the previous experience has been offered as an important source of managerial learning (Seibert 1996). Reflection is defined as "an intentional cognitive process in which the person attempts to increase his or her awareness of personal experiences and, therefore, his or her ability to learn from them" (Hall 2002, 260). Reflection could be both about "content reflection" (thinking about *what* we perceive), and "process reflection" (thinking about *how* we perceive) (Mezirow 1991).

Seibert (1996) has found that managers do engage in reflection on their everyday experiences, and their reflection and learning are connected to the context in which action occurs. Furthermore, managers think about themselves as well as their job experiences, the former of which has been identified as an important metacompetency, which implies the ability to change one's sense of identity to fit with the changes in one's experiences and environment (Hall 1986).

Also, consider the issue of "negative transfer" or interference, whereby performance of the subsequent job is inhibited by the previous learning (Ellis 1965, 15). Potential problems might emerge for learning when the new and the old jobs are apparently the same or similar, but in fact, may require different responses. Thus, the person may inappropriately apply the lessons from the old position in the new one. However, this negative transfer is less likely to be a problem under conditions of high novelty, when the two jobs are un-related and it is clear to the person that it is necessary to explore and find new behaviors.

International Assignments

Among the variety of experiences that contribute to the development of executive adapt-ability, international assignments are probably the most pronounced ones. Global assign-ments involve adapting to a different business environment and social culture. The intensity and complexity of today's global economy challenges corporate executives in many ways. People's lives, their identities, social networks, and career goals and prospects are trans-formed by the experience of living in another country. Hall (1986) identifies international assignments as an important source of both task learning and personal learning, which cause people to become more adaptable and to extend their identities.

Since magnitude of change in an assignment is associated with how much people stretch themselves to be able to perform the job effectively, global assignments will probably bring one of the greatest opportunities to learn from the experience. Therefore, although previous work identified adaptability as a necessary individual characteristic for effective performance in international assignments, it is also something that can further develop as a result of having global experiences. Hall, Zhu, and Yan (2001) discussed international assignments as a means of leadership development that are more challenging than domestic executive development, since they expose managers to novel situations and a high level of uncertainty: "it is the process of experiencing surprises, where one's standard 'routines' no longer work, that stimulates a cycle of exploration, experimentation with new behaviors and reflection on these new skills. In this way, the person develops not only new skills, but also a new understanding of oneself – a *transformed identity*" (Hall, Zhu, and Yan 2001, 335; emphasis in original).

McCall and Hollenbeck (2002) identified the top six key events in the lives of inter-national executives. We believe that those key lessons are very critical sources for the development of executive adaptability. The list, in the order of priority determined by the number of international managers who mentioned the event, as outlined by McCall and Hollenbeck at the winter 2000 meeting of the Executive Development Roundtable at Boston University, includes (Karaevli 2000):

- *The significant other people.* These experiences resulted from a relationship with another person or people, whether good or bad. These people were most frequently bosses, superiors, peers, subordinates, customers, friends, or spouses. The most fre-quently reported lessons involved learning about one's own likes and dislikes, strengths and weaknesses. Support from others increased people's confidence. Negative experiences with bosses could improve one's skill in dealing with superiors. Good bosses taught lessons in developing others. Other people could be particularly important early in a career and in situations where learning about international context was important. Particularly valuable were good bosses from another culture.

- *Business turnaround.* These events involved fixing a business or function in trouble, and often included culture shock, career shift, and occasionally an educational or developmental event. Lessons learned in these assignments included belief in oneself, learning to listen to others and see the world through their eyes, running a business, staying focused, building a team, making tough calls on people, managing the interface with headquarters, and managing one's own career. These assignments have one of the highest potentials for learning possibilities.

- *Culture shock.* These events focused almost exclusively on the impact of being in a new or different culture, where the purpose of the assignment was less important than the cultural learning. Most often the cultural discontinuity was a surprise or even a shock. These experiences were frequently associated with turnarounds and joint ventures. Culture shock is the primary source of lessons about culture – all three categories are heavily represented (learning a foreign language, specific cultural lessons, and generic cultural lessons). Related lessons included listening, seeing the world through others' eyes, being open and genuine, being flexible and adapting to the situation, and establishing credibility.

- *Special project, consulting, roles, and staff advisory jobs.* These events include temporary and short-term assignments and special projects, often on top of a regular job. They usually involved giving advice or conducting a study rather than bottom-line responsibility, were often limited in duration, and were usually well defined. They often occurred in conjunction with early work, and often included culture shock. Major lessons were learned on how to run a business from both a strategic and operational perspective, confidence in oneself, and specific knowledge based on the content of the task.

- *Developmental and educational experiences.* These were formal educational experiences and jobs or projects that had primarily an educational or exposure purpose. Included here were rotational programs, internal training programs, and various external programs (e.g., Harvard, INSEAD, CCL), both degree and nondegree. Frequently they involved culture shock. People learned how to be flexible and adapt, both to the other participants and to the demands of the programs. From a content perspective, participants learned about international business. When the program involved action learning or projects, people also gained team-building skills. From some academic programs they learned how to develop people.

- *Career shift.* This is defined as a major change in career direction; for example, changing organizations or vocations, or switching to a new function. Such moves often involved considerable risk or personal sacrifice. These events were commonly associated with family stress, changes in scope, and even joint ventures. Most career shifts involved responsibility for something new, and therefore taught lessons in running a business. Most involved a change in culture, so lessons in culture also accompanied these shifts. Depending on the nature of the change, lessons might include managing the family, taking risks, or developing people. Successful transition was a big confidence builder.

As it is evident from the key events that were identified by McCall and Hollenbeck (2002), global assignments bring probably the highest magnitude of change and variety, and therefore, learning and development opportunity.

The Subjective Perceptions of Change in Career Transitions

The outcomes of career transitions have traditionally been identified as affective responses and coping (Brett 1980; Latack 1984), identity changes (Hall 1971, 1976, 1986, 1995; Ibarra 1999), and some behavioral outcomes in the form of adaptations to new settings (Van Maanen and Schein 1979). Although she hypothesized that a high degree of change in a role transition can cause job stress because it creates role ambiguity (uncertainty on how a job should be done) and role overload (the perception that the new job is beyond one's resources and capabilities), Latack (1984) did not find any significant relationship between the magnitude of career transition and role ambiguity. Furthermore, as opposed to her expectations, she found that rather than being overloaded by a major career transition, employees are less prone to perceptions of job overload than their colleagues who made minor transitions or no transition at all.

Therefore, rather than examining the effects of role variables, such as role ambiguity and role overload, which are mostly related concepts to "adjustment" (Nicholson 1984) or "adaptation" (Ibarra 1999; Van Maanen and Schein 1979), we want to focus on the developmental and learning outcomes of experiencing various job transitions. However, it is also expected that how much managers identify with a particular role will affect their *subjective* perceptions of the magnitude, and therefore the process and outcomes of the transitions. In fact, in her qualitative study of 19 new managers, Hill (1992) found that the promotion to a managerial level entailed a role identity transformation from a specialist to a generalist, and this change in identity presented a considerable challenge to new managers. This implies that how much an individual identifies himself or herself with the previous role will affect both the difficulty and the attractiveness of transition to the individual, both of which may bring personal development opportunity (Nicholson 1984) as well as potential stress that may tax adaptive capacities (Latack 1984).

More specifically, Hill found that there were two key ways in which first-time managers' identities were transformed as they moved into their new roles. First, they moved from being specialists and doers to generalists and agenda-setters. That is, rather than directly performing technical tasks themselves, they orchestrated diverse tasks and people. Psychologically, they had to switch their identification with their individual specialist tasks to identification with the business or with the role of manager.

A related identity transformation for these emerging managers was moving from seeing oneself as an individual actor to seeing oneself as a network builder. Psychologically, this meant switching from defining success through one's independent task accomplishment to valuing the accomplishments of others and to valuing interdependence.

To make this transformation work, Hill (1992, 6) found that these managers had to master four key tasks:

- Learning what it means to be a manager
- Developing interpersonal judgment
- Gaining self-knowledge
- Coping with stress and emotion

Much of this learning, then, is identity learning, or learning about oneself, and some is learning more about what the role requires. Interestingly, only one of these tasks relates to a specific competency area (interpersonal judgment). And, as Hill found, most of this learning did not happen intellectually; it happened experientially:

> The lessons were learned as the managers confronted the daily litany of interactions and problems in their new assignments. And they were learned incrementally, gradually. Sometimes the managers were aware that they were learning, but most often they were not. The learning consisted principally of "gradual and tacit change"; with the accumulation of evidence and experience came the erosion of one set of beliefs, attitudes, and values and buildup of another.
>
> *(Hill 1992, 7–8)*

Pacing of Career Experiences

The duration or exposure to prior knowledge is a critical element in order for an individual to successfully transfer learning from the previous experience. Learning-set theory points out the importance of a sufficient number of practicing related problems before a particular problem is reliably learned (Harlow 1949, 1959). Similarly, managerial succession and learning studies have suggested that developing new competencies need not only a variety of experiences, but also sufficient time at each assignment (Gabarro 1987; McCall, Lombardo, and Morrison 1988). Gabarro (1987) has indeed found that sometimes executives do not stay in important assignments long enough to learn much from them at all.

Therefore, pacing of the career experiences (frequency of job transitions and the time spent in an assignment) is important for the development of executive adaptability, in the sense that experience which comes too fast can overwhelm the managers and lead to an inability to transform experience into meaningful learning (Eisenhardt and Martin 2000). On the other hand, an infrequent experience can lead managers to forget what was learned previously and may result in little knowledge accumulation (Argote 1999).

Career Stage

Early career is particularly important for the development of adaptability. Early career is a time when an individual needs to develop action skills, so that he or she can apply the concepts and competencies that were acquired in school (Hall 2002). Although specializing is important early in a career, the person should also be rotated to a new specialty after a few years in order to avoid becoming too narrow (Hall 2002). We argue that the advantages of having variety of experience for the development of adaptability will be particularly pronounced when the experiences are acquired early in an individual's career. A maximum variety of jobs greatly improves a person's flexible, strategic and political thinking.

However, we also believe that job transitions at early career stage should be planned very carefully. If individuals are assigned to both unrelated functional areas and institutional contexts (e.g., firm, industry, national culture) from their previous jobs at the same time without developing the "confidence that one's successes are one's own" (Hall 2002), this may lead to low work satisfaction and organizational commitment, as well as possibly discouraging individuals from exploring and learning. We believe that unrelated functional experience early in a career will result in individuals striving too much to develop new technical skills at the expense of developing socio-emotional competencies, which are necessary for the development of executive adaptability.

Context of the Career Experiences

Previous research has shown that the rate of change in the organizational environment in which experience takes place affects the consequences of that experience. Environments differ in terms of rate and instability of change and exist on a continuum of stable to dynamic (Child 1972; Dess and Beard 1984; Simerly and Li 2000). As the rate of environmental change increases, executives need to develop adaptive capacities to deal with uncertainty associated with reduced knowledge available for decision making (Milliken 1987).

Therefore, in moderately dynamic environments, experience in related, but different situations, has been argued to be effective in sharpening managerial capabilities. In other words, through frequent, but low-magnitude changes, managers can elaborate their capabilities in current situations and extend them to related new ones (Eisenhardt and Martin 2000; Haleblian and Finkelstein 1999). However, it seems that a small number of assignments that are very different from each other will help managers to *reflect* on their learning and will thus be more effective for developing adaptability in highly changing environments.

Discussion

At this point the reader may be wondering where the list of personality or individual difference factors is in figure 3.1. This is a good point at which to make explicit one of the major themes in our argument: Adaptability is primarily a developmental construct! This is not to say that people are not born with some predisposition to be either more less adaptable, but for practical purposes it is more fruitful to focus on the ways that adaptability can be acquired.[2]

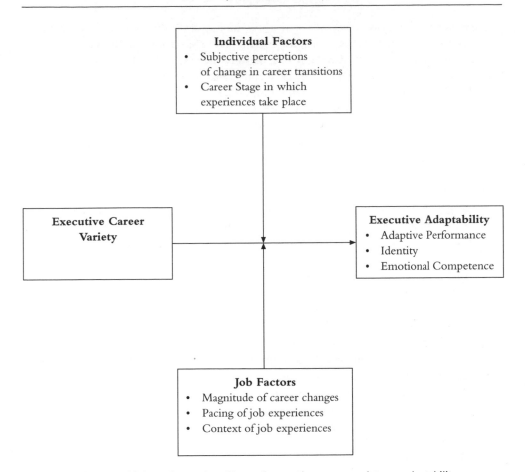

Figure 3.1: Factors which moderate the effects of executive career variety on adaptability

Our point is that individuals are capable of far greater personal change than they or anyone else might imagine. As Morrison and Hall's (2002) literature review reports, studies of individuals dealing with aging, with physical challenges, with international cultural transitions, and a variety of other unexpected environmental changes at various points in their adult lives show consistent evidence of high ability and motivation to change in some people.

And what accounts for differences between those people with high ability and motivation to change versus those with low ability and motivation? We would argue that a major predictive factor is differences in the variety of their career experiences. It is variety that forces the person to move out of routine behavior patterns and stretches him or her to explore new ways of being – both new behaviors and new ways of seeing the self. And, as these explorations and new behaviors and views of the self result in success, the result is a series of positive learning cycles which result in the person seeing himself or herself as a more adaptable and protean person (Hall 2002). Morgan McCall (1998) makes the similar argument when he shows how the "right stuff" in a leader is the result of developmental experiences, rather than inborn personal qualities. In a similar vein, Bunker and Webb (1992) found that the most adaptive managers were those who had had the most stressful life experiences. And furthermore, these adaptive managers tended to see these experiences as challenges and positive opportunities, rather than as stressors.

Thus, it appears that organizations that need to build their adaptable capacity would do well to *manage for career variety* as part of their leadership development activities. Let us consider some of the implications of the career variety or adaptability model in figure 3.1. As you will see, some of these may be counterintuitive.

- *Select for development, not performance.* One of the strongest barriers to organizational adaptability is the widespread practice of selecting managers and executives on the basis of their proven track record of competence in the tasks of the target job. In our view, this competency-based approach is just building rigidity into the organization, as future leaders are chosen with the same skills as past leaders. Rather, it makes more sense to select a person who has a *different* set of past career experiences, along with high *learning ability and potential* to excel. This person will experience the "stretch" of this novel job and will be stimulated and motivated to master it. On the other hand, the person who has already had experience doing a job like this one will find nothing new and challenging here. She or he will be more likely to fall back on previously learned (i.e., old) career routines and will be *less* likely to be a star performer in this assignment than the more diversely experienced candidate.

- *Build career variety into assignments at an early stage.* Research going back to the middle of the last century has shown clearly that a person's initial assignments represent a critical period for learning (much like the first few years of a child's experience) (Berlew and Hall 1966; Howard and Bray 1988; Livingston 1976; Morrison 1977). Attitudes toward self and work, as well as skills and performances, are not only learned more easily at this early stage than later, but they are also more deeply internalized and thus more enduring. The time to grow leaders who will be adaptive in their forties and fifties is not when they have reached senior levels of responsibility but when they are just starting their careers.

  However, this is also a counterintuitive notion. It flies in the face of the conventional wisdom that managers need to grow their specialized skills at the beginning of their careers and should thus be given assignments that promote depth rather than breadth. Our reply to this notion is that this focus on depth is in fact growing premature obsolescence and resistance to change. Get young managers used to moves that constantly put them in a steep learning curve, and they will learn to love change.

- *Follow the Mae West rule: Opt for variety over familiarity.* Mae West was one of the first sex symbols in American films. In one of her films she opined, "When I have to choose between two evils, I prefer the one I haven't tried yet!" We would argue that this rule applies well in career management, both for individuals and for organizations. When a person is being considered for two assignments, one involving work that she has done before and one involving work that is new to her, we would argue for the one that she hasn't tried yet. One of the most powerful ways to produce varied career experience is to opt for assignments in which the learnings are unrelated to learning from previous assignments. We know now from research at the Center for Creative Leadership what kinds of assignment tend to produce what kinds of lessons (McCall, Lombardo, and Morrison 1988), so we now have an empirical basis for knowing when an assignment is truly "different."

- *"Mine" the experience: Build in reflection.* Contrary to popular belief, experience is not the best teacher. What produces learning is not the experience per se but rather the *reflecting* that the person does on the experience. Unfortunately, because of the fast pace of contemporary work life, most people do not have the luxury of taking time to do much reflecting on a recently completed assignment. So, if someone does not *make reflection part of the person's job*, much of the learning from a key assignment will be lost, just like water poured into the sand. Reflection provides a container, a base for learning, much like a bowl placed on that sand, which will capture the learning. A number of activities to promote reflection can be found in Seibert (1999) and Hall (2002). Specific tools, such as Learning Logs, key questions to promote reflection, peer-coached reflection, and group processes to capture shared experiences, have been shown to help extract the lessons of career experience (Hall 2002).

- *Help the person become aware of identity change.* Out of a good reflection on a past assignment, one important outcome should be the person's increased awareness of changes in the person's view of self. We have found that it is relatively easy for a person to become aware of new skills and behaviors, but it is much more difficult to have perspective on changes in the self. Individual reflection can be useful here, but we also advocate the following step.

- *Use Peer Coaching to promote identity change.* In addition to individual reflection through journals and Learning Logs, relational methods can add a power multiplier effect. We have found that one of the easiest and most motivational of the relational methods is Peer Coaching. This is simply a process in which two individuals who have been through a recent experience meet to share their reactions to the experience, the lessons that they took from it, and their thoughts and plans for next steps in their development. It usually works best when the first step is individual reflection, in writing shared with the Peer Coach. Then the next step is a conversation with the Peer Coach. Each person acts as a coach to the other.

- *Manage the pacing of career variety.* We know from the work of Gabarro (1987) that there is a natural "life cycle" of the learning to be drawn from a particular assignment. The more complex and challenging the assignment is, the longer that life cycle of learning may be. Unfortunately, however, we also know from Gabarro's work that in practice the organization generally moves the person on to the next assignment before the full learning potential of the assignment is reached. It is possible, however, that a person can be left too long in an assignment, long after the learning has stopped. This can happen, for example, when a person has mastered the role and has become an excellent performer, so that there is a need to retain her in the position.

The implication of this idea is that when the plans for the person's assignment are being made, there should be an attempt to determine the optimal length of the assignment for the person's learning, and this should be a factor in when to end the assignment. We realize that staffing and business needs are important and cannot be ignored, but we are saying that the optimal learning time should be added as an explicit criterion in the decision about when to end the assignment.

Conclusion

The purpose of this chapter has been to introduce the concept of career variety as an important factor in the development of contemporary careers. Much the same way as job challenge was stressed years ago as a strong predictor of career performance, now that adaptability is so important in a turbulent environment, career variety should be encouraged as a way of building adaptive capacity. Put another way, just as diversity in an organization's workforce builds a stronger employee base, diversity in a person's career experience builds a more adaptive leader capable of handling a variety of complex, unforeseen situations. In addition, we know that there are several characteristics of individuals and jobs that can interact to heighten the positive impact of career variety, and these should be used more explicitly as components of a developmentally based executive selection system.

NOTES

Work on this chapter was supported in part by a dissertation grant to Ayse Karaevli by the Boston University Executive Development Roundtable.

1   For the purposes of this analysis, following Hall (2002), we will us the terms self, self-concept, and identity synonymously. Self and identity, as used in the psychology literature, are reflexive concepts, meaning that they refer to the person's image or view of him or herself.
2   See Morrison and Hall (2002) for a review of the personality factors that are related to adaptability.

REFERENCES

Abernathy, W. J., and Wayne, K. 1974. Limits of the learning curve. *Harvard Business Review* 52 (5):109–19.

Argote, L. 1999. *Organizational Learning: Creating, Retaining, and Transferring Knowledge.* Boston: Kluwer Academic.

Arthur, M. B., and Rousseau, D. M. 1996a. Introduction: The boundaryless career as a new employment principle. In M. B. Arthur and D. M. Rousseau (eds.), *The Boundaryless Career: A New Employment Principle for a New Organizational Era.* New York: Oxford University Press.

Ashford, S. J., and Tsui, A. S. 1989. Self-regulation for managerial effectiveness. *Academy of Management Journal* 34:251–80.

Ashforth, B. E. 2001. *Role Transitions in Organizational Life: An Identity Based Perspective.* Hillsdale, NJ: Lawrence Erlbaum.

Baltes, P. B., and Baltes, M. M. 1990. Psychological perspectives on successful aging: The model of selective optimization with compensation. In P. B. Baltes and M. M. Baltes (eds.), *Successful Aging: Perspectives from the Behavioral Sciences*. Cambridge: Cambridge University Press.

Bandura, A. 1986. *Social Foundations of Thought and Action: A Social-Cognitive View*. Englewood Cliffs, NJ: Prentice Hall.

Bartunek, J. M., Gordon, J. R., and Weathersby, R. P. 1983. Developing complicated understanding in administrators. *Academy of Management Review* 8:273–85.

Berlew, D. E., and Hall, D. T. 1966. The socialization of managers: Effects of expectations on performance. *Administrative Science Quarterly* 11:207–23.

Brett, J. M. 1980. Job transfer and well-being. *Journal of Applied Psychology* 67:450–63.

Bunker, K. A., and Webb, A. D. 1992. *Learning how to Learn from Experience: Impact of Stress and Coping*. Report 154. Greensboro, NC: Center for Creative Leadership.

Callister, R. R., Kramer, M. W., and Turban, D. B. 1999. Feedback seeking following career transitions. *Academy of Management Journal* 42:429–38.

Carpenter, M. A., Sanders, G. W., and Gregersen, H. B. 2001. Bundling human capital with organizational context: The impact of international assignment experience on multinational firm performance and CEO pay. *Academy of Management Journal* 44:493–511.

Child, J. 1972. Organization structure, environment and performance: The role of strategic choice. *Sociology* 6:2–22.

Dess, G. G., and Beard, D. W. 1984. Dimensions of organizational task environments. *Administrative Science Quarterly* 29:52–73.

Eisenhardt, K. M., and Martin, J. A. 2000. Dynamic capabilities: What are they? *Strategic Management Journal* 21:1105–21.

Ellis, H. C. 1965. *Transfer of Learning*. New York: Macmillan.

Featherman, D. L., Smith, J., and Peterson, J. G. 1990. Successful aging in a post-retired society. In P. B. Baltes and M. M. Baltes (eds.), *Successful Aging: Perspectives from the Behavioral Sciences*. Cambridge: Cambridge University Press.

Gabarro, John J. 1987. *The Dynamics of Taking Charge*. Boston: Harvard Business School Press.

Gardner, H. 1983. *Frames of Mind: The Theory of Multiple Intelligences*. New York: Basic.

Gick, M. L., and Holyoak, K. J. 1987. The cognitive basis of knowledge transfer. In S. M. Cormier and J. D. Hagman. *Transfer of Learning: Contemporary Research and Applications*. San Diego: Academic.

Gist, M. E., and Mitchell, T. R. 1992. Self-efficacy: A theoretical analysis of its determinants and malleability. *Academy of Management Review* 17:183–211.

Gist, M. E., Schwoerer, C., and Rosen. B. 1989. Effects of alternative training methods on self-efficacy and performance in computer software training. *Journal of Applied Psychology* 74:884–91.

Glaser, R., and Chi, M. T. H. 1988. Overview. In M. T. H. Chi, R. Glaser, and M. J. Farr (eds), *The Nature of Expertise*. Hillsdale, NJ: Lawrence Erlbaum.

Goleman, D. 1998. *Working with Emotional Intelligence*. New York: Bantam.

Goleman, D. 2001. An EI-based performance. In C. Cherniss and D. Goleman (eds.), *The Emotionally Intelligent Workplace*. New York: John Wiley.

Haleblian, J., and Finkelstein, S. 1999. The influence of organizational acquisition experience on acquisition performance: A behavioral learning perspective. *Administrative Science Quarterly* 44 (1):29–56.

Hall, D. T. 1971. A theoretical model of career subidentity development in organizational settings. *Organizational Behavior and Human Performance* 6:50–76.

Hall, D. T. 1976. *Careers in Organizations*. Glenview, IL: Scott, Foresman.

Hall, D. T. 1986. Dilemmas in linking succession planning to individual executive learning. *Human Resource Management* 25 (2):235–65.

Hall, D. T. 1995. Executive careers and learning: Aligning selection, strategy, and development, *Human Resource Planning* 18:14–23.

Hall, D. T. 1996. Protean careers of the twenty-first century. *Academy of Management Executive* 10 (4):8–16.

Hall, D. T. 2002. *Careers in and out of Organizations.* Thousand Oaks, CA: Sage.

Hall, D. T., Zhu, G., and Yan, A. 2001. Developing global leaders: To hold them, let them go! *Advances in Global Leadership* 2:327–49.

Harlow, H. F. 1949. The formation of learning sets. *Psychological Review* 56:51–65.

Harlow, H. F. 1959. Learning set and error factor theory. In S. Koch (ed.), *Psychology: A Study of Science.* Vol. 2. New York: McGraw-Hill.

Hesketh, B., and Neal, A. 1999. Technology and performance. In D. R. Ilgen and E. D. Pulakos (eds.), *The Changing Nature of Performance: Implications for Staffing, Motivation, and Development.* San Francisco: Jossey-Bass.

Hill, L. A. 1992. *Becoming a Manager: Mastery of a New Identity.* Boston: Harvard Business School Press.

Howard, A., and Bray, D. W. 1988. *Managerial Lives in Transition: Advancing Age and Changing Times.* New York: Guilford.

Huy, Q. N. 1999. Emotional capability, emotional intelligence, and radical change. *Academy of Management Review* 24:325–45.

Ibarra, H. 1999. Provisional selves: Experimenting with image and identity in professional adaptation. *Administrative Science Quarterly* 44:764–91.

Kahn, W. A. 2001. *Developing Self-Reliance through Secure Relationships at Work.* Technical report, Executive Development Roundtable, Boston: Boston University School of Management.

Kanfer, R., and Ackerman, P. L. 1989. Motivation and cognitive abilities: An integrative/aptitude treatment interaction approach to skill acquisition. *Journal of Applied Psychology* 74:657–89.

Karaevli, A. 2000. *Strategies and Tactics of Global Leadership Development.* Technical report on Winter 2000 Meeting, Executive Development Roundtable, Boston: Boston University School of Management.

Katz, D. 1974. Skills of an effective administrator, *Harvard Business Review* 52 (5):90–102.

Katz, D., and Kahn, R. L. 1978. *The Social Psychology of Organizations.* New York: John Wiley.

Kram, K. E. 1996. A relational approach to career development. In D. T. Hall and associates (eds.), *The Career Is Dead – Long Live the Career: A Relational Approach to Careers.* San Francisco: Jossey-Bass.

Latack, J. C. 1984. Career transitions within organizations: An exploratory study of work, nonwork, and coping strategies. *Organizational Behavior and Human Performance* 34:296–322.

Leonard-Barton, D. 1992. Core capabilities and core rigidities: A paradox in managing new product development. *Strategic Management Journal* 13:111–26.

Levinthal, A. A., and March, J. G. 1993. The myopia of learning. *Strategic Management Journal* 14:95–112.

Livingston, J. S. 1976. Pygmalion in management. *Harvard Business Review* 47 (July/August): 81–9.

London, M., and Mone, E. M. 1999. Continuous learning. In D. R. Ilgen and E. D. Pulakos (eds.), *The Changing Nature of Performance: Implications for Staffing, Motivation, and Development.* San Francisco: Jossey-Bass.

Louis, M. R. 1980. Career transitions: Varieties and commonalties. *Academy of Management Review* 5:329–40.

McCall, M. W., Jr. 1998. *High Flyers: Developing the Next Generation of Leaders.* Boston: Harvard Business School Press.

McCall, M. W., Jr., and Hollenbeck, G. P. 2002. *Developing Global Executives: The Lessons of International Experience*. Boston: Harvard Business School Press.

McCall, M. W., Jr., Lombardo, M. M., and Morrison, A. M. 1988. *The Lessons of Experience*. Lexington, MA: Lexington Books.

McCarthy, J. 1999. *Using Emotional Intelligence in Executive Development*. Technical report on Winter 1999 Meeting, Executive Development Roundtable, Boston: Boston University School of Management.

Mezirow, J. 1991. *Transformative Dimensions in Adult Learning*. San Francisco: Jossey-Bass.

Milliken, F. J. 1987. Three types of perceived uncertainty about the environment: State, effect, and response uncertainty, *Academy of Management Review* 12:133–43.

Morrison, R. F. 1977. Career adaptivity: The effective adaptation of managers to changing role demands. *Journal of Applied Psychology* 62:549–58.

Morrison, R. F., and Hall, D. T. 2002. Career adaptability. In D. T. Hall, *Careers in and out of Organizations*. Thousand Oaks, CA: Sage.

Mumford, M. D., Costanza, D. P., Baughman, W. A., Threlfall, K. V., and Fleishman, E. A. 1994. Influence of abilities on performance during practice: Effects of massed and distributed practice, *Journal of Educational Psychology* 86:134–44.

Murphy, P. R., and Jackson, S. E. 1999. Managing work role performance: Challenges for twenty-first century organizations and their employees. In D. R. Ilgen and E. D. Pulakos (eds.), *The Changing Nature of Performance: Implications for Staffing, Motivation, and Development*. San Francisco: Jossey-Bass.

Neale, M. A., and Northcraft, G. B. 1989. Experience, expertise, and decision bias in negotiation: The role of strategic conceptualization. In B. Shepard, M. Bazerman, and R. Lewicki (eds.), *Research on Negotiation in Organizations*. Vol. 2. Greenwich, CT: JAI.

Nicholson, N. 1984. A theory of work role transitions. *Administrative Science Quarterly* 29:172–91.

Norburn, D. 1989. The chief executive: A breed apart, *Strategic Management Journal* 10 (1):1–15.

Phillips, S. D. 1997. Toward an expanded definition of adaptive decision making. *Career Development Quarterly* 45 (3):275–87.

Pulakos, E. D., Arad, S., Donovan, M. A., and Plamondon, K. E. 2000. Adaptability in the workplace: Development of a taxonomy of adaptive performance. *Journal of Applied Psychology* 85 (4):612–24.

Reuber, R. A. 1997. Management experience and management expertise. *Decision Support Systems* 21:51–60.

Robinson, G., and Wick, C. 1992. Executive development that makes a business difference. *Human Resource Planning* 15 (1):63–76.

Salovey, P., and Mayer, J. D. 1990. Emotional intelligence. *Imagination, Cognition and Personality* 9 (3):185–211.

Schilling, M. A., Ployhart, R. E., Vidal, P., and Marangoni, A. 2002. Learning by doing something else: Variation, relatedness, and the learning curve. Working paper, Systems Research Center, Boston: Boston University School of Management.

Seibert, K. W. 1996. The nature of managerial reflection in learning from developmental job experiences in organizations. Unpublished doctoral dissertation, Boston University School of Management, Boston.

Seibert, K. W. 1999. Reflection-in-action: Tools for cultivating on-the-job learning conditions. *Organizational Dynamics* 27 (3):54–65.

Shepard, H. A. 1984. On the realization of human potential: A path with a heart. In M. B. Arthur, L. Bailyn, D. J. Levinson, and H. A. Shepard (eds.), *Working with Careers*. New York: Columbia University, Graduate School of Business.

Simerly, R. L. and Li, M. 2000. Environment and capital structure. *Strategic Management Journal* 21:31–49.

Smith, E. M., Ford, J. K., and Kozlowski, S. W. J. 1997. Building adaptive expertise: Implications for training design. In M. A. Quinones and A. Ehrenstein et al. (eds.), *Training for a Rapidly Changing Workplace.* Washington, DC: American Psychological Association.

Super, D. E. 1957. *The Psychology of Careers.* New York: Harper and Row.

Thompson, K. R., Hochwarter, W. A., and Mathys, N. J. 1997. Stretch targets: What makes them effective, *Academy of Management Executive* 11 (3):48–60.

Tushman, M. L., and Romanelli, E. 1985. Organizational evolution: A metamorphosis model of convergence and reorientation. Research in L. L. Cummings and B. M. Staw (eds.), *Research in Organizational Behavior.* Vol. 7. Greenwich, CT: JAI.

Van Maanen, J., and Schein, E. H. 1979. Toward a theory of organizational socialization. *Research in Organizational Behavior* 6:287–365.

4

Tridimensional Leadership Theory: A Roadmap for Flexible, Adaptive Leaders

GARY YUKL

Introduction

Organizations with a turbulent environment and diverse missions need leaders who are flexible enough to adapt their leadership style to different situations and changing conditions. The leaders must be able to analyze the situation, determine what pattern of leadership behavior is needed to influence processes that are important for unit performance, and then carry out the behavior in a skillful way (Yukl 2002). A relevant theory of leadership can serve as a valuable tool for diagnosing the situation and determining the most relevant aspects of leadership behavior.

Theories in which the same pattern of leadership behavior is optimal for all situations cannot provide the guidance needed by leaders confronted with changing situations and new challenges. Well-known theories that emphasize universal rather than situational aspects of leadership include transformational leadership (Bass 1985, 1996), charismatic leadership (Conger and Kanungo 1998; Shamir, House, and Arthur 1993), and leader–member exchange (Graen and Cashman 1975; Graen and Uhl-Bien 1991). These theories have made some important contributions to our understanding of effective leadership, but they say little about flexible, adaptive leadership.

A new theory called "tridimensional leadership" builds on earlier theories but offers several advantages. This new theory includes a wider range of behaviors, it specifies intervening processes that mediate the effects of leader behavior on unit performance, and it identifies contextual variables that determine what types of leader behavior are most relevant in particular situations. The theory was developed to explain the contributions of leadership to the effectiveness of an organization, but it also provides insights about effective leadership of organizational subunits (e.g., divisions, departments, teams). The constructs and propositions of tridimensional leadership theory will be explained in this chapter, and the new theory will be compared to some of the earlier theories of effective leadership in organizations.

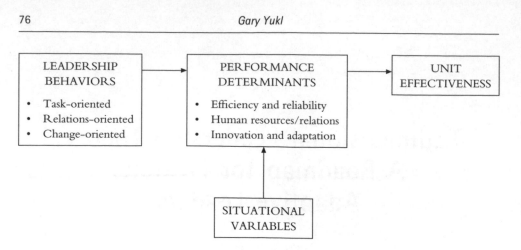

Figure 4.1: Primary relationships in the tridimensional leadership theory

Overview of the Theory

Tridimensional leadership theory includes several distinct types of constructs, including unit effectiveness, performance determinants, situational variables, and leadership behavior. Figure 4.1 depicts the primary relationships among the four types of constructs. Unit effectiveness is defined as the long-term prosperity and survival of the organizational unit, and relevent measures include net profits, profit margin, sales growth, and market share. Three key determinants of unit effectiveness include (1) efficiency and reliability, (2) human resources and relations, and (3) innovation and adaptation to changes in the environment. The primary situational variables are the type of organization or unit, and the amount of environmental volatility and uncertainty. Leadership behavior is described in terms of three broad metacategories (task-oriented, relations-oriented, and change-oriented) and the specific behaviors that comprise each metacategory. The causal relationships among the key variables are summarized in the following propositions:

1. Unit effectiveness is determined primarily by the three types of performance determinants.
2. The importance of each performance determinant depends on relevant aspects of the situation and the competitive strategy of the organization.
3. The primary effect of task leadership is on efficiency and reliability.
4. The primary effect of relations leadership is on human relations and human resources.
5. The primary effect of change leadership is on innovation and adaptation to the environment.
6. The leadership behaviors sometimes influence the other performance determinants in a positive or negative way.
7. Effective leaders integrate the behaviors in a way that is consistent with the situation.
8. Leadership is most difficult when all three performance determinants are very important.

Determinants of Unit Performance

The performance determinants emphasized in tridimensional leadership theory are derived from organization theory (e.g., Katz and Kahn 1978; Lawrence and Lorsch 1969; Miller and Friesen 1984; Quinn and Rohrbaugh 1983). Each performance determinant includes processes that mediate the influence of leadership behavior on unit effectiveness. The clustering of components is based on similarities in how they mediate the effects of leadership, not on the correlations among the components (they may or may not be higher intercorrelated). The performance determinants have independent effects on unit performance, but in addition there are complex interdependencies among the performance determinants themselves.

Efficiency and Reliability

Efficiency involves using people and resources to carry out essential operations in a way that minimizes costs. The performance of a unit will be better when there is high productivity and low cost of operations. Efficiency can be increased by improving the productivity of the unit members (e.g., by using better work methods). Efficiency can also be improved by redesigning work processes and coordinating unit activities to avoid unnecessary activities, duplication of effort, and wasted resources. New technology often provides an opportunity to improve efficiency, despite the initial cost of acquiring the necessary equipment or software.

Reliability means the unit is able to maintain established standards of quality for the production and delivery of its products and services (e.g., avoid unnecessary delays, errors, quality defects, or accidents). Reliability can be improved by using extra resources to ensure that quality standards are maintained, products or services are delivered on time, and accidents are avoided. However, this approach for increasing reliability is likely to reduce efficiency. In contrast, interventions such as reengineering and total quality management seek to improve both efficiency and reliability simultaneously. For example, it is sometimes possible to redesign products (e.g., by reducing the number of parts) so that they are easier to make as well as less prone to quality defects. It is sometimes possible to redesign production processes (e.g., by simplifying work flows) to reduce costs as well as errors and delays. It is sometimes possible to redesign services (e.g., by using information technology) to make them more reliable but less expensive to deliver. Many improvements in efficiency and reliability can be achieved by making incremental changes in work processes, but sometimes incremental changes are insufficient and major changes are necessary.

Human Resources and Relations

Human relations include cooperation, mutual trust, and organizational commitment. Collective work is performed more effectively when unit members are strongly committed to task objectives, they agree about the best way to accomplish the objectives, and they co-operate with each other in carrying out their interdependent work roles. Human resources include the task-relevant skills and experience of unit members. There is a direct effect of human relations and resources on unit effectiveness. Performance will be better when unit members understand what must be done and how to do it.

Human relations and resources may also affect the other performance determinants. Efforts to improve efficiency, reliability, innovation, and adaptation depend in part on the skills and motivation of unit members. For example, it is difficult to improve efficiency or reliability if members resist change because they distrust higher management. It is difficult to implement new technology or work processes if members lack the skills to operate the equipment or use the work processes.

Innovation and Adaptation

Unit performance also depends on responding in appropriate ways to external threats and opportunities. When changes in the external environment affect the capacity of the unit to carry out its mission, successful adaptation requires recognition of threats and opportunities, creative problem solving, and the willingness to make appropriate changes in processes, products, services, or the competitive strategy of the organization (i.e., the approach for achieving acceptance of its products and services). Adaptation is enhanced by accurate interpretation of information about the environment; collective learning by members (understanding of processes and causal relationships); knowledge management (retention and diffusion of new knowledge within the organization); flexibility of work processes (capacity to change them quickly as needed); and availability of discretionary resources (to support new initiatives and crisis management).

Although adaptation to the external environment often requires major changes in products or services (to make them more appealing to customers), the changes may also involve the other performance determinants. For example, major improvements in efficiency or reliability may be required to compete effectively with companies that can pay lower wages for employees. Major improvements in human resources (e.g., through innovative practices and policies) may provide a competitive advantage for an organization that is very dependent on the skills and commitment of its members for providing high quality products and services.

Situational Variables

All three types of performance determinants are relevant for all organizations, but their importance will differ across organizations and over time. The importance of each performance determinant depends on relevant aspects of the situation. Insights about conditions that influence the importance of the performance determinants comes primarily from organization theory and theories of strategic management (Miller 1990; Miller and Friesen 1984; Tushman and Romanelli 1985; Zajac, Kraatz, and Bresser 1999). These theories tell us that the importance of each performance determinant depends on the type of organization or subunit, the amount of uncertainty and volatility in the external environment, and the organization's competitive strategy. Even though leaders can change the strategy, whatever strategy is in effect at a given time will influence the relative importance of the performance determinants.

Importance of Efficiency and Reliability

When resources are used efficiently, the cost of operations will be lower and profits higher. Efficiency is more important for the survival of an organization when there are limited funds available to support operations than when there are surplus funds. Efficiency is especially important when the competitive strategy of the organization is to offer its products and services at a lower price than competitors. This strategy is most common for basic products or services with little differentiation (e.g., petrochemicals, cement, lumber, grocery supermarkets, printing and photocopying services, low budget hotels). It is not possible to keep prices low if the cost of operations is high. Although it is desirable for all organizations to keep costs low, it is less important when the competitive strategy is to provide a unique product or service for which there is high demand and no direct competition.

Reliability of products or services is especially important when there are serious consequences of errors, such as injuries, accidents, financial loss, and damage to property. Examples of organizations for which reliability is likely to be important include medical labs, pharmaceutical companies, hospitals, financial services. When reliability is a major determinant of repeat business, it may be important even for organizations with relatively inexpensive, standard types of products or services (e.g., fast-food restaurants, express mail companies, auto repair shops). Reliability is also important when the the organization's activities involve the risk of serious accidents that can destroy expensive equipment and kill or injure employees, customers, and other people (e.g., airlines, nuclear power plants, amusement parks, military combat units).

Importance of Adaptation

Innovative change is more important when the external environment is volatile and uncertain than when it is relatively stable and predictable. Uncertainty is greater when there is rapid technological change, political and economic turmoil, or new threats from competitors or external enemies. An appropriate response to emerging threats or opportunities usually requires some innovation in products, services, or operating processes. Examples of organizations with volatile, uncertain environments include telecommunications companies, computer products companies, research laboratories, police forensics laboratories, military combat units, and recently deregulated industries (e.g., financial services, energy utilities).

Another condition that makes innovation more important for the organization is a competitive strategy that emphasizes unique, leading-edge products or services designed to satisfy the changing needs of customers and clients. For the strategy to be effective, there must be frequent innovation and rapid response to threats and opportunities. Examples of organizations that need to be very responsive to changing customer preferences, new technology, and new initiatives by competitors include fashion clothing, pharmaceutical companies, medical equipment companies, computer companies, advertising agencies, and the entertainment industry.

Importance of Human Resources and Relations

Human resources are especially important when the work is complex and difficult to learn, new members require extensive training, and successful performance requires a high level of member skill and motivation (e.g., hospitals, consulting companies, legal firms, research universities, special forces combat teams). Human relations are more important when it is difficult to recruit and train competent replacements for people who leave. Acquiring and retaining key members is especially important when the competitive strategy emphasizes services by celebrities or unique experts who, if dissatisfied, can find jobs in competing organizations (or start their own). Finally, human relations are also more important when there is high role interdependence among members of the unit and effective unit performance requires a high level of cooperation and teamwork.

The conditions that increase the importance of reliability or innovation can also increase the importance of human relations and resources. When successful performance requires high reliability and mistakes can have serious consequences, there is a need for high commitment and vigilance, even if the work itself is repetitive and easy to learn (e.g., security guards, food preparation employees, employees who process financial transactions, employees who screen passengers at airports). Finally, the conditions that increase the importance of innovation may also increase the importance of human resources if the organization depends on members with special expertise as a major source of new ideas.

Situational Variables for Subunits

The performance determinants are relevant for the effectiveness of organizational subunits as well as for the overall organization, but the priorities may vary from one type of subunit to another. In most organizations the relative importance of efficiency, innovation, and human relations will be different across specialized subunits, consistent with the ideas of differentiation proposed by organization theorists such as Lawrence and Lorsch (1969).

Adaptation to the environment is more likely to be important in boundary spanning subunits (e.g., marketing, purchasing) and subunits with a primary mission of innovation (e.g., research, product development). Innovation is also important for many specialized teams with nonroutine tasks, such as disaster relief crews, special forces teams in the military, product development teams, management consulting teams, and task forces formed to deal with a crisis.

Efficiency is likely to be more important in subunits responsible for highly structured activities. Examples include mass or large-batch production, engineering, maintenance, accounting, contract administration, payroll administration. Reliability is more important in subunits with activities that directly affect the quality of the organization's products or services, or the health and safety of members and outsiders.

Potential Tradeoffs

It is common for one determinant to be more important than the others, but sometimes they are all very important. The most difficult challenge for leaders occurs when more than one determinant is highly important and there are tradeoffs among them. In this situation, attempts to maximize one determinant may have adverse effects on one or both of the other determinants.

Efficiency versus Adaptation

Efficiency can be increased by refining work processes, establishing norms and standard procedures, investing in specialized personnel, facilities, or equipment, and organizing around the strategy. However, these practices tend to reduce flexibility and make it more difficult to change strategies and work processes at a future time in response to environmental threats and opportunities. When efficiency is the dominant concern, leaders tend to focus effort and resources on refining the existing strategy rather than in discovery of new approaches (Miller 1990). Opportunities may be overlooked until long after they are feasible to exploit. Emerging threats may be discounted until they are finally so serious that it will be more difficult and costly to deal with them.

Conversely, major changes in strategies or work processes are likely to cause a period of lower efficiency (Lord and Maher 1991). A substantial investment of extra resources is usually required to implement major change. There will be a period of difficult adjustment and relearning by individuals and groups, which will cause a temporary decline in efficiency and reliability. Additional costs may result from effort and resources diverted to political activity, as people try to protect their power and status in the organization.

Efficiency versus Human Relations

There is a potential tradeoff between efficiency and human relations. Providing a high level of compensation and benefits may increase member satisfaction and willingness to remain in the organization, but operating costs will increase and net earnings will be lower. Achieving high efficiency requires controlling costs, which cannot be done if the organization is overly generous about allocating resources for the personal benefit of members. To achieve high efficiency, the organization must avoid unnecessary costs for lavish salaries and benefits, luxurious working conditions, or unproductive people.

Conversely, some approaches for improving efficiency can degrade human relations and resources. Cutting spending on benefits can improve efficiency but may reduce organizational commitment and increase turnover. For example, extensive downsizing to reduce the number of employees can increase efficiency, but it tends also to reduce the satisfaction and commitment of the remaining employees, especially when they are asked to do more for the same compensation.

Innovation versus Human Relations

There is a potential tradeoff between adaptation and human relations. Successful adaptation to a changing, environment usually requires a substantial investment of resources diverted from other uses. In the middle of an economic crisis for the organization, fewer resources are available to satisfy the individual needs of members. Leaders must ask for sacrifices and make unpopular changes that affect members. When leaders are preoccupied with making changes, there is less time for people-oriented concerns such as being supportive and developing member skills other than those directly relevant for the change. There will be less tolerance of people who lack the competencies or commitment necessary to implement change successfully. Controversial changes will increase conflict, distrust, and dysfunctional political activity.

Major change is likely to be very stressful for members of the organization. There will be significant effects on roles, relationships, power, and status. People may be uprooted and moved to different locations. Important aspects of the old culture may be lost. Expertise that was important may become irrelevant. If the change is not considered necessary or appropriate, there will be attempts to reverse or delay it. Even when change is not resisted, the disruptive effects of implementing a major change can undermine commitment to the organization and increase turnover among members who have more attractive options for employment.

Conversely, when the organization uses a large proportion of its surplus funds to improve compensation and benefits for members, there will be less investment in activities that promote future adaptation, such as research and product development. When there is a high priority for protecting member privileges, benefits, and job security, necessary steps to implement major change successfully may be avoided. For example, the organization may be unwilling to reassign or dismiss members whose skills have become obsolete, or members who refuse to accept the changes.

Leadership Behavior

Tridimensional leadership theory uses a hierarchical taxonomy of leadership behavior with three behavior metacategories (task-oriented, relations-oriented, and change-oriented). The metacategories are differentiated by the primary objective (e.g., efficiency, relations, adaptation) of the component behaviors. Each metacategory includes specific component behaviors (see table 4.1), most of which correspond closely to behaviors identified in research on effective leadership over the past half century (Yukl, Gordon, and Taber 2002).

Table 4.1 Hierarchical taxonomy of leader behavior

Task Behavior
- Plan short-term activities
- Clarify task objectives and role expectations
- Monitor operations and performance

Relations Behavior
- Provide support and encouragement
- Provide recognition for achievements and contributions
- Develop member skill and confidence
- Consult with members when making decisions
- Empower members to take initiative in problem solving

Change Behavior
- Monitor the external environment
- Explain why change is necessary
- Propose an innovative strategy or new vision
- Encourage innovative thinking
- Take risks to promote necessary change
- Facilitate collective learning

A distinction was made between task and relations behavior in the early leadership research (e.g., Fleishman 1953; Halpin and Winer 1957), and subsequent research identified key component behaviors for the broadly defined task and relations metacategories (see Yukl 2002; Yukl, Gordon, and Taber 2002). The component task behaviors include short-term planning, clarifying role expectations, and monitoring operations. The component relations behaviors include supporting, recognizing, developing (coaching, facilitating learning), consulting, and empowering (delegating).

Change-oriented behavior was not recognized as a separate metacategory until more recently. Evidence for the construct validity of this metacategory is provided by studies involving factor analysis of behavior description questionnaires (Ekvall and Arvonen 1991; Yukl 1998). Yukl, Gordon, and Taber (2002) identified some of the specific component behaviors, and other components are suggested by theories of change management (Beer 1988; Kotter 1996; Nadler et al. 1995). The component change behaviors include monitoring the environment, explaining why change is needed, envisioning beneficial change, encouraging innovation, taking risks to promote change, and facilitating collective learning within the unit.

Effects of the Behavior Metacategories

The primary effect of each behavior metacategory is on a different determinant of organizational effectiveness. Task behaviors are most useful for maintaining stable and reliable operations, utilizing personnel and resources efficiently, and making small incremental improvements in quality and productivity. Change behaviors are most useful for adapting to change in the environment, responding to threats and opportunities, adjusting to changing conditions, and implementing major innovations in strategy, processes, products, or services. Relations behavior are most useful for improving relationships, increasing cooperation and teamwork, increasing job satisfaction and motivation, and building identification with the organization.

In addition to these primary effects, each type of behavior may also have positive or negative effects on the other performance determinants. These side effects are often unintended, especially when negative. They may result from inappropriate forms of leadership behavior, or they may reflect inherent incompatibilities and tradeoffs among the performance determinants themselves.

A few studies provide evidence that each behavior metacategory is correlated with criteria of leadership effectiveness (Ekvall and Arvonen 1991; Yukl 1998). Evidence for the relevance of the specific component behaviors is provided by survey field studies using criteria of leadership effectiveness such as subordinate performance and satisfaction (e.g., Conger and Kanungo 1998; Kim and Yukl 1995; Lowe, Kroeck, and Sivasubramaniam 1996; Podsakoff et al. 1990; Yukl, Wall, and Lepsinger 1990). Unfortunately, these studies did not include some of the relevant component behaviors for the three metacategories. For example, most research on transformational leadership deals with less than half of the component behaviors, despite the claim to be a "full range" model (see critique by Yukl 1999). Moreover, most prior studies on effects of leadership behavior did not measure the organizational-level performance determinants or relevant situational variables (e.g., environmental volatility).

One of the most relevant studies for a key proposition of tridimensional leadership theory was conducted by Waldman et al. (2001). These researchers found that transformational leadership by CEOs was related to company profits when there was high uncertainty in the external environment (as perceived by respondents) but not when there was little uncertainty. Although the measure of transformational leadership included only a few of the change-oriented behaviors, the results provide indirect support for the proposition that this type of behavior is more relevant in a volatile, uncertain environment.

Flexible, Adaptive Leadership

The optimal pattern of leadership behavior should reflect the relative priorities of the three performance determinants. The challenge for leaders is to find an appropriate balance among the different types of behavior, and to determine which component behaviors are most relevant for a particular situation.

Even in situations where one performance determinant is dominant, some behaviors relevant for the other performance determinants will be necessary. A prosperous organization in a relatively stable environment has less need for adaptation, but some change-oriented behavior is still desirable. Examples include encouraging innovative thinking and collective learning to facilitate incremental improvements, and monitoring the environment to permit early detection of threats and opportunities when they eventually occur. For an organization in a turbulent, uncertain environment, change-oriented behavior has top priority, but some task behaviors are still necessary. Leaders must plan the action steps and resources needed to implement a new strategy, clarify new role expectations for people, and monitor the progress of change. The organization structures and management systems may need to be redesigned to support the new strategy and achieve coordination among different parts of the organization. As people learn how to conduct operations in new ways, this learning needs to be codified into standardized procedures to improve efficiency and reliability.

The leadership role is especially difficult when all three performance determinants are important. In this situation, effective leadership requires the integration of many diverse behaviors and the skillful balancing of behaviors that involve tradeoffs in terms of their positive and negative effects on the performance determinants.

The conditions that affect the importance of a performance determinant can change over time, and the appropriate pattern of leadership behavior will change as well. Effective leaders must be able to understand the immediate situation, recognize what behaviors are appropriate, know how to do the behaviors skillfully, and be willing to do them. The difficulties of leadership are increased when the situation is rapidly changing, or there is a need to carry out multiple missions involving different situations. As the level of turbulence and uncertainty continues to increase for most organizations, there is a greater need for flexible, adaptive leadership at all levels of management.

Comparison to Other Leadership Theories

The most prominent theories of leadership effectiveness involve either charismatic or transformational leadership. After a brief description of these theories, I will compare them to tridimensional leadership theory.

Transformational Leadership

The theory of transformational leadership (Bass 1985, 1996) differentiates between two types of leadership that are defined primarily in terms of the leader's effects on followers and the behaviors used to influence followers. Transformational leadership involves motivating followers by making them more aware of the importance of task outcomes, inducing them to transcend their own self-interest for the sake of the organization or team, and activating their higher-order needs. The transformational behaviors include individualized consideration, inspirational motivation, intellectual stimulation, and idealized influence (Bass and Avolio 1990). Transactional leadership involves an exchange process that may result in follower compliance with leader requests but is not likely to generate enthusiasm and commitment to task objectives. The transactional behaviors include providing contingent recognition and rewards, active monitoring, and passive monitoring (management by exception).

Charismatic Leadership

Theories of charismatic leadership describe how leaders arouse enthusiasm and commitment in followers by articulating a compelling vision, increasing follower confidence
about achieving it, and linking the task or mission to the values, ideals, and self-concept
of followers (Conger and Kanungo 1998; Shamir, House, and Arthur 1993). Attribution
of exceptional qualities to the leader is likely if the leader articulates a compelling vision
and strategy, the leader takes personal risks to get the strategy implemented, and the
strategy appears to be succeeding. Charismatic leaders can have a tremendous influence on
an organization, but the consequences are not always beneficial (e.g., Conger and Kanungo
1998; Sankowski 1995). The key leadership behaviors in the Conger and Kanungo (1998)
theory include sensitivity to the environment, sensitivity to member needs, articulation
of a compelling vision, personal risk taking, and exhibiting nontraditional behavior.
The behaviors in the Shamir et al. (1993) theory are less clearly defined, and they have not
been measured in a consistent way from one study to another.

Similarities and Differences

Tridimensional leadership theory is compatible with theories of transformational and charismatic leadership, but it explains leadership processes at a different level of conceptual analysis.
Tridimensional leadership theory is primarily concerned with explaining the influence of
leaders on organizational processes, whereas charismatic and transformational leadership
theories are primarily concerned with explaining the influence of leaders on subordinate
motivation and perceptions. The collective influence processes in tridimensional leadership
theory subsume the dyadic processes emphasized in the other two theories, but there is no
explicit description of these dyadic processes. For example, according to tridimensional
leadership theory, a leader can improve the performance of an organization (or subunit) by
increasing subordinate commitment, but the theory does not describe the psychological
processes responsible for this influence.

All three theories identify relevant leadership behaviors, but somewhat different behaviors
are emphasized in each theory. Table 4.2 compares tridimensional leadership to popular
versions of transformational leadership (Bass 1996) and charismatic leadership (Conger and
Kanungo 1998). With regard to change-oriented behavior, the other two theories have a
behavior similar to envisioning change. However, only transformational leadership has a
behavior similar to encouraging innovative thinking, and only charismatic leadership theory
has behaviors similar to external monitoring and taking personal risks. Neither theory has
behaviors similar to explaining the need for change or facilitating collective learning.
In both of the other theories there is a relations behavior similar to supporting, but
only transformational leadership theory has counterparts for developing and recognizing.
Except for monitoring (in transformational leadership theory), the task behaviors are not
explicitly included in the other two theories.

Table 4.2 Correspondence among behaviors in three leadership theories

Tridimensional	Transformational	Charismatic
CHANGE BEHAVIORS		
Envisioning change	Inspirational motivation	Strategic vision articulation
Encourage innovative thinking	Intellectual stimulation	NI
Monitoring environment	NI	Sensitivity to environment
Taking personal risks	NI	Personal risk taking
Explaining need for change	NI	NI
RELATIONS BEHAVIORS		
Supporting	Individualized consideration	Sensitivity to member needs
Developing	Individualized consideration	NI
Recognizing	Contingent reward behavior	NI
Consulting	NI	NI
Empowering	NI	NI
TASK BEHAVIORS		
Monitoring performance	Active monitoring	NI
Short-term planning	NI	NI
Clarifying	NI	NI

Note: NI indicates the behavior is not included in this theory.

A few behaviors identified in the other theories did not meet the criteria for inclusion in tridimensional leadership theory (i.e., the behavior must be effective, clearly defined, and observable). Two examples are passive monitoring and idealized influence, which are behaviors in the Bass (1996) version of transformational leadership theory. Passive monitoring is an ineffective behavior for influencing organizational performance, and idealized leadership is confounded with the effects of the behavior on follower perceptions and motivation. Nontraditional behavior, which is part of Conger and Kanungo's (1998) charismatic leadership theory, was excluded because it is difficult to define and measure. What is considered "traditional" varies considerably across organizations, cultures, and types of leadership positions. Moreover, a nontraditional behavior can become traditional after a leader uses it repeatedly.

As noted earlier, the three theories also differ in another important respect. Charismatic and transformational theories emphasize universal aspects of leadership behavior. A few scholars (e.g., Pawar and Eastman 1997; Shamir and Howell 1999) have identified conditions that can facilitate or limit leader influence on individual followers, but there has been little effort to identify the variables that determine what type of leadership behavior is most relevant for organizational effectiveness. In tridimensional leadership theory there is more emphasis on the contingency factors in effective leadership. All leaders must use some aspects of task, relations, and change behavior, but the appropriate amount and the mix of component behaviors will depend on the situation, which changes over time.

A final difference among the theories is the locus or source of leadership. Charismatic and transformational leadership theories emphasize the importance of an individual leader, whereas tridimensional theory emphasizes the importance of leadership processes without any assumption that there is only one leader. In tridimensional theory, some or all of the behaviors may be distributed or shared among multiple leaders. For example, while some leadership functions may be carried out by the chief executive officer of the organization or the unit, other relevant functions may be carried out by other members of the executive team, or by subordinate leaders at a lower level. In self-managed teams, the behaviors may be widely shared among the members of the team.

Discussion

Tridimensional leadership theory explains how leaders contribute to the effectiveness of an organization. The theory describes a complex process in a parsimonious way. In order to keep the theory from becoming too complicated, I did not include all types of variables that are relevant for understanding effective leadership.

Excluded Variables

Tridimensional leadership theory does not include leader traits or skills. Examples of skills that are probably relevant for flexible, adaptive leadership include emotional intelligence, cognitive complexity, systems thinking, situational awareness, behavioral flexibility, and technical knowledge. Examples of traits that are probably relevant for leaders include emotional maturity, a socialized power orientation, achievement motivation, self confidence, and internalized values consistent with the culture of the organization (Yukl 2002). Since the effects of these traits and skills are usually mediated by leadership behavior, it did not seem necessary to include them explicitly at this time.

The dyadic influence processes that explain how leaders motivate followers were not included because they represent a micro level of analysis that is not essential for understanding the basic propositions of tridimensional leadership theory. As noted earlier, how leaders influence follower motivation is already described in some other leadership theories.

The concept of power was not explicitly included in the model, because it is relative to the individuals who are attempting to exert or resist influence and to the type of decision or action one attempts to influence (Yukl 2002). Moreover, power can increase or diminish as people interact with each other. It is obvious that a powerful leader has a greater opportunity to influence the performance determinants, but the model does not assume that unit effectiveness depends on the actions of a single, "heroic" leader.

Finally, the initial version of tridimensional leadership theory does not include all relevant constructs from the literature on strategic management or organization theory. If necessary, the leadership theory can be expanded at a later time to include other micro and macro variables (e.g., organization structure, culture, environmental complexity).

Benefits

Tridimensional leadership theory offers a number of benefits for researchers and practicing managers:

1. It provides a parsimonious model for understanding flexible, adaptive leadership in teams and organizations.
2. It provides important insights about the relevance of the specific leadership behaviors in different situations.
3. It provides a better understanding of the results from research on effective leadership by CEOs and managers of organizational subunits.
4. It identifies some leader behaviors not included in transformational and charismatic leadership theories.
5. It provides relevant knowledge that could be used to improve leadership training and development.
6. It provides a basis for relating leadership theory to organization theory, strategic management theory, and change management theory.

Recommended Research

Empirical research is needed to directly test the propositions of tridimensional leadership theory. A variety of different research methods will be needed, including survey field studies, comparative case studies, and field experiments. The survey field studies can provide data to test the basic propositions, and use of samples representing different situations would enable one to test the moderating effects of the situational variables. Comparative case studies would provide qualitative information on the way effective leaders balance and integrate the three types of behavior in different situations. Field experiments in which leader behavior is manipulated with a training intervention could provide evidence of the leader's causal influence on the performance determinants. The use of multiple methods in research on the theory will provide a way to assess causal relationships and evaluate method bias. Research to test and refine the theory has already begun, but much more will be needed.

REFERENCES

Bass, B. M. 1985. *Leadership and Performance beyond Expectations*. New York: Free Press.
Bass, B. M. 1996. *A New Paradigm of Leadership: An Inquiry into Transformational Leadership*. Alexandria, VA: US Army Research Institute for the Behavioral and Social Sciences.

Bass, B. M., and Avolio, B. J. 1990. *Multifactor Leadership Questionnaire*. Palo Alto, CA: Consulting Psychologists Press.

Beer, M. 1988. The critical path for change: Keys to success and failure in six companies. In R. H. Kilmann and T. J. Covin (eds.), *Corporate Transformation: Revitalizing Organizations for a Competitive World*. San Francisco: Jossey-Bass.

Conger, J. A., and Kanungo, R. 1998. *Charismatic Leadership in Organizations*. Thousand Oaks, CA: Sage.

Ekvall, G., and Arvonen, J. 1991. Change-centered leadership: An extension of the two-dimensional model. *Scandinavian Journal of Management* 7:17–26.

Fleishman, E. A. 1953. The description of supervisory behavior. *Personnel Psychology* 36:1–6.

Graen, G. B., and Cashman, J. F. 1975. A role making model of leadership in formal organizations: A developmental approach. In J. G. Hunt and L. L. Larson (eds.), *Leadership Frontiers*. Kent, OH: Kent State University Press.

Graen, G. B., and Uhl-Bien, M. 1991. The transformation of work group professionals into self-managing and partially self-designing contributors: Toward a theory of leadership-making. *Journal of Management Systems* 3 (3):33–48.

Halpin, A. W., and Winer, B. J. 1957. A factorial study of the leader behavior descriptions. In R. M. Stogdill and A. E. Coons (eds.), *Leader Behavior: Its Description and Measurement*. Columbus, OH: Bureau of Business Research, Ohio State University.

Katz, D., and Kahn, R. L. 1978. *The Social Psychology of Organizations*. New York: John Wiley.

Kim, H., and Yukl, G. 1995. Relationships of self-reported and subordinate-reported leadership behaviors to managerial effectiveness and advancement. *Leadership Quarterly* 6:361–77.

Kotter, J. P. 1966. *Leading Change*. Boston: Harvard Business School Press.

Lawrence, P. R., and Lorsch, J. W. 1969. *Organization and Environment: Managing Differentiation and Integration*. Homewood, IL: Richard D. Irwin.

Lord, R. G., and Maher, K. J. 1991. *Leadership and Information Processing: Linking Perceptions and Performance*. Boston: Unwin-Hyman.

Lowe, K. B., Kroeck, K. G., and Sivasubramaniam, N. 1996. Effectiveness correlates of transformational and transactional leadership: A meta-analytic review of the MLQ literature. *Leadership Quarterly* 7:385–425.

Miller, D. 1990. *The Icarus Paradox*. New York: HarperCollins.

Miller, D., and Friesen, P. H. 1984. *Organizations: A Quantum View*. Englewood Cliffs, NJ: Prentice Hall.

Nadler, D. A., Shaw, R. B., Walton, A. E., and Associates. 1995. *Discontinuous Change: Leading Organizational Transformation*. San Francisco: Jossey Bass.

Pawar, B. S., and Eastman, K. K. 1997. The nature and implications of contextual influences on transformational leadership: A conceptual examination. *Academy of Management Review* 22:80–109.

Podsakoff, P. M., MacKenzie, S. B., Morrman, R. H., and Fetter, R. 1990. Transformational leader behaviors and their effects on follower's trust in leader, satisfaction, and organizational citizenship behaviors. *Leadership Quarterly* 1:107–42.

Quinn, R. E., and Rohrbaugh, J. 1983. A spatial model of effectiveness criteria: Towards a competing values approach to organizational analysis. *Management Science* 29:363–77.

Sandowsky, D. 1995. The charismatic leader as narcissist: Understanding the abuse of power. *Organizational Dynamics* 23 (4):57–71.

Shamir, B., and Howell, J. 1999. Organizational and contextual influences on the emergence and effectiveness of charismatic leadership. *Leadership Quarterly* 10:257–84.

Shamir, B., House, R. J., and Arthur, M. B. 1993. The motivational effects of charismatic leadership: A self-concept theory. *Organization Science* 4:1–17.

Tushman, M. L., and Romanelli, E. 1985. Organizational evolution: A metamorphosis model of convergence and reorientation. In L. L. Cummings and B. M. Staw (eds.), *Research in Organizational Behavior.* Vol. 7. Greenwich, CT: JAI.

Waldman, D. A., Ramirez, G. G., House, R. J., and Puranam, P. 2001. Does leadership matter? CEO leadership attributes and profitability under conditions of perceived environmental uncertainty. *Academy of Management Journal* 44:134–44.

Yukl, G. 1998. An evaluative essay on current conceptions of effective leadership. *European Journal of Work and Organizational Psychology* 8:33–48.

Yukl, G. 1999. An evaluation of conceptual weaknesses in transformational and charismatic leadership theories. *Leadership Quarterly* 10:285–305.

Yukl, G. 2002. *Leadership in Organizations,* 5th ed. Upper Saddle River, NJ: Prentice Hall.

Yukl, G., Gordon, A., and Taber, T. 2002. A hierarchical taxonomy of leadership behavior: Integrating a half century of behavior research. *Journal of Leadership and Organization Studies* 9:15–32.

Yukl, G., Wall, S., and Lepsinger, R. 1990. Preliminary report on validation of the managerial practices survey. In K. E. Clark and M. B. Clark (eds.), *Measures of Leadership.* West Orange, NJ: Leadership Library of America.

Zajac, E. J., Kraatz, M. S., and Bresser, R. K. F. 1999. Modeling the dynamics of strategic fit: A normative approach to strategic change. *Strategic Management Journal* 21:429–53.

Part II

Leading Others

5

Principles and Advice for Understanding and Promoting Effective Teamwork in Organizations

EDUARDO SALAS, MARY P. KOSARZYCKI, SCOTT I. TANNENBAUM, AND DAVID CARNEGIE

In today's business environment, senior managers routinely deal with a variety of issues ranging from internal organizational structural demands to external challenges and opportunities. For example, external threats from the environment can include increased global competition from developing countries that employ low-paid, highly skilled workers; unforeseen political, legal, and economic pressures (e.g., disturbed economic conditions that followed the 9–11 terrorist attack); labor market shortages (e.g., low unemployment, lack of workers with certain technology-related skills but abundance of untrained/poorly trained workers); customer and client fickleness (e.g., increased use of Internet as an alternative to retail stores); and technological advances that support innovation while making obsolete long-established manufacturing, marketing, and information-processing systems (e.g., Internet training replaces classroom training, enterprise-wide databases obviate need for mid-level analysts). Senior managers also face unrelenting internal challenges, including pressures to control costs (e.g., huge increases in insurance premiums, and ethical dilemmas, such as those that result from constant shareholder pressure for increased share value). The ultimate aim of senior managers is to deal with environmental volatility in a manner that enhances shareholder value and ensures the survival of the organization.

In the past decades, executives have increasingly employed teams as a tactic to combat the challenges presented by a turbulent marketplace (Hackman 1990). Through the use of teams, organizations can adapt successfully to changes by capitalizing on the synergy that effective teams produce. An important challenge for senior managers, then, is to understand how to create the conditions that will facilitate effective work teams. It has long been recognized that, even under the best of conditions, managing and motivating employees is a formidable task. Placing individuals into team settings, in which the individuals must coordinate their efforts and work together interdependently to complete their assignments, only serves to add another layer of complexity to the issues that senior managers must address. However, senior managers can benefit from the research conducted by cognitive, industrial/organizational, and social psychologists, who have identified many of the mechanisms important for effective teamwork (Guzzo and Dickson 1996).

In this chapter, we review the research literature on teams, distilling some basic, high-level principles for understanding team effectiveness. Based on the research review and the authors' experiences with a wide range of teams, the chapter culminates with a practical synthesis – advice – describing what makes highly effective teams successful in work organizations.

Why Do we Care about Teams?

When one individual does not have the skills, training, or resources to handle complex situations, organizations rely on teams of individuals who can work together to accomplish the goals. Some visible examples of teams are aviation cockpit crews, military command and control teams, battlefield crews, emergency room and operating room teams, emergency medical teams (EMT), law enforcement SWAT teams, oil platform teams, nuclear power plant teams, and top management teams. Because these teams typically process complex, ambiguous information, operate under time pressure, and experience high workloads in rapidly changing situations, these teams require high levels of coordination among members (McIntyre and Salas 1995). Such teams are typically hierarchical in organization. Team leaders use team member input, that is, information, to evaluate risks and make decisions, as well as to implement the leaders' subsequent action plans (McIntyre and Salas 1995). The success of the mission depends on the quality of the information and the smooth coordination between members of the team (Hackman 1990).

Organizations use teams for a number of reasons, but principally because teams offer a myriad of benefits beyond those possible from the efforts of individuals. Most importantly, synergy results when the efforts of many individuals are combined, which in turn produces enhanced outcomes. For example, in manufacturing settings fewer employees are needed to cover fluctuating workloads when individual tasks are transformed into flexible team tasks (Kelly 1982). Furthermore, the use of teams means that continuity of effort is possible despite turnover of personnel. Finally, teams are better equipped to handle the increased environmental and technological complexity that organizations face. Such complexity requires the increased cognitive resources that a team can mobilize as well as a team's capacity for greater coordination; for example, across functions, departments, and divisions.

While a single individual might struggle with the cognitive demands required to attend to, process, synthesize, and communicate complex information, a team of individuals could share the cognitive load and then integrate the products of their subtasks into a unified outcome. For example, in knowledge organizations such as financial-service firms, analysts are constantly bombarded by a stream of financial data that they must scan, process, analyze, and then recommunicate, using the appropriate format, to internal managers and customers, as well as to external clients. Moreover, the information processing is attended by the stress of operating under significant time pressure. In such a dynamic, data-rich, and time-constrained setting, a team arrangement may be the most appropriate organizational arrangement.

History has shown that teams can accomplish great goals. In their analysis of what they call Great Groups, Bennis and Biederman (1997) describe seven creative work teams whose output had an enduring impact on US culture. Included in their list were the team of artists at Walt Disney studio that in 1937 created the animated film *Snow White and the Seven Dwarfs*; the teams at Apple and at Xerox's Palo Alto Research Center responsible for designing user-friendly computers; the 1992 Clinton campaign team; Lockheed's Skunk Works teams that designed the innovative stealth airplane; the team that founded the Black Mountain College experimental arts school; and the Manhattan Project team that designed the atom bomb. Bennis and Biederman contend that it was the collaboration among the team members that led to their innovative output.

Research on Teams, Teamwork and Team Effectiveness

In the 1930s, Harvard researchers studied small groups at the Hawthorne Plant of Western Electric and published their findings about the power of informal group norms, which set off a flurry of research on small-group performance. Until recently, small work groups were the common arrangement when individuals worked together in organizations. As a result, research on small "groups" continued, but little or no research was conducted on work "teams." The distinction between them is that small groups engage in minimal or no task interdependency (e.g., department of individual contributions), while members of work teams are highly task interdependent (e.g., an assembly unit).

Salas et al. (1992) identified a number of unanswered questions concerning the nature of teamwork. Major questions remained about how best to manage teams and to train teamwork skills. One industry that started to examine teamwork issues closely in the 1980s was the aviation industry. Their interest in teamwork was related to the need to focus on increasing cockpit safety after a series of widely publicized airplane disasters. The disasters were attributed in part to cockpit crew error and poor crew coordination (Foushee 1984). The resulting research aimed to discover how best to train teamwork in high-reliability teams and resulted in the development of a training technique known as Crew Resource Management (CRM). Not only have commercial and military airlines widely adopted CRM training, but CRM training has spread to other high-reliability organizations, such as offshore oil platforms and operating rooms (Salas, Bowers, and Edens 2001).

The US military also has been responsible for stimulating interest in teamwork. After a series of tragedies resulting from poor military decision making (e.g., the USS *Vincennes* affair, in which an American vessel shot down a civilian Iranian airliner carrying 290 passengers and crew members), the military commissioned research to understand the relationship between stress, decision making, and team performance (Cannon-Bowers and Salas 1998). From one of the major research efforts, the Tactical Decision-Making Under Stress (TADMUS) project, came research that shed light onto relevant team processes and provided direction for ameliorating the effects of stress on team performance.

Industry, too, has experimented with team arrangements to solve business problems. For example, many organizations have adopted self-managing teams. Self-managing teams (SMTs) are typically charged with discovering operational shortcuts to reduce new-product development and production cycle times and to solve problems. Until it closed in the early 1990s after some 30 years of operation, Swedish auto manufacturer Volvo's plant in Kalmar was one of the earliest and best known examples of team-based manufacturing (Mueller, Procter, and Buchanan 2000).

In summary, recent needs of the military and industry to solve practical problems by applying research findings led to an increase in theoretical proposals and empirical studies on teams and teamwork (Sundstrom et al. 2000). The goal of the research was to understand how team members work together and to identify the specific characteristics that distinguish teams that function most effectively. On the one hand, it is clear that teams can accomplish great things, but it is equally apparent that subfunctioning teams have the potential to fail spectacularly. Only when individuals truly work together as a team, employing both taskwork and teamwork skills, can they accomplish their common goal. In the next section, we elaborate on what a team is and how teamwork contributes to effective team functioning.

Defining Teams, Teamwork, and Team Effectiveness

The terms "team," "teamwork," and "team effectiveness" can mean different things to different readers. Such definitional ambiguity can lead to confusion when senior managers are discussing teams but using the terms loosely. For example, a senior manager might suggest using a team to solve a problem, and conceive of the team as being composed of individuals whose activities will be highly interdependent. However, if the managers assigned the responsibility of creating and maintaining the team interpret the word "team" merely as a general label for any small group of workers, the "team" that is assembled will likely lack the requisite competencies and organizational support needed to be effective. Therefore, before we describe the characteristics of effective teams, we review definitions of teams, teamwork, and teamwork effectiveness to establish a common understanding of the terms.

What Is a Team?

A team has been defined as "a distinguishable set of two or more people who interact, dynamically, interdependently, and adaptively toward a common and valued goal/ objective/mission, who have each been assigned specific roles or functions to perform, and who have a limited life-span of membership" (Salas et al. 1992, 4). A team differs from a work group by a matter of degree, especially of interdependence among members. For example, Sundstrom et al. (2000) use the same definition to describe both work groups and work teams: "interdependent collections of individuals who share responsibility for specific outcomes for their organizations (Sundstrom, DeMeuse, and Futrell 1990, 120)."

In addition, team members see themselves, and appear to others, as a social unit. The major difference between work groups and teams is that teams require greater interdependency among members than do traditional work groups. In other words, they rely on each other and share needs with each other more often than groups do. For example, members of a work group may individually make recommendations to their manager, whereas members of a team would be more likely to offer a team recommendation based upon input from all members.

Many kinds of teams exist. For convenience, teams are typically divided into categories based on the type of task being undertaken by the team. One very popular typology (Sundstrom, De Meuse, and Futrell 1990) describes four types of teams; other authors use slightly different categorization schemes (Cohen and Bailey 1997). The well-known Sundstrom et al. (1990) typology includes the following categories of teams:

- Action and negotiation teams, such as sports teams, expeditions, negotiation teams, cockpit crews, firefighters, surgery teams, military tank crews, investigative units, rescue units, and professional musician groups (Sundstrom et al. 1990).
- Advice and involvement teams, such as committees, advisory councils, review panels. These teams are also referred to as parallel teams (Cohen and Bailey 1997).
- Production and service teams, such as manufacturing crews, assembly teams, maintenance crews, data processing groups. Work teams is the label given these teams by Cohen and Bailey.
- Self-managing teams, also known as semi-autonomous, autonomous, empowered, or self-directing teams. Once led by supervisors, current variations of these teams allow employees to assume some of the supervisor's decision-making responsibility (Cohen and Bailey 1997).
- Project and development teams, such as planning teams, research groups, engineering teams, task forces, development teams, (a.k.a. project teams in Cohen and Bailey).

In their typology, Cohen and Bailey (1997) also add a category for management teams. Management teams are responsible for the overall performance of the subunits managed by the team members. These five major types of teams are differentiated by the nature of their major task. In table 5.1 we summarize the main characteristics of the five major types of teams as described by Sundstrom, De Meuse, and Futrell (1990) and Cohen and Bailey (1997).

Throughout the remainder of this chapter, we conclude each section with several principles that summarize the key points discussed. We offer these principles as generalized statements that will serve both to describe teams and to focus the reader's attention on critical information. For a table consolidating all of the principles put forth within this chapter, refer to table 5.1.

Principle 1: Teams are characterized by high task interdependency.

Principle 2: All teams are not created equal.

Table 5.1 Types of teams and their characteristics

Type of team	Characteristics	Outcomes
Action, negotiation, and performing teams (Sundstrom et al.)	Experts with specialized skill sets Engage in complex, challenging, time-limited events Highly interdependent roles Requires rapid, coordinated task behavior (Kozlowski et al. 1996)	Performance event
Advice and involvement teams (Sundstrom et al.) a.k.a. parallel teams (Cohen and Bailey 1997)	Employee involvement groups Have limited authority restricted to making recommendations to upper management	Problem solving Improvement activities
Production and service (Sundstrom et al.) a.k.a. work teams (Cohen and Bailey)	Provide services or produce goods Typically stable, full-time, well-defined membership (Cohen 1991) Led by supervisors or self-managed Self-managed teams are typically cross-trained	Improved productivity Reduced costs Improved quality
Project and development teams (Sundstrom et al.) a.k.a. project teams (Cohen and Bailey)	Limited team life Produce non-repetitive, one-time outputs Require cross-functional knowledge, expertise, judgment Members disband or receive new assignments following project completion	Produce either incremental improvements or novel ideas Perform many concurrent activities Result in rapid development time
Management teams (Cohen and Bailey)	Subunit managers provide strategic management Hierarchically organized (Cohen and Bailey)	Provide combined expertise Responsible for organizational performance (Cohen and Bailey)

What Is Teamwork?

To be effective, team members need both taskwork and teamwork skills (McIntyre and Salas 1995). Taskwork refers to activities with tools, tasks, machines, and systems that support the team's operations. Each team member must know how to do his or her job; that is, the team member must possess the taskwork competencies (i.e., knowledge, skills, attitudes) that allow the individual to perform the task successfully (Salas and Cannon-Bowers 2001). In addition, each team member must possess skills that are related to the relational aspects of being a team member. Teamwork is the activity that supports the relationships, functional interactions, communication, coordination, and cooperation of team members. More succinctly, taskwork is what teams are doing, and teamwork is how they are doing it together (Marks et al. 2002). Thus, individuals must know how to work together and be "team players." We describe the competencies comprising teamwork in a later section of this chapter.

Principle 3: Team effectiveness is a function of both taskwork and teamwork.

Principle 4: Teamwork is a set of related competencies that supports taskwork.

What Is Team Effectiveness?

A team's effectiveness is not determined solely by the output it produces. Some authors have suggested that team effectiveness actually has three major dimensions (Cohen and Bailey 1997). The first dimension addresses the quality and quantity of the team's outputs, which can include productivity, efficiency, quality, turnaround time, innovation, and customer satisfaction. A second team effectiveness dimension concerns the attitudes of members. Team members can experience either positive or negative commitment, satisfaction with the team process, and willingness to work on future team projects (Hackman and Oldham 1980). The final dimension is behavioral outcomes such as safety, turnover, and absenteeism (Cohen and Bailey). A team with high "output," that is, demonstrating decreased commitment and turnover, is not a team that can maintain long-term success. Clearly, the effectiveness of team outcomes can impact various levels within an organization: individuals, the team itself, the division in which the team is embedded, and the organization.

Principle 5: A team's effectiveness can only be understood by examining multiple criteria.

In the following section, we present the major principles that characterize effective work teams. Using findings from empirical research as well as theoretical propositions put forth by leading scientists, we describe key attributes of effective teams. We also explain how the factor influences team performance.

When Teams Work.... and why

Although the volume of research conducted to understand and describe teams has been steadily growing, the literature is still deficient in many respects. However, in spite of its limitations, the team–research literature gives us enough information so that we can confidently offer principles about effective team functioning. These principles are general conclusions that can serve to guide senior management in making decisions about whether to use a team, how to organize a team, and what support is required for a team to maximize its success.

According to a popular typology (Sundstrom et al. 2000), characteristics of effective teams can be sorted into the following five broad categories:

1. the organizational context in which the team operates;
2. the size and member composition of the team;
3. the design of the team's work;
4. interactions and processes among team members; and
5. interactions between the team and its external contacts.

We use this typology as an organizing framework to present the principles of effective team functioning. Within each category, we summarize general findings about how the category influences team performance. We include information from specific studies to illustrate the points made.

Organizational Context

No team operates in a vacuum. Every team is embedded in an organization which in turn can legitimatize and reinforce the team, its purpose, and its output. Teams are shaped to varying degrees by the features of the organization, such as its reward and recognition system, the training it provides, how performance is measured, the information systems available to the team, the facility which houses employees, and external environmental factors, such as technology, industry, competitors, and markets (Sundstrom 1999). Additional contextual factors that affect teams include organization-wide supervisory practices and leaders' roles (Sundstrom, De Meuse, and Futrell 1990; Sundstrom et al. 2000).

An organization's culture powerfully shapes the perceptions of individual team members and the team as a whole as to the kinds of behaviors that are expected, accepted, and rewarded (Schein 1996). Furthermore, the organization's communications can impact team performance. For example, a clear organizational mission statement helps team members recognize the contribution of their efforts to the organization's goals, which focuses their efforts by giving them a shared purpose.

Another organizational system that impacts team performance is the reward system. Reward systems tell team members which behaviors will be rewarded and which will be punished. If the reward system reinforces individualistic behavior, then team effectiveness will be compromised as group goals are sacrificed for increased personal outcomes. In one study, service technician groups who received group-based rewards showed the best performance when the team members had high task interdependence; that is, they relied on each other extensively to complete the task (Wageman 1995). Rewards don't always need to be financial. In one instance, telecommunications teams rated their performance high when they received management recognition, which is a nonmonetary reward (Cohen, Ledford, and Spreitzer 1996). However, changes in reward systems may often be more effective when combined with other interventions. For example, when rewards were combined with performance feedback and goal-setting interventions, aircraft maintenance teams (service teams) showed a large increase in productivity (Pritchard et al. 1988).

Performance evaluation systems also signal team members about the types of behaviors that the organization values. If the performance evaluation system fails to reward team members for participation in team projects, or worse, if team participation is seen as a reason for failure to meet nonteam personal goals, a team member's willingness to participate on team projects may be strongly discouraged. In addition to the performance appraisal system, an organization's training and development efforts are also influential because they inform teams about the skills that the organization considers most important. For example, a global financial services firm demonstrated significant change in this area by explicitly rewarding – through annual appraisals – partners who participated in team projects relating to campus recruitment, monitoring, and educational activities. The presence or lack of training in teamwork skills sends a subtle signal to team members and their managers about the necessity of such skills.

Teams are attentive to their surroundings, too. The physical environment includes the resources and equipment that team members need to accomplish their goals (e.g., production equipment, computers and communication technology, etc.). The equipment, technology, and resources available to the team can help or hinder the team's efforts to meet its goals. A team will evaluate the degree of organizational support that is being provided to them, and based on that judgment, will form impressions of how important the team's activities are to management. Leaders and supervisors, who have a powerful impact on teams, typically demonstrate those management behaviors that are reinforced by the larger organization. To the extent that the organization supports teams, managers and supervisors will tend to support teams.

External environmental factors include the technology used within the organization, the industry in which the organization competes, its turbulence, its competitors, and its markets. These factors can influence a team in two major ways. First, they can shape the nature and composition of a team. For example, in a dynamic industry such as financial services, organizations require flexible, adaptive teams composed of highly motivated specialists. Other external factors also influence teams as they work toward accomplishing their goals (Cohen and Bailey 1997; Sundstrom 1999). For example, teams within financial-services firms require state-of-the-art telecommunications support to provide them with instant information about activities in global financial markets. In this case, a financial-service organization could compensate for external conditions by ensuring that teams have the best possible technological support. Team success is directly affected by the extent to which an organization can anticipate and respond to the influence of environmental factors.

In summary, we make two general conclusions about the information presented in this section. First, teams may operate without experiencing direct congruence between their needs and support from the organization. Second, to the extent that the organization systematically ensures congruence among the different organizational systems and the needs of teams, team outcomes will be improved. To paraphrase John Donne, "no team is an island, entire of itself."

Principle 6: When an organization shows that it values teamwork, teams are more likely to perform "as a team."

Principle 7: Teams explicitly and implicitly evaluate whether the organization values teamwork.

Principle 8: Rewards, and what is measured in the organization, tell teams which behaviors are valued and need to be exhibited.

Team Composition and Size

Because teams are composed of multiple individuals, team composition variables affect team performance. A team's effectiveness can be influenced by its size as well as by each member's traits, such as personality, ability, and demographic characteristics (Sundstrom et al. 2000). Other important factors are the team's collective expertise, diversity, ability, heterogeneity, and membership stability.

Determining the appropriate number of team members with which to staff a team is a judgment call. A team's size must be balanced between having too few members and having too many. Too few members results in decreased availability of member expertise while having too many members results in performance decrements due to negative social processes, such as process loss (Steiner 1972) and social loafing (Cohen and Bailey 1997).

One of the most critical factors underlying team success is individual-member competencies (knowledge, skills, attitudes) because each team member must be capable of carrying out his or her assigned role (McIntyre and Salas 1995). Individual team members must have the appropriate task knowledge; that is, they must know what to do, when to do it, and how to do it. They must also have adequate work experience to perform their roles (McIntyre and Salas). Poor team member composition (on any number of dimensions) leads to suboptimal results (Barrick et al. 1998; LePine et al. 1997).

Another individual characteristic, personality traits, can also impact team performance (Sundstrom et al. 2000). Some studies found that higher levels of the personality trait of conscientiousness were associated with higher performance for two kinds of service teams, assembly teams, and maintenance teams (Barrick et al. 1998; Neuman and Wright 1999; Neuman, Wagner, and Christiansen 1999).

The functional diversity of team members has been both positively and negatively associated with team effectiveness (Sundstrom et al. 2000). Functional diversity refers to the total number of job functions or specialties of team members. In some cases, functional diversity has a positive relationship with group effectiveness. For example, in a study of service teams, greater functional diversity was positively related to members' self-ratings of performance (Gladstein 1984). In project teams, it was positively associated with effectiveness ratings (Ancona and Caldwell 1992b). Furthermore, supervisors rated team effectiveness higher in those employee involvement (advisory) groups that had greater functional diversity (Magjuka and Baldwin 1991). However, functional diversity has shown mixed results in top management teams. Studies have shown that greater functional diversity is related to lower company performance (Haleblian and Finkelstein 1993), although other studies have shown inconsistent relationships (Smith et al. 1994). In contrast, other studies found that top management teams with greater functional diversity demonstrated greater strategy planning flexibility (Bartel 1994).

Principle 9: Team composition matters.

Principle 10: The right composition depends on the requirements of the task.

Team Work Design

Recently, researchers have recognized the impact of work design on team outcomes (Bell and Kozlowski 2002). How a work team is designed directly influences team outcomes and indirectly affects team processes and interpersonal relations (Cohen and Bailey 1997). Work design refers to work features, such as task characteristics, equipment, and reporting relationships (Sundstrom et al. 2000). Reporting relationships concern the degree to which the team manages itself, the limits of its decision-making authority, and its level of autonomy.

The layout of the physical/space plan of the equipment with which a team works determines whether team members will have opportunities to talk together, observe each other's behavior, and anticipate problems. Proper space and equipment can facilitate information sharing and team cohesiveness.

Task interdependence among members has complex effects on team effectiveness (Sundstrom et al. 2000). Studies of task interdependence have been done mainly with service teams. For example, in a study of information technology teams, high task interdependence was positively associated with team member satisfaction and with objectively measured team performance (Janz, Colquitt, and Noe 1997). In a study of clerical teams, task interdependence was positively related to productivity, and higher goal interdependence was associated with higher performance ratings by managers (Campion, Medsker, and Higgs 1993). The study also found that outcome interdependence was positively related to the satisfaction of team members.

However, the relationships found between task interdependence and performance are complex. For example, service technician teams that were highly interdependent showed high performance only if a group-based reward system was in place (Wageman 1995). But teams that had low interdependence and an individual-based rewards system also showed high performance. The conclusion that can be drawn is that the relationship between task interdependence and performance is influenced by many other factors (Sundstrom et al. 2000).

A team's performance can be directly affected by its level of autonomy. For example, in service teams, a clear positive relationship between autonomy and performance was established (Campion, Medsker, and Higgs 1993; Cohen and Ledford 1994). However, for project teams, greater autonomy was negatively related to performance (Kim and Lee 1995), which may have been due to the high frequency of contact between project teams and individuals outside the team. One aspect of autonomy is the degree to which a team sets its own goals. Goal-setting focuses team member attention and thereby directly impacts the team's performance. Teams that set their own goals will have a greater investment in reaching those goals. For production teams, research showed that goal-setting interventions increased quality, but had no impact on production quantity (Buller and Bell 1986).

Principle 11: The nature of the task sets major team boundaries.

Principle 12: The team's physical layout matters.

Principle 13: The task determines how much interdependence is required.

Within-Team Processes

A key defining characteristic of a team is that team members interact among themselves. Therefore, the category of within-team processes include interpersonal team processes such as communication, collaboration, coordination, and conflict (Sundstrom et al. 2000). The elements in this category are frequently referred to as "teamwork behaviors" (McIntyre and Salas 1995). Also included are cohesion, perceived potency or collective efficacy, group norms, social integration, and other group characteristics. Cohen and Bailey (1997) refer to these as group psychosocial traits, which include a team's beliefs, shared understandings, or emotional tone. Team mental models are also considered a within-team process (Cannon-Bowers, Salas, and Converse 1993).

Group psychosocial traits are group-level phenomena that directly influence outcomes (Sundstrom et al. 2000). They also affect how team members relate both to one another and to contacts outside of the team. Relationships among members, which are affected by team members' status and roles, are included in this category. If team leaders are also members of the team, then roles of the leader, such as feedback or goal setting, are included in the category. If the team's role requires coordination, then both the within-group-processes and team-work-design categories are pertinent to the team's interpersonal processes.

Successful interdependency requires team members to have the skills to communicate effectively (McIntyre and Salas 1995). Effective communication may require closed-loop communication in which the sender sends the message, the recipient receives and acknowledges receipt of the message, and the sender verifies that the message received was the one sent. In emergency or unexpected situations, clear and accurate exchange of information between members may mean the difference between success or failure. Even in nonemergency situations, poor communication can result in negative outcomes. For example, on a noisy trading floor, large sums of money have been lost because directions to buy/sell were executed in the wrong direction or with the wrong stocks. Not only must communication be clear, but communication and information sharing must be fostered. The team leader and team members must discourage the "hoarding" of information that might occur if team members are trying to protect their individual power.

Group norms determine how individual team members will work together (Seashore 1954). An obvious example is the informal production norms that can prove more powerful than official organization norms (Roethlisberger and Dickson 1939: Hawthorne studies). One performance value (attitude) that acts as an enabling condition for teams is the willingness of the team members to see themselves as team players, working together toward group success (McIntyre and Salas 1995). Team members should value team success more than individual success. When the members of a team are not prepared to work together, poor team outcomes result (Mohrman, Cohen, and Mohrman 1995). Another interpersonal process that affects team performance is how members view conflict among the team members and the conflict-reduction strategies they use. For example, in both management and production teams, relationship-based conflict was found to decrease member satisfaction, although it had no effect on team performance (Jehn 1995).

The degree of a team's social integration also affects its outcomes. In a hierarchically organized team, members have different status. The formal and informal social structure influences member behavior (Sundstrom et al. 2000). Frequently, low-status team members will hesitate to question or contradict higher-status members, even if doing so would help team effectiveness. Training can teach individuals to be more assertive in the presence of their superiors. For example, Crew Resource Management training is used to teach flight crew members how to bring safety issues proactively to the attention of the captain (Helmreich et al. 1986).

Cohesion in groups and teams has been well studied (Sundstrom et al. 2002). Cohesiveness is the degree to which members are attracted to the group and are loyal to teammates. For project and production teams, higher team cohesion has been shown to have a positive relation with performance (Gully, Devine, and Whitney 1995). However, those effects were not found with service teams or bank management teams (David, Pearce, and Randolph 1989; George and Bettenhausen 1990). Also, there was no relationship between cohesion and turnover among members of service teams (George and Bettenhausen 1990). So, although cohesion in project teams can predict team effectiveness, cohesion does not predict well for service teams. Possibly cohesion only predicts well if teams have group norms that favor production (Seashore 1954).

Group efficacy or perceived potency is a very strong predictor of how well teams will perform (Sundstrom et al. 2000). Collective efficacy and group potency are related concepts that refer to the perception of team members that the team can accomplish its tasks (Guzzo et al. 1993). Studies conducted with production, project, and service teams have found that higher collective efficacy is positively associated with higher ratings of performance by observers. Similar results have been shown for clerical and customer service teams (Campion, Medsker, and Higgs 1993; Hyatt and Ruddy 1997).

Another important attitude is that team members promote interdependence among the members (McIntyre and Salas 1995). Members must understand that their subtasks are interconnected and that overall task success depends on the success of each subtask. Each team member must understand how his or her role functions in relation to the roles of others. The value underlying this attitude is that members depend on each other and that interdependence is appropriate and essential.

Teams develop through a sequential process (Sundstrom, De Meuse, and Futrell 1990). Teams, especially intact teams whose members have worked together as a team, will change and develop over time (McIntyre and Salas 1995). For the team, fundamental aspects of teamwork, such as the closed-loop communication mentioned above, can improve with training, practice, and experience. Role definition and problem solving are two more examples of team interventions that affect team development.

Roles need to be clear because clear roles contribute to expectations, serve to assign accountability for major critical activities that must occur, and reduce ambiguity. In fact, research has shown that team building efforts that focus on clarifying team roles are not effective (Salas et al. 1999; Tannenbaum, Beard, and Salas 1992). Role definition can contribute to improved team coordination. Team processes that enable team members to learn about other team members' tasks can be very beneficial (McIntyre and Salas 1995). Each team member needs to be competent to a certain degree in the general team tasks and highly competent in tasks upon which his or her own task depends. Individuals must know what behaviors to monitor, what information to feed back, and how to back up their teammates.

Members must monitor each other's performance (McIntyre and Salas 1995). This behavior both improves the team's performance and establishes psychological trust among the team members. Team members should demonstrate back-up behavior; that is, offer to help others. Team members must be willing and inclined to both offer and accept help from others. Back-up behavior can only be feasible if team members have the required skills or expertise in others' tasks. In addition to monitoring teammates' performance, team members should provide feedback.

Feedback should be freely sought and provided by team members (McIntyre and Salas 1995). Feedback sources are both external and internal to the team. Feedback serves to keep team members focused and keep goals aligned, and it also allows for corrective action as needed. As a result of monitoring, team members can provide feedback. To provide high-quality feedback, team members must be able to overcome issues of status, tenure, and rank. Being able to do so depends on the team's climate, which is often a result of leader behaviors that set a norm of accepting criticism. Feedback is important because it makes members aware of their strengths and weaknesses, a preliminary stage to acquiring needed competencies. A source of feedback information can be regular team "debriefs," which are an opportunity for team members to discuss outcomes and explore ways in which to improve similar future situations. Research has shown that teams that conduct effective debriefs perform better (Tannenbaum et al. 1996). "Situation updates" must be provided within the team. Communication (both implicit and explicit) provides a basis for coordinating team member efforts.

Common goals must be established early in the team's life. When goals are shared among team members, they serve to facilitate team processes by providing direction. Goals also help team members to attain value congruency among themselves. Ideally, goals are aligned both with individual goals and with the organization's goals. As well as goals, teams need a road map, a plan, for accomplishing their goals. The road map keeps the attention of members directed toward goals. Team leaders can use the road map as a point of comparison between the plan and the actual status of the team's progress. Along with the creation of goals and shared values, shared mental models are constructed. They serve to keep team members coordinated by managing expectations of other members' behaviors (Cannon-Bowers, Salas, and Converse 1993).

Teamwork requires that team members possess a repertoire of skills. In addition, team members must be flexible and able to adapt to the circumstances as they affect the team. They are aided by the establishment of clear task processes. Clear processes are valuable because routinization of procedures reduces uncertainty and administrative and other systems provide structure, which allows the team to divert resources to nonroutine issues. Personal adaptability is also important. For example, team leaders may engage in behaviors ranging from democratic to autocratic depending on the needs of the moment.

Principle 14: Communication skills and processes (e.g., closed-loop feedback) are essential.

Principle 15: Team players must value the team's goal.

Principle 16: Teams must believe that collectively they can reach their goal.

Principle 17: Teams can improve their processes through training, practice, and experience.

Principle 18: Clear member roles facilitate coordination.

Principle 19: Team debriefs are powerful team performance enhancers.

Principle 20: Monitoring and back-up behaviors are the core of teamwork.

Principle 21: Team members must be able to recognize and be ready to adapt as the situation changes.

External Team Processes

Team members not only engage in interpersonal processes among themselves; they also interact with agencies outside the team (Sundstrom et al. 2000). External contacts may include managers, peers, customers, staff, and suppliers. Such boundary-spanning interactions require coordination and communication processes as described above (Sundstrom, De Meuse, and Futrell 1990).

The boundaries by which a team defines itself serve to differentiate it from other teams and from other parts of the organization. Temporal factors also influence team outcomes (Sundstrom, De Meuse, and Futrell 1990). Both the expected life span of the team as well as the amount of time that the team spends working together affect how team members view the importance of the team.

Many studies have been conducted on the relationship between external contacts and team performance in project teams. Evidence suggests that the type and frequency of external communication may predict performance, under certain conditions (Ancona 1990; Ancona and Caldwell 1992a; Katz 1982). Whether external communication is related to team effectiveness seems to depend on the type of team (Sundstrom et al. 2000). For example, project teams that reported high amounts of external communication were judged to be effective (Ancona and Caldwell 1992a).

A number of external interaction strategies (informing, parading, and probing: Ancona 1990) have been identified. For educational consultant teams, a correlation was found between probing and ratings of their performance (Ancona). In new product development teams, the amount of external communication was positively associated with budget and schedule adherence (Ancona and Caldwell 1992a). Innovation efficiency was also positively related to more frequent external communications (Ancona and Caldwell).

Principle 22: Boundary-spanning requires communication and coordination skills.

Principle 23: Contacts outside the team can facilitate team innovation.

Team Leadership

Although the topic of leadership as it relates to team performance belongs in the categories of organizational context or within-group processes, we have added a separate section for it in recognition of the powerful influence leadership can have on a team. The two major responsibilities of leaders are achieving the team's goal and maintaining the team as a viable entity. Researchers have been interested in identifying a leader's managerial role but have recently emphasized understanding the social, interpersonal-oriented aspects of leadership. Team leaders must maintain a balance between administrative duties and interpersonal relationships, which is affected by such factors as the type and nature of the task, member characteristics, and so on.

Leadership is important because leaders can exert a powerful influence on the cognitive, motivational, affective, and coordination aspects of team processes (Zaccaro, Rittman, and Marks 2001). For example, through their instructions and explanations, leaders can shape team members' cognitions, such as shared mental models (Klimoski and Mohammed 1994). Leaders can influence the motivation levels of team members by exhibiting behaviors that support the formation and maintenance of the team's cohesion and collective efficacy (Kozlowski et al. 1996). Team members also share affective feelings, which leaders can influence. For example, leaders can reduce the stress level in a team by reducing negative mood and building positive mood (George 1995). Finally, team leaders coordinate team members' activities by maximizing member contributions, guiding team members to acquire successful interaction patterns, and spreading the patterns through standardization (Kozlowski et al. 1996).

For many types of teams, the leader must have at least some technical/operational competence. With low technical competence, leaders are forced to rely more on team members. A leader can model appropriate team and task behavior for team members, which in turn establishes the teamwork climate. Effective leaders are committed to the team and place the success of the team ahead of their own personal success. Another characteristic of effective leaders is their sensitivity to gaining and maintaining respect from team members, which makes them better able to influence team members' attitudes and behaviors (McIntyre and Salas 1995).

A leader's duties includes establishing performance goals and a clear focus, setting expectations for individuals and the team, assigning roles to members, ensuring that the team has needed personnel and material resources, and removing barriers to performance (Klimoski and Zaccaro 2002). Furthermore, leaders monitor the progress of a team towards its goal, providing feedback and fine-tuning schedules and plans in a timely and appropriate manner. The leader also represents the team to external agents. In the boundary-spanning role, leaders frame and publicize the team's achievements, negotiate for resources, and bring information back to the team. Essentially, they "market" the team and its capabilities to a wider audience. The patterns of a leader's activities change over the life cycle of the team and its phase in the task activities.

Depending on the type of team, a leader can be the assigned team leader who has decision-making responsibility (McIntyre and Salas 1995). The leadership role can also be filled by a senior team member or assigned leader assistant who provides team management and leadership. In some cases, the distributed expertise of individual members can substitute for the leader role (Klimoski and Zaccaro 2002). For self-managed teams, the leadership role is split among the members, according to their level of expertise, their willingness and interest in leading, and the time they have available to assume leadership duties. At different times in the life of a self-managed team, the leadership role will rotate among the members.

Team leadership affects team performance. Leaders model teamwork behavior, which in turn gains support from team members. Some teams can work around poor team leaders, but generally poor leaders cannot protect and grow their teams (McIntyre and Salas 1995). Leader behavior also influences the willingness of team members to monitor and provide feedback behavior.

Leaders must keep the team focused on its mission. Leaders must also frame events so that team members do not become discouraged after a failure. At the same time, leaders must not encourage undue optimism that leads team members to become overconfident of their abilities. Leaders vary on their readiness to lead and on their technical competence with team operations. Leaders who are not technically ready or are not ready to lead cause disorder. Team members interpret unreadiness as due to insignificance of the team or of the team task. But if leaders are both technically ready and leadership ready, they can give direction and convey the importance of the team's assignment.

Leaders must be knowledgeable enough that they can be self-confident and open to input from team members with special expertise. Leaders must know enough about team operations, based on both their own knowledge and experience and that of team members to maintain an understanding of the big picture. Leaders who feign expertise and worry about face saving may resist help and feedback, which can be counterproductive. Leaders must provide feedback and recommendations for improvement, but can do so only to the extent they have expertise in operational and technical details.

A leader's style can influence a team's feedback processes. Team effectiveness is hampered by an overtly tough leadership style (e.g., micromanaging, personal overconfidence regarding technical mastery of team tasks, and autocratic style of managing). For example, team members may find it difficult to provide such leaders with constructive criticism because leaders will reject it, become defensive, or resist it. Team members, in turn, learn to stop providing it. Further problems for team members may include the perceived need to screen negative information which may be unpalatable to the manager for fear of being blamed for it. The ultimate result may be that the team orientation of members may deteriorate. Respected team leaders are more effective than those who are not respected. Alienated team members (i.e., who do not like the leader) do not support or help the leader, which can lead to failure of teamwork.

Team leaders must be strong problem solvers. Typically, individuals in leadership positions have greater expertise or experience than other team members. The greater the personal and organizational resources upon which they can call for assistance, the more likely they will tap into resources that will lead to optimal solutions. This characteristic is especially important in knowledge-intensive environments, in which the complexity is high and leaders experience constant conflict in prioritizing.

Leaders must be flexible. If opportunities arise, the leader must not only recognize the opportunity, but be able to analyze the threats associated with it and evaluate the probability of success if a new path is followed. They must be able to respond to circumstances quickly and change priorities accordingly. Leaders must have the cognitive resources necessary to deal with complexity in the environment. Leaders may experience role ambiguity, especially when they must balance the team's interests against those of the larger organization. Leaders must be able to manage (diffuse, reduce, or cope with) role ambiguity.

Team leaders must be able to implement effectively. Whenever ideas, equipment, or procedures change, leaders must proactively ensure, whether through their own activities or those of the team members, that follow through and monitoring occur. Good ideas that fail to be implemented are of no benefit to the team's functioning.

Principle 24: Team leadership can make a large difference in team performance.

Principle 25: Team leaders model desirable behaviors.

Summary

In table 5.2, we have summarized the key principles that describe effective teams. However, it is important to remember that all teams are not created equal. They vary on a number of dimensions, including maturity, level of development, and cohesiveness. Teamwork fundamentals, such as back-up behavior and within-team interdependence,

Table 5.2   Principles for understanding teamwork

Principle

Principle 1: Teams are characterized by high task interdependency.
Principle 2: All teams are not created equal.
Principle 3: Team effectiveness is a function of both taskwork and teamwork.
Principle 4: Teamwork is a set of related competencies that supports taskwork.
Principle 5: A team's effectiveness can only be understood by examining multiple criteria.
Principle 6: When an organization shows that it values teamwork, teams are more likely to perform "as a team."
Principle 7: Teams explicitly and implicitly evaluate whether the organization values teamwork.
Principle 8: Rewards, and what is measured in the organization, tell teams which behaviors are valued and need to be exhibited.
Principle 9: Team composition matters.
Principle 10: The right composition depends on the requirements of the task.
Principle 11: The nature of the task sets major team boundaries.
Principle 12: The team's physical layout matters.
Principle 13: The task determines how much interdependence is required.
Principle 14: Communication skills and processes (e.g., closed-loop feedback) are essential.
Principle 15: Team players must value the team's goal.
Principle 16: Teams must believe that collectively they can reach their goal.
Principle 17: Teams can improve their processes through training, practice, and experience.
Principle 18: Clear member roles facilitate coordination.
Principle 19: Team debriefs are powerful team performance enhancers.
Principle 20: Monitoring and back-up behaviors are the core of teamwork.
Principle 21: Team members must be able to recognize and be ready to adapt as the situation changes.
Principle 22: Boundary-spanning requires communication and coordination skills.
Principle 23: Contacts outside the team can facilitate team innovation.
Principle 24: Team leadership can make a large difference in team performance.
Principle 25: Team leaders model desirable behaviors.

change over time through training, practice, and experience (Salas and Cannon–Bowers 2001).

How Can Management Support Teams?

The purpose of this chapter is also to familiarize managers, executives, and those in human resources with the factors that lead to effective team performance. In general, a key role of senior leaders is to ensure that organizational support systems are aligned with performance requirements. We acknowledge that aligning systems and subsystems often requires a significant effort from an organization. A successful team is composed of individuals with the requisite team and task competencies. The burden is on management to create a system that motivates individuals to acquire those competencies. Some other management issues associated with the use of teams within organizations are discussed below.

Caveats: When a Team Is Not the Solution

Forming a team is not the best solution to every organizational problem. Sometimes an individual possesses the unique knowledge or expertise that can solve a problem. Teams require a great deal of support; they need management attention and effort. In one sense, using teams has become a sort of management fad, due to the well-publicized (and well-deserved) success of high-profile teams. But before forming a team, managers must ask whether the resources required will justify the costs incurred. Ensuring team effectiveness often requires changing organizational systems to support the teams, but the cost and effort involved in doing so just to have teams is not sufficient rationale. Furthermore, teams may not always be able to reach the perfect solution. For example, after time-consuming research and deliberation, a Total Quality Management (TQM) team might recommend structural changes to existing equipment as a way to increase machine output. However, if the management team determined that the strategic solution were to purchase new equipment based on breakthrough technology, then the TQM team's efforts would have been pointless. One potential outcome that could have long-term negative effects for the organization would be the creation of a perception by team members that future efforts on their part would be equally valueless. Such a perception might result in less employee enthusiasm toward team membership.

We offer another example of a situation in which a team may not be the answer. If a few individuals on the team do the majority of the work, then the efforts of the individuals and not teamwork is making the team successful. Highly experienced or well-prepared members can show outstanding performance. However, the result may be team dependence on a star performer who may in turn become overloaded or unavailable. Before creating teams, senior management must address the issue of unequal individual skills.

Teams Require an Investment

Teams don't just happen. The creation of teams must be a result of deliberation: purposeful and planned. Moreover, teams require ongoing support, which can be expensive. In addition, because team members are composed of idiosyncratic humans, every team has its own personality: culture, norms, and standards, which may or may not align with the organization's culture.

Some Practical Advice

In this section, we translate what we know about effective teamwork into a list of the characteristics that describe effective teams. In developing the contents of the list, we

Table 5.3   Characteristics of highly effective teams

Highly effective teams . . .
Have a clear, common purpose
Differentiate between higher and lower priorities
Ensure team member roles are clear but not overly rigid
Manage conflict well – team members confront each other effectively
Involve the right people in decisions
Examine and adjust the team's physical workplace to optimize communication and coordination
Back up and fill in for each other
Distribute and assign work thoughtfully
Communicate often "enough." Ensure that fellow team members have the information they need
   to be able to contribute
Conduct effective meetings
Establish and revise team goals and plans
Consciously integrate new team members
Identify teamwork and task work requirements
Ensure that, through staffing and/or development, the team possesses the right mix of
   competencies
Effectively "span" boundaries with stakeholders outside the team
Negotiate for the resources needed to succeed
Regularly provide feedback to each other, both individually and as a team ("de-brief")
Select team members who value teamwork
"Deal" with poor performers
Strongly believe in the team's collective ability to succeed
Have members who understand each others' roles and how they fit together
Trust other team members' "intentions"
Periodically diagnose team "effectiveness," including its results, its processes, and its vitality
   (morale, retention, energy)
Are neither too large nor too small
Have mechanisms for anticipating and reviewing issues/problems of members
Have a "critical mass" that actively supports what the team is trying to accomplish
Have team members who believe the leader cares about them
Are led by someone with good leadership skills and not just technical competence

relied both on our practical experiences as well as on the steadily increasing collection of team-related empirical research findings. Necessarily broad, the items in this list are useful because they have been found repeatedly in effective teams and are considered to be predictors of team effectiveness.

We suggest that managers, executives, and human resource professionals use the contents of table 5.3 as a checklist to perform a quick diagnosis of the presence or absence of "team success" factors. However, we caution readers when reviewing table 5.3 to remember two of the initial principles that we proposed. First, teams differ on many dimensions, which means that the organizational setting, composition of the team, and team processes must be taken into account as influences on team effectiveness. Second, both taskwork and teamwork are required for team success. Team members must be able to perform their primary tasks, but must do so as "team players."

Concluding Remarks

We began this chapter by noting that senior managers face a myriad of challenges from both external and internal sources. To meet those challenges, senior managers increasingly rely on the synergy that is an output of the efforts of effective work teams. However, management faces a significant challenge when using teams because of the need to identify and provide the conditions that are essential for successful teamwork. Specifically, teams are influenced by a number of factors at the individual, the team, and the organizational level, all of which must be explicitly addressed by management. As long as teams can contribute to desirable organizational outcomes, senior managers must support teams wherever their use makes a meaningful contribution to organizational goals.

NOTES

Correspondence concerning this article should be addressed to Eduardo Salas, PhD, Department of Psychology, University of Central Florida, PO Box 161390, Orlando, FL 32816-1350, 407-882-1325 (telephone), 407–658–5059 (fax). Electronic mail may be sent via Internet to esalas@pegasus.cc.ucf.edu.

The views expressed herein are those of the authors and do not reflect the opinions of the organizations.

REFERENCES

Ancona, D. G. 1990. Outward bound: Strategies for team survival in the organization. *Academy of Management Journal* 33:334–65.

Ancona, D. G., and Caldwell, D. F. 1992a. Bridging the boundary: External activity and performance in organizational teams. *Administrative Science Quarterly* 37:634–65.

Ancona, D. G., and Caldwell, D. F. 1992b. Demography and design: Predictors of new product team performance. *Organization Science: A Journal of the Institute of Management Sciences* 3: 321–42.

Barrick, M. R., Stewart, G. L., Neubert, J. M., and Mount, M. K. 1998. Relating member ability and personality to work-team processes and team effectiveness. *Journal of Applied Psychology* 83:377–91.

Bartel, A. P. 1994. Productivity gains from implementation of employee training programs. *Industrial Relations* 33:411–26.

Bell, B. S., and Kozlowski, S. W. J. 2002. A typology of virtual teams. *Group and Organization Management* 27:14–49.

Bennis, W., and Biederman, P. W. 1997. *Organizing Genius: The Secrets of Creative Collaboration.* Reading, MA: Addison-Wesley.

Bettenhausen, K. L. 1991. Five years of groups research: What we have learned and what needs to be addressed. *Journal of Management* 17:345–81.

Blake, R. R., and Mouton, J. S. 1964. *The Managerial Grid: Key Orientations for Achieving Production through People.* Houston, TX: Gulf.

Blickensderfer, E., Cannon-Bowers, J. A., and Salas, E. 1998. Cross-training and team performance. In J. A. Cannon-Bowers and E. Salas (eds.), *Making Decisions under Stress: Implications for Individual and Team Training.* Washington, DC: APA.

Buller, P. F. and Bell, C. 1986. Effects of team building and goal setting on productivity: A field experiment. *Academy of Management Journal* 29:305–28.

Campion, M. A., Medsker, G. J., and Higgs, A. C. 1993. Relations between work group characteristics and effectiveness: Implications for designing effective work groups. *Personnel Psychology* 46:823–50.

Cannon-Bowers, J. A., and Salas, E. 1998. Individual and team decision making under stress: Theoretical underpinnings. In J. A. Cannon-Bowers and E. Salas (eds.), *Making Decisions under Stress: Implications for Individual and Team Training.* Washington, DC: APA.

Cannon-Bowers, J. A., Salas, E., and Converse, S. 1993. Shared mental models in expert team decision-making. In N. J. Castellan, Jr. (ed.), *Current Issues in Individual and Group Decision-Making.* Hillsdale, NJ: Lawrence Erlbaum.

Cannon-Bowers, J. A., Salas, E., Blickensderfer, E., and Bowers, C. A. 1998. The impact of cross-training and workload on team functioning: A replication and extension of initial findings. *Human Factors* 40 (1):92–101.

Cohen, S. G. 1991. New approaches to teams and teamwork. In J. R. Galbraith, E. E. Lawler, and Associates (eds.), *Organizing for the Future: The New Logic for Managing Complex Organizations.* San Francisco: Jossey-Bass.

Cohen, S. G., and Bailey, D. E. 1997. What makes team work: Group effectiveness research from the shop floor to the executive suite. *Journal of Management* 23 (3):239–220.

Cohen, S. G., and Ledford, G. E. 1994. The effectiveness of self-managing teams: A quasi-experiment. *Human Relations* 47:13–43.

Cohen, S. G., Ledford, G. E., and Spreitzer, G. M. 1996. A predictive model of self-managing work team effectiveness. *Human Relations* 49:643–76.

David, F. R., Pearce, J. A., and Randolph, W. A. 1989. Linking technology and structure to enhance group performance. *Journal of Applied Psychology* 74:233–41.

Eden, D. 1985. Team development: A true field experiment at three levels of rigor. *Journal of Applied Psychology* 70:94–100.

Fleming, J. L., and Monda-Amaya, L. E. 2001. Process variables critical for team effectiveness. *Remedial and Special Education* 22 (3):158–71.

Foushee, H. C. 1984. Dyads and triads at 35,000 feet. *American Psychologist* 39:885–893.

George, J. M. 1995. Leader positive mood and group performance: The case of customer service. *Journal of Applied Social Psychology* 25:778–94.

George, J. M., and Bettenhausen, K. 1990. Understanding prosocial behavior, sales performance, and turnover: A group-level analysis in a service context. *Journal of Applied Psychology* 75:698–709.

Gillespie, D. F., and Birnbaum, P. H. 1980. Status concordance, coordination, and success in interdisciplinary research teams. *Human Relations* 33:41–56.

Gladstein, D. L. 1984. Groups in context: A model of task group effectiveness. *Administrative Science Quarterly* 29:499–517.

Greene, C. N. 1989. Cohesion and productivity in work groups. *Small Group Behavior* 20:70–86.

Gully, S. M., Devine, D. J., and Whitney, D. J. 1995. A meta-analysis of cohesion and performance: Effects of levels of analysis and task interdependence. *Small Group Research* 26 (4):497–520.

Guzzo, R. A., and Dickson, M. W. 1996. Teams in organizations: Recent research on performance and effectiveness. *Annual Review of Psychology* 47:307–38.

Guzzo, R. A., Yost, P. R., Campbell, R. J., and Shea, G. P. 1993. Potency in groups: Articulating a construct. *British Journal of Social Psychology* 32:87–106.

Hackman, J. R. 1990. *Groups that Work (and Those that Don't): Creating Conditions for Effective Teamwork*. San Francisco: Jossey-Bass.

Hackman, J. R., and Oldham, G. R. 1980. *Work Redesign*. Reading, MA: Addison-Wesley.

Haleblian, J., and Finkelstein, S. 1993. Top management team size. CEO dominance, and firm performance: The moderating roles of environmental turbulence and discretion. *Academy of Management Journal* 36:844–63.

Helmreich, R. L. 1984. Cockpit management attitudes. *Human Factors* 26:583–9.

Helmreich, R. L., Foushee, H. C., Benson, R., and Russini, W. 1986. Cockpit resources management: Exploring the attitude performance linkage. *Aviation, Space, and Environmental Medicine* 57:1198–200.

Hyatt, D. E., and Ruddy, T. M. 1997. An examination of the relationship between work group characteristics and performance: Once more into the breech. *Personnel Psychology* 50:553–85.

Janz, B. D., Colquitt, J. A., and Noe, R. A. 1997. Knowledge worker team effectiveness: The role of autonomy, interdependence, team development, and contextual support variables. *Personnel Psychology* 50:877–904.

Jehn, K. A. 1995. A multimethod examination of the benefits and detriments of intragroup conflict. *Administrative Science Quarterly* 40:256–82.

Katz, R. 1982. The effects of group longevity on project communication and performance. *Administrative Science Quarterly* 27:81–104.

Keller, R. T. 1986. Predictors of the performance of project groups in R and D organizations. *Academy of Management Journal* 29:715–26.

Kelly, J. 1982. *Scientific Management, Job Redesign, and Work Performance*. London: Academic.

Kim, Y., and Lee, B. 1995. R&D project team climate and team performance in Korea. *R&D Management* 25:179–97.

Klimoski, R., and Mohammed, S. 1994. Team mental model: Construct or metaphor? *Journal of Management* 20:403–37.

Kosarzycki, M. P., Salas, E., DeRouin, R., and Fiore, S. M. In press. Distance learning in organizations: A review and assessment of future needs. In D. Stone (ed.), *Human Resources Technology*. Vol. 3 in JAI series "Advances in Human Performance and Cognitive Engineering Research."

Kozlowski, S. W. J., Gully, S. M., McHugh, P., Salas, E., and Cannon-Bowers, J. A. 1996. A dynamic theory of leadership and team effectiveness: Developmental and task contingent leader roles. In G. Ferris (ed.), *Research in Personnel and Human Resources Management*. Vol. 14. Greenwich, CT: JAI.

Kozlowski, S. W. J., Gully, S. M., Salas, E., and Cannon-Bowers, J. A. 1996. Team leadership and development: Theory, principles, and guidelines for training leaders and teams. In M. Beyerlein (ed.), *Advances in Interdisciplinary Studies of Work Teams: Team Leadership*. Vol. 3. Greenwich, CT: JAI.

Labianca, G., Brass, D. J., and Gray, B. 1998. Social networks and perceptions of intergroup conflict: The role of negative relationships and third parties. *Academy of Management Journal* 41:55–67.

Lawler, E. E., III. 1994. *Motivation in Work Organizations*. San Francisco: Jossey-Bass.

LePine, J. A., Hollenbeck, J. R., Ilgen, D. R., and Hedlund, J. 1997. Effects of individual differences on the performance of hierarchical decision making teams: Much more than g. *Journal of Applied Psychology* 82:803–11.

Likert, R. 1961. *New Patterns of Management*. New York: McGraw-Hill.

Magjuka, R. J., and Baldwin, T. T. 1991. Team-based employee involvement programs: Effects of design and administration. *Personnel Psychology* 44:793–812.

Marks, M. A., Sabella, M. J., Burke, C. S., and Zaccaro, S. J. 2002. The impact of cross-training on team effectiveness. *Journal of Applied Psychology* 87 (1):3–13.

McGregor, D. 1960. *The Human Side of Enterprise*. New York: McGraw-Hill.

McIntyre, R. M., and Salas, E. 1995. Measuring and managing for team performance: Emerging principles from complex environments. In R. A. Guzzo, and E. Salas (eds.), *Team Effectiveness and Decision Making in Organizations*. San Francisco: Jossey-Bass.

Mohrman, S. A., Cohen, S. G., and Mohrman, A. M., Jr. 1995. *Designing Team-Based Organizations*. San Francisco: Jossey-Bass.

Mueller, F., Procter, S., and Buchanan, D. 2000. Teamworking in its context(s): Antecedents, nature and dimensions. *Human Relations* 53 (11):1387–424.

Neuman, G. A., and Wright, J. 1999. Team effectiveness: Beyond skills and cognitive ability. *Journal of Applied Psychology* 84:376–89.

Neuman, G. A., Wagner, S. H., and Christiansen, N. D. 1999. The relationship between work-team personality composition and the job performance in teams. *Group and Organization Management* 24:28–45.

Pritchard, R. D., Jones, S., Roth, P., Stuebing, K., and Ekeberg, S. 1988. Effects of group feedback, goal setting, and incentives on organizational productivity. *Journal of Applied Psychology* 73:337–58.

Roethlisberger, F. J., and Dickson, W. J. 1939. *Management and the Worker*. Cambridge, MA: Harvard University Press.

Salas, E., and Cannon-Bowers, J. 2001. The science of training: A decade of progress. *Annual Review of Psychology* 52:471–99.

Salas, E., Bowers, C. A., and Edens, E. 2001. *Improving Teamwork in Organizations: Applications of Resource Management Training*. Mahwah, NJ: Lawrence Erlbaum.

Salas, E., Dickinson, T. L., Converse, S. A., and Tannenbaum, S. I. 1992. Toward an understanding of team performance and training. In R. W. Swezey and E. Salas (eds.), *Teams: Their Training and Performance*. Norwood, NJ: Ablex.

Salas, E., Rozell, D., Driskell, J. D., and Mullen, B. 1999. The effect of team building on performance: An integration. *Small Group Research* 30:309–29.

Schein, E. H. 1996. *Organizational Culture and Leadership*. San Francisco: Jossey-Bass.

Seashore, S. E. 1954. *Group Cohesiveness in the Industrial Work Group*. Ann Arbor, MI: Institute for Social Research.

Seers, A., Petty, M. M., and Cashman, J. F. 1995. Team-member exchange under team and traditional management. *Group and Organization Management* 20:18–38.

Smith, K. G., Smith, K. A., Olian, J. D., Sims, H. P., Jr., O'Bannon, D. P., and Scully, J. A. 1994. Top management team demography and process: The role of social integration and communication. *Administrative Science Quarterly* 39:412–38.

Steiner, I. D. 1972. *Group Process and Productivity*. New York: Academic.

Sundstrom, E. (ed.). 1999. *Supporting Work Team Effectiveness*. San Francisco: Jossey-Bass.

Sundstrom, E., De Meuse, K. P., and Futrell, D. 1990. Work teams: Applications and effectiveness. *American Psychologist* 45 (2):120–33.

Sundstrom, E., McIntyre, M., Halfhill, T., and Richards, H. 2000. Work groups: From the Hawthorne studies to work teams of the 1990s and beyond. *Group Dynamics: Theory, Research, and Practice* 4:41–67.

Tannenbaum, S. I., Beard, R. L., and Salas, E. 1992. Team building and its influence on team effectiveness: An examination of conceptual and empirical developments. In K. Kelley (ed.), *Issue, Theory, and Research in Industrial/Organizational Psychology*. Amsterdam: Elsevier.

Tannenbaum, S. I., Salas, E., and Cannon-Bowers, J. A. 1996. Promoting team effectiveness. In M. West (ed.), *Handbook of Work Group Psychology*. Chichester: John Wiley.

Tsui, A. S., and Gutek, B. A. 1999. *Demographic Differences in Organizations: Current Research and Future Directions*. Lanham, MD: Lexington Books.

Tziner, A., and Eden, D. 1985. Effects of crew composition on crew performance: Does the whole equal the sum of its parts? *Journal of Applied Psychology* 70:85–93.

Volpe, C. E., Cannon-Bowers, J. A., Salas, E., and Spector, P. 1996. The impact of cross training on team functioning. *Human Factors* 38:87–100.

Wageman, R. 1995. Interdependence and group effectiveness. *Administrative Science Quarterly* 40:145–80.

West, M. A. 1996. Preface: Introducing work group psychology. In M. A. West (ed.), *Handbook of Work Group Psychology*. New York: John Wiley.

Zaccaro, S. J., and Klimoski, R. 2002. The Interface of leadership and team processes. *Group and Organization Management* 27:4–13.

Zaccaro, S. J., Rittman, A. L., and Marks, M. A. 2001. Team leadership. *Leadership Quarterly* 12:451–83.

6

Work–Related Values and Experiences of Generation X Professionals and Managers

MARY C. MATTIS, PAULETTE R. GERKOVICH, RACHEL GONZALEZ, AND NICOLE H. JOHNSEN

Background

A new generation of professionals is working in American and Canadian corporations and professional firms today. Currently in their mid-20s to mid-30s at the time of this research, this group comprises the future leadership of business.

While we recognize that no group is monolithic in its experiences and worldview, Catalyst embarked on this study to understand this generation's motivations and to determine whether widely held assumptions about this generation of professionals are myths or realities. We chose to focus on the generation of people born between 1964 and 1975 – the so-called Generation X – because they are uniquely positioned to teach us about how the workplace is changing or should change to attract, retain, develop, and advance new talent. Ultimately, the expectations that this cohort brings to the workplace will affect succeeding generations of professionals as well as those more senior members of companies who are their managers and mentors.

In the decades since Ryder's (1965) seminal work, cohort analysis has been used to examine social, psychological, and political outcomes as varied as homicide rates (O'Brien, Stockard, and Isaacson 1999); value changes in cadets at the US Military Academy (Franke 2001; Priest and Beach 1998); women's attitudes toward abortions (Lynxwiler and Gay 2001); the link between left-oriented activism and cohabitation (Wilhelm 1998); life-course experiences (Anisef and Axelrod 2001); drug use and treatment initiation patterns (Joshi, Grella, and Hser 2001); trends in enrollment and completed schooling of men relative to those of women (Card and Lemieux 2001); women's rights activism (Duncan and Stewart 2000); returning home in young adulthood (Goldscheider et al. 1999); fertility rates (Lesthaeghe and Willems 1999); and political beliefs and behavior (Alwin 1998). A number of researchers have used cohort analysis to examine marriage and family change, a component of this research (Sweeney 2002; Flouri and Buchanon 2001; Goldstein and Kenney 2001; Schoen and Standish 2001; Brewster and Padavic 2000; Whittington, Averett, and Anderson 2000; Rogers and Amato 1997; Moffit and Rendall 1995; Ravenera, Rajulton, and Burch 1995), however, scant research is available that employs cohort analysis to examine work-related experiences and attitudes of corporate professionals and managers (Lauterbach and Sacher 2001; Sterling et al. 2001; Whittington, Averett, and Anderson 2000; Pencavel 1998).

Ryder defined a cohort as "the aggregate of individuals (within some population definition) who experienced the same event within the same time interval." As Ryder observed, the cohort record is not merely a summation of a set of individual histories; rather, each cohort has a distinctive composition and character reflecting the circumstances of its unique origination and history. Ryder observed that while most cohort research uses date of birth as the defining event, it is "only a special case of the more general approach" of cohort analysis. He went on to note that "The proposed orientation to temporal differentiation of cohorts emphasize[s] the context prevailing at the time members of the cohort experience critical transitions. The approach can be generalized beyond the birth cohort to cohorts identified by common time of occurrence of any significant and enduring event in life history" (1965, 845, 847).

Using this approach, the strategic focus for using cohort as a concept in the study of social change is the *context* under which each cohort is launched on its own path; that is, the temporal context differentiates cohorts. The same point can be made from the opposite direction, by observing types of major change, the extent to which participation is age specific and, therefore, cohort differentiating.

This understanding of a generation as a distinct subgroup shaped by the historical and social context of its origination and history has become a part of American popular culture as well. In the US, terms such as "Baby Boom" and "Generation X" are commonly used to describe two cohorts of Americans who have been shaped by unique historical and cultural forces. While there has been little comparative research on these two cohorts, "Boomers" and "Gen-Xers," as they are referred to, are viewed by the media and portrayed in literature and film as fundamentally different from each other in their worldviews. Boomers, for instance, are frequently portrayed as money-hungry, acquisitive, Wall Street types, who plundered the economy and the environment in pursuit of their fortunes. While Boomers are portrayed as workaholics, Gen-Xers are shown to be the opposite, seeking self-fulfillment and meaning in their work lives, and greater balance in their commitments to careers and self and family.

Much has also been made of the hostility between Gen-Xers and Boomers. Gen-Xers accuse Boomers of selling out on their social and political beliefs so prominently displayed in the 1960s and early 1970s. Boomers see Gen-Xers as narcissistic and lacking in competitive drive. Living literally and figuratively in the shadow of bloated Baby Boom, Generation X has also experienced a different opportunity structure, the higher echelons of which is still largely occupied and controlled by Boomers. Stereotypes and assumptions about intergenerational differences between Boomers and Gen-Xers disguise the reality that each cohort contains considerable *intra*-generational diversity related to gender, class, race/ethnicity and temporal context. The first wave of Boomers who came of age during a period that included the Civil Rights Movement, the antiwar movement and the women's movement, may have little in common with the last wave of Boomers who reached young adulthood in the late 1970s and early 1980s.

Nonetheless, anecdotal data from focus groups and interviews in companies conducted by Catalyst confirms some inter-cohort tension around specific workplace issues. For example, some younger women report that they do not view senior women in their companies as relevant role models. In turn, senior women in companies are puzzled and hurt by a developing chasm between themselves and younger women with whom they expected to have supportive mentoring relationships.

Younger women's rejection of senior women's career choices seems to center around their perception that these women "sacrificed" or "traded off" a personal life, marriage and/or children for a successful career. They do not see themselves making the same choices; therefore, they do not see what senior women have to offer them as mentors. Older senior women believe they have information and experience to impart to younger women which they gained through their pioneering ascent to senior positions in male-dominated corporate work environments and cultures.

Anecdotal data also suggests that intergenerational tensions exist between senior male managers and younger male professionals/managers in corporations and firms. Younger men in companies today are far more likely than early generations of male professionals and managers to have dual-career marriages and partnerships and are more likely than senior men to expect greater flexibility and support from their company to manage the work/life commitments they share with their partners/spouses. Older male managers, whose wives did not work outside the home, have little experience of managing flexibility and are less likely to understand why corporations should accept responsibility for providing support for work/life balance.

Research Objectives

The business and popular presses have devoted considerable attention to these and other perceived differences in the work-related values and goals of Generation X and generations who preceded them in the workplace. This has generated concern within corporations. Work-related stereotypes and assumptions that have been put forward about Generation X professionals and managers include

- *Generation X wants work/life balance.* Since they are more likely than generations before them to have been raised in dual-career, single-parent, or stepparent families, it is assumed that they resent the amount of time their parents spent at work (Lynch 2001) and are wary of workaholism (Filipczak 1994).
- *Generation X has low organizational commitment.* By the time this generation entered the workforce, they had witnessed a decade of corporate downsizing. This was followed by the dismantling or outright failure of many high tech and dot-com businesses (Brown 2001). Consequently, it is assumed that they view the so-called *psychological contract* between employer and employee as obsolete and have been

stereotyped as job–hoppers (Loomis 2000). Further, it is believed that this generation has little patience for steady, measured career progression and that they expect immediate gratification from their organizations in the form of high compensation, early and frequent promotions, company-sponsored training and development opportunities, and workplace amenities that previous generations of workers never imagined.

- *Generation X expects support from their employers for work/life balance.* They were the first generation of women raised to believe that they could have *careers* as opposed to *jobs*. Furthermore, they expect to be able to *have it* all – fulfilling careers and a good marriage/family life.
- *The Generation X men are supportive of women's career aspirations.* Many men in this cohort had mothers who worked outside the home. They graduated from business and other graduate programs with substantial numbers of women. They were socialized alongside of women who were told they were equal to men.

Companies and firms naturally are concerned about these proposed differences between Generation X professionals (and those following in their footsteps) and generations of workers before them. If they are so different from their predecessors, what changes in performance managers and other human resources strategies will be needed to motivate and manage them effectively? Dual purposes of this research were to confirm or dispel existing stereotypes about today's professionals, and, in doing so, to assist companies and their employees to identify strategies to manage and leverage the talents of this cohort.

The Importance of Generation X to Corporate Competitiveness

During the last ten years, there has been a steady decline in the United States and Canada in the absolute number of people aged 25 to 34, the pipeline from which organizations draw their entry- and mid-level professionals and managers. Today this group comprises just 20 percent of the US adult population compared to the Baby Boomers' 41 percent share (US Census Bureau 2000; Canadian Social Trends 2000). This cohort, then, represents a "seller's market" when it comes to their attractiveness to business organizations. Even though organizations are currently continuing to downsize, this group represents a scarce resource moving into the future. Therefore, it is critically important that employers understand their work-related motivations and expectations in order to attract, retain and develop the best and brightest for future leadership roles.

At the same time that the labor pool of this generation has shrunk, the percentage of women in the pool has increased. During the last half of the twentieth century, there was a steady increase in the proportion of women aged 25 to 34 who work – from 36 percent in 1960 to 76 percent in 2000 (Bureau of Labor Statistics 2001).

Unlike the United States, Canada did not have a Baby Boom phenomenon. As a consequence, the percentage of individuals in the age groups 20 to 39 and 40 to 59 in Canada – 9 million and 8.5 million, respectively – are almost equal (Statistics Canada 2000). However, there are other factors operating in Canada that present a compelling business case for Canadian companies to examine their recruitment strategies for today's

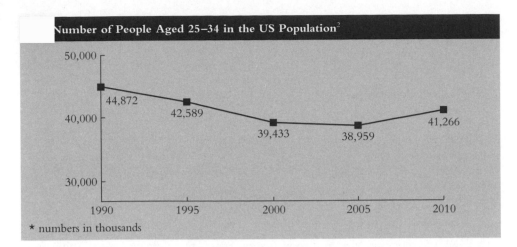

Figure 6.1: Number of people aged 25–34 in the US population*

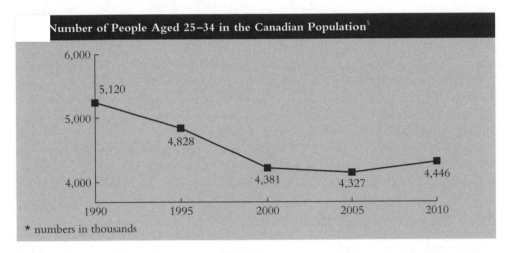

Figure 6.2: Number of people aged 25–34 in the Canadian population*

professionals, especially with regard to women: adult women's employment rates have tripled in just over 50 years, while men's have fallen by one-fifth; women outnumber men at university in Canada and the percentage of women enrolled full-time in Canadian universities is continuing to grow (Canadian Social Trends 2000).

Furthermore, the representation of people of color in the US labor pool is increasing rapidly and is projected to continue to grow through succeeding generations. The 2000 US Census shows that Americans under the age of 18 are 15 percent African-American, 1 percent Native American, 3 percent Asian-American, 17 percent Hispanic, 61 percent non-Hispanic white, and 3 percent multiethnic or other. Today, and into the future, companies seeking the best and brightest need to cast their nets broadly to attract women

Table 6.1   Ten participating businesses, by industry

Industry	Number/Location of Companies	Percent of Respondents
Technology and Communications	2 (1 Canada; 1 US)	17
Financial Services	1 (US)	13
Retail	1 (US)	12
Professional services	2 (US)	14
Consumer goods	1 (US)	8
Heavy manufacturing	2 (1 Canada; 1 US)	26
Wholesale electronics	1 (US)	10

and people of color, and to identify organization factors that influence the recruitment of this diverse candidate pool.

Methodology and Profile of Respondents

Ten companies and firms participated in the research, two Canadian business organizations and eight from the US. Surveys were mailed to a random sample of employees born between the years 1964 and 1975 in each of the ten companies. Follow-up mailings followed several weeks later. Industry sectors represented in the study and the percentage of respondents from each sector are shown in table 6.1.

Individual demographics. Of the 1,263 respondents, 71 percent are women and 19 percent are men. Seventy-eight percent of the respondents are from the US and 22 percent are from Canada. Eighteen percent (227) are people of color, 71 percent of whom are women. Nearly one-third of all respondents had earned graduate degrees. Two percent of respondents describe their sexual identify as gay/lesbian or bisexual.

Household and family demographics. A majority (71 percent) of respondents were married or living with a partner at the time they responded to the survey. Thirty-six percent had children. Not surprising, individuals born between 1964 and 1969 were more likely to be married/partnered than those born between 1970 and 1975 (76 percent compared to 66 percent), and to have children (51 percent compared to 20 percent).

US and Canadian household and family demographics. US and Canadian respondents differed somewhat in their household and family status. For example, US women and men are equally likely to have a spouse or partner (72 percent and 73 percent, respectively) whereas Canadian women respondents were more likely than Canadian men respondents to be married/partnered (74 percent compared to 64 percent). Another statistically significant difference between the US and Canadian respondents was that US men were much more likely than Canadian men to have children (47 percent compared to 34 percent).

Household income. As would be expected, the average household income of respondents varied considerably by age. Those born between 1964 and 1969 reported a greater household income (US $114,246; Cdn $90,675) than younger respondents born between 1970 and 1975 (US $89,654; Cdn $76,658).

Professional profile. Nearly one-third of respondents held line positions (positions that involve profit-and-loss or direct client responsibility) in their organizations; 46 percent held staff roles (positions that provide functional support to the line operation); the remainder (23 percent) had jobs involving both line and staff responsibilities. This is the first survey conducted by Catalyst in which women participants are not disproportionately represented in staff positions (30 percent compared to 33 percent of men). A small percentage of women respondents (5 percent) worked part time; no men reported working part time.

Women and men respondents had been with their organization for an average of five years. As would be expected, younger respondents had shorter tenure (four years) than older respondents (six years), with no significant differences observed in the tenure of men and women.

Family background. About one-fourth of the men and one-fifth of the women grew up in families that included at least one stepparent. Respondents' fathers were more highly educated than their mothers; 57 percent of fathers had earned bachelor's degrees compared to 40 percent of mothers. Seventy percent of respondents had fathers who were employed in business in a professional or managerial capacity compared to only 37 percent whose mothers were employed in such a capacity.

Findings

A paramount goal of this research was to provide employing organizations with advice about how to attract, retain, develop, and advance new generations of professionals. Therefore, the findings presented in the following pages are grouped under the solutions-oriented headings of attracting, retaining, and developing and advancing new generations of professionals.

Attracting Generation X Professionals to Business Organizations

Reasons for joining. The overwhelming majority of men and women who participated in this research were attracted to their current organizations for traditional reasons. Roughly two-thirds placed high importance on job security, challenging the assumption that members of this generation are job-hoppers and have low organizational commitment. This is particularly interesting given the survey was distributed during late summer 2000 – a time when job opportunities were reputedly abundant. However, this generation is not entirely traditional. For example, over one-half report that the perception of a fun and innovative organizational culture was a factor in their decision to join their current organization.

Compensation valued over time off. Compensation is clearly important to Gen-Xers – when asked whether they would prefer that a promotion take the form of time off or money, most chose money. However, there are age differences. Not surprisingly, younger

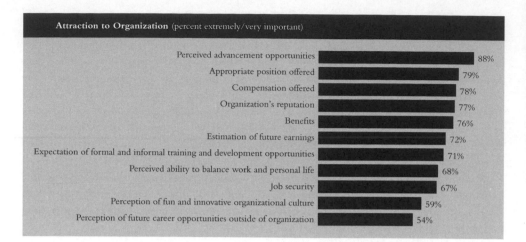

Figure 6.3: Attraction to organization

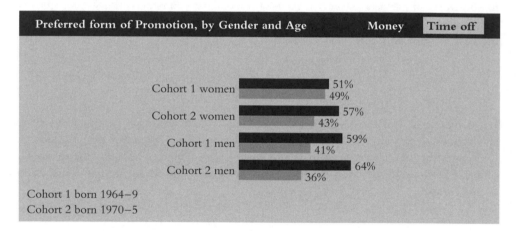

Figure 6.4: Preferred form of promotion, by gender and age

respondents (born between 1970 and 1975), who are less likely to be married and/or have children, were significantly more likely than older respondents (1964–9) to say they would prefer money to time off.

Value placed on personal and family commitments. Findings from this study also show that this generation of professionals values personal and family commitments more highly than work commitments. Thus, the ability of companies and firms to offer programs that support such values will provide a competitive advantage in recruiting, as well as retaining this (and it is assumed future) generation of professionals.

While majorities of men and women rate personal and family values and goals as extremely important, women are significantly more likely than men to give this response.

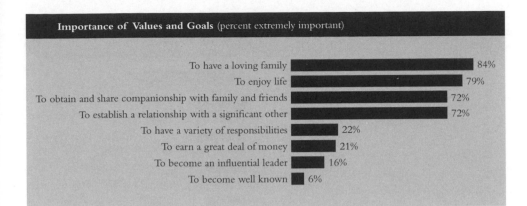

Figure 6.5: Importance of values and goals

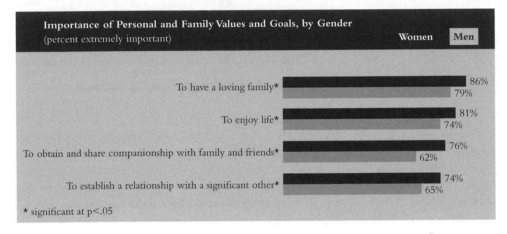

Figure 6.6: Importance of personal and family values and goals, by gender

Although the overall percentages are smaller, statistically significant differences related to gender were also observed regarding work-related goals, with men placing more importance on these goals than women; for example, 27 percent of men compared to 18 percent of women said it was extremely important to them "to earn a great deal of money"; and 22 percent of women versus 13 percent of men believe it is extremely important to become an influential leader.

Experience with work/life balance. Almost two-thirds of respondents (29 percent) reported that the interference of their jobs on their personal lives was "severe" or "very severe"; another 43 percent described this interference as "moderate"; while 28 percent said it was "minimal." This finding suggests that either companies and firms represented in this study are not offering the range of policies/programs needed to support younger professionals' personal and family goals or that such policies and programs are not producing the desired outcome.

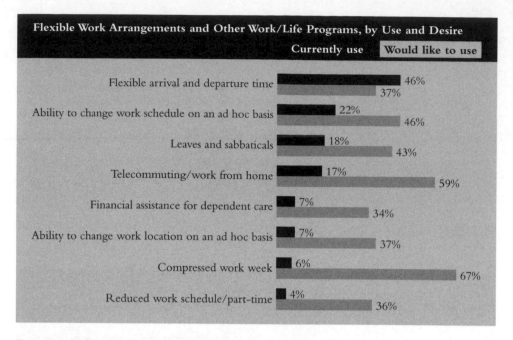

Figure 6.7: Flexible work arrangements and other work/life programs, by use and desire

Younger professionals want flexibility. Both men and women respondents expect their employers to provide policies and programs that will help them manage their work and personal commitments. It is important for organizations to recognize that this is not just a "women's issue" – overall, substantial percentages of both men and women report that they want flexibility. Therefore, offering programs that allow flexibility regarding when and where work gets done will provide a competitive advantage in recruiting this generation of professionals.

Women professionals responding to the survey were significantly more likely than men to report that they would use the following types of flexible work arrangements:

- Flexible arrival and departure times (40 percent of women compared to 32 percent of men).
- Ability to change work schedule on an *ad hoc* basis (48 percent of women compared to 32 percent of men).
- Telecommuting/work from home (61 percent of women compared to 54 percent of men).
- Reduced work schedule/part-time arrangement (42 percent of women compared to 22 percent of men).

With the exception of flexible arrival and departure times – used by about one-third of the respondents – far more men and women would like to use flexible work arrangements of every type specified in the question than currently use them (see figure 6.7). This finding suggests that flexibility is and will continue to be an important criterion for younger professionals, especially women, in their selection of a company or firm.

While majorities of men and women desire flexible work arrangements to attend to childcare responsibilities, they also specified a variety of other motivations for wanting flexibility at work – to attend school, to address overwork, to attend to their personal health or to personal interests unrelated to family responsibilities; however, men were significantly more likely than women to cite reasons that were not related to childcare responsibilities; for example, 47 percent of male respondents compared to 37 percent of female respondents cited continuing or returning to school as a motivation to adopt a flexible work arrangement; and 39 percent of men versus 31 percent of women cited a personal reason unrelated to family.

Access to technology. In today's workplace, access to technology is related to the ability to work effectively, but in particular it is related to the ability to telecommute effectively. Telecommuting may be an especially attractive form of flexibility for women because it provides more options around when and where they work, allows greater flexibility for childcare arrangements, and reduces the distance between themselves and their children during working hours. So it is not surprising that women are much more likely than men to report that access to technology (50 percent of women compared to 41 percent of men) and the ability to telecommute (32 percent of women compared to 17 percent of men) are extremely important to their job satisfaction.

Contrary to stereotypes of Generation X, nontraditional amenities such as gym membership, convenience services at job site, employee lounges, and subsidized meals are not reported to be overly important to their job satisfaction. The one exception to this rule is a casual dress code – cited as "extremely" or "very important" by 54 percent of respondents to the survey.

Recruitment strategies. When it comes to attracting younger professionals to companies, these findings suggest that they have many traditional needs for job security, benefits, and advancement opportunities. However, they are also seeking more than these traditional incentives and rewards, asking companies to fundamentally rethink the way that work is done. They want increased flexibility, including the ability to telecommute, and access to technology. In addition, there is a high desire for organizational cultures that are fun and innovative and that provide a casual dress code.

Retaining Generation X Professionals in Business Organizations

While recruiting new talent is a competitive process, organizations frequently report that the retention of high-potential professionals and managers is even more difficult. Replacement costs related to turnover of both younger professionals and seasoned managers are substantial. Other less visible costs include the impact on productivity and on the morale of project teams and work units; discontinuity of customer/client service with the resulting negative impact on customer/client satisfaction; and loss of intellectual capital with the associated possibility that a former employee may become a future competitor.

Commitment to Current Organization	
	percent strongly agree
I really care about the fate of this organization	85%
I am willing to put in a great deal of effort beyond what is normally expected in order to help this organization be successful	83%
I am extremely glad that I chose this organization to work in over others I was considering	75%
I talk up this organization to my friends as a great place to work	62%
I find that my values and the organization's values are similar	61%
I feel a strong sense of "belonging" at my current organization	58%
I would be very happy to spend the rest of my career with my current organization	47%

Figure 6.8: Commitment to current organization

Findings from the survey show that contrary the assumption that younger professionals have low levels or organizational commitment, they are highly committed and loyal to their current employers. A surprising 47 percent reported they would be happy to spend the rest of their careers in their current organizations.

Intention to stay. Almost one-third of respondents (29 percent of women and 32 percent of men) reported that they intend to stay with their current organization for more than ten years; 16 percent intend to stay between five and ten years; and 20 percent intend to stay between three to five years. In contrast, 34 percent report that they intend to leave in less than three years. No significant differences were observed by gender in response to this question.

Catalyst assessed differences between the group of employees who intend to stay with their organization more than zero years (defined here as "stayers") and those who intend to leave in less than three years (defined here as "leavers"). Research demonstrates that respondents' expressed intentions to leave their organizations are highly correlated to actual turnover (Steele and Nestor 1984; Kraut 1975).

What differentiates stayers from leavers? Top reasons leavers gave for why they might leave their organizations are similar to the reasons they gave for joining their current organizations: increased intellectual stimulation; greater advancement opportunities; and increased compensation

Although women are no more likely then men to be categorized as leavers, women who fell into the leaver category are significantly more likely than men leavers to regard the following as extremely or very important reasons for why they might consider leaving their organizations:

- More flexibility in work arrangements (61 percent of women; 45 percent of men)

- Ability to work fewer hours (52 percent of women; 30 percent of men)
- Ability to telecommute (51 percent of women; 37 percent of men)

Who is most likely to leave? People of color, both men and women, are significantly more likely to be found among leavers (44 percent compared to 31 percent of white respondents) than among stayers (20 percent as opposed to 32 percent of white respondents). With one exception, "leavers" who are people of color generally report the same reasons for intending to leave their organizations as white "leavers," the exception being that they are much more likely than white employees to cite a desire for increased visibility (68 percent compared to 49 percent).

Respondents with expectations of their organizations that were not met were also significantly more likely than other respondents to be found among leavers. For example, 45 percent of leavers do not feel that their work/life balance expectations were met, compared to only 28 percent of stayers. Companies need to take this finding seriously given that both men and women respondents assigned greater importance to personal and family goals and values than to work-related goals and values.

Perceptions of fairness. Findings from this study show that women and men have significantly different perceptions of the "fairness" of their organizational culture.

- 42 percent of women compared to 11 percent of men reported that "women have to outperform men to get the same rewards in my organization"
- 30 percent of women compared to 62 percent of men said "women are paid a comparable salary to men for similar work in my organization"
- 10 percent of women compared to 30 percent of men reported that "all other things being equal, a woman will be promoted over a man in my organization"

Retention strategies. These findings suggest that there are a number of organizational factors that, if addressed, could reduce the potential for companies and firms to lose valuable professionals. These include failure to meet expectations that attracted professionals to the organization in the first place, especially the expectation of support for work/life balance; perceived lack of fairness of performance measurement and remuneration; and lack of flexibility and related programs that enable employees, especially women, to use flexible work arrangements.

Developing and Advancing Generation X Professionals

When looking at organizational initiatives relating to career development and advancement, overwhelming majorities of respondents agreed that factors such as supervisor support, performance feedback, high-potential identification and development, and developmental planning are important. In addition to effective performance-management policies and strategies, over three-fourths (78 percent) of men and women rated flexible work policies and programs as extremely or very important to their advancement and job satisfaction.

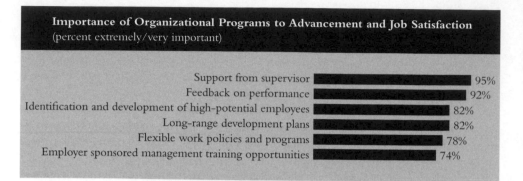

Figure 6.9: Importance of organizational programs to advancement and job satisfaction

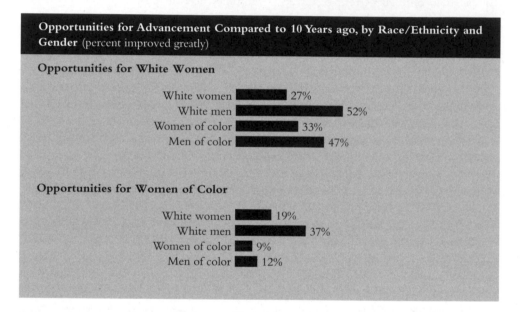

Figure 6.10: Opportunities for advancement compared to 1990, by race/ethnicity and gender

Progress and prospects for a new generation of women professionals. Findings show that men and women respondents have very different perceptions of the changes in opportunities for white women and women of color to advance in their organizations that have taken place in their organizations. Overall, white men are the most likely to believe that opportunities for both groups of women have greatly improved since 1990.

Men's perceptions that there has been a great deal of improvement in opportunities for women to advance in their organizations may explain the fact that in response to another question they are *much less likely to agree or strongly agree* with the business case for

Table 6.2 Respondents' recommendations for the advancement of women

Respondents' Recommendations for the Advancement of Women	Percent of women's comments	Percent of men's comments
Provide mentors, role models, and networks	22	13
Provide work/life programs and support for them	19	6
Improve corporate culture and leadership commitment	14	7
Provide other organizational strategic programs	11	15
Provide skill development and enhanced opportunities	10	7
Support for a meritocratic workplace	10	17
Increase diversity awareness; debunk stereotypes	6	3
Already doing a good job	4	8
Do nothing specifically for women	4	23

Note: see notes at end of chapter for a full description of these categories.

companies to advance women. This is reflected in men's responses to the following statements about why companies and firms should work to increase the representation of women in senior leadership roles:

- Women have unique perspectives to contribute to decision making and problem solving (79 percent of women agree or strongly agree compared to 60 percent of men).
- Women possess unique leadership skills (73 percent of women agree or strongly agree compared to 47 percent of men).
- Women are a significant consumer base whose buying power is increasing (66 percent of women compared to 54 percent of men agree or strongly agree).

These differences in perceptions of men and women concerning changes in opportunities may also be an expression of backlash from men about corporate diversity initiatives which, they believe, reduce their own opportunities.

Recommendations for accelerating women's advancement. "If you could change one thing in your organization in order to accelerate the advancement of women to senior positions, what would it be?" Analyses of write-in responses to this open-ended question underscore the disparity between men and women regarding the diversity imperative. Over 75 responses with recommendations were submitted by survey participants, with 75 percent coming from women. Results are shown in table 6.2.

Close to one-fourth of male respondents (23 percent) recommended *doing nothing* specifically for women to accelerate their advancement to senior positions compared to only 4 percent of women who gave this response. Again, this may be an indicator of male perceptions that increasing opportunities for other groups will, in turn, reduce their own opportunities.

Challenges for women in dual-career couples. Many people assume that male Gen-Xers, especially those in dual-career couples, take increasing responsibility for sharing the work associated with family commitments and supporting their spouses'/partners' career goals. Numerous findings from this study suggest otherwise. And, surprisingly, the differences between men and women in dual-career couples on these issues are the same for those respondents with and without children. These differences include:

- Men who have children and are in dual-career relationships are more likely to work 50 or more hours per week than are their female counterparts (50 percent compared to 42 percent).
- Women are more likely than men to leave their jobs to relocate with a spouse/partner (13 percent compared to 7 percent of men).
- Women were much more likely than men to report that they either employed outside services for domestic help (41 percent compared to 16 percent of men), relied on supportive relatives other than their spouses/partners (36 percent compared to 27 percent of men), or postponed having children to achieve work/life balance (32 percent compared to 21 percent of men).
- Women with children use reduced work schedule/part-time arrangements more than men with children (15 percent compared to 1 percent of men).
- Women are much more likely than men to believe they will work part time in their current organizations during the next five years (19 percent compared to 2 percent of men).
- Of those respondents with a spouse or partner who works full time, far more men than women say that their own careers are primary careers (53 percent of men compared to 29 percent of women). In contrast, women are significantly more likely than men to report that neither their own nor their spouses' or partners' careers are primary.

Development and advancement strategies. Business organizations are competing for talent. Attracting and recruiting new generations of professionals are the first steps in competing for the best and brightest. Organizations must also develop their current employees into tomorrow's leaders. Respondents in this study tell us that when their expectations of

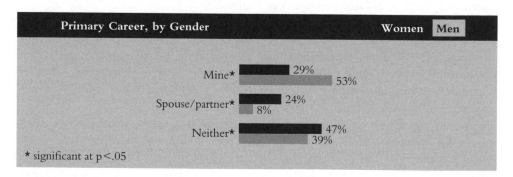

Figure 6.11: Primary career, by gender

certain organizational programs and policies go unmet, they are more likely to leave. Providing such programs will increase commitment and reduce turnover.

Findings in this section on development and advancement show that men and women essentially want the same policies and programs from their employers. When it comes to development and advancement, effective performance-management strategies are key to this generation.

Findings presented in this section also suggest that companies have a good deal more work to do to level the playing field for both white women and women of color and to communicate the business case for doing so in a way that will reduce the likelihood of male backlash.

This and other Catalyst research shows that recruitment, retention, development, and advancement strategies are interdependent – companies and firms need to do well on all four fronts to achieve positive people management outcomes (Catalyst 2000). We have seen that retaining new generations of professionals involves providing a comprehensive mix of concrete policies and programs supporting work/life balance, access to technology and flexibility, and an attractive organizational culture.

Conclusions. Findings from this research show that the majority of Generation X professionals are committed and loyal to their employers. Contrary to assumptions covered in the popular and business press, business organizations have the opportunity to retain this cohort long term; however, they should not take this group's organizational commitment and loyalty for granted. Generation X professionals are interested in advancement, but not at any cost. Among other things, they expect support from their organizations for work/life balance, flexibility, effective performance-management strategies, an innovative and fun organizational culture and a casual dress code.

Recommendations for Business Organizations

Recruitment

Communicate to candidates what they can expect from your organization.

- Talk about your organization's successes in providing work/life policies and programs, flexibility, and valuing diversity on campuses, at job fairs, and at meetings of professional and affinity groups/networks.
- Provide written descriptions of work/life and flexible work arrangement policies and programs in recruitment brochures.
- Include women and people of color on every recruiting team to facilitate questions about work/life policies and programs, as well as questions about other aspects of the work environment and culture.

Mean what you say about your organization.

- This research shows that individuals whose expectations of their organization are unmet are significantly more likely to report they intend to leave. Do not make promises to candidates that you cannot meet. Describe your policies, programs, work environment, and culture accurately, providing data on use of various programs where available.

In recruitment efforts, provide visibility for successful women and people of color in your organization.

- Ensure that women and people of color are included among speakers that represent your company at high-profile business and civic events.
- Nominate and sponsor women and people of color for business- and community-based membership organizations.
- Feature women and people of color prominently in your organization's communication vehicles such as annual reports, recruitment brochures, and on your website. Work with local and national media outlets to publish announcements of promotions and other accomplishments of senior women and people of color and to include them in appropriate feature stories about key organizational developments and events.
- Encourage women and people of color to represent your organization in external mentoring programs.
- Offer internships and scholarships as a recruitment tool.

Retention

Create a flexible work environment.

- Develop and communicate your organization's support for employees' efforts to balance their work and personal lives.
- Confront managers' anxieties about flexible work arrangements. Train and reward all levels of management for developing their staff, leveraging corporate policies, and addressing the work/life needs of employees – both men and women.
- Reward managers who are role models for your organization's flexibility policies and programs.
- Provide a range of alternatives to traditional work arrangements that are both formal (part-time schedules, telecommuting, compressed workweek) and informal (e.g., flexible arrival and departure times).
- Focus on results, not line-of-sight management. Catalyst's research has consistently shown that "face time" is an ineffective measurement of performance, especially for those with alternative work arrangements.
- Provide training and support for professionals with flexible arrangements and their supervisors. Highlight information about who is eligible; the process for negotiating an arrangement; guidelines regarding benefits, compensation, commissions, performance review, and promotions when using flexible options; technology to support the arrangement; and best practices and success stories within your organization.

- Provide systems and structures that support flexibility and reasonable job demands, rethinking headcount and billable-hour systems, unclear performance ranking and rating systems that emphasize face-time, and rigid career path criteria and timeframes that fail to address the changing needs and expectations of younger professionals.

Provide support for employees' dependent care needs.

- Develop and communicate your organization's business rationale for supporting employees' dependent care needs.
- Monitor the dependent care needs of your workforce that change over time.

Development and Advancement

Create and communicate development strategies.

- Identify and communicate to high-potential employees your organization's interest in their development.
- Provide company-sponsored formal and informal training and development opportunities and ensure that women and people of color are represented among individuals who are sponsored for in-house training, executive MBA programs and other leadership development programs.
- Offer rotational programs that provide high-potential professionals with a breadth of functional and divisional experience.
- Implement a formal mentoring program.
- Encourage and fund participation in professional organizations and developmental and educational opportunities outside of your organization.
- Implement succession planning that reaches down into and across functional units to identify women and people of color early in their careers and track their development and advancement.
- Develop effective performance-management strategies and train managers to use them.
- Retain high-potential employees by tuition reimbursement and time off to attend school.

Provide customized career planning and management.

- Provide manager training.
- Create checkpoints for employee input and dialogue about their career goals.
- Use assessment tools to identify areas of strengths and areas for improvement.
- Track the development and advancement of high-potential employees and hold managers accountable in this area.
- Reward successful managers.

Implement a casual dress code.

Address perceptions of reverse discrimination.

- Document and articulate the issues; for example, failure to retain or develop women and people of color.
- Communicate the specific business rationale for organizational initiatives to retain and advance women and people of color.
- Position your effort in terms of "inclusion" rather than "diversity."
- Articulate and model top-level commitment.
- Hold managers accountable for results and reward them for being a part of the solution.

Assess your organization's work environment/culture to ensure that professionals in every age group feel valued and have meaningful opportunities to contribute.

- Analyze data from employee surveys by age group.
- Include representatives from all age groups on task forces and committees that advise senior management decisions.
- Ensure that company social events are inclusive of all age groups.

Level the playing field for women and people of color.

- Use surveys, focus groups and post-departure interviews to assess the inclusiveness of your organizational culture and work practices.
- Communicate and demonstrate your organization's commitment to women and people of color.
- Provide effective, mandatory diversity training throughout the organization.
- Hold managers accountable for the retention, development, and advancement of women and people of color.
- Integrate inclusiveness goals and values into routine organizational practices such as recruitment, new-hire orientation, management training, career, development, and succession planning.

NOTES

The authors acknowledge the work on this project of the following Catalyst staff: Sheila W. Wellington, Marcia Kropf, PhD, Nancy Kane, Susan Black, PhD, Nancy Guida, Elizabeth McCormick, Regina Chung, and Jan Combopiano. In addition, we would like to thank the companies that funded this research: Ernst & Young and GE Fund.

Table 6.2 categories:

- Provide work/life programs and support for them: includes flexible work arrangements and work/life programs to improve balance, as well as addressing negative stereotypes relating to having a family and being a mother.

- Provide other organizational strategic programs: includes recruitment, succession planning, career pathing, and high potential programs.
- Provide skill development and enhanced opportunities: includes opportunities for high visibility and high risk assignments, development and rotational assignments, and training.
- Increase diversity awareness; debunk stereotypes: includes diversity-specific training and tearing down general stereotypes about women and work.

REFERENCES

Alwin, D. 1998. The political impact of the baby boom: Are there persistent generational differences in political beliefs and behavior? *Generations* 22 (1):46–54.

Anisef, P., and Axelrod, P. 2001. Baby boomers in transition: Life-course experiences of the "Class of '73," in V. W. Marshall, W. R. Heinz, H. Kruger, and A. Verma (eds.), *Restructuring Work and the Life Course*. Toronto: University of Toronto Press.

Brewster, K. L., and Padavic, I. 2000. Change in gender-ideology, 1977–1996: The contributions of intracohort change and population. *Journal of Marriage and the Family* 62 (2):477–87.

Brown, Eeryn. 2001. The humbled generation, *Fortune*, April 2, 93–5.

Bureau of Labor Statistics. 2001. *Employment and Earnings, January 1961 and January 2001.*

Canadian Social Trends. 2000. No. 57, summer, 8.

Canadian Social Trends. 2000. No. 59, winter, 6–7.

Card, D., and Lemieux, T. 2001. Going to college to avoid the unintended legacy of the Vietnam War, *American Economic Review* 91 (2):97–102.

Duncan, L., and Stewart, A. 2000. A generational analysis of women's rights activists. *Psychology of Women Quarterly* 24 (4):297–308.

Filipczak, B. 1994. It's just a job: Generation X at work, *Training*, April, 21–7.

Flouri, E., and Buchanan, A. 2001. What predicts traditional attitudes to marriage? *Children and Society* 15 (4):263–71.

Franke, Volker C. 2001. Generation X and the military: A comparison of attitudes and values between West Point cadets and college students. *Journal of Political and Military Sociology* 29 (1): 92–119.

Goldscheider, F., Goldscheider, C., and St. Clair, P. 1999. Changes in returning home in the United States, 1925–1985. *Social Forces* 78 (2):695–720.

Goldstein, J. R., and Kenney, C. 2001. Marriage delayed or marriage foregone? New cohort forecasts of first marriage for US women. *American Sociological Review* 66 (4):506–19.

Joshi, V., Grella, C., and Hser, Y-I. 2001. Drug use and treatment initiation patterns: Differences by birth-cohorts. *Journal of Drug Issues* 32 (4):1039–62.

Kraut, Allen. 1975. Predicting turnover of employees from measured job attitudes. *Organizational Behavior and Human Performance* 13 (2):233–43.

Lauterbach, W., and Sacher, M. 2001. The first years in the labor market: Four birth cohorts in comparison. *Kölner Zeitschrift für Soziologie und Sozialpsychologie* 53 (2):258–82.

Lesthaeghe, R., and Willems, P. 1999. Is low fertility a temporary phenomenon in the European Union? *Population and Development Review* 25 (2):211–28.

Loomis, Judi E. 2000. Generation X. *Rough Notes*, September, 52–4.

Lynch, S. 2001. Taking stock of Gen X: It's fallen sharply. *Washington Post*, April 25, 21–7.

Lynxwiler, J., and Gay, D. 2001. Cohort variations and women's attitudes toward legal abortion. Unpublished paper presented at a meeting of the Southern Sociological Society (SSS).

Moffit, R., and Rendall, M. 1995. Cohort trends in the lifetime distribution of female family leadership in the United States. *Demography* 32 (August):407–24.

O'Brien, R. M., Stockard, J., and Isaacson, L. 1999. The enduring effects of cohort characteristics on age-specific homicide rates, 1960–1995. *American Journal of Sociology* 104 (4):1061–95.

Pencavel, J. 1998. The market work behavior and wages of women: 1975–94. *Journal of Human Resources* 33 (4):771–804.

Pit-Catsouphes, M., and Googins, B. 1999. The evolving world of work and family: New stakeholders, new voices. *Annals of the American Academy of Political and Social Science* 562, March. Thousand Oaks, CA: Sage.

Priest, R. F., and Beach, J. 1998. Value changes in four cohorts at the US Military Academy. *Armed Forces and Society* 25 (1):81–102.

Ravenera, Z. R., Rajulton, F., and Burch, T. K. 1995. A cohort analysis of home-leaving in Canada, 1910–1975. *Journal of Comparative Family Studies* 26 (summer):179–93.

Riggs, A., and Turner, B. 2000. Pie-eyed optimists: Baby-boomers the optimistic generation? *Social Indicators Research* 52 (1):73–93.

Rogers, S., and Amato, P. 1997. Is marital quality declining? The evidence from two generations. *Social Forces* 75 (March):1089–100.

Ryder, Norman. 1965. The cohort as a concept in the study of social change. *American Sociological Review* 30 (6):843–61.

Schoen, R., and Standish, N. 1995. The retrenchment of marriage: Results from marital status life tables for the United States. *Population and Development Review* 27 (3):553–63.

Steele, Robert P., and Nestor, K. 1984. A review and meta-analysis of research on the relationship between behavioral intentions of employee turnover. *Journal of Applied Psychology* 69 (4):673–86.

Sterling, R. C., Gottheil, E., Glassman, S. D., Weinstein, S. P., Serota, R. D., and Lundy, A. 2001. Correlates of employment: A cohort study. *American Journal of Drug and Alcohol Abuse* 27 (1):137–46.

Sweeney, K. A. 2002. Payoff of education: The effect of wife's education on economic dependency in marriage. Differences among Black, Mexican American and White women in the US. Unpublished paper presented at a meeting of the Southern Sociological Society (SSS).

US Census Bureau. 2000. Census 2000.

Whittington, L., Averett, S., and Anderson, D. 2000. Choosing children over career? Changes in postpartum labor force behavior of professional women. *Population Research and Policy Review* 19 (4):339–55.

Wilhelm, Brenda. 1998. Changes in cohabitation across cohorts: The influence of political activism. *Social Forces* 77 (1):289–313.

7

Managing Contingent Workers: Adapting to New Realities

CATHERINE E. CONNELLY AND DANIEL G. GALLAGHER

As market and competitive conditions change rapidly, organizations are adapting by building and managing increasingly more flexible and responsive workforces. From a Human Resources Management (HRM) perspective, this shift towards increased organizational flexibility is often most visible in short- and long-term adjustments to the size of the organization's workforce. Practices such as the increased assignment of required overtime hours or reduced work schedules and layoffs are common short-term HRM adjustments to staffing imbalances. More permanent numerical adjustments to organizational staffing levels also exist in the form of increased recruitment and hiring or the opposite and increasingly visible phenomenon of organizational "downsizing" and resultant employment loss.

It is important to note that HRM practices designed to assist in meeting the broader survival and profitability goals of organizations that operate in less stable and predicable markets are not limited solely to issues of numerical flexibility as measured by the size of the workforce at a particular time. As noted by a number of writers, employment flexibility may also be addressed in other dimensions such as time, location, compensation, and function (e.g., Brewster, Mayne, Tregaskis 1997; Deery and Mahony 1994; Friedrich et al. 1998; Lautsch 1999; Reilly 1998; Sparrow 1998). Temporal flexibility focuses on when the work is performed (e.g., flextime, shift scheduling), whereas locational flexibility refers to the use of workers outside the boundaries of the traditional workplace (e.g., telecommuting) (Cooper and Burke 2002). In contrast, financial flexibility describes compensation plans that are based partly on profit-sharing arrangements where employment earnings vary with firm performance. A further form of HRM-focused flexibility exists in what has been labeled as functional flexibility, where the focus is based on a more efficient allocation of labor by internally moving workers to tasks or functions where human resources are needed. Efforts to maximize this functional flexibility as a means of adjusting to market shifts in product or service demands have been closely tied with other HRM practices such as cross-training, multi-skilling, skill-based pay plans, and the redesign of task allocation (Reilly 1998).

It appears that concurrent with the broader organizational concern of being able to operate effectively within more competitive and rapidly changing market conditions, many organizations have begun to adopt HRM-based strategies which have moved toward an reliance on the use of temporary or contingent employment contracts (e.g., Delsen 1999; Gallagher 2002; Gallie et al. 1998; Kalleberg 2000; Zeytinoğlu 1999). Most interestingly, surveys conducted to determine the reasons and extent to which employers hire workers on short-term or temporary contracts, invariably rank staffing "flexibility" as their primary motivation (Nollen and Axel 1996). Often, flexibility in the ability to expand and reduce the size of the workforce through the use of temporary hiring arrangements is closely followed or intertwined with "cost-containment" as the underlying advantage associated for use of short- or fixed-term contracts. The extent to which cost-containment is linked to broader governmental labor policies or union contracts which impose tariffs associated with hiring, layoff, and termination of "regular" employees is an issue of continued debate. It is also important to note that, beyond issues of numerical flexibility, the hiring of workers on fixed-term contracts can often represent a means by which an organization can gain access to particular sets of knowledge, skills, and abilities which are absent or in limited supply in the organization. In essence, temporary or contingent workers can in fact provide organizations with a form of increased functional flexibility.

As recently noted by Gallagher (2002), a considerable diversity exists in the form of contingent employment contracts, as well as the types and levels of skills that can be secured by organizations on a short-term basis. From a definitional perspective, a widely cited view of "contingent work" involves conditions under which workers "do not have explicit or implicit contracts for long-term employment and one in which the minimum hours can vary in a non-systematic manner" (Polivka and Nardone 1989, 11). However, similarly situated workers may have different perceptions of what they see as their implicit contract with the employing organization. In fact, these perceptions of the implicit contract may also have implications in terms of what a contingent or temporary worker may expect from the organization in return for performance. As reflected in much of the psychological contract research (Rousseau 1995), the way in which individuals perceive the work arrangement or "the deal" may be more important to understanding the attitudes and behaviors of workers than the ability to precisely classify workers into well-defined employment categories (McLean Parks, Kidder, and Gallagher 1998). Despite such definitional limitations, Gallagher (2002) and Gallagher and McLean Parks (2001) suggest that three forms or types of employment arrangements exist that comfortably fit the above noted definition of contingent work.

First, the most commonly recognized form of contingent work arrangements is a worker who is hired on an as needed basis through the services of an intermediary organization such as a "temporary-help service firm" (THS) (e.g., Adecco or Manpower). Within these arrangements there is often a contractually explicit understanding that an assignment or dispatch is for a fixed duration or time or until a specific project has been completed. As suggested in the literature and in practice, the temporary-help service industry has not only increased dramatically in popularity in the past decade, but has also expanded in scope well beyond the stereotypical image of temporary clerks and day laborers. In fact, there are a growing number of temporary help firms that specialize in the short-term placement of workers in professional positions such as accounting, engineering, and medical occupations. For many client organizations, temporary-help service firms represent an established vehicle for assisting them in adjusting to numerical and functional staffing demands on a "just in time" basis.

A second general form of contingent work arrangement exists in the form of "direct-hire," "zero-hour," or "in-house" arrangements with the immediate employer organization (Gallagher 2002). In practice, direct-hire contingent workers may have an ongoing relationship with a single employing organization, perhaps with an implicit or explicit understanding that a more permanent contract may result later, but there is a general absence of a predicable or systematic work schedule. Entirely consistent with the goal of numerical flexibility, direct-hire temps are assigned and removed from work as changes in product or service demands dictate.

The third and increasingly more popular form of contingent employment exists in the organizational use of "independent contractors." Independent contractors or "freelance" workers are legally defined as self-employed persons who sell their services to a client organization on a fixed term or project basis. Most often, independent contractors are highly educated and professionally trained workers who have skills that are in short supply within an organization or for which the organization has an immediate but not a long-term ongoing need. These workers generally set their own hours and decide how the work will be completed. A growing number of independent contractors can be found in "knowledge based" occupations and areas requiring substantial technological skills (e.g. information technology). It has also become an increasingly common management practice in some industries to remove or terminate some workers from more permanent employment positions but to rehire these same individuals as nonemployee independent contractors under fixed term or project-based contracts. As evidenced in the case of the Microsoft Corporation, the propriety of such arrangements is questionable when the level of client control for all practical purposes constitutes a form of "dependent" rather independent contractor arrangement (Greene 2000; Marin 2000). In some circumstances, independent contractors may rely upon intermediary client-contractor matching services for the location of contractual assignments.

The Management Challenge

From both a management and an academic perspective it is interesting, and perhaps even ironic, to note that the dramatic growth in contingent work arrangements as a strategy for enabling firms to become more numerically and functionally flexible comes at the same time that practitioner- and research-based publications have emphasized the financial and competitive value of organizational HRM policies and practices which focus on the importance of employment security and organizational attachment. Most notably, a growing body of both HRM and more general management literature since the mid-1980s has begun to emphasize the economic and competitive advantages of management practices that are focused less on the "control" of human assets within an organization, and more on the development of "commitment" building strategies (e.g., Walton 1985; Eisenhart 1985; Arthur 1994).

As generally envisioned and practiced, control-based HRM practices are intended to reduce labor costs and to improve efficiency by enforcing employee compliance through specific rules and procedures and even offering "rewards" on the basis of some measurable output criteria. Arthur (1994) notes that these control-based HRM policies are most likely to exist where managers have relatively complete knowledge of the work processes so that they may set clear performance standards and easily measure employee performance. These conditions enable employers to directly monitor and reward employee behavior or the specific outcomes of that behavior (Arthur 1994; Ouchi 1979).

In contrast to control-based HRM practices, "commitment" based HR systems seek to encourage desirable employee attitudes and behaviors by building psychological linkages between organizational and employee goals. Rather than emphasizing monitoring and controlling, commitment-based approaches are based on HRM strategies which seek to develop committed employees who are encouraged to use their discretion to carry out their job tasks in ways that are consistent with organizational goals (Arthur 1994; Organ 1988). As noted by Arthur (1994), commitment-based HRM strategies or systems were generally chacterized by higher levels of employee involvement in managerial decision making, training in group problem solving or teamwork, general training, and minimal status differences. Research by Wood (1999) also suggests that commitment-based models of workforce management exist as the underlying basis for increasing more touted practices as "high-commitment management," "high involvement management," or "high-performance management." The evolution of commitment-based models of HRM has advanced even further to broaden focus away from excessive emphasis on employee attitudes and toward an emphasis on the importance of skill formation, work structuring, pay methods, and other HR practices that may influence performance (Wood 1999). Today, a considerable amount of research and practitioner attention seen in books and seminars is directed toward the development of "High Performance Work Systems" (HPWS) (e.g., see Huselid 1995; Becker and Huselid 1998). This theory emphasizes the importance of "bundles" or "clusters" of HRM practices that enable employees as a means of more effectively utilizing human assets in the implementation of corporate strategy and the attainment of organizational goals. For example, firms are encouraged to enhance job security if they provide extensive training; it is wasteful to invest in the skills of employees who are about to be terminated.

The advocacy of high-performance work systems or HPWS, and associated management practices as an effective and established means of enhancing firm performance is well established by Pfeffer (1994) in his work *Competitive Advantage through People*. In a more recent articulation of the underlying principles of HPWS and commitment-based models of HRM, Pfeffer and Veiga note, we read, "Simply put, people work harder because of the increased involvement and commitment that comes from having more control and say in their work; people work smarter because they are encouraged to build skills and competence; and people work more responsibly because more responsibility is placed in hands of employees farther down the organization" (1999, 40).

One of the most intriguing aspects of the work of Pfeffer (1994) and Pfeffer and Veiga (1999) is their identification of organizational HRM practices that are essential ingredients in the development of a high-performance work environment. Listed among the practices or strategies noted by Pfeffer and Veiga for enhanced organizational performance through the more effective use of human assets are selective hiring, increased employment security, self-managed teams with decentralized decision making, high compensation based upon organizational performance, extensive training investments, reduction in status differences within the organization, and the open sharing of information within the organization. More recent research by Barling, Loughlin, and Kelloway (in press) has even sought to extend the components of a HPWS by the inclusion of an organizational emphasis on workplace safety and transformational leadership styles.

On the surface there appears to be a contradiction between the trend toward the use of "contingent" workers as a means of facilitating organizational flexibility and the managerial advice found in the commitment-based and HPWS models of human resource management within organizations. For example, how can an organization rely on an increasing number of temporary workers and at the same time espouse a philosophy of employment security? What is the meaning of "commitment" in the context of short-term or contingent contracts? To what extent can or should managers be willing to invest in the HPWS practices of training or information sharing with workers who the organization has made contractually distinct from the more permanent or "core" workers?

In the following sections of this chapter, we will identify and discuss the issues and related challenges that are faced by organizations that use contingent workers as part of their overall HRM strategy to ensure staffing flexibility. Particular emphasis will be placed on how the use of contingent workers affects the importance of such managerial strategies as commitment building, the application of high-performance work practices (e.g., employment security, job design, and reduced status distinctions), as well as the usefulness of transformational leadership behaviors. Included within this discussion will be both the identification of relevant organizational research that may be applicable to the issues that are being faced by both workers and managers, as well as a number of suggestions for managers who are attempting to balance the dual objectives of creating staffing flexibility while also fostering high-involvement and high-performance workplaces. In the concluding section, our attention will be directed to identifying a number of ongoing challenges that organizations will face in association with the increased use of contingent workers.

Commitment Building: Commitment to What?

For most managers, the proposition of moving away from a "control" based approach to a "commitment" based HRM strategy is not likely to be met with open opposition. For that matter, most organizations would prefer to be known for having a "highly committed workforce" rather than priding itself as a place of employment where workers are "closely controlled and monitored." However, for organizations that are employing more contingent workers as part of their staffing strategies, there might well exist a need to rethink the meaning and applicability of "commitment" based approaches to the management of human resources.

To date, a tremendous amount of literature on the topic of commitment has been developed. As noted by Meyer and Allen (1997) and Mowday, Porter, and Steers (1982), commitment has largely been viewed from the perspective of a worker's attachment and identification with the goals and values of the organization for which they work (i.e., organizational commitment). In short, people feel a sense of organizational commitment when there is a congruence between organizational practices and their own personal values and objectives. In addition to this notion of an "affective" commitment to the organization, there is also evidence to suggest that workers may be committed to an organization for less positive reasons such as a lack of practical alternatives or because of organizational policies that have created an excessive personal investment or sunk cost that prevents them from leaving the organization (i.e., continuance commitment). For others, organizational commitment may also reflect a "normative" feeling of obligation or responsibility to remain attached to the organization.

It is also extremely important to recognize, particularly in the context of the growing popularity of contingent contracts, that "organizational commitment" and "commitment" in general are viewed as monolithic concepts. However, as noted by Reichers (1985), workers may hold a particular level of commitment to the organization and at the same time hold varying levels of commitment to multiple constituencies within the organization. Objects or foci of a worker's organizational commitment may include co-workers, a team leader, a unit manager, or the top management of the organization. Not unexpectedly, there are circumstances where a worker might hold a high level of commitment to their immediate work team but a lower level of commitment to either top management or to the organization in general. Managers should note research findings that suggest that commitment is an important aspect of an employment relationship because commitment at both the organizational and subunit levels is related to positive attitudinal and behavioral outcomes such as improved attendance, retention, extra-role behaviors, and most importantly job and organizational performance. Equally important for organizations interested in building commitment-based HRM practices, is the existence of a substantial body of literature that indicates that worker commitment can be positively (and negatively) influenced by management practices (Meyer and Allen 1997).

Also important to our understanding of the ultimate influence of commitment among the contingent component of an organization's workforce is the recognition that despite all the attention that has been given to it, organizational commitment (and subcomponents) is only one aspect of commitment within the broader context of "work commitment." As noted by Morrow (1993), "commitment" can be operationalized and understood not only in the context of a worker's attachment to the employer organization, but also in the context of such considerations as an individual's attachment to "employment" in general (i.e., the importance of having work), "job commitment" (i.e., the position in which that person is employed and the tasks associated with it), and "occupational" or "professional commitment" (i.e., a desire to remain within a particular line of work and an attachment to the values and mission of a particular profession, e.g., nursing, teaching, engineering, etc.). This is an important consideration given the fact that especially in the face of poor workplace relationships, workers' performance may be a function of their occupational or professional commitment.

For organizations that are faced with the task of managing both contingent and "regular" workers, the above-noted dimensionality of "commitment" and the implications for building or maintaining a "commitment" based HRM system is particularly important. Most notably, contingent workers can be both highly committed and, when properly assisted by management, can direct that commitment to the benefit of the organization in terms of performance (e.g. Pearce 1993; Van Dyne and Ang 1998). The key task for managers is to understand the underlying motivations of their contingent workers and the foci of their commitment. Central to this task is the need to further recognize that the form or nature of the contingent employment relationship may have an impact on the nature and importance of the different forms of commitment.

One contingent employment situation where the issue of commitment may appear at first blush to be outside the traditional paradigm rests in the case of temporary or contingent workers that are hired through the services of a temporary help service (THS) firm. First of all, there is an inherent temptation for managers to believe that attempts to build "organizational commitment" or expectations of any commitment from THS workers to the client organization are a misallocation of effort. This belief may in part rest on the proven association between organizational commitment and retention (reduced turnover), and the related lack of a felt necessity to develop commitment if the goal of using temporary workers is to actually avoid long-term retention and to actually ensure turnover by the design of the employment contract. However, as recently noted by Gallagher and McLean Parks (2001), commitment among THS workers is both meaningful and complex. Most notably, similar to most "regular" forms of employment, THS workers do have a measurable level of "organizational" commitment, but the meaning of the term "organization" has greater complexity given the presence of a "triangular" employment relationship between the temporary worker, the THS organization and the client organization that is using the services of the temporary worker. For managers in client organizations that engage the services of THS firm employees, commitment has meaning both in terms of the temporary worker's short-term attachment to the client firm (albeit even continuance-based) and also their commitment to the "job" to which they have been assigned. In one regard, the ability of managers within the client organization to develop or cultivate the temporary workers' levels of organizational and job related commitment may be hampered by the fact that a number of the proximal antecedents of commitment (e.g., wages, benefits, training) are in fact mostly under the control of the THS firm. However, managers in the client organization should recognize that they can in fact still influence the level of commitment that the temporary worker holds towards the client organization and (even more importantly) the job that they have been assigned to perform. Included among those commitment-building capabilities are functions such as efforts to effectively orient the temporary worker to their work environment, a careful articulation of all duties and performance expectations, just and fair treatment, and an effort to explain to temporary employees where they fit into the overall mission of the organization (Feldman, Doerpinghaus and Turnley 1994; Feldman 1995).

In the case of "direct-hire" temporaries, the complexity of a client–employer relationship is absent and there is a clearly more identifiable "employer–employee relationship." Therefore, for the most part, what we know about commitment building strategies that have been applied to more "traditional" or "regular" workers can also be applied to direct-hire temporary workers. Perhaps the greatest issue of concern is the disinclination of some managers to invest in the development of the organizational and job commitment of direct-hire temporary workers. The flip side of this coin is the potential disinclination of direct-hire temporary workers to be responsive to their managers' commitment building strategies.

In many cases the level of attention that managers give towards enhancing the commitment of temporary workers may be a function of the perceived motivations of both the workers and the organization. For example, some workers may take on direct-hire temporary positions as a means of gaining access to more permanent jobs in the organization, but other workers may have voluntarily chosen to become temporary workers, perhaps in order to maintain a balance between employment and nonemployment commitments such as family or educational responsibilities. As will be noted elsewhere, organizations themselves may use temporary work arrangements (both direct-hire and via THS firms) as a means of prescreening potential permanent employees. In all cases, however, worker identification with the goals and objectives of the organization or the jobs that they perform after they have been granted permanent employment could be negatively affected by any managerial neglect which preceded the transition to more permanent employment. Conversely, managerial avoidance of commitment building strategies in a "temp to perm" environment could conceivably result in the organization's loss (turnover) of the very workers that it had hoped to retain for permanent employment.

Finally, in the case of independent contractors, the notion of building commitment to an "employer" organization has little practical meaning for those who are actually self-employed. However, managerial treatment of independent contractors may be realized in terms of the contractor's commitment to the client organization. In this regard, it may become important for managers in client organizations to better understand the relative importance of the foci of commitment among independent contractors. As noted by Gallagher and McLean Parks (2001), the job-related performance of independent contractors may be most closely tied to their level of commitment to the profession in which they are employed. Recent research by Ang and Slaughter (2001) has found that even in adverse client–contractor relationships, contractor performance and willingness to engage in extra-role behaviors are closely related to the contractors' level of commitment. From a managerial perspective, a client organization may not necessarily be able to influence professional commitment, but managers in client organizations should be sensitive to providing a work context that enables independent contractors to fully realize their professionalism and autonomy. Furthermore it is especially important for managers to consider the issue of commitment building or "rebuilding" in the situation where employees are involuntary moved from the status of permanent employee to independent contractor (Ho and Ang 1998). Most notably, managers need to consider the extent to which the feelings of commitment that were developed under the preexisting psychological contract between the worker and the organization have been seriously undermined by the employment dissolution and transfer to a more contingent arrangement.

In general terms, "commitment" still has meaning for workers who are employed under contingent rather than more traditional long-term employment relationships. For managers who are responsible for contingent workers, the key task is to recognize that commitment is not a unitary concept, and that these contingent workers may value or be more sensitive to different foci of organizational and work commitment. Although some managers might assume that contingent workers are less likely to become committed to a client organization, it is worth recognizing that this commitment is a function of the characteristics of the job itself as well as the workers' treatment by their supervisor (e.g., McDonald and Makin 2000). In recognition of this, organizations should consider the use of such tactics as selective hiring, reduced status distinctions, effective job design and transformational leadership to enhance contingent workers' commitment to the organization.

Choosing Wisely

As noted by Pfeffer and Veiga (1999), organizations that are serious about profitability through the effective use of people need to expend considerable effort to ensure that they recruit the right people in the first place. There is no reason to suggest that an emphasis on selective hiring of longer-term or "regular" employees is not applicable in organizations that also employ contingent or temporary workers. However, the issue of concern is the extent to which managers can in fact apply selective hiring standards to those workers for which they are offering short-term contracts (THS workers and independent contractors) or jobs with unpredictable work schedules (e.g., direct-hires).

In reality, the nature of the selection and screening processes applied to engaging the services of contingent workers may be a function of the types of jobs for which they are being recruited, their type of contract, and the motivations of both the contingent worker and organization. As previously noted, the decision by an organization to use contingent workers as part of its overall staffing strategy reflects in large part the objectives of maintaining numerical and functional flexibility. However, it is also possible that the use of contingent workers may actually serve as a form of selective hiring. Most notably, access to more permanent positions, especially at the entry levels, may be extended primarily to workers who have unofficially undergone a "probationary period" as a direct-hire or THS worker. In effect, not only may contingent workers provide organizations with a means to meet fluctuating staffing needs, but they may also provide management a longer look at potential hires. This strategy has been described as an excessively long interview, and it may unfortunately place "probationary" workers under undue pressure in that they face constant scrutiny from supervisors, peers, and clients over a protracted time period.

Using contingent workers as a form of selective hiring also involves a number of practical and ethical considerations for organizations that employ such an approach. First, from a practical perspective, a heavy reliance on hiring contingent workers through "temp to perm" arrangements has the unintended consequence of seriously reducing the potential labor pool from which the organization recruits potential employees. In particular, the majority of the labor force in most developed countries consists of individuals whose first employment priority is to seek long-term and secure employment opportunities with a particular employer. As a result, temp to perm recruitment and hiring would reduce an organization's access to the preponderance of potential candidates that are outside the contingent labor market. Second, even within the contingent market, there are a significant number of workers who are not interested in securing more permanent employment. As a result, transitioning contingent workers to more permanent positions may not be possible when it is inconsistent with the employment objectives of the temporary worker. Thirdly, although the use of a "temp to perm" hiring strategy may facilitate an organization's ability to attract direct-hire temps (and even independent contractors), there is also a danger that contingent workers may feel betrayed and therefore less committed to the organization if an implied transition to more permanent employment is not realized.

From a practical perspective, the unwillingness of an organization to move certain direct-hire contingents to permanent positions may place managers in the position of having to give increased attention to how to "selectively remove" contingent workers whose interests in longer-term employment are not supported by their qualifications or their performance. In many respects, this also suggests the need for organizations to be honest with contingent workers in terms of the true likelihood that they will actually be considered or advantaged in the selection process for permanent positions within the organization. Finally, in cases where organizations are using a temp to perm recruitment and hiring strategy, it also appears that managers should not underestimate the importance of the initial hiring process under the assumption that poor selection of temporary workers can be easily mitigated by more immediate termination of the temporary workers' contracts. In contrast, if direct-hire temporary arrangements exist as an alternative or primary means of staffing for entry level positions, then management should extend serious consideration to the types of selective hiring strategies for the procurement of permanent workers (Pfeffer and Veiga 1999).

In contrast to the level of discretion and control that managers may exercise in engaging direct-hire temporary workers, the hiring of temporary workers through the services of a THS firm (e.g., Adecco, Manpower, etc.) provides a different set of challenges. Most notably, although a client organization may occasionally request the services of a specific temporary worker, the responsibility of "selecting" an appropriate temporary worker for an assignment rests with the THS firm. For organizations, the emphasis moves away from the process of hiring the best individual in favor of engaging the services of the most appropriate THS firm(s) and achieving the best match in terms of expectations and abilities. Managers will need to direct their attention to the ongoing monitoring of the workers' performance (Pfeffer and Baron 1988). From a practical perspective, the ability to secure THS dispatched temporary workers with the desired knowledge, skills, and abilities to perform assigned tasks becomes a dual responsibility of the client and the THS firm organizations.

For managers within client organizations, effective temporary worker selection is partly a function of their ability to clearly articulate to the THS firm the nature of the tasks involved in the job and the job-related skill specifications. However, unlike the case of direct-hire contingent workers, the screening and selection process rests with the THS firm. Although, incorrect "matches" may be remedied by the "return" of the temporary to the THS, such mismatches still represent effective losses of time and efficiency. The magnitude of the dysfunctional consequences of the misalignment of need versus skills may vary according to the level of responsibility associated with the temporary position (e.g., a day laborer vs. a nurse or an accountant). From a strategic perspective, organizations who frequently seek staffing flexibility through the use of THS firms may need to address the issue of the extent to which they are willing to contract with a single or multiple THS firms (Feldman et al. 1994). At issue is the question as to whether or not the staffing function can be more effectively managed if the organization enters into an exclusive or limited partnership with one or a few THS firms.

For client organizations, exclusive or limited contracting arrangements with particular THS firms may restrict supply sources, but they may conversely have the benefit of developing a more detailed understanding by the THS firm of the needs of the client organization. An extensive use of contingent workers who are hired through THS firms may also create a situation where temporary managers from the THS firm are actually assigned "on-site" supervisory responsibilities for the other temporary workers. Such an arrangement has the potential of producing an element of ambiguity in terms of where the ultimate responsibility rests for certain human resource management functions. In addition, there is also the potential for managers to direct increased attention to the task of managing the external managers.

Finally, it is also important to note that the task of meeting numerical or functional staffing requirements through the use of independent contractors presents management with some very basic selection or hiring issues, the most visible of which is the extent to which an organization knows if or which independent contractor actually has the skills sought by the client organization. Similar to the challenges faced by organizations in the subcontracting or outsourcing of work, the task of effectively securing "independent contractors" should require managers to exercise considerable diligence in the "hiring process." As noted by Lacity and Willcocks (1998), contractual arrangements should involve a clear written statement of the end product as well as explicit completion deadlines. A further challenge to organizations that employ independent contractors is the ability to access information from other clients or sources concerning the skills, credentials, and past projects of potential candidates. In effect, the use of independent contractors may actually increase the importance of organizations using social networks with professional associations and other employers to assess the suitability and fit of specific independent contractors to the needs of the client organization.

But Someone Has to Do it

Stereotypically, contingent workers perform repetitive and menial tasks that are of minimal value to the organization. Unfortunately, for many workers, this stereotype is not very far from the truth. Although organizations may have originally employed contingent workers mostly to fill in for permanent workers who were sick or on leave, organizations today are likely to engage contingent workers to perform specific tasks or projects. Although some of these projects require specialized skills and are crucial for the performance of the organization as a whole, many of these projects are in fact those that no one currently employed in the organization has an interest in completing. Many contingent workers can be stuck with dirty jobs that no one else wants to do.

Managers who argue that assigning contingent workers less interesting jobs is their prerogative are not incorrect. However, there are a number of negative organizational consequences of having workers with low-quality jobs, and there are also a number of simple ways in which managers can make a job more intrinsically motivating. Managers who already recognize the negative effects on their organizations of offering low-quality jobs may be familiar with the work of Fisher (1993), who explored how boring jobs may result in more safety violations, sabotage, and theft, as well as other research that links poorly designed jobs to low performance and motivation (e.g., Hackman and Oldham 1980). These managers may also be concerned with their employees' health, in recognition of the fact that a worker's lack of decision latitude, coupled with heavy job demands, can result in job strain, job dissatisfaction, and high blood pressure (Karasek 1979; Schaubroeck and Merritt 1997).

In general, directly hired temporary workers may be placed in jobs of the lowest quality of all contingent workers. They tend to perform repetitive tasks that comprise only a subset of a project and they are given only a limited understanding of the finished products of their work. In fact, Rogers (1995, 147) reports, "temporaries consistently report being assigned to 'scut work', or 'dreg work'." They may be allocated repetitive tasks such as filing, photocopying, or stuffing envelopes that are perceived as being extremely monotonous. More seriously, contingent workers may be hired to perform the most dangerous jobs on a work site (Collinson 1999). This is particularly important for managers to recognize because these workers also tend to be less experienced, have less safety training, and have less knowledge about the site-specific safety procedures (e.g., location of the fire extinguisher and safety exits, knowledge of the evacuation procedures, etc.) and therefore face a higher level of individual and contextual risks (Rousseau and Libuser 1997).

The issues faced by THS firm temporary workers are again related to the type of work they are performing. Like the direct-hires, many temporary workers will have jobs that are of poorer quality than those of their permanent counterparts. However, as previously noted, a number of temporary workers enjoy jobs with high skill variety, task significance, task identity, autonomy, and feedback, such as nursing, translation, and accounting. The job design challenge for these workers lies in clarifying their roles and managing the expectations of their clients in conjunction with the expectations of their service firms. Although some of the onus is certainly on the individual to balance their competing responsibilities, managers in the client organization also have an important role to play. In fact, Feldman et al. (1994) note how many client firms fail to state the terms of the contract or assignment in advance. This is highly problematic in that role clarity has been identified as an important element of job design that has a significant effect on worker health and well-being (Parker, Chmiel, and Wall 1997) as well as performance (Fried et al. 1998).

In general, independent contractors are assumed to have interesting, well-designed, high-quality jobs. Indeed, these workers are indeed usually highly skilled and by definition enjoy an elevated level of autonomy in comparison to most other workers, but a recent study by Ang and Slaughter (2001) suggests that this is not always the case. They found that managers tended to assign their software developer contractors tasks that were more limited in scope than those assigned to the permanent employees. Managers who hire independent contractors may be concerned about controlling the output of these workers, but if they have selected qualified individuals, they should trust that their output will be acceptable if they are given sufficient opportunity to demonstrate their skill. In this circumstance, once a contractual understanding has been reached, management focus might be best directed to reviewing scheduled outcomes rather than focusing on the process.

As mentioned, there are a number of simple strategies that managers may adopt in order to improve the job quality of the tasks allocated to the contingent workers engaged by the organization. For example, managers can increase workers' motivation by increasing their perceptions of the importance of their job to the organization or by explaining how it fits into the larger organizational context. Furthermore, particularly in the case of direct-hire temporary workers, managers can use job rotation, job enrichment, or job enlargement to reduce monotony and enhance skill sets while benefiting from more motivated workers with better performance and safety behaviors. For direct-hire temps, such strategies may also facilitate a transition to a more permanent position within the organization.

Organizational Castes

Although contingent workers may, because of their indeterminate status, face a certain degree of social stigma in our society (Zeytinoğlu 1999), they may also be stigmatized by their permanent colleagues in their workplaces. Contingent workers may be treated rudely or receive insufficient information with which to perform their tasks. These status distinctions, however, are detrimental to their performance and to the performance of many of the permanent workers who witness this treatment. Management should be aware of the possible pressures of such distinctions and consider developing strategies for reducing them wherever possible.

Some contingent workers report that they are excluded from the social interaction of their permanent counterparts. For example, one worker reported, "in the company [I am assigned to] they make me feel so much like an outsider, a nobody. Whenever the whole office does something together, I am not included. It is as if I do not exist" (Feldman et al. 1994, 54). Similarly, another worker explained that "whenever there was going to be a company party or something, the temps had to stay and work . . . you could tell where the second-class citizenship started" (Rogers 1995, 150). While social isolation is naturally unpleasant, other contingent workers report being barred from activities related to their jobs. According to one Silicon Valley professional, it was regarded as affront to their integrity to be excluded from team and staff meetings because the employer did not want them to have access to proprietary data (Gerber 1999). Such slights, even if they are unintentional, are detrimental to worker morale and make effective teamwork difficult. These perceived injustices may also have lasting consequences, in terms of reduced commitment and performance, for contingent workers who become permanent employees. Also, as noted, such unfair treatment may have a "spillover effect" on the perceptions of more permanent employees regarding organizational fairness.

Contingent workers' sense of being "second-class citizens" may also be reinforced by more tangible status differentials, such as inadequate safety equipment. This has the dual effect of both increasing resentment along with the likelihood of serious injuries and it also provides easy identification of whose health and safety is valued by the organization. As a driller observed, "company men look down their nose [*sic*] at us, they think they're of a higher status" (Collinson 1999, 588). These contract workers were also seen wearing the second-hand thermal jackets of the permanent company employees. The consequences of these status distinctions are more serious than hurt feelings or reduced organizational commitment; occupational injuries and fatalities are more common among contingent workers than permanent employees (Kochan et al. 1994; Park and Butler 2001).

In order to resolve these issues, managers should endeavor to reduce the status distinctions that result in these social tensions. Some of these initiatives may be relatively simple yet they should yield significant results. For example, relationships between temporary workers and their permanent colleagues improved and turnover decreased by approximately one-third when temporary workers at a Midwestern auto manufacturing plan were finally issued uniforms that bore the worker's name (von Hippel et al. 1997).

Another managerial strategy to reduce status distinctions between workers with different employment relationships entails the full integration of contingent workers within the organization, so that permanent employees are not accorded any special privileges or considerations aside from their job security. In fact, the contract workers may even be paid more than their permanent contractors. Lautsh (1999) compares this approach to that of a complete segregation policy, where contingent workers are kept separate from the "core" group of employees and enjoy far fewer rights and freedoms. While these "ghettoized" workers had lower productivity than their permanent counterparts, the "assimilated" contingent workers had equal performance and greater perceptions of procedural and interactional justice. However, it is also crucial to note that in many countries, positive efforts to integrate temporary workers (especially THS firm workers) may be seriously discouraged by the principle of "co-employment." By assuming too much control through a more complete integration of temporary workers into the workplace, the client firm may unintentionally become legally responsible for a number of legislative rights which are afforded to their "regular workers" (e.g., benefits, severance pay, notice of termination, etc.) and which the organization had sought to avoid by using contingent workers. The fair treatment and integration of contingent workers is legally undermining the organization's flexibility and cost reduction for which many contingent workers are hired in the first place.

Again, in deciding how to structure their organizations, managers should also consider how the introduction of contingent workers into the organization might affect the attitudes and behaviors of permanent employees (Feldman et al. 1994). Permanent employees may see their duties change once contingent workers have been brought into the organization; for example, Ang and Slaughter (2001) found that managers broadened the job descriptions of the permanent employees in order to compensate for the limited scope of the tasks that were allocated to the independent contractors. If these extra responsibilities are not recognized or compensated, a certain level of resentment is understandable. Indeed, while the hiring of additional permanent employees increases the morale of all workers, engaging the services of additional contingent workers actually tends to decrease morale and trust (Morishima and Feuille 2000).

Leading to High Performance

Many managers engage contingent workers specifically in order to avoid the time, energy, and resources that are required to develop and motivate employees; they prefer to simply exercise their option to discontinue the contracts of workers whose performance is unsatisfactory. They see limited value in the leadership of workers who are, by their definition, not supposed to be with the firm long term, and who may easily transport their skills elsewhere. The contemporary reality, however, is that these "temporary" workers may remain at the firm for years while "permanent" workers may be downsized and thus have a shorter tenure. In addition, organizations must realize that contingent workers have the potential to contribute greatly to their work environment while they are there, and that this potential should be leveraged. Managers who refuse to lead or motivate their workers are assuming that their performance is easy to monitor and correct. Alternately, they may assume that a promise of eventual permanent employment is a sufficient motivator. However, all workers (including contingent workers) have the discretion to engage in organizational citizenship behaviors such as outstanding performance, providing assistance to other employees, and being generally helpful to the organization. Similarly, all workers have the potential to engage in organizational retaliatory behaviors, such as sabotage, theft, and aggression and violence towards other employees. For these reasons, managers should use transformational leadership to motivate and develop their contingent workers.

While a "control" based management strategy may require less effort, a "commitment" based strategy fostered by transformational leadership will result in tangible benefits to the organization. In fact, a number of studies suggest that managers who engage in transformational leadership behaviors reap any number of positive outcomes. For example, transformational leadership has been shown to have direct positive effects on organizational commitment, trust in management, and group cohesion, organizational citizenship behavior (Koh, Steers, and Terborg 1995) and sales performance (Barling, Weber, and Kelloway 1996). Although there are proven benefits to using transformational leadership to manage permanent employees and volunteers, there is some evidence that managers have not applied these techniques towards their contingent workers.

As identified by Avolio (1999), transformational leadership is comprised of four dimensions: intellectual stimulation, idealized influence, inspirational motivation, and individualized consideration. We may examine each in turn and identify how each aspect may be particularly problematic for contingent workers.

As noted earlier, many contingent workers are often given unchallenging tasks even if they are in fact highly qualified. This management strategy is not compatible with the intellectual stimulation component of transformational leadership, which suggests that managers should encourage subordinates to think for themselves. For example, a supervisor may answer questions with more questions, or encourage their employees to contradict their boss in order to fully explore all relevant issues (Avolio 1999). Contingent workers, particularly those with low status in the organization, may find it politically difficult to contradict their supervisors or to suggest new ways of performing their duties. This might be particularly problematic for lower-skilled THS firm workers, in that "following directions" may be part of the culture of some segments of the THS firm industry.

Inspirational motivation, another component of a transformational leadership strategy, is exhibited by managers who instill in their followers a clear vision of the future by painting an optimistic future and by creating positive expectations that in turn become self-fulfilling prophecies (Avolio 1999). Similarly, idealized influence is an element of transformational leadership that is apparent when a manager sets an example by showing determination, displaying extraordinary talents, showing dedication to "the cause," and creating a sense of joint mission (Avolio 1999). Essentially, these leaders are good role models whose values and behaviors allow followers to learn by example. In contrast, Rogers (1995) identifies a number of situations where contingent workers are given no direction and are even physically isolated from other workers. Because contingent workers have fewer interactions with their supervisors, they have fewer opportunities to learn by example or to be told of an optimistic vision of the future. Instead, contingent workers are exposed to management behaviors that correspond more closely with "laissez-faire" management, where "leaders" do little if anything to encourage or motivate their employees.

Individualized consideration is the fourth integral component of an effective transformational leadership style. Transformational leaders delegate projects in order to create learning experiences, and treat each follower with respect and as a unique individual (Koh et al. 1995). In addition, according to Avolio (1999), leaders with individualized consideration skills answer followers' questions with minimal delay, show that they are concerned for their followers' well-being, assign tasks on the basis of individual needs and abilities, encourage two-way exchanges of ideas, are available when needed, constantly encourage self-development, and effectively mentor, counsel, and coach peers and followers. In contrast, we have noted earlier that contingent workers are frequently denigrated or treated rudely by their managers. Contingent workers in higher-status jobs may be more immune to such egregious displays of disrespect, but they may still not be treated with the same regard as the permanent employees in an organization. This management behavior is inconsistent with the individualized consideration element of transformational leadership.

Direct-hire temporary workers may face some of the same issues as their permanent counterparts, but their situation may be exacerbated by the transitory nature of their relationships with their superiors. Their supervisors may not invest in the relationship if they feel that the duration is too short for the subunit to benefit from any increases in performance. Alternately, some managers may believe that the assigned tasks are insufficiently complex for the worker to benefit from any coaching. However, managers who use transformational leadership can benefit from having workers with more positive attitudes towards the organization and who are more likely to exhibit enthusiasm and extra-role behaviors.

Contingent workers who are affiliated with a THS firm will face the same obstacles as direct-hires and independent contractors, but having two "supervisory" relationships (i.e., with the client firm and with the THS firm) further complicates their situation. Each firm may assume that the other is responsible for motivating and managing the worker, and so the temporary worker may receive little encouragement or support from either organization. Because they have no control over the actions of the temporary service firm, managers who employ temporary workers should apply transformational leadership strategies to encourage the maximum performance from their contingent workers.

Independent contractors do not face the obstacles posed by multiple agency, but they may still be less likely to receive transformational leadership than their permanent colleagues. Because, by definition, these contingent workers are responsible for deciding how their work may be accomplished, managers who deal with them may be hesitant to infringe on their autonomy by offering suggestions or encouragement related to the tasks at hand. This reluctance is understandable in that the services of an independent contractor may have been engaged specifically so that the client firm's managers did not need to allocate time and resources toward their motivation, development, or guidance. However, independent contractors should not be subjected to negative management behaviors, such as management by exception (MBE) where managers wait for a worker to make a mistake and then correct it (Avolio 1999). Managers should be clear in their expectations and pay particular attention to providing individualized consideration (e.g., being available to answer questions, demonstrating concern, allowing a two-way exchange of ideas, etc.) even if they are not able to offer specific guidance.

Although some managers who lead contingent workers may assume that these individuals require only the most rudimentary supervision this attitude is worth reexamining. Because organizations are becoming increasingly reliant on contingent workers, because contingent workers may remain at an organization for far longer than anticipated, and for the reason that contingent workers may have a significant impact on the functioning of the organization, managers should use transformational leadership to motivate these workers. In addition, the treatment of contingent workers is readily observable by permanent workers who may form negative attitudes towards the organization if they perceive any mistreatment. Managers who are conscientious will reap the benefits of increased organizational commitment, trust in management, organizational citizenship behavior, and performance.

Conclusions and Future Challenges

The employment of workers on fixed term or project-based contracts is not a new phenomenon. As noted by Cappelli (1999), many employment contracts prior to the rise of industrialization were based entirely upon short-term or almost daily hire labor agreements. In addition, in many craft-based occupations such as construction and entertainment (e.g., movies, theatre, etc.) the notion of project-based employment still remains a primary staffing technique. However, over the last two decades there has been a significant growth in the use of contingent work contracts throughout the world in an increasing range in types and sizes of manufacturing, financial, service sector, and knowledge-based organizations.

As noted in this chapter, this increased use of contingent workers presents a broad array of challenges for the task of managing the entire workforce within an organization. Most fundamental to these managerial challenges are philosophical and practical questions pertaining to the relative value of "control" versus "commitment" based models for the management and development of an organization's human resources. In particular, the increasing proportion of functions being performed within an organization by contingent "workers" rather than by "employees" raises questions concerning the extent to which organizations may be tempted or encouraged to follow a "dualistic" approach to workforce management. In effect there may be a "primary" and highly visible core organization where management believes in and practices such HPWS and commitment-based principles as selective hiring, job security, extensive training, information sharing, contingent pay, and reduced status differences (Pfeffer and Veiga 1999). At the same time, there may simultaneously be a parallel or "shadow" organization that is populated by contingent workers and managed through control-based strategies such as rigid job structures, detailed performance contracts, and close monitoring by management or designated agents.

These "dualistic" strategic approaches to the management of mixed contingent/noncontingent workforces may exist by design or by passive neglect. As previously noted, this dualistic approach may in some countries reflect legitimate legal concerns regarding the maintenance of an "arm's length relationship," in order to avoid the determination and the potential liability related to a "co-employer" or "dependent worker" affiliation. In other cases, management's treatment of contingent workers might not be a reflection of any systematic policy but rather a function of day-to-day management practices, which may be a result of the biases or beliefs that some managers hold about the potential contributions of short-term or contingent workers. Although there is some preliminary research on the topic, organizations still need to gain more insight into the possible consequences of pursuing a dualistic or differential treatment of contingent and noncontingent workers. A practical concern is the extent to which contingent workers perceive inequities in their treatment as well as the impact of such managerial treatment on their performance. In effect, do control-based strategies for managing contingent workers guarantee the underutilization of their skills and value to the organization? From a broader perspective, it is also important to determine the organizational consequences of how the treatment of contingent workers is perceived by the "regular" employees and how such perceptions affect the existing or the desired organizational culture?

As an alternative to operating under the principle of a dual workforce (the regulars vs. the contingents), managers may be fully aware of many of the issues raised in this chapter and pursue a more seamless integration of contingent and noncontingent workers. Such managers will be, however, faced with the challenge of doing so while maintaining their intended goals of using contingent workers to achieve numerical and functional flexibility and of being in compliance with any existing governmental policies, which actually mandate certain forms of differential treatment. Furthermore, any discussion of efforts to more effectively use the skills and talents of contingent workers through increased workplace integration or similar treatment to those of "regular" workers once again needs to consider differences that exist among the forms, types, and motivations of contingent workers. Most notably, managers cannot be misled into believing that there is a single prescription or set of policies that can lead to the more effective integration of an organization's contingent workforce. As noted at the onset and throughout the preceding discussion, aside from the application of basic principles of fairness, dignity and respect, strategies concerning the management of contingent workers may need to be customized to the type of contingent work arrangement and the objectives that the organization is seeking to achieve. The issues associated with the selection, assignment, evaluation, and potential eventual advancement of "direct-hire" temporaries can be very different than the management issues associated with contracted THS temporaries or independent contractors. Furthermore, at the individual worker level, what contingent workers expect in terms of treatment from an organization and its managers is dependent on individuals' level of professional skills and their motivations for performing contingent work. In many respects, the psychological contracts between contingent workers and their organizations may be more diverse in scope than what exits among more traditional or "regular" workers.

Finally, the challenge of managing contingent workers is also reflected in a recent essay by Peter Drucker (2002) that identifies and discusses the trend by organizations to increasingly relinquish their responsibility for HRM functions through the use of outsourcing, leased workforces (professional employee organizations; i.e., PEOs), and THS firms. Despite the prescribed benefits of having another party manage the organization's human resources, Drucker notes that "Every organization must take management responsibility for *all* the people whose productivity and performance it relies on – whether they're temps, part-timers, employees of the organization itself, or employees of its outsourcers, suppliers, and distributors" (2002, 75).

In the context of contingent work, the task facing managers might well fit within what Drucker refers to as the need to develop skills of an "orchestral director." Most notably, today's managers are placed in the position of having to manage human assets that are internal, external, and tangential to the organization's traditional employment structure. To address this world of increased use of contingent workers, the HR skills of managers must extend beyond traditional models of workforce management towards a consideration of how to collaboratively manage the internal workforce as well as a consideration of how to manage the integration of the external and internal workforces. Such a responsibility will also require a consideration of how managers can more effectively collaborate with external THS managers and self-employed independent contractors. Of particular interest in the future will be the extent to which existing managerial skills that were developed by working with external product suppliers and customers can be applied to the more effective management of the sources of contingent workers. These challenges are complicated by the varying sources and motivations of external workers, the increased labor market flexibility and volatility, and the growth of knowledge-based enterprises that has increased the dependence of managers on the skills of human resources external to the firm.

It is apparent that the organizational landscape has shifted. In recognition of this, managers will need to develop new strategies; although contingent work is by its nature temporary, its ascendancy is likely permanent.

REFERENCES

Ang, S., and Slaughter, S. A. 2001. Work outcomes and job design for contract versus permanent information systems professionals on software development teams. *MIS Quarterly* 25:321–50.

Arthur, J. B. 1994. Effects of human *resource* systems on manufacturing performance and turnover. *Academy of Management Journal* 37:670–87.

Avolio, B. J. 1999. *Full Leadership Development: Building the Vital Forces in Organizations.* Thousand Oaks, CA: Sage.

Barling, J., Loughlin, C., and Kelloway, E. K. In press. Development and test of a model linking safety-specific transformational leadership and occupational safety. *Journal of Applied Psychology.*

Barling, J., Weber, T., and Kelloway, E. K. 1996. Effects of transformational leadership training on attitudinal and financial outcomes: A field experiment. *Journal of Applied Psychology* 81:827–32.

Becker, B. E., and Huselid, M. A. 1998. High performance work systems and firm performance: A synthesis of research and managerial implications. In G. Ferris (ed.), *Research in Personnel and Human Resources* 16. Greenwich, CT: JAI.

Brewster, C., Mayne, L., and Tregaskis, O. 1997. Flexible working in Europe: A review of the evidence. *Management International Review* 37:85–103.

Cappelli, P. 1999. *The New Deal at Work.* Boston: Harvard Business School Press.

Collinson, D. L. 1999. "Surviving the rigs": Safety and surveillance on North Sea oil installations. *Organization Studies* 20:579–600.

Cooper, C. L., and Burke, R. J. (eds.). 2002. *The New World of Work: Challenges and Opportunities.* Oxford: Blackwell.

Deery, S. J., and Mahony, A. 1994. Temporal flexibility: Management strategies and employee preferences in the retail industry. *Journal of Industrial Relations* 36:332–52.

Delsen, L. 1999. Changing work relations in the European Union. In I. U. Zeytinoğlu (ed.), *Changing Work Relationships in Industrialized Economies.* Amsterdam: John Benjamins.

Drucker, P. 2002. They're not employees, they're people. *Harvard Business Review* February, 70–7.

Eisenhart, K. M. 1985. Control: Organizational and economic approaches. *Management Science* 31:134–49.

Feldman, D. C. 1995. Managing part-time and temporary employment relationships: Individual needs and organizational demands. In M. London (ed.), *Employees, Careers, and Job Creation.* San Francisco: Jossey-Bass.

Feldman, D. C., Doerpinghaus, H. I., and Turnley, W. H. 1994. Managing temporary workers: A permanent HRM challenge. *Organizational Dynamics* (fall):49–63.

Fisher, C. D. 1993. Boredom at work: A neglected concept. *Human Relations* 46:395–417.

Fried, Y., Ben-David, H. A., Tiegs, R. B., Avital, N., and Yeverechyahu, U. 1998. The interactive effect of role conflict and role ambiguity on job performance. *Journal of Occupational and Organizational Psychology* 71:19–27.

Friedrich, A., Kabst, R., Weber, W., and Rodehuth, M. 1998. Functional flexibility: Merely reacting or acting strategically? *Employee Relations* 20:504–23.

Gallagher, D. G. 2002. Contingent Work Contracts: Practice and Theory. In C. L. Cooper and R. J. Burke (eds.), *The New World of Work: Challenges and Opportunities.* Oxford: Blackwell.

Gallagher, D. G., and McLean Parks, J. 2001. I pledge thee my troth . . . contingently: Commitment and the contingent work relationship. *Human Resource Management Review* 11:181–208.

Gallie, D., White, M., Cheng, Y., and Tomlinson, M. 1998. *Restructuring the Employment Relationship.* Oxford: Oxford University Press.

Gerber, S. Z. 1999. Independent contractors: The impact of perceived fair treatment on measures of commitment, organizational citizenship behavior and intent to stay. Paper presented at the Academy of Management Meeting, August, 1999, Chicago.

Greene, B. 2000. Independent contractors: An attractive option? University of Otago, Dunedin, New Zealand. Unpublished research paper.

Hackman, J. R., and Oldham, G. R. 1980. *Work Redesign.* Reading, MA: Addison-Wesley.

Heckscher, C. 2000. HR strategy and nonstandard work: Dualism versus true mobility. In F. Carré, M. A. Ferber, L. Golden, and S. L. Herzenberg (eds.), *Nonstandard Work.* Champaign, IL: Industrial Relations Research Association.

Ho, V. T., and Ang, S. 1998. Spillover of psychological contract: When employees become contract labor in an outsourcing context. Paper presented at the Academy of Management Meeting, August, 1998, San Diego.

Huselid, M. A. 1995. The impact of human resource management practices on turnover, productivity, and corporate financial performance. *Academy of Management Journal* 38:635–73.

Kalleberg, A. M. 2000. Nonstandard employment relations: Part-time, temporary and contract work. *Annual Review of Sociology* 26:341–65.

Karasek, R. A. 1979. Job demands, job decision latitude, and mental strain: Implications for job redesign. *Administrative Science Quarterly* 24:285–308.

Kochan, T. A., Smith, M., Wells, J. C., and Rebitzer, J. B. 1994. Human resource strategies and contingent workers: The case of safety and health in the petrochemical industry. *Human Resource Management* 33:55–77.

Koh, W. L., Steers, R. M., and Terborg, J. R. 1995. The effects of transformational leadership on teacher attitudes and student performance in Singapore. *Journal of Organizational Behavior* 16:319–33.

Lacity, M. C., and Willcocks, L. P. 1998. An empirical investigation of information technology sourcing practices: Lessons from experience. *MIS Quarterly* 22:363–408.

Lautsch, B. A. 1999. Boundary labor markets: A grounded theory of contingent work. Working paper, Simon Fraser University, Burnaby, British Columbia, Canada.

Marin, E. 2000. The perspectives for a new and comprehensive vision of the protection of workers. *Proceedings of the Twelfth World Congress of the International Industrial Relations Research Association* 1:151–9, Tokyo.

Matusik, S. F., and Hill, C. W. L. 1998. The utilization of contingent work, knowledge creation, and competitive advantage. *Academy of Management Review* 23:680–97.

McDonald, D. J., and Makin, P. J. 2000. The psychological contract, organizational commitment and job satisfaction of temporary staff. *Leadership and Organizational Development Journal* 21:84–91.

McLean Parks, J., Kidder, D. L., and Gallagher, D. G. 1998. Fitting square pegs into round holes: Mapping the domain of contingent work arrangements onto the psychological contract. *Journal of Organizational Behavior* 19:697–730.

Meyer, J. P., and Allen, N. J. 1997. *Commitment in the Workplace: Theory, Research, and Application.* Thousand Oaks, CA: Sage.

Morishima, M., and Feuille, P. 2000. Effects of the use of contingent workers on regular status workers: A Japanese–US comparison. Paper presented at the Twelfth World Congress of the International Industrial Relations Research Association, May, 2000, Tokyo.

Morrow, P. C. 1993. *The Theory and Measurement of Work Commitment.* Greenwich, CT: JAI.

Mowday, R. T., Porter, L. W., and Steers, R. M. 1982. *Employee–Organizational Linkages: The Psychology of Commitment, Absenteeism and Turnover.* New York: Academic.

Nollen, S. D., and Axel, H. 1996. *Managing Contingent Workers.* New York: American Management Association.

Organ, D. W. 1988. *Organizational Citizenship Behavior: The Good Soldier Syndrome*. Lexington, MA: Lexington Books.

Ouchi, W. G. 1979. A conceptual framework for the design of organizational control mechanisms. *Management Science* 25:833–48.

Park, Y., and Butler, R. J. 2001. The safety costs of contingent work: Evidence from Minnesota. *Journal of Labor Research* 22:831–49.

Parker, S. K., Chmiel, N., and Wall, T. D. 1997. Work characteristics and employee well-being within a context of strategic downsizing. *Journal of Occupational Health Psychology* 2:289–303.

Pearce, J. L. 1993. Toward an organizational behavior of contract laborers: Their psychological involvement and effects on employee coworkers. *Academy of Management Journal* 36:1082–96.

Pfeffer, J. 1994. *Competitive Advantage through People: Unleashing the Power of the Workforce*. Boston: Harvard University Press.

Pfeffer, J., and Baron, N. 1988. Taking the work back out: Recent trends in the structures of employment. In B. M. Staw and L. L. Cummings (eds.), *Research in Organizational Behavior* 10:257–303.

Pfeffer, J., and Veiga, J. F. 1999. Putting people first for organizational success. *The Academy of Management Executive* 13:37–48.

Polivka, A. E., and Nardone, T. 1989. The definition of contingent work. *Monthly Labor Review* 112:9–16.

Reichers, A. E. 1985. A review and reconceptualization of organizational commitment. *Academy of Management Review* 10:465–76.

Reilly, P. A. 1998. Balancing flexibility – meeting the interests of employer and employee. *European Journal of Work and Organizational Psychology* 7:7–22.

Rogers, J. K. 1995. Just a temp: Experience and structure of alienation in temporary clerical employment. *Work and Occupations* 22:137–66.

Rousseau, D. M. 1995. *Psychological Contracts in Organizations: Understanding Written and Unwritten Agreements*. Thousand Oaks, CA: Sage.

Rousseau, D. M., and Libuser, C. 1997. Contingent workers in high-risk environments. *California Management Review* 39 (2):103–23.

Schaubroeck, J., and Merritt, D. E. 1997. Divergent effects of job control on coping with work stressors: The key role of self-efficacy. *Academy of Management Journal* 40:738–54.

Sparrow, P. 1998. The pursuit of multiple and parallel organizational flexibilities: Reconstituting jobs. *European Journal of Work and Organizational Psychology* 7:79–95.

Van Dyne, L., and Ang, S. 1998. Organizational citizenship behavior of contingent workers in Singapore. *Academy of Management Journal* 41:692–703.

von Hippel, C., Mangum, S. L., Greenberger, D. B., Heneman, R. L., and Skoglind, J. D. 1997. Temporary employment: Can organizations and employers both win? *Academy of Management Executive* 11:93–104.

Walton, R. E. 1985. From control to commitment in the workplace. *Harvard Business Review* 63:76–85.

Wood, S. 1999. Getting the measure of the high-performing organization. *British Journal of Industrial Relations* 37:391–417.

Zeytinoğlu, I. U. (ed.) 1999. *Changing Work Relationships in Industrialized Economies*. Amsterdam: John Benjamins.

Part III

Leading on Issues

8

Integrity–Based Governance: Responding to the Call for Corporate Governance Reform

JERRY GOODSTEIN

Introduction

There is a crisis in corporate governance and it is not likely to fade for some time. This issue is not one of competitiveness or competence. The crisis is one of corporate integrity. In the wake of Enron, Arthur Andersen, WorldCom, Global Crossing, and a host of other corporate scandals, investors and the public are questioning how well corporate leaders and board members have fulfilled their most fundamental ethical and legal responsibilities.

Changes in the law will help regain some of this lost trust and confidence, but governing boards will need to do more if the real goal is to demonstrate to employees, investors, and other stakeholders that these boards are serious about corporate integrity.

In order for corporate boards to truly answer the public call for greater integrity, corporate boards should use this opportunity to move to an integrity-based model of corporate governance.

Integrity-based governance meets the responsibilities to shareholders and stakeholders as given definition through the mission and values of the firm. Corporate boards demonstrate a true commitment to ensuring that the structures and processes that reinforce ethical behavior toward stakeholders are in place and that the values that underlie ethical behavior and corporate integrity are at the heart of strategic and policy decision making and stakeholder relationships.

The central goal of this chapter is to advance an integrity-based perspective of corporate governance. I begin first with a brief overview of the two prevailing paradigms of corporate governance: agency theory and stakeholder theory. I then elaborate the concept of corporate integrity and its essential connection to the core ideology of the corporation. Within this discussion, I highlight important social constraints and limits on what constitutes corporate integrity. The chapter then moves to an exploration of the roles and responsibilities corporate boards and managers must assume within an integrity-based system of governance. Moving away from the corporation to its institutional context, I consider how the roles and expectations of shareholders and other stakeholders, including legal institutions, will need to be defined within this integrity-based system of governance. I close with a consideration of some of the critical challenges and opportunities associated with integrity-based governance.

Current Perspectives on Corporate Governance

Agency Theory and Stakeholder Theory

Two perspectives have dominated theory and research in the corporate governance literature. One major stream of work in the literature on corporate governance is rooted in agency theory (Berle and Means 1932; Fama and Jensen 1983; Jensen and Meckling 1976; Eisenhardt 1989). As Tirole suggests, from an agency perspective governance involves developing institutions and mechanisms to "defend shareholder interests" (2001, 1). Significant theoretical and empirical attention has been given to evaluating how to best create institutions, for example, incentive systems (Beatty and Zajac 1994; Eisenhardt 1989; Dalton and Daily 2001), or board structures and processes (Kosnik 1990; Johnson, Hoskisson, and Hitt 1993), which best address managerial opportunism. At the core of this perspective is the alignment of corporate behavior and decision making with the interests of shareholders – typically defined in terms of maximizing wealth and profits.

The stakeholder perspective on corporate governance challenges the assumption that shareholder interests should be the focus for corporate governance (Donaldson and Preston 1995; Evan and Freeman 1993; Freeman 1984; Freeman and Evan 1990). Stakeholder theorists argue that stakeholders have a legitimate right to have their interests considered in corporate policy and decision making. Conger et al. (2001, 173) press this point by arguing "all organizations must recognize the value that multiple key stakeholders create in the corporation, and they must give each of these stakeholders a voice in the boardroom."

Alignment requires governing bodies to fulfill the interests of a broad range of stakeholders, including shareholders. Rather than maximizing shareholder wealth, one can point to a different goal – maximizing organizational wealth (Blair 1995) or furthering corporate social performance (Berman, Wicks, Kotha, and Jones 1999; Waddock and Graves 1997; Johnson and Greening 1999). If agency theory emphasizes maximization of shareholder interests, stakeholder theory is ultimately about balancing an array of interests reflected within the corporate stakeholders.

Neither agency theory nor stakeholder theory gives weight to how a corporation's specific and unique mission and values might influence corporate governance. Agency theory directs managers and governing boards in all corporations to act on behalf of shareholders and aim to maximize shareholder wealth. Stakeholder theory directs managers and governing boards in all corporations to account for and attempt to balance stakeholder interests. Whether a given corporation might prioritize shareholder interests differently, or how a corporation defines its primary stakeholders, is not acknowledged. Nor do stakeholder theorists attend to the potential for stakeholder "interests" to evolve into stakeholder "demands," putting into the question the meaning of stakeholder accountability (Selznick 1992, 352).

The challenge for corporate governance in the future is not to be "investor" focused or "stakeholder" focused. Rather, governance must be "integrity-based" with a central focus on reinforcing a context that furthers the corporate mission and core values. Governing boards must ask not only what is the bottom line, but how did we get there? In particular, in achieving the bottom line, how well did the corporation fulfill the commitments inherent in the corporate values? Putting the core values at the center of corporate governance gives boards the ability to better serve shareholders and critical stakeholders while at the same time establishing limits on how far the corporation will go to meet shareholder and stakeholder interests.

Integrity-Based Governance

What does corporate integrity mean and what are the merits of integrity-based governance, particularly in relation to the current dominant models of agency theory and stakeholder theory? To act with integrity is for a corporation to strive for a "coherent integration of identity and responsibility" (Paine 1997, 98) in its decisions, actions, and policies. Corporations achieve this crucial integration in the corporate governance context through a process of alignment. Corporate boards and executive leadership ensure that corporations respond to environmental and organizational contingencies in a way that is legitimate from an internal perspective, guided by the corporation's core ideology, and an external perspective, consistent with stakeholder interests and widely held social norms and laws (Collins and Porras 1994, 1997; McCoy 1985; Paine 1994, 1997; Selznick 1957, 1992).

To govern with the goal of corporate integrity in mind is to reflect on fundamental questions of organizational identity (Albert and Whetten 1985; Collins and Porras 1994; Freeman and Gilbert 1988; Selznick 1992): What is the fundamental purpose and basic direction of the corporation? What are our unifying principles and values? What do we stand for?

The answers to these questions are given definition and meaning through the core ideology – in words and in deeds. Corporate integrity requires "fidelity to self-defined principles" (Selznick 1992, 322). The mission and values of a corporation are the foundation of internal legitimacy and define those principles of organizational identity that are "core, enduring, and distinctive" (Albert and Whetten 1985, 265) about the organization. McCoy argues that "what the company stands for and wants to maintain," in essence the core ideology of the corporation, represents "what the company interests really are" (1985, 146).

In some instances, for example Johnson & Johnson or Hewlett-Packard, the core ideology emerges early in the life cycle of the organization as a reflection of the founders (Collins and Porras 1994). Many companies do not identify a core ideology until after the initial start-up phase. In addition, there may be situations in which the core ideology is not explicitly defined, an issue I take up at a later point.

This internal dimension of corporate integrity and legitimacy, with its focus on self-defined values, acknowledges and respects the autonomy and plurality of corporate missions and values. Donaldson and Dunfee (1999) argue in their integrated social contracts theory that there are varying degrees of moral free space for corporations operating within economic communities. Corporations, through their core ideologies, can articulate preferences for different sets of values. Not all corporations are obligated to pursue shareholder wealth, for example, as the number one institutional priority (Collins and Porras 1994; Donaldson and Dunfee 1999). Stakeholders can be recognized, but in varying ways and given varying priority depending on the core ideology of the organization (Collins and Porras 1994). The firm must remain responsive to meeting stakeholder interests, but responsiveness takes place within the context of the firm's core ideology.

Allowing for diversity in the core ideologies of corporations does not imply that there are no limits on what constitutes corporate integrity. Corporations cannot rely solely on a measure of self-consistency in determining corporate integrity. To do so would allow for corporations to justify corporate involvement in unethical practices such as "exploitive child labor, corporal punishment for employees, or barbarously unsafe working conditions" (Donaldson and Dunfee 1999, 44) on the grounds of internal legitimacy and consistency with self-defined core ideologies.

Corporations must therefore fulfill the requirements of external or social legitimacy by meeting key stakeholder needs, attending to basic rules and norms within society, and fulfilling the broader claims of law and morality, such as fundamental human rights (Donaldson and Dunfee 1999). Such "hypernorms" (Donaldson and Dunfee 1999) establish the outer limits of how far organizations can extend and apply their core ideologies before violating legitimate societal norms.

The core ideology must also be one that is authentic; that is, widely shared and respected by organizational members and stakeholders (Donaldson and Dunfee 1999; Paine 1994). Core ideologies that are defined and applied by executive leadership and governing boards in a narrow and self-serving manner, for example, would not likely gain the acceptance of most organizational participants or stakeholders.

Self-governance, a crucial element of individual and corporate integrity (Paine 1994, 1997; Selznick 1992), therefore takes place within a larger societal context, "For institutions, as for persons, self-regulation does not mean freedom to do as one pleases. Rather it implies the exercise of options that will strengthen the enterprise, release its energies, and enhance its integrity. All this takes place within a moral order, not in opposition to it or in disregard to its claims" (Selznick 1992, 344–5). Integrity-based governance emphasizes the "knowledge of limits as well as of potentialities" (Selznick 1957, 27). As will be discussed in detail later, governing boards play an essential role in integrity-based governance by ensuring that corporate decisions, policies, and practices meet the demands of internal and external legitimacy.

In summary, integrity-based governance makes the core ideology a central focus of defining the best interests of the corporation. Firms can legitimately depart from a dominant focus on shareholder maximization of wealth as *the* focal point of governance (of concern to agency theorists) and at the same time other firms can maintain a strong focus on maximization of shareholder wealth (of concern to stakeholder theorists). Given that multiple missions and values are possible, integrity-based governance emphasizes the importance of corporations having defined a core ideology that identifies the best interests of a given firm and its stakeholders. Corporate integrity further demands that the core ideology does not contradict fundamental societal norms and legal constraints. Finally, integrity-based governance requires an alignment of actions and expectations – the corporation declares what it stands for, communicates this clearly to a broad range of stakeholders, and the firm's actions and policies (reinforced by organizational processes and structures) are guided by the core ideology.

Why Integrity-Based Governance?

Paine (1994) and Collins and Porras (1994) provide evidence that supports the potential importance of an integrity-based approach to governance that places its emphasis on the mission and values of the firm. They found in separate studies that when the core ideology is articulated and deeply integrated into the primary structures, systems, and processes of an organization, there are important outcomes for a variety of stakeholders. Paine (1994, 117) found a commitment to corporate integrity (defined in different ways for the three corporations she studied) "contributed to competitiveness, positive workforce morale, as well as solid sustainable relationships with . . . key constituencies."

Collins and Porras (1997, 55) further found that visionary companies that had achieved superior financial performance in comparison with other companies in similar industries distinguished themselves by having a core ideology more deeply integrated into all aspects of the organization. They went on to argue that the core ideology, when institutionalized into the culture and translated into specific mechanisms, acts as a kind of "internal compass," keeping the corporation focused on how the organization has defined its true and enduring interests.

The core ideology also facilitates adaptation and change by providing a base of continuity around which a visionary company can evolve, experiment, and change. Collins and Porras (1997, 55) note "By being clear about what is core (and therefore relatively fixed), a company can more easily seek variation and movement in all that is not core."

Integrity-based governance therefore emphasizes both responsiveness and responsibility, what Selznick (1992, 338) identifies as "reflexive responsibility." Changes in strategy, structure, policies, and practices can and will take place, but there will be an emphasis on ensuring that when change is necessary "revision takes place in a principled way, that is, while holding fast to values and purposes" (Selznick 1992, 338).

How does integrity-based governance influence the critical roles and responsibilities of governing boards, the managers they oversee, and the nature of their fiduciary duties? What implications does this perspective have for the expectations of shareholders, and stakeholders, including legal institutions? Below I turn my attention to these questions.

Integrity-Based Governance: New Roles and Responsibilities

The board of directors plays a pivotal role in reinforcing integrity-based governance and holding executive leadership accountable for meeting shareholder and other stakeholder interests as given definition and priority in the core ideology. Governing boards must first ensure that the mission and values are defined in a way that reflects the firm's identity and its critical stakeholder commitments. Corporations must identify a core purpose and set of values that can guide the corporation over time, helping the firm adapt to the environment, establishing limits on behaviors, and orienting the firm to act in ways that truly create value for investors, employees, customers, and other stakeholders over time. Without an explicit mission and core set of values, short-term competitive pressures or the power and influence of opportunistic actors can whipsaw a corporation. Corporate boards may take on a position of being "responsive" without being responsible, particularly to the long-term interests of shareholders and stakeholders.

How does a corporate board bring together responsiveness and responsibility within an integrity-based model of governance? One of the most critical roles of contemporary governing boards is their involvement in strategic decision making and implementation (Conger et al. 2001). Integrity-based governance compels the board to consider major strategic plans within the context of the core ideology. In addition to being concerned about the potential profitability of potential strategic initiatives, market share implications, and various legal issues associated with these initiatives, boards of directors would draw explicit attention to the alignment of these potential initiatives with the core ideology.

For example, a corporation's governing board and leadership team will determine whether the corporation should pursue a major strategic alliance based on the consistency of this strategic initiative with the core ideology of the corporation. For Seattle-based Starbucks Corporation, this would involve evaluating whether the strategic alliance helps Starbucks better fulfill its mission to "Establish Starbucks as the premier purveyor of the finest coffee in the world while maintaining our uncompromising principles while we grow." The board of directors and executive leadership would explicitly confront a series of questions related to Starbucks' key principles (found on the Starbucks website www.starbucks.com):

> Provide a great work environment and treat each other with respect and dignity.
> Embrace diversity as an essential component in the way we do business.
> Apply the highest standards of excellence to the purchasing, roasting and fresh delivery of our coffee.
> Develop enthusiastically satisfied customers all of the time.
> Contribute positively to our communities and our environment.
> Recognize that profitability is essential to our future success.

Board deliberation and evaluation would fully acknowledge the implications of these decisions in terms of how well they have advanced corporate integrity: Will this alliance meet the standards of excellence associated with the purchasing, roasting, and delivery of coffee? Does the alliance contribute to the profitability of the corporation? In expanding the board's role in this way, the role of the board becomes one of framing strategic decision making in terms of the character or identity of the corporation, keeping executive leadership focused on what, "what we should 'do' in order to become what we want to 'be'" (Selznick 1957, 144).

Within the framework of integrity-based governance, the board must ultimately hold executive leaders accountable for ensuring to the extent possible that they align corporate decisions and policies with the core ideology of the firm (Collins and Porras 1994; McCoy 1985). The core ideology provides the context within which leadership serves shareholder and stakeholder interests. Governing boards assess the performance of strategies in light of measures that reflect the core ideology.

The governing board at Starbucks, to return to this specific example, will need to assess the performance of the strategic alliance in ways that capture critical dimensions of the core ideology; for example, "excellence" in purchasing, roasting, and delivering coffee, "enthusiastically satisfied customers," and "profitability." Integrity-based governance provides a means for the board and the CEO to establish critical limits in its interactions with stakeholders. Without this kind of anchor for alignment it is possible for corporations and governing boards to lose their sense of direction, responding in a fragmented manner to stakeholders who may at times exercise their power and influence in their efforts to have their needs and interests served.

This shift in the board's strategic role and responsibilities has important implications for CEO evaluation and compensation. A good deal of recent reform in CEO evaluation and compensation has been oriented toward emphasizing a longer-term performance horizon (Conger et al. 2001). Integrity-based governance moves in this important direction by linking CEO evaluation and compensation directly to the achievement of a set of measures that relate to the long-term mission and core values. Boards reward CEOs based on overall firm performance and specifically on how well these executives have managed the values that shape corporate performance over time (McCoy 1985).

Corporate boards adopting an integrity-based governance perspective must establish measurable performance objectives for CEOs that reflect strategic goals (where the corporation is going) and core values (how the corporation gets to where it is going). As Collins (2002) argues, this board responsibility is fundamental to building value for shareholders and other stakeholders. The board must avoid the peril of submitting to executive leaders who respond in a misguided manner to the pressures of opportunistic "shareflippers" (Collins 2002, 216) with no long-term interest in the corporation. Compensation committees can reinforce this longer time horizon by basing salary increases, bonuses, or the granting of stock options directly on the achievement of these objectives. When a CEO's actions represent a significant departure from the demands of corporate integrity, the board of directors may be motivated to recommend searching for a new CEO.

Corporate boards should hold CEOs accountable as well for developing the necessary systems, structures, and processes to reinforce the mission and core values in the organization. The success of integrity-based governance and firm performance depends on how well corporate leadership has institutionalized the core ideology within the corporation and among critical stakeholders (Collins and Porras 1994; Epstein 1987; Paine 1994). CEOs that pay attention to the institutionalization of the core ideology demonstrate a commitment to the success of the institution, rather than personal success, and in this sense exemplify the kind of "Level 5" leadership associated with "great" companies (Collins 2002).

Corporate boards will need to attend to how well the firm's executive leadership has guided the development of systems (e.g., control systems, information systems) and processes (e.g., performance appraisal, budget and strategic planning) that make the core values a central focus for decision making and evaluation. Corporate integrity cannot be a function of an isolated program or department. As Paine (1994, 112) argues, "A formal ethics program can serve as a catalyst and a support system, but organizational integrity depends on the integration of the company's values into its driving systems."

Conger et al. (2001) and Waddock (2001), among others, argue that corporate boards and organizations can undertake social audits as a strategy to assess the depth and perform- ance of this integration. Waddock defines the central focus for this form of monitoring accountability: "Social auditing involves assessing internal corporate practices and/or stakeholder perceptions of corporate practices to determine how well a company is living up to its vision and values" (2001, 223).

CEOs have an important responsibility within this integrity-based perspective on cor- porate governance that governing boards must monitor – to communicate on a continual basis to shareholders and stakeholder groups and make as transparent as possible the nature and significance of the core ideology in corporate policy and strategic decision making (Paine 1997). This ensures that shareholders and stakeholders have clear expectations regarding the values and long-term focus that will drive leadership actions (Drucker 2002). As will be discussed in greater depth below, an integrity-based governance system can motivate shareholders and nonshareholder stakeholders to ultimately align with corpora- tions based on the extent to which there is a congruence of expectations and values. This effort to communicate serves as a form of signaling (Spence 1974), identifying for share- holders and other stakeholders important values and commitments the firm has made and intends to uphold.

There is a challenge inherent in moving toward an integrity-based governance system, specifically developing measures that assess the alignment of firm and CEO behavior with the core ideology. Corporations have had far more experience developing measures of profitability and wealth (Blair 1995). As Drucker notes, the governance context in the twenty-first century will require these new measures: "Today's leaders have to accept the fact that the interest of shareholders as expressed in yesterday's Dow Jones Industrial Average is not what whey are running the company by. Not only governance, but its related concepts and tools, will need to be confronted and transformed over the next fifteen years" (Drucker 2002, 81–2).

Innovative corporations have developed ways to translate corporate values into specific criteria; for example, in values-based performance evaluation of employees (Pfeffer 1998) or in the development of balanced scorecards (Kaplan and Norton 1996). The practice of internal and external auditing has also advanced, providing firms with specific methodo- logies for creating mission and values-based measures of performance (Waddock 2001; Waddock and Smith 2000). CEOs and governing boards will need to assume responsibil- ity for ensuring that these mission and values-based-measures are in place. Without these measures, the underlying basis for determining alignment and integrity is put in question and managerial accountability is undermined.

An integrity-based approach to governance should prompt boards of directors to evalu- ate existing structures (e.g., board committees) and processes (board decision making, executive evaluation) to determine whether these structures and processes promote ac- countability to the core ideology. Governing boards may need to reconsider, for example, how well critical board decision-making processes allow for a more direct integration of the core ideology into corporate decision-making and policy functions (Epstein 1987; Paine 1997).

Some healthcare organizations have put in place a process known as "mission discernment" (Gallagher and Goodstein 2002; Goodstein and Carney 1999). This process brings the mission and values to bear on critical strategic and policy choices for healthcare organizations such as joint ventures with physician groups, the development of new products or services, or internal reorganizations.

Mission discernment begins when a member of the organization given the responsibility to coordinate the process brings individuals together to deliberate. These individuals should have the relevant capabilities to address the key issues associated with a particular proposal, and represent key stakeholders. Mission-driven values guide the discussion. The participants discuss how the proposal under discussion may or may not be responsive to the interests of the multiple stakeholders affected potentially by a pending decision: patients, employees, other providers, payers, vendors, and the community. The coordinator of mission discernment incorporates the results of the deliberations along with the financial, marketing, and legal analyses associated with a proposal into a unified business plan. The governing board of the healthcare organization then undertakes a review and discussion of the business plan, incorporating all these considerations.

Governing boards should also consider the role of required board committees in supporting integrity-based governance. The responsibilities of the board audit committee can be modified, for example, in some important ways. Traditional financial auditing can be combined with a form of social or responsibility auditing; for example, as is done by The Body Shop (Waddock 2001). Boards can develop new committees, such as corporate integrity committees, with the goal of evaluating the effectiveness of the firm's overall corporate integrity strategy.

In order for leadership and governing boards to pursue corporate integrity, these individuals must truly understand what is at the heart of the core ideology and hone their judgment and decision-making skills regarding how to address these considerations in the context of important governance choices. This is a significant governance challenge requiring discernment and a commitment to interpret and bring the mission and values to bear on major corporate decisions and policies in a manner that is independent of self-interest. It is ultimately through this commitment to corporate integrity, to the company's best interests, that executive leadership and directors will, as McCoy notes, "develop information with reference to these interests, shape criteria for appraising them, and discover ways to integrate this deepened conception of corporate self-interest into policy formulation" (1985, 146).

Integrity-Based Governance: New Expectations

Shareholders and Stakeholders

An integrity-based perspective on corporate governance clearly has important implications for shareholders and other stakeholders. As noted above, there is a responsibility for governing boards and corporate leadership to communicate the nature of the firm's core ideology to constituencies. There is a reciprocal responsibility that shareholders and other stakeholders must fulfill by acknowledging the entire range of the values of the corporations they are involved with, not just those that are consistent with their own interests.

Shareholders, in particular, might argue that an integrity-based governance system undermines their legal rights as shareholders. Shareholders expect corporations to act in ways that enhance shareholder wealth, and when this does not occur shareholders expect that the courts will hold managers and governing boards accountable. As Blair (1995) points out, however, there is ambiguity in the interpretation of the law. The fiduciary principle does not clarify the situation given that, "under the laws of most states, managers and directors owe their fiduciary duties to the corporation as a whole, rather than to individual shareholders or to individual classes of shareholders" (Blair 1995, 58). Twenty-nine states have challenged the primacy of shareholder financial interests through the passage of other constituency statutes that provide greater opportunities for internalizing stakeholder interests into corporate governance discussions (Luoma and Goodstein 1999).

Investment – whether in more direct forms, for example ownership (shareholders), capital investment (suppliers), investment of human resources (employees), or in more indirect forms, for example community-based tax incentives (community) – does not provide these groups with an exclusive or unambiguous legal right to assume that the corporation will act only in their interest. Rather, shareholders and other stakeholders should understand that governing boards and executive leadership, as fiduciaries, are obligated to act in the company's best interests. This way of understanding shareholder responsibility conflicts with current shareholder-oriented perspectives on governance where shareholders "need not accept, and for the most part do not accept, responsibility for the enterprise as a going concern" (Selznick 1992, 318).

The appropriate question therefore for shareholders and other stakeholders to ask within this integrity-based conception of corporate governance is not, "Has the organization or leadership acted to maximize my interests?" but rather, "Has the organization acted with integrity?" This central question brings to the fore the nature of the implicit contract and expectations in integrity-based governance between shareholders and key stakeholders on one hand, and governing boards and the managers they oversee on the other. Shareholders can expect fidelity on the part of directors and managers, but they must recognize that directors and managers will look to the core ideology as the locus of the company's interests in relation to shareholders and other stakeholders. Managers and boards can still fail to fulfill their fiduciary and broad governance responsibilities to shareholders. However, violations of duty are in essence violations of corporate integrity. Shareholders and stakeholders must evaluate failures of obligations in specific terms, with reference to the core ideology of the corporation, rather than in general terms; that is, failure to maximize shareholder wealth.

Two kinds of situations may be important to note in light of the above discussion. The first situation may occur when shareholders and stakeholders acknowledge the nature of the core ideology but believe that the firm, through action or inaction, has violated crucial elements of this core ideology. Under these conditions, a legitimate response by shareholders and stakeholders is the exercise of voice and loyalty (Hirschman 1970).

Shareholders and stakeholders can express and press their concerns in a variety of forums, such as the media, shareholder resolutions, direct communication, and, when necessary, in the courts through shareholder lawsuits (Blair 1995).

There is another basic situation where certain shareholders and stakeholders fundamentally do not understand the nature of the firm's core ideology. Under these circumstances, certain groups of shareholders may question why the firm has taken particular actions. In this situation, the appropriate response is exit. Governing boards should not be obligated to meet the expectations of individuals or groups whose interests represent a significant departure from the core ideology of the organization. To do so would lead to a kind of opportunistic behavior that undermines corporate integrity.

What emerges from this kind of orientation to governance is a more "visible hand" or marketplace of values where shareholders and other stakeholders seek relationships based on demonstrated consistency of values, and not necessarily the pursuit of short-term advantages (Dunfee 1998). Over time, loyalty will prevail as stakeholders gravitate to those organizations that fulfill the demands of corporate integrity and act in a manner consistent with their own values as well. Shareholders, stakeholders, and society at large, through the mechanisms of exit, voice, and loyalty, will determine what is and is not valued and which corporations will survive and thrive over time.

Legal Institutions

As with shareholders and stakeholders, this shift in orientation for corporate governance is likely to prompt questions and concerns within legal institutions and among legal scholars. Questions will arise as to how to determine when directors and management have acted in ways that contradict the company's best interests, particularly when corporations have defined these interests differently. What will represent a legitimate shareholder suit? Will such an approach create even more legal uncertainty, rather than provide the compelling focus noted earlier?

These questions are important ones to pose and an extensive discussion is beyond the scope of this chapter. A beginning point for discussion, however, is to recognize that an integrity-based conception of corporate governance does fit within the existing framework of law. Integrity-based governance does not require fundamental substantive change in corporate governance law. As I argued earlier, making the core ideology the primary focus for determining corporate action in a particular context is thoroughly consistent with the current legal definition of fiduciary duty and its emphasis on directors acting in the company's best interests and promoting corporate welfare (Balotti and Hinsey 2000). The legislatures in 29 states that have adopted other-constituency statutes have also provided governing boards with greater flexibility to consider a broader array of interests beyond those of shareholders when undertaking their oversight and decision-making functions.

There is therefore no inherent contradiction implied by moving to an integrity-based conception of corporate governance. Rather, what is at issue is what has been at issue for decades, the interpretation of what constitutes "the company's best interests." I have tried to argue for why the pursuit of corporate integrity, defined in terms of the alignment of corporate action with the core ideology, is a legitimate and productive strategy for addressing this central issue of corporate governance.

To the extent that legal institutions and scholars see merit to moving in this direction, there is an opportunity for further development of an institutional framework to support this movement. An integrity-based system of governance fits quite well with a reflexive orientation of the law (Teubner 1983). Orts captures the emphasis of this perspective on legal procedures and processes rather than substantive change: "Reflexive law considers methods by which to embed the quality of reflexivity or self-reflection within institutions" (1995, 780).

Within a reflexive law tradition the substance of the goals that corporations pursue in particular domains, for example labor relations or the environment, largely remains at the discretion of firms. External control is deemphasized, and there is an emphasis on self-regulation and critical self-reflection (Selznick 1992; Teubner 1983). Conger et al. (2001, 8) note that the courts have been giving increased emphasis to the processes and procedures by which corporations and corporate boards arrive at their decisions. This emphasis leaves open the substance of what is decided in favor of ensuring that board processes fulfill their central duties. These duties include those of diligence (i.e., being informed and careful in securing and processing information), obedience (i.e., staying within the law and within corporate bylaws and charter), and loyalty (i.e., avoiding conflicts of interest that could compromise the objectivity of directors).

Orts (1995) and Hess (1999) specifically note how legal scholars and practitioners have adopted this reflexive orientation to the domain of environmental law. The focus, as Orts notes, is "to establish incentives and procedures that encourage institutions to think critically, creatively, and continually about how their activities affect the environment and how they may improve their environmental performance" (1995, 780). Orts (1995) further identifies a number of sources of external elements relevant to establishing an institutional framework for supporting reflexive practices – voluntarism, public disclosure, third-party certification, participation by public interest groups, and, internally, procedures for institutional self-reflection and self-criticism.

Within the corporate governance domain, parties could develop legal initiatives to support integrity-based governance by creating incentives for internal and external audits, mission-values integration into governance decision making, and other aspects of governance reform. These legal innovations would complement the current wave of corporate governance reforms that increase board and CEO accountability for ensuring the integrity of financial information disclosed to shareholders and other stakeholders. As in the case of the passage of other-constituency-statutes, political support and legitimating would be crucial to the implementation of these initiatives by corporations.

Conclusion

This chapter has only begun to outline the elements of a framework for integrity-based corporate governance. Each of these elements, for example, clarifying the nature of corporate integrity in the context of governance, defining new roles and responsibilities for governing boards and shareholders/stakeholders, and developing internal and external mechanisms and institutional supports to further integrity-based governance, require much more theoretical and empirical development. Below I briefly outline some of the questions and issues prompted by this perspective.

If corporate integrity is the central goal of corporate governance, and this proposition clearly may require further elaboration beyond this chapter, what are the theoretical extensions that link the achievement of corporate governance goals to other outcomes, such as firm competitive advantage? What theoretical relationships connect the internal and external mechanisms noted earlier, such as internal and external audits or corporate social policy processes, to corporate integrity? How can core ideologies act as effective signals to shareholders and stakeholders, influencing their decisions on developing relationships and potentially creating a new kind of market ecology?

Each of these theoretical issues, and many others that this integrity-based governance perspective might raise, lead naturally to empirical research. Researchers, as well as governing boards, must confront the fundamental challenge of how to measure "alignment." What are appropriate indices of managerial opportunism within an integrity-based governance perspective? What organizational structures and processes enhance corporate integrity? Do firms that achieve corporate integrity over time maintain a sustainable competitive advantage? What is the relationship between corporate integrity and reputation?

There are important practical hurdles to the acceptance and institutionalization of integrity-based governance. Despite the issues I noted earlier when corporations do not have an explicit core ideology, there are firms that do not have a clear mission or core values. Under these circumstances, there is no foundation for integrity-based governance. The leadership of these firms may believe that such statements are unnecessary and a waste of time. However, in a climate where the trust and confidence of investors and the public in corporate governance has eroded, these leaders will be hard pressed to convince demanding shareholders and stakeholders that they have put in place the necessary elements to restore and sustain trust and corporate integrity.

Integrity-based governance alters both responsibilities and expectations for managers, governing boards, shareholders and other stakeholders, and the courts. It requires a deepened sense of knowledge about any given corporation and it demands a great deal, particularly of governing boards. Swimming against the strong tide of current shareholder and stakeholder governance perspectives will be difficult.

In the end, some might criticize this emphasis on corporate integrity as a potential "smokescreen" for executives and governing boards to act in self-interested ways. Decades ago, Selznick warned of a kind of utopianism where those, "who purport to be institutional leaders attempt to rely on overgeneralized purposes to guide their decisions." When standards such as values are poorly defined and "too general to permit responsible decision-making," then there is a danger that utopianism can slip into opportunism as "immediate exigencies will dominate the actual choices that are made" (1957, 157). There is also the potential that executives and board members interpret the mission and values in ways that are self-serving.

The recent corporate fraud legislation significantly raises the costs for executives and board members whose actions may violate the law. Shareholders and stakeholders are in a better position now to go beyond these laws and require governing boards to act in ways that promote corporate integrity. Shareholders and stakeholders should utilize their power and influence to keep CEOs and governing boards focused on long-term interests. It is important that stakeholders hold executive leadership and governing boards accountable for putting in place systems and processes throughout the corporation to reinforce corporate integrity. Governing boards are responsible for monitoring how well executives have integrated the mission and values into corporate policies and practices and stakeholder relationships. Shareholders and stakeholders should strongly criticize efforts that appear to be motivated by short-term manipulation of the bottom line and stock price, and, when necessary, they should put pressure on CEOs and board members to be let go or to resign.

These issues, and others as well, represent important theoretical, empirical, and practical challenges that governance scholars and practitioners will confront in shifting to an integrity-based governance system. In light of the governance crisis that plagues the corporate sector, there may not be a choice. It should be clear that the bottom line for CEOs and boards of directors in this new governance context must be corporate integrity.

REFERENCES

Albert, S., and Whetten, D. A. 1985. Organizational identity. *Research in Organizational Behavior* 7:263–95.

Balotti, R. F., and Hinsey, J. 2000. Director care, conduct, and liability: The model business corporation act solution. *Business Lawyer* 56:35–61.

Beatty, R. P., and Zajac, E. J. 1994. Top management incentives, monitoring, and risk sharing: A study of executive compensation, ownership and board structure in initial public offerings. *Administrative Science Quarterly* 39:313–36.

Berle, A., Jr., and Means, G. 1932. *The Modern Corporation and Private Property*. Chicago: Commerce Clearing House.

Berman, S. L., Wicks, A. C., Kotha, S., and Jones, T. M. 1999. The relationship between stakeholder management models and firm financial performance. *Academy of Management Journal* 42 (5):488–506.

Blair, M. M. 1995. *Ownership and Control*. Washington, DC: Brookings Institution.

Collins, J. C. 2002. *Good to Great*. New York: HarperBusiness.

Collins, J. C., and Porras, J. I. 1994, 1997. *Built to Last*. New York: HarperBusiness.

Conger, J., Lawler, E., and Feingold, D. 2001. *Corporate Boards*. San Francisco: Jossey-Bass.

Dalton, D. R., and Daily, C. M. 2001. Director stock compensation: An invitation to conspicuous conflict of interest? *Business Ethics Quarterly* 11 (1):89–108.

Donaldson, T., and Dunfee, T. 1999. *Ties that Bind: A Social Contracts Approach to Business Ethics*. Boston: Harvard Business School Press.

Donaldson, T., and Preston, L. E. 1995. The stakeholder theory of the corporation: Concepts, evidence, and implications. *Academy of Management Review* 20:65–91.

Drucker, P. F. 2002. *Managing in the Next Society*. New York: St. Martin's Press.

Dunfee, T. W. 1998. The marketplace of morality: Small steps toward a theory of moral choice. *Business Ethics Quarterly* 8 (1):127–46.

Eisenhardt, K. M. 1989. Agency theory: An assessment and review. *Academy of Management Review* 14:57–74.

Epstein, E. M. 1987. The corporate social policy process: Beyond business ethics, corporate social responsibility, and corporate social responsiveness. *California Management Review* 24 (3):99–114.

Evan, W. F., and Freeman, R. F. 1993. A stakeholder theory of the modern corporation: Kantian capitalism. In T. Beauchamp and N. Bowie (eds.), *Ethical Theory and Business*. Englewood Cliffs, NJ: Prentice Hall.

Fama, E., and Jensen, M. 1983. Separation of ownership and control. *Journal of Law and Economics* 26:301–25.

Freeman, R. E. 1984. *Strategic Management: A Stakeholder Approach*. Englewood Cliffs, NJ: Prentice Hall.

Freeman, R. E., and Evan, W. F. 1990. Corporate governance: A stakeholder interpretation. *Journal of Behavioral Economics* 19:337–59.

Freeman, R. E., and Gilbert, D. R. 1988. *Corporate Strategy and the Search for Ethics*. Englewood Cliffs, NJ: Prentice Hall.

Gallagher, J. A., and Goodstein, J. 2002. Fulfilling institutional responsibilities in health care: Organizational ethics and the role of mission discernment. *Business Ethics Quarterly* 12 (4):433–50.

Goodstein, J., and Carney, B. 1999. Actively engaging organizational ethics in healthcare: Four essential elements. *Journal of Clinical Ethics* 10 (3):224–9.

Hess, D. 1999. Social reporting: A reflexive law approach to corporate social responsiveness. *Journal of Corporation Law* 25 (1):41–76.

Hirschman, A. O. 1970. *Exit, Voice, and Loyalty*. Cambridge, MA: Harvard University Press.

Jensen, M., and Meckling, W. 1976. Theory of the firm: Managerial behavior, agency costs, and ownership structure. *Journal of Financial Economics* 3:305–60.

Johnson, R. A., and Greening, D. W. 1999. The effects of corporate governance and institutional ownership type on corporate social performance. *Academy of Management Journal* 42 (5):564–76.

Johnson. R. A., Hoskisson, R. E., and Hitt, M. A. 1993. Board of director involvement in restructuring: The effects of board versus managerial controls and characteristics. *Strategic Management Journal* 14:33–50.

Jones, T. M. 1995. Instrumental stakeholder theory: A synthesis of ethics and economics. *Academy of Management Review* 20:404–37.

Kaplan, R. S., and Norton, D. P. 1996. *The Balanced Scorecard: Translating Strategy into Action*. Boston: Harvard Business School Press.

Kosnik, R. 1990. Effects of board demography and directors' incentives on corporate greenmail decisions. *Academy of Management Journal* 37:1207–51.

Luoma, P., and Goodstein, J. 1999. Stakeholders and corporate boards: Institutional influences on board composition and structure. *Academy of Management Journal* 42 (5):553–63.

McCoy, C. 1985. *The Management of Values*. Berkeley: University of California Press.

Orts, E. 1995. A reflexive model of environmental regulation. *Business Ethics Quarterly* 5:779.

Paine, L. S. 1994. Managing for organizational integrity. *Harvard Business Review* (March–April): 106–17.

Paine, L. S. 1997. *Leadership, Ethics, and Organizational Integrity*. Chicago: Irwin.

Pfeffer, J. 1998. *The Human Equation*. Boston: Harvard Business School Press.

Selznick, P. 1957. *Leadership in Administration*. Berkeley: University of California Press.

Selznick, P. 1992. *The Moral Commonwealth*. Berkeley: University of California Press.

Spence, A. M. 1974. *Market Signaling*. Cambridge, MA: Harvard University Press.

Swanson, D. 1999. Toward an integrative theory of business and society: A research strategy for corporate social performance. *Academy of Management Review* 24 (3):506–21.

Teubner, G. 1983. Sustantive and reflexive elements of modern law. *Law and Society Review* 17 (2):239–85.

Tirole, J. 2001. Corporate governance. *Econometrica* 69 (1):1–35.

Waddock, S. A. 2001. *Leading Corporate Citizens*. Boston: McGraw-Hill.

Waddock, S. A., and Graves, S. B. 1997. The corporate social performance-financial performance link. *Strategic Management Journal* 18:303–19.

Waddock, S. A., and Smith, N. 2000. Corporate responsibility audits: Doing well by doing good. *Sloan Management Review* 41 (2):75–83.

9

The Successful Navigation of Uncertainty: Sustainability and the Organization

DAVID WHEELER

Sustainable development meets the needs of the present without compromising the ability of future generations to meet their own needs.
World Commission on Environment and Development 1987

Introduction: Globalization, Uncertainty and Sustainability

Few commentators or indeed ordinary citizens doubt that we live in a world of increasing uncertainty, complexity, and paradox. This has significant implications for organizations, their senior management teams, and their strategies (Stacey 1992; Levy 1994; Sanders and Carpenter 1998; Courtney 2001). The twin effects of globalization and technological change are both intrinsic causes of that uncertainty and accelerators of other phenomena, for example, political, economic, social, and ecological drivers and constraints, which in turn further exacerbate uncertainty (Reich 2001; World Resources Institute et al. 2002). In his wide ranging popular treatise on globalization *The Lexus and the Olive Tree*, Thomas Friedman (2000) provided a parallel analysis to Francis Fukuyama (1999) in noting the end of social order as we came to know it in the middle years of the twentieth century, when cold war political certainties and cultural barriers and norms prevailed. For most of the last century the world seemed locked into an Orwellian pact regarding what was acceptable or unacceptable for citizens, nongovernmental agencies and businesses to engage in. At least for business, ideological and technological changes at the end of the twentieth century altered that forever (Govindarajan and Gupta 2001).

From the perspective of this chapter, Friedman made two especially interesting conceptual assertions. First, he drew attention to the need to employ six particular perspectives in navigating the new global realities: financial, political, cultural, national security, technological, and environmental. Second, he classified potential societal responses to the challenges of a globalized world on a two by two matrix according to attitudes to globalization (separatist or integrationist) and attitudes to social inclusion (for or against social welfare safety nets). Friedman concluded that for globalization to be "sustainable" it required both an integrationist and a social inclusion mindset. In his somewhat upbeat final chapter Friedman quotes John F. Kennedy, "If a free society cannot help the many who are poor, it cannot save the few who are rich," before offering his own prescription: "what is needed . . . is a new social compact that both embraces free markets but also ensures that they benefit, and are tolerable for, as many people as possible. . . . If you are not willing to spend what it takes to equip the have-nots and turtles in your society to survive in this new system, they will eventually produce a backlash that will choke off your country from the world" (2000, 44).

Recent events in Palestine, Afghanistan, New York, and Washington seem to have lent greater authority to Friedman's analysis; as has the commentary of mainstream economists such as Joseph Stiglitz, former Chief Economist of the World Bank. Stiglitz, a 2001 Nobel Laureate states, "Globalization today is not working for many of the world's poor. It is not working for much of the environment. It is not working for the stability of the global economy. . . . What is needed is a policy for sustainable, equitable and democratic growth. That is the reason for development . . . This sort of development won't happen if only a few people dictate the policies a country must follow" (2002, 214). It is safe to assume that not many of Mr Stiglitz's predecessors would have spoken out in such political terms immediately following their tenure at such an august establishment. However, it is not uncommon for such language to be used by politicians and business leaders today (Watts and Holme 1999). And management theorists have begun to explore what it might mean for multinational companies to engage more effectively with the world's 4 billion poor who exist on less than US $1,500 per capita per annum, or indeed with communities rather closer to home (Prahalad and Hart 2001; Mintzberg, Simons, and Basu 2002). It seems we have entered an era where it is deemed appropriate for mainstream practitioners and commentators to deploy powerful rhetoric on globalization, democracy, sustainable development, and strategic management.

The language may be new and the messengers increasingly senior and influential, but the thinking is not novel. In 1987, in one of the seminal reports ushering in the concept of sustainable development *Our Common Future*, the World Commission on Environment and Development (1987) based much of their analysis on an assumption that a world of endemic poverty and inequity is more likely to suffer ecological and other crises. And of course there is a rich tradition of doom laden commentary from radical environmentalists and social activists going back to the early 1970s, for example, the Club of Rome report *Limits to Growth* (Meadows et al. 1972). These analyses typically manifest themselves in dire predictions of catastrophe, and more recently, trenchant antiglobalization, antibusiness rhetoric (Korten 1995; Klein 2000). But what does seem relatively new in this field is the increasing linkage of environmental and social dislocation to questions of geopolitics, democracy, and security, thus illustrating the adoption of multiple perspectives referred to by Friedman – in this case by opponents and critics as well as practitioners of globalization.

Recent popular titles on this theme include *Jihad vs McWorld* in which Benjamin Barber (1995), describes the seemingly bizarre conflict and interdependence or "dialectic" of consumer capitalism and religious fundamentalism. In *Resource Wars* (2001) Michael Klare describes a "new geography" of conflict for the twenty-first century where wars will be fought by powerful nations and their clients over the oil, water, minerals, and timber resources required to fuel advanced capitalist economies. This thinking has led American commentators such as Carl Frankel to see a strong convergence between the ideal of sustainability and security, particularly since the apocalyptic events of September 11, 2001. Writing just one month after the tragedy Frankel contrasted the relative security and wealth of most ordinary Americans with that of three-quarters of humanity and employed one of President Bush's more graphic allusions in asserting "the goal of sustainable development is to moderate global capitalism such that the tensions and hostilities it induces are eliminated, while its basic strengths (open society, global citizenship, etc.) are retained. . . . To the extent that sustainability erases global capitalism's shadowy side, it helps 'drain the swamp' that breeds terrorism" (Frankel 2001, 42).

On the subject of drainage, many believe that water resources will prove particularly problematic in economic, political, and security terms in the first few decades of the twenty-first century. Public institutions are failing to deliver acceptable water services in much of the developed and developing world (World Resources Institute et al. 2002). Meanwhile, the entry of multinational water service businesses such as Vivendi, Suez Lyonnaise des Eaux and even Enron into the business through privatization and "public private partnerships," has unleashed a vibrant political and economic debate over ownership of resources and responsibility for services – a global market estimated by the World Bank to be worth US $1 trillion. Indicative titles here include *Blue Gold: The Battle against Corporate Theft of the World's Water* (Barlow and Clarke 2002) in which two influential members of Canadian civil society refer approvingly to "water warriors" – local activists opposing privatization – and set out a ten point plan for "water security" which includes the need to "confront" the IMF and the World Bank, "challenge" the "Lords of Water" (*sic*) and "fight" for legislation. Using equally stirring language, in *Water Wars: Privatization, Pollution and Profit* influential Indian scientist and activist Vandana Shiva (2002) makes clear she also has the World Bank and the IMF as well as the WTO, GATS and the "water giants" in her sights. With this political and economic context, the decreasing physical availability of water for basic needs such as drinking and agriculture – let alone industrialization – makes for highly unstable future scenarios.

Of course it may be argued that the changes associated with the world's entry into a chaotic, post-cold war, postindustrial, globalized economy are nothing inherently new in terms of the human experience. The upheavals caused by the Age of Enlightenment, the advent of scientific approaches to agriculture and medicine, the industrial revolution itself, accompanied by the transition from mercantile to free trade, the era of mechanization and standardization – all of these major transitions had far reaching political, economic, social, and ecological impacts. In addition they were all associated with scientific and technological breakthroughs and were often accompanied by security issues, social dislocation, and no little suffering on the part of "stakeholders" who got caught out or left behind (Wheeler and Sillanpää 1997). Just like globalization, these revolutions in human understanding and practice were the cause of major philosophical, religious, and political debate and resulted in significant protest, cultural and artistic commentary, and critique. Thus it may be argued that perhaps the only differences now are the scale and visibility of the changes: the number of people impacted and the complexity of the interactions. And the only salient political challenge is how human institutions may navigate the changes so that society evolves to a new state.

In this chapter we are not going to rehearse the arguments of those who would seek to roll back the tide of free markets and technological change in the hope of minimizing harm and distress to people and the environment – the analysis of the angry, the dispossessed, the disenfranchised, and the pessimistic. Nor are we going to contrast current events and their likely outcomes with previous major upheavals in the hope of predicting the eventual, successful "muddling through" by global policymakers and the institutions they control – the analysis of the content, the technocentrics, the optimists or the simply contrarian. Doubtless, all these perspectives have their merits. Instead, we are going to explore the position of the manager in an organization needing to effectively navigate these monumental challenges while still engaging in the act of creating value – for the organization and for society. In doing this we will not take a moral posture, but we will seek to reinforce and support both of Friedman's assertions in our exploration of the links between sustainable globalization and the pursuit of oganizational sustainability; namely, that to be successful navigators of uncertainty, managers need to (1) explore and employ multiple perspectives; and (2) mirror emerging societal norms with respect to social integration and ecological protection.

Capturing Friedman's six perspectives, but reclassifying them somewhat, we may construct a mental model for organizational sustainability that appears something like figure 9.1. In the figure we treat globalization and technological change as somewhat neutral, or at least non-negotiable factors – powerful but essentially technical phenomena without intrinsic "value"; both may deliver social, environmental, and economic value or destroy it – either way they represent a context that is hard to disavow or disinvent. In contrast, we depict four elements of the global system that are subject to dynamic, values-based negotiation and resolution by any organization wishing to exhibit sustainability: the political (including security), the social, the economic, and the ecological. Our model implies that the sustainable organization must be in dynamic interaction with all four elements in order to navigate globalization and technological change effectively. It also implies that to be sustainable, an organization needs to simultaneously harness the drivers and minimize constraints in service of economic, social, and ecological gain – maximizing the so-called triple bottom line (Elkington 1998).

We will now set the context for the practical implications of following through on this analysis, starting with a few words about societal expectations, linking these in turn to questions of organizational governance, mission, and strategy.

From Context to Organizational Sustainability: Social Attitudes, Governance, Mission, and Strategy

Social Attitudes

Around the world, ordinary citizens want it all, and they want it now (Environics 2002; World Resources Institute et al. 2002). They want economic development, they want

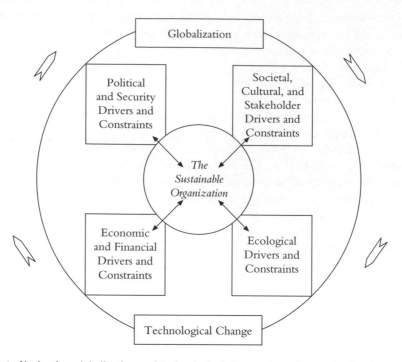

Figure 9.1: Navigating globalization and technological change through organizational sustainability

consumer goods, they want social justice, and they want an environment that allows them and their children to breathe freely, drink safe water, and consume safe food. And even as they lose faith in established institutions such as the church and the state, they want corporations to act in a socially responsible manner. The mass media (print, TV, and Internet) now extend well into the former communist and isolationist countries of the world, and thus demonstrate, minute by minute, day by day, precisely what is possible in terms of Western lifestyles and standards of living. Thus, although half the population on the planet has yet to make a telephone call (World Resources Institute et al. 2002), there are not many places on the planet where Coca-Cola, Disney, Microsoft, Nestlé, Shell or Unilever products are not advertised or cannot be found and purchased.

The polling firm Environics International conducts annual surveys of public opinion on issues of globalization and social and environmental change focused on G20 countries. November 2001 results conducted on behalf of the World Economic Forum (Environics 2002) revealed that there are common aspirations and fears across the world. For example citizens support both a war on poverty and a war on terrorism. It also emerged in late 2001 that notwithstanding the awful events of September 11 that year, environmental pollution and natural resource depletion concerns outweighed fears of war and armed conflict as the number one issue considered "very serious for you and your family" – 63 percent versus 61 percent across G20 countries. In comparison, 42 percent were concerned with overpopulation and 32 percent with the growing power of global companies.

Leadership roles are available for those institutions willing to act on issues that concern ordinary people – including business and government – but civil society organizations are currently seen as most legitimate. Sixty five percent of G20 respondents trust NGOs to operate "in the best interests of society" versus religious groups and churches (58 percent), the press and media (52 percent), large national companies (49 percent), trade or labor unions (46 percent), their national government (45 percent), and global companies (40 percent).

These data provide something of a challenge to both private corporations and national governments, whose legitimacy lags well behind that of civil society organizations and even the "fourth estate." And so it is interesting to note that Environics found a strong correlation (r = 0.68) between support for globalization and trust in global companies, with countries like Germany, Japan, Nigeria, South Korea, and Sweden most associated with higher levels of trust in companies in addition to seeing the effects of globalization as broadly positive. At the other end of the spectrum were countries such as Argentina, France, and Spain, with intermediate countries including Canada, Chile, Great Britain, Mexico, India, Turkey, and the US. Outliers were Brazil, Italy, and Russia, all of whom exhibited low trust in corporations but moderate empathy with globalization.

In larger polling, that is beyond the G20, attitudes to the role of companies in society were divergent across the continents. Only 11 percent of North Americans believed that the role of large companies was to "focus on making profits in ways that obey all laws" (the conventional wisdom espoused most eloquently by Milton Friedman), compared with 39 percent who wanted companies to "set higher standards and build a better society" (49 percent wanted both). The percentages espousing the conventional wisdom in other continents were Europe (21 percent), Latin America (27 percent), Eurasia (28 percent), Asia (34 percent), and Africa (32 percent).

If we accept the premise that business needs to operate with the support not just of governments but also within the "rules of the game," which we might now interpret as observing both legal and civil norms, that is with the support of its direct stakeholders and society at large, what does this information mean to the busy manager charged with creating value in terms of governance, mission, strategy, and organization? We might also reasonably apply a similar query to individuals charged with organizational leadership roles in the public and civil society sectors. In the following sections we will tend to focus on issues relating to for-profit organizations, but we will make more general comments where appropriate.

First, we must recognize that for businesses, corporate governance practice and company law does not really help very much at all – at least in English-speaking jurisdictions dominated by the requirements for short-term economic value added. Second, we must clarify what we mean by organizational purpose (or mission or strategic intent) and the creation of value. Third, we must decide what we mean by strategy.

Only then can we talk about the practical implications of sustainability for management and organization.

Governance

Given recent events in the US and the effective demise of two of the world's most overhyped and overvalued companies, Enron and WorldCom, together with their accountants Arthur Andersen, it is unsurprising that even the President of the United States entered the fray on corporate governance and corporate ethics (Bush 2002). However, amid anger from stakeholders, calls for retribution from Congress, and skittishness in capital markets, it seemed less than likely that legislators would recognize that here was evidence of a potential systems failure rather than simply evidence of individual and collective venality which required summary punishment. Thus, most of the prescriptions for addressing the blip in confidence in capitalism which these events precipitated were concerned with tightening rules surrounding disclosure, removing conflicts of interest for accountants, and the distribution of punitive justice for wrongdoers.

A systems-based analysis aimed at generating more sustainable models for corporations might look at the ambiguities and contradictions inherent in corporate governance practices around the world – the fact that although there is some convergence in such practices in OECD countries, there also remain significant differences in corporate law, governance practices and accounting standards between English-speaking and non-English speaking jurisdictions (Charkham 1995; Clarke and Monkhouse 1994). Such an analysis would take into account broader cultural issues, and the fact that the most common governance form in the private sector, that is family owned enterprise, is not amenable to economic rational-based systems of governance (Lubatkin, Lane, and Schulze 2001). Indeed, it might go further and draw attention to the contradiction that managers are supposed to act as usually rational but self-interested agents,[1] when in practice they respond to context (Lubatkin, Lane, and Schulze 2001), exhibit differences between attitude and behaviours (Ghoshal and Moran 1996), and drive value increasingly through the quality of relationships with the organization's stakeholders – in particular customers, employees, and business partners (Kay 1995; Wheeler and Sillanpää 1997; Svendsen et al. 2001).[2] We might examine the inherent contradiction of conventional governance systems and the roles of board directors being largely concerned with the exercise of controls through risk management practices, that is avoiding liability and loss or dealing with crisis or failure (Chatterjee and Harrison 2001), rather than actively promoting innovation and the creation of value for all stakeholders – key factors on which companies are increasingly assessed in the marketplace. Finally, we might also posit that only a systemic understanding of the role and purpose of the firm in a globalized economy would allow managers to discharge their obligations effectively in different jurisdictions – both in the developed and the developing world.

Managers hoping for a systems-based, global review of governance practices with an outcome that might help them navigate these ambiguities and contradictions should probably not hold their breath. There is little or no evidence that powerful jurisdictions like the US would welcome such a fundamental review of the capitalist project. Nor is there much evidence that international bodies such as the OECD, the G8, the WTO, or others with an interest in promoting free trade would have the legitimacy to undertake the task.

Thus we should probably not look to governance systems to resolve contradictory signals to managers at the national or international level. Happily, a rather more promising and grounded approach may be on offer at the level of the organization, to which we now turn.

Purpose, Mission, or Strategic Intent: Stakeholder Perspectives and the Creation of Value

As noted above it is becoming increasingly clear that the market valuation of companies and indeed the economic success of civil society and public organizations is becoming more dependent on intangible assets such as intellectual capital, social capital, human capital (including quality of management), and what many refer to simply as "reputation" (Stewart 1997; Teece 2000; Adler and Kwon 2002; Nahapiet and Ghoshal 1998; Pfeffer 1994; Blair and Kochan 2000; Hitt et al. 2001; Fombrun 1996, 2001). This is a general phenomenon, but understandably, these assets are especially valued in the resource extractive industries where externally determined "right to operate" is so essential (Wheeler, Fabig, and Boele 2002a) and in the world of new technologies where intangible assets such as intellectual capital, "business webs," and "relational capital" usually account for the overwhelming majority of the market value of the firm (Tapscott, Ticoll, and Lowy 2000; Sawhney, Gulati, and Paoni 2001). In for-profit organizations the trend is manifested in the increasing divergence of market-to-book ratios, the difference being accounted for by indirect valuation of intangible assets, notably intellectual capital. Employing this analysis, Dess and Lumpkin (2001) have developed a framework for leveraging human capital, linking it to other organizational resources for the purpose of reinforcing "core value-creating activities." We can hypothesize that organizations that manage their intangible assets well are more likely to succeed in a competitive environment as they will be better at generating the loyalty and support of customers, clients, investors, employees, and other stakeholders (Reichheld 1996). This explains the growing interest in "stakeholder capitalism" deriving from the seminal work of Freeman (1984) and the current vogue for trying to develop robust measures of intangible assets (Svendsen et al. 2001).[3] It may also explain – at least in part – the growing interest in consumer attitudes and behaviours with respect to ecological and social issues (Coddington 1993; Charter and Polonsky 1999).

Clearly, economic or market valuation of companies and their brands and the economic success of civil society and public organizations reflects one very important dimension of value creation, but it does not provide a full picture. Evaluation of an organization in the absolute sense is highly dependent on who is being asked to provide the judgment. Thus customers might value the economic utility of the product or service they buy from an organization, but they may also value the experience and implicit esteem conferred by the product, the social and ecological values of the organization, or indeed any one of a number of intangible factors contributing to self-actualization.

Different individual stakeholders will apply different factors in their judgments about what constitutes value for them in their relationship with an organization and its outputs; moreover these judgments may change over time. So, without attempting to be wholly postmodern in our analysis, we can safely assume that it is not possible for an individual manager or an organization either to control or to reduce the complexity of the discourse around the organization, nor indeed to dictate what proportion of economic and noneconomic factors may be in play at any one time. An organization's identity (as defined by Albert and Whetton 1985) is certainly part of an ongoing, reflective internal conversation that may in turn inform strategy (Dutton and Dukerich 1991). But it is also the product of a more pluralistic, externally mediated discourse that may be outside the realm of the organization's ability to control (Gioia 1998). It is possible to acknowledge the power of different constituencies within and external to the firm (Pfeffer 1994), map these stakeholders and their relative degrees of power, influence, and salience (Harrison and St John 1996; Johnson and Scholes 1999; Mitchell, Agle, and Wood 1997) and even audit the quality of their relationships with the firm over time (Wheeler and Sillanpää 1998). But these practices do not reduce complexity; they simply make explicit the challenge of managing it.

Given the above, I believe it is very important for organizations to be clear on at least three things:

1. what is the *purpose* of the firm; that is, its mission or "strategic intent" in Hamel and Prahalad's (1989) terms;
2. in whose *interests* is the firm run; that is, its orientation both to investors and other stakeholders and to the natural environment – here we know there are significant practical and cultural variables at play (Pfeffer and Salancik 1978; Yoshimori 1995); and
3. its *commitment to maximizing* value – however this may be defined by different actors at different points in time; that is, the organization's commitment to holistic performance and delivery.

Of these, perhaps the third is most relevant to the day-to-day role of the manager. It is also where management systems – objective setting, management accounting, performance management, and measurement – make the difference between aspiration and reality. In recent years there has been a good deal of attention devoted to strategic, holistic management and measurement systems, from total quality to balanced scorecard approaches integrating data on financial performance, customer satisfaction, employee development, societal expectations, and environmental performance (Kaplan and Norton 1996, 2001; Fiksel, McDaniel, and Mendenhall 1999).

In defining purpose, declaring interests and committing to the creation of value for stakeholders there is no need in each case to resolve hierarchies of interests, trade-offs between interests, or indeed assumptions about "win-win" outcomes between different stakeholders. All these need to be dealt with in real time. It is enough simply to acknowledge who the organization is in relationship with and commit to maximize the quality of their experience given that not everyone can have everything at all times. Strategic apportionment of benefits is typically an annual management function, linked to the budget planning horizon, not the role of the mission and purpose of the firm and it would

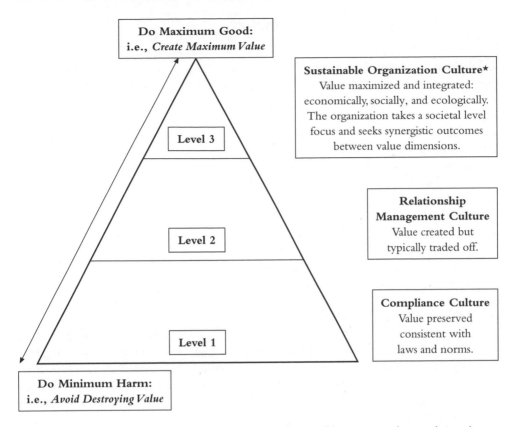

Figure 9.2: Framework for classifying organizational cultures with respect to the creation and distribution of value

be a mistake to imply otherwise. Sometimes workers lose their jobs; investors do not always receive dividends; sometimes customers lose a valued product or service. Good managements handle these events well, and high-performing, that is sustainable companies, make sure that key relationships experience "value-add" over the long term (Kotter and Heskett 1992).

Employing the creation of value in a world of diverse stakeholders as the central organizing principle, and drawing on the business ethics literature, Wheeler, Colbert and Freeman (2002b) sought to embrace concepts as diverse as economic value added, stakeholder theory, sustainability, and corporate social responsibility in a simple two-dimensional model. Depicted above (figure 9.2), it remains to be seen whether this navigational tool proves helpful to managers in the longer run, but a commitment to value creation – *as defined by stakeholders as well as the organization* – seems to be a useful and unifying notion on which any sound organizational strategy may be based.

Strategy

Of all the many standard definitions of strategy, the one that may have closest relevance to the subject of this chapter is that of Johnson and Scholes, who assert "Strategy is the *direction* and *scope* of an organization over the *long term*: which achieves *advantage* for the organization through its configuration of *resources* within a changing *environment*, to meet the needs of *markets* and to fulfil *stakeholder* expectations" (1999, 10; original emphasis). The highlighted terms distinguish key elements of strategy; they also draw attention to the long-term, dynamic, and inclusive nature of effective strategy making. The definition is also helpful in that it links advantage to the firm (i.e., value to investors and managers) to needs of markets and stakeholders (i.e., value to customers, employees, business partners, etc.). Thus it ties very appropriately to our placing value creation at the centre of our thinking on mission and purpose. And for advocates of the resource-based view of strategy (Wernerfeld 1984; Barney 1991) it implies that resources may be broadly defined; for example to include exogenously (i.e., marketplace) determined forms of intangible asset co-owned, co-developed or co-negotiated with stakeholders and other agents consistent with the perspective of Pfeffer and Salancik (1978) and contemporary views of institutional theory (Oliver 1997; Dacin, Goodstein, and Scott 2002).[4]

Thinking of strategy this way helps break down the false dichotomy provided to us by ideologists and some "economic value add" activists (and indeed company law in English-speaking countries) that the interests of investors should be considered primary and separate from those of other stakeholders. Moreover, it is consonant with perspectives on governance and company purpose in non–English-speaking jurisdictions; and it is closer to the day-to-day reality of most real-world managers who have a *de facto* daily need to manage multiple relationships in complex systems and observe accountabilities to a wide range of internal and external stakeholders (Demb and Neubauer 1992).

Regardless of where we might place legal or moral rights and responsibilities respectively on stakeholders and the organization (a subject that we do not address here), the Johnson and Scholes definition requires managers and organizations to (1) develop sensitivities to multiple perspectives within a changing and uncertain external environment; and (2) exhibit capabilities to respond to these perspectives through the building of value-adding relationships that permit stakeholder expectations to be fulfilled – thus addressing the two Friedman criteria for successful navigation of globalization described earlier. The Johnson and Scholes approach also resonates with more dynamic, stakeholder inclusive, learning-based approaches to strategy – what Mintzberg, Ahlstrand, and Lampel (1998) would refer to as "descriptive" rather than the more conventional "prescriptive" planning-based approaches to strategic management.

Whatever approach to strategic management is favoured at any point in time, there is general agreement that there is a clear distinction between strategy formulation (analysis and choice) and implementation.

In terms of strategy formulation and sustainability, an especially useful navigational tool emerged in 2002, which resonates with both the multiperspective requirements of globalization and the dynamic, negotiated space between the foundation of civil norms

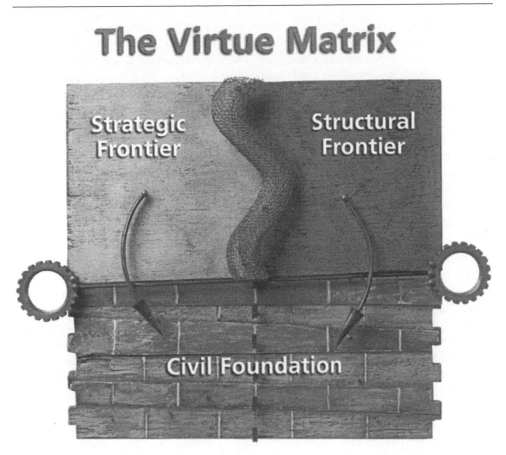

Figure 9.3: The Virtue Matrix

and expectations (equivalent to level 1 on the Wheeler, Colbert and Freeman 2000b model depicted in figure 9.2), and the discretionary versus nondiscretionary choices (levels 2 and 3 in figure 9.2) that organizations may elect to exercise. In his "Virtue Matrix" (depicted above in figure 9.3), Roger Martin (2002) attempted to drive strategic clarity into the discussion of corporate social responsibility – a concept which is becoming increasingly influential in European public policy terms (Parkinson 1999; European Commission 2001) but which still causes some agonizing in corporate circles. Corporate Social Responsibility (CSR) (like the stakeholder approach) can be viewed as wholly normative or morally driven, or it can be advanced as solely instrumental to the interests of the firm, or indeed a combination of the two. CSR can be construed as philanthropy (the notion which so offended Milton Friedman), or it can be seen as good marketing, and again a hybrid of the two. In constructing his Virtue Matrix, Martin sought to make explicit the shifting boundaries of what firms may choose to do in different jurisdictions based on what civil society and the organization's stakeholders may deem appropriate. Martin stressed the need for leadership and vision in navigating the inconsistencies in standards; that is, the depth of the "civil foundation" in the developed versus developing world, which he referred to as "globalization's most troubling dilemma" (2002, 11).

With respect to strategy implementation, and applying similar assumptions about the value of dynamic, pluralistic (i.e., stakeholder-inclusive and learning-based) approaches to strategy in complex environments, Wheeler, Sutherland, and Kelly (2000) used a deductive and empirical approach to identify seven characteristics of corporate and operational strategy implementation that could be used to define the degree to which corporate strategy successfully embraced principles of global sustainability. These included assessments of corporate mission and objectives, corporate capability for change and the development of new markets, capability for learning, operational orientation to key external stakeholders, operational orientation to employees, and operational orientation toward the natural environment. The framework was applied successfully to ten North American firms and in an in-depth analysis of Royal/Dutch Shell's strategy (Wheeler et al. 2000, 2001).

Happily, it would seem that apart from being globally appropriate and practical, these models, based as they are on dynamic, pluralistic approaches to strategy, also coincide with the notion of maximizing economic value over the long term. The economic value (defined as revenue, stock price appreciation, and income) of developing effective, balanced relationships with key stakeholders in private sector firms in the US was established quite conclusively by Kotter and Heskett (1992). Similarly, Collins and Porras (1994) demonstrated a clear correlation between long-term stock price performance and key elements of internal culture. There is now growing evidence of synergy between economic, social and/or environmental performance emanating from a range of research studies (e.g., Waddock and Graves 1997; Berman et al. 1999; Roman, Hayibor, and Agle 1999). These are backed by empirical evidence from specialist stock market indices in North America and Europe which demonstrate consistent share price premia for companies that perform well in their sector on social and/or environmental issues (Feltmate, Schofield, and Yachnin 2001). In this author's experience, proponents of "sustainable development investing" (investment analysts that pick companies which will win economically in the future on the basis of their social and environmental today) have no illusions about the causality of the correlations; they simply point to good social and environmental management as surrogate indicators for effective overall management – managements that can routinely and effectively deal with multiple, complex demands and prosper.

Implications for Organization and Management

In the foregoing section we observed the strong case to be made for corporate responsiveness to the social and environmental concerns of publics around the world; we noted the inadequacy of current approaches to governance in English-speaking jurisdictions in addressing these concerns; we made a case for managements making clear their commitments on these questions, with particular emphasis on the centrality of creating value for stakeholders *in their terms*; and we drew attention to the value of pluralistic approaches to organizational strategy that tend to rely on dynamic, stakeholder-inclusive, and learning-based rather than prescriptive approaches.

We will now build on these insights to construct a approach to management and organization consistent with notions of sustainable globalization (Friedman 2000) and organizational sustainability (the subject of this chapter). There seem to be at least four key areas of organization that encompass the challenge. Managers must establish and nurture

1. organizational *connectivity* – taking a societal level, systems-based perspective and placing the organization cognitively and consciously in a global political, economic, social, and ecological context (see also figure 9.1);
2. organizational *commitments* to the creation of value across a range of economic, social, and ecological factors, manifested in missions, codes, strategies, objectives, and measures that are meaningful for the organization and its stakeholders;
3. organizational *culture* – which embraces values, beliefs, and assumptions consistent with the organization's roles and responsibilities in a complex, globalized world (see also figure 9.2); and
4. organizational *capabilities* – which allow managers, employees, and other stakeholders to learn from, understand, and navigate complex situations and challenges, employing multiple perspectives and tailored behaviours as appropriate.

We have already discussed connectivity and commitments (to mission, strategy, and the delivery of stakeholder value) at some length earlier in the chapter. In summary these may be deemed to be consistent with a systems-based, pluralistic approach to external political, economic, social, and ecological drivers and influences and a holistic approach to commitments and performance. So let us now turn to internal issues of culture and capabilities.

Organizational Culture

Schein (1985) first introduced the notion that organizational culture consists of three layers or dimensions: values, which may typically be made explicit in corporate statements and literature; beliefs, which may be manifested in codes, rules, and norms; and taken-for-granted assumptions – the tacit paradigm of the organization; that is, "how we do things around here." Culture and organizational values impact directly on strategic management processes (Johnson 1992) and can be a source of significant differentiation and competitive advantage (Barney 1986; O'Reilly and Pfeffer 2000); conversely we also know that similar institutions may converge in terms of mindsets and beliefs (DiMaggio and Powell 1983), which tends to minimize opportunities for differentiation. While varying in the way they deal with the forces of convergence (Oliver 1991), managers can become "captive" to insitutionalized organizational arrangements creating barriers to innovation and change (Scott 1995). Meanwhile, the values, interpretations, and perceptions of senior managers and teams themselves are influential with respect to (1) strategic choice and performance (Hambrick and Mason 1984; Daft and Weick 1984; Starbuck and Milliken 1988); (2) attitudes to globalization (Carpenter and Frederickson 2001); and (3) organizational culture, responses to stakeholder influence and the exercise of power (Finkelstein and Hambrick 1996; Agle, Mitchell, and Sonnenfeld 1999).

If managers and organizations are intimately and iteratively linked through a variety of internal cultural and strategic systems and processes, how does this observation relate to the navigation of globalization?

There is no shortage of influential prescriptions and imperatives for organizations operating globally (Ohmae 1989; Bartlett and Ghoshal 1989; Porter 1990; Trompenaars and Hampden-Turner 1998). Empirical prescriptions and imperatives tend to place sensitivity to cultural diversity at their core and stress the need for strategic, organizational, and cognitive flexibility. Organizations and managers need to develop what Gupta and Govindarajan (2002) describe as a "global mindset" which "combines an openness to and awareness of diversity across cultures and markets with a propensity and ability to synthesize across this diversity" (Govindarajan and Gupta 2001, 116). Based on long-term studies of more than 100 global corporations these authors believe such a mindset is important to all businesses and all employees regardless of chosen markets, products, and services or individual roles. They also draw on the literature describing team performance to stress the importance of "cognitive diversity" in teams; thus reinforcing the Friedman assertion on the importance of multiple perspectives in navigating globalization.

The correlation between indicators of top management team diversity and globalization posture has been established empirically by Carpenter and Frederickson who concluded that these correlations were "consistent with the upper echelons view that the diverse perspectives, skills, and information networks that are presumed to accompany international experience and educational and tenure heterogeneity may equip firms to manage the complexity and high information-processing demands associated with expansive global strategic postures" (2001, 545). Again, we might describe this as a pluralistic approach.

Let us now turn to the organizational capabilities underpinning cultural and cognitive pluralism and what this means for the management of change in turbulent environments.

Organizational Capabilities

Organizational change is perhaps least understood and least researched at the international level where there is a special need for pluralistic thinking both in theory and practice (Pettigrew, Woodman, and Cameron 2001). The need for flexibility and adaptation over the longer term has long been recognized, even in naturally bureacratic organizations. This contrasts with the shorter-term need that even the most anarchic organizations have for some level of predictability in routines and processes. Kilduff and Dougherty remind us that in J. D. Thompson's *Organizations in Action* (Thompson 1967) management was seen as "a kind of roller coaster ride" involving "shooting at a moving target of co-alignment in which the several components of that target are themselves moving" (2000, 777).

Today we would refer to the importance of constantly evolving or "dynamic" organizational capabilities (Teece, Pisano, and Shuen 1997) – particularly in the context of international or globalized organizational strategy (Tallman 2001).

There is a rapidly growing body of thoughtful research and theory building in the field of ecological sustainability and organizational change (Starik and Marcus 2000). Perhaps understandably, early researchers coming from an ecocentric or natural environment perspective tended to explore the phenomenon of corporate "greening"; for example, the introduction of environmental management systems and pollution control mechanisms either at a conceptual or at a technical level. However, more recently there has emerged a more systematic and in-depth attempt to place the concept of "environmental strategy" or "sustainability strategy" more firmly in the context of the mainstream organizational literature (Hart 1995, 1997; Starik and Rands 1995; Christman 2000; Sharma 2000). In addition, a number of authors have drawn particular attention to the importance of certain capabilities for organizations to become environmentally or ecologically sustainable.

The most recurrently cited organizational capabilities for ecological sustainability may be summarized thus:

1. leadership (e.g., Egri and Herman 2000), which here might include the importance of creating a global and institutional context and culture for the organization (Welford 1997), legitimation of a sustainability vision or frame (Zietsma and Vertinsky 2002), an appropriate measure of pluralistic behaviour (Jones 2000), and permission for sustainable actions (Ramus and Steger 2000);
2. learning, including adaptation and innovation (e.g., Hart 1995; Sharma and Vredenburg 1998; Boons and Berends 2001; Senge and Carstedt 2001), which in less incrementalist prescriptions embraces neo-Schumpeterian concepts such as the "creative destruction" of environmentally inefficient organizations and processes and their replacement with more sustainable ones (Hart and Milstein 1999); and
3. stakeholder inclusion and network building or "boundary spanning" (Wheeler and Sillanpää 1998; Clarke and Roome 1999; Sharma and Vredenburg 1998; Madsen and Ulhøi 2001; Sharma 2001).

Although less well developed, we might catalogue an equivalent list of capabilities for the nexus between organization and the social dimension of sustainability (i.e., societal and intergenerational fairness and equity) that tends to play out in the literatures on social issues in management, business, society, corporate social responsibility, and business ethics. This would likely have a stronger emphasis on the normative ethical role of the manager, but it would certainly include the three organizational capabilities listed above, predicated on a strategic "stakeholder approach" (Freeman and McVea 2001).

According to Johnson and Scholes (1999), at the strategic level, capabilities can be described as threshold competencies (i.e., a minimum level of competency is required for the effective running of the organization's value chain) or core competencies (which confer competitive advantage) – a concept popularized by Prahalad and Hamel (1990).

We might question which of the organizational capabilities associated with organizational sustainability listed here – leadership, learning/adaptation/innovation, and stakeholder inclusion – might be "core competencies" for different organizations in different circumstances at different points in time. In the oil and gas industry, companies like Shell and BP have decided to pursue all three in their competitive strategies; Exxon Mobil and Chevron Texaco have not (at least to 2002), but would presumably claim some level of threshold competency in each case.

Of the three capabilities, perhaps the importance of stakeholder inclusion and network building as a source of competitiveness is the most contentious. Some level of competence is required in stakeholder relations in most organizations: for example investor relations, customer relations, and employee relations. But there are successful organizations that do not move beyond compliance or basic relationship-management (tiers 1 and 2 in the model depicted in figure 9.2) in terms of stakeholder involvement. It is harder to argue that leadership and learning are optional capabilities in rapidly changing environments (de Geus 1997; Senge et al. 1999; Teece, Pisano, and Shuen 1997; McGrath 2001; Tidd, Bessant, and Pavitt 2001). However, the strong case made for pluralism in organizational culture (see above) adds some weight to the idea that systematic inclusion of employees and business partners with different cultural and cognitive influences helps organizations navigate globalization.

Summary of Implications for Organization and Management and Conclusions

When we take these organizational components and map them onto the requirements of management, the diagram below emerges, with connectivity, commitments, culture, and capabilities all requiring simultaneous attention (figure 9.4).

If we accept that minimum requirements of the sustainable *organization* are the maintenance of appropriate levels of connectivity, commitment, culture, and capability, and if we accept that the context for sustainability is a situation of rapid and potentially large-scale change, then the individual charged with this multifaceted set of responsibilities in a world of major change requires a powerful toolkit for *management*. In recent years, two linked frameworks have emerged that may help the manager navigate the multidimensional challenge of directing a human institution through turbulence to organizational sustainability. Both draw on principles consistent with the foregoing analysis, in particular the pluralistic real world nature of management.

The first is the notion of complexity, popularized by Stacey (1992, 1993, 1995), Levy (1994), and others, and developed in leadership terms by Wheatley (1992) and related to organizational culture and change respectively by Frank and Fahrbach (1999) and Dooley and Van de Ven (1999). Owing much to insights derived from various scientific and mathematical observations of uncertainty and change in physical and biological systems systems, these authors assert that complex systems are characterized by high levels of interaction leading to nonlinear phenomena, self-organization and adaptation. Consituents

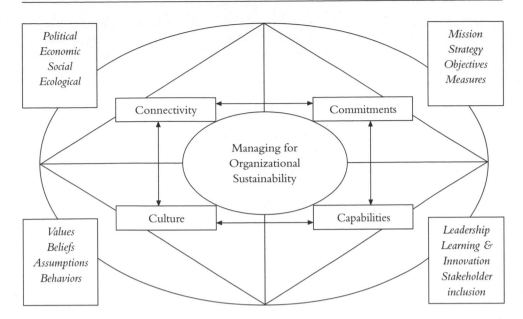

Figure 9.4: Managing for organizational sustainability

of complex systems may coexist at the "edge of chaos" for purposes of maximizing adaptability in the event of unpredictable or catastrophic change. Or constituents may self-organize and co-evolve to allow new patterns and a new order to emerge. In this sense complexity and chaos are separable, although the two concepts are frequently linked. But in both cases, interaction or enactment with other actors is the key to remaining competitive and adaptive during incremental or catastrophic change and transition to a new state.

Complementary to this approach is the growing interest in studying paradox in management, which seeks to make explicit the cognitive and practical tensions of dealing with multiple responsibilities and multiple relationships or enactments in uncertain environments.[5]

Marianne Lewis (2000) attempted to capture the fundamentals of management of paradox, developing a simple framework which could lead to acceptance, confrontation, or transcendance of dramatic change, describing the act of "managing paradox" as "capturing its enlightening potential." Lewis went on to explore paradoxes of learning (e.g., tensions between the old and the new), paradoxes of organization (e.g., tensions between control and flexibility), and paradoxes of belonging (e.g., tensions between the self and others). Much of Lewis's analysis derived from the learning and innovation literature, the performance and empowerment literature, and studies of individuality, diversity, and the challenges posed by globalization. Thus, looming large over Lewis's review was the thinking of Morgan (1986), Quinn (1988), Argyris (1993), and Argyris and Schön (1978, 1996), all of whom emphasized the need for managers (1) to identify and surface the cognitive models running in their organization; (2) where appropriate to "reframe" problems, if necessary employing broader constructions which can hold apparently contradictory, that is paradoxical, positions; and (3) to develop the capability for complex conversation and narrative.

If we see the manager as a person responsible for ensuring organizational sustainability: political, economic, social, and ecological (i.e., consistent with notions of sustainable development and the stewardship theory of the firm), then it is axiomatic that their capabilities must mirror

1. the complexity and pluralism of a globalized world in which change is discontinuous and the future highly uncertain;
2. the complexity and pluralism of organizations that need to interact effectively with multiple components of a globalized world in order to create value for the firm and its stakeholders.

We know that organizations respond to ecological and social issues for a variety of reasons; drivers include (1) regulatory, (2) stakeholder-mediated, (3) economic opportunity, and (4) internal, ethical reasons; for example, leadership and corporate values (Vredenburg and Westley 1993; Bansal and Roth 2000). Clearly organizations and senior managers deal with threats and opportunities differently, depending on the strategic type of the organization and the availability of discretionary or "slack" resources (Chattopadhyay, Glick, and Huber 2001). And as noted earlier, the values and cognitive models of managers appear to be central to determining the nature of the strategic response of organizations to external and internal drivers. Zietsma and Vertinsky (2002) identified six prototypical cognitive frames that managers may bring in their responses to environmental issues: the [natural] environment can be framed as (1) not the firm's responsibility, (2) a threat, (3) a technical issue, (4) an opportunity, (5) a societal duty, and (6) a personal commitment. Similar to the arguments of Wheeler, Colbert, and Freeman (2002b) with respect to cultural orientation to relationships in the context of sustainable value (the three tiers in figure 9.2), and citing Starbuck and Milliken (1988) and Argyris and Schön (1978), these authors argue that strategic response frames are not mutually exclusive nor static but are subject to organizational sense making and learning processes driven by perceived incongruencies between mental models and actual experience.

Thus perhaps one of the most important roles of the senior managers and *leadership* of the sustainable organization must be to help the organization frame external events appropriately and develop appropriate strategic responses consistent with a viable vision of the future. In support of this strategic frame and vision, *managers* must be capable of managing and nurturing the four components of the sustainable organization (connectivity, capabilities, culture, and commitment) in terms of their own abilities to lead, learn, and engage with drivers, influences, and different actors impacting the organization externally and internally. Managers of the sustainable organization must be pluralistic and inclusive in their own mental models and behaviours, and consequently must be able to deal with paradox when pluralism and inclusivity lead to contradictory signals and outcomes, framing suitable metacontexts for the organization and its stakeholder in order for them to make sense of their roles in paradoxical situations. Happily, there is no shortage of complexity and paradox in our globalized world today to enable a manager to choose such a metacontext to help illuminate the complex and explain the inexplicable.

NOTES

1   This notion is backed by corporate law in English-speaking countries as well as by simplistic versions of transaction cost theory (Williamson 1975) and agency theory (Jenson and Meckling 1976).

2   To reinforce this point, while value resides increasingly in relationships, the obverse also holds true; the collapse of the Enron pack of cards can be described very effectively as a classic example of the shadow side of building social capital with stakeholders: helpful when it exists; disastrous when it evaporates – in this case almost overnight.

3   Popular indices have emerged from both the worlds of human resource consulting (Watson Wyatt 2000) and brand consulting (Aaker and Joachimsthaler 2000) to capture the value of intangible assets. Indeed it may be argued that the surge in interest in branding, which many commentators now stress as crucial for success in the global, digital economy (Reich 2001; Wind et al. 2002), is entirely driven by this thinking. British futurist and commentator Charlie Leadbeater (1999) describes brands as essential "shortcuts to trust" in a world of complexity and information overload.

4   It is interesting to note that the resource-based view (RBV) approach was comprehensively critiqued in terms of its contribution to strategic management by Priem and Butler (2001) as containing "a theory of sustainability [*sic*] but *not* a theory of competitive advantage (i.e., value creation)," partly because of RBV's inability to encompass and define externally determined value. In the context of this chapter, this is one of the primary strengths of RBV. A consistent, if more conventional argument for RBV focusing on "captured value" was advanced by Makadok and Coff (2002).

5   It may be worth noting here that de Wit and Meyer (1998) constructed their entire *Strategy* textbook on ten paradoxes of strategic management.

REFERENCES

Aaker, D. A., and Joachimsthaler, E. 2000. *Brand Leadership*. New York: Free Press.

Adler, P. A., and Kwon, S.-W. 2002. Social capital: Prospects for a new concept. *Academy of Management Review* 27 (1):17–40.

Agle, B. R., Mitchell, R. K., and Sonnenfeld, J. A. 1999. Who matters to CEOs? An investigation of stakeholder attributes and salience, corporate performance, and CEO values. *Academy of Management Journal* 42 (5):507–25.

Albert, S., and Whetton, D. A. 1985. Organizational identity. In B. M. Staw and L. L. Cummings (eds.), *Research in Organizational Behaviour* 7. Greenwich, CT: JAI.

Argyris, C. 1993. *Knowledge for Action: A Guide to Overcoming Barriers to Organizational Change*. San Francisco: Jossey-Bass.

Argyris, C., and Schön, D. A. 1978. *Organizational Learning: A Theory of Action Perspective*. Reading, MA: Addison-Wesley.

Argyris, C., and Schön, D. A. 1996. *Organizational Learning II: Theory, Method, and Practice*. Reading, MA: Addison-Wesley.

Bansal, P., and Roth, K. 2000. Why companies go green: A model of ecological legitimacy. *Academy of Management Journal* 43 (4):717–36.

Barber, B. R. 1995. *Jihad vs. McWorld: How Globalism and Tribalism are Reshaping the World.* New York: Ballantine.

Barlow, M., and Clarke, T. 2002. *Blue Gold: The Battle against Corporate Theft of the World's Water.* Toronto: Stoddart.

Barney, J. B. 1986. Organizational culture: Can it be a source of sustained competitive advantage? *Academy of Management Review* 11 (3):656–65.

Barney, J. B. 1991. Firm resources and sustained competitive advantage. *Journal of Management* 17:99–120.

Bartlett, C. A., and Ghoshal, S. 1989. *Managing across Borders: The Transnational Solution.* Boston: Harvard Business School Press.

Berman, S. L., Wicks, A. C., Kolha, S., and Jones, T. M. 1999. Does stakeholder orientation matter? The relationship between stakeholder management models and firm financial performance. *Academy of Management Journal* 42 (5):488–506.

Blair, M. M., and Kochan, T. A. (eds.). 2000. *The New Relationship: Human Capital in the American Corporation.* Washington, DC: Brookings Institution.

Boons, F., and Berends, M. 2001. Stretching the boundary: the possibilities of flexibility as an organizational capability in industrial ecology. *Business Strategy and the Environment* 10 (2):115–24.

Bush, G. 2002. Presidential comments on corporate responsibility. Available at http://www.whitehouse.gov/news/releases/2002/07/20020709-1.html (accessed 19 July 2002).

Carpenter, M. A., and Frederickson, J. W. 2001. Top management teams, global strategic posture, and the moderating role of uncertainty. *Academy of Management Journal* 44 (3):533–45.

Charkham, J. 1995. *Keeping Good Company: A Study of Corporate Governance in Five Countries.* Oxford: Oxford University Press.

Charter, M., and Polonsky, M. J. 1999. *Greener Marketing: A Global Perspective on Greening Marketing Practice.* Sheffield: Greenleaf.

Chatterjee, S., and Harrison, J. S. 2001. Corporate governance. In M. A. Hitt, R. E. Freeman, and J. S. Harrison (eds.), *Handbook of Strategic Management.* Oxford: Blackwell.

Chattopadhyay, P., Glick, W. H., and Huber, G. P. 2001. Organizational actions in response to threats and opportunities. *Academy of Management Journal* 44 (5):937–55.

Christman, P. 2000. Effects of "best practices" of environmental management on cost and advantage: The role of complementary assets. *Academy of Management Journal* 43 (4):663–80.

Clarke, S., and Roome, N. 1999. Sustainable business: Learning-action networks as organizational assets. *Business Strategy and the Environment* 8 (5):296–310.

Clarke, T., and Monkhouse, E. (eds.). 1994. *Rethinking the Company: Forces Shaping Business in the Next Century.* London: Pitman.

Coddington, W. 1993. *Environmental Marketing.* New York: McGraw-Hill.

Collins, J. C., and Porras, J. 1994. *Built to Last: Successful Habits of Visionary Companies.* London: Random House.

Courtney, H. 2001. *20/20 Foresight: Crafting Strategy in an Uncertain World.* Boston: Harvard Business School Press.

Dacin, M. T., Goodstein, J., and Scott, W. R. 2002. Institutional theory and institutional change: Introduction to the special research forum. *Academy of Management Journal* 45 (1):45–57.

Daft, R., and Weick, K. 1984. Toward a model of organizations as interpersonal systems. *Academy of Management Review* 9:284–96.

de Geus, A. 1997. *The Living Company: Growth, Learning and Longevity in Business.* London: Nicholas Brealey.

Demb, A., and Neubauer, F. F. 1992. *The Corporate Board: Confronting the Paradoxes*. Oxford: Oxford University Press.

Dess, G. G., and Lumpkin, G. T. 2001. Emerging issues in strategy process research. In M. A. Hitt, R. E. Freeman, and J. S. Harrison (eds.), *Handbook of Strategic Management*. Oxford: Blackwell.

de Wit, B., and Meyer, R. 1998. *Strategy: Process, Content, Context*. London: Thomson.

DiMaggio, P., and Powell, W. W. 1983. The iron cage revisited: Institutional isomorphism and collective rationality in organizational fields. *American Sociological Review* 48:147–60.

Dooley, K. J., and Van de Ven, A. H. 1999. Explaining complex organizational dynamics. *Organization Science* 10 (3):359–72.

Dutton, J. E., and Dukerich, J. M. 1991. Keeping an eye on the mirror: Image and identity in organizational adaptation. *Academy of Management Journal* 34:517–54.

Egri, C. P., and Herman, S. 2000. Leadership in the North American environmental sector: Values, leadership styles, and contexts of environmental leaders and their organizations. *Academy of Management Journal* 43 (4):571–604.

Elkington, J. 1998. *Cannibals with Forks: The Triple Bottom Line of Twenty-First Century Business*. Gabriola Island, BC: New Society.

Environics. 2002. *CSR Monitor and Global Issues Monitor Surveys*. Toronto: Environics.

European Commission. 2001. *Promoting a European Framework for Corporate Social Responsibility. Green Paper*. Luxembourg: Office for Official Publications of the European Commission.

Feltmate, B. W., Schofield, B. A., and Yachnin, R. W. 2001. *Sustainable Development, Value Creation and the Capital Markets*. Ottawa: Conference Board of Canada.

Fiksel, J., McDaniel, J., and Mendenhall, C. 1999. Measuring progress towards sustainability: Principles, process, and best practices. Proceedings of the Eighth International Greening of Industry Network Conference, November 1999, Chapel Hill, NC.

Finkelstein, S., and Hambrick, D. C. 1996. *Strategic Leadership: Top Executives and their Effects on Organizations*. Eagan, MN: West.

Fombrun, C. J. 1996. *Reputation: Realizing Value from the Corporate Image*. Boston: Harvard Business School Press.

Fombrun, C. J. 2001. Corporate reputations as economic assets. In M. A. Hitt, R. E. Freeman, and J. S. Harrison (eds.), *Handbook of Strategic Management*. Oxford: Blackwell.

Frank, K. A., and Fahrbach, K. 1999. Organization culture as a complex system: Balance and information in models of influence and selection. *Organization Science* 10 (3):253–77.

Frankel, C. 2001. Sustainability and September 11th. *Green@Work* (November–December):42–3.

Freeman, R. E. 1984. *Strategic Management: A Stakeholder Approach*. Boston: Pitman.

Freeman, R. E., and McVea, J. 2001. A stakeholder approach to strategic management. In M. A. Hitt, R. E. Freeman, and J. S. Harrison (eds.), *Handbook of Strategic Management*. Oxford: Blackwell.

Friedman, T. 2000. *The Lexus and the Olive Tree: Understanding Globalization*. New York: Anchor/Random House.

Fukuyama, F. 1999. *The Great Disruption: Human Nature and the Reconstitution of Social Order*. New York: Free Press.

Ghoshal, S., and Moran, P. 1996. Bad for practice: A critique of the transaction cost theory. *Academy of Management Review* 21 (1):13–47.

Gioia, D. A. 1998. From individual to organizational identity. In D. A. Whetton and P. A. Godfrey (eds.), *Identity in Organizations*. Thousand Oaks, CA: Sage.

Govindarajan, V., and Gupta, A. K. 2001. *The Quest for Global Dominance: Transforming Global Presence into Global Competitive Advantage*. San Francisco: Jossey-Bass.

Gupta, A. K., and Govindarajan, V. 2002. Cultivating a global mindset. *Academy of Management Executive* 16 (1):116–26.

Hambrick, D., and Mason, P. 1984. Upper echelons: The organization as a reflection of its top managers. *Academy of Management Journal* 15:514–35.

Hamel, G., and Prahalad, C. K. 1989. Strategic intent. *Harvard Business Review* 67 (3):63–76.

Harrison, J. S., and St. John, C. H. 1996. Managing and partnering with external stakeholders. *Academy of Management Executive* 10 (2):46–59.

Hart, S. L. 1995. A natural-resource-based view of the firm. *Academy of Management Review* 20:986–1014.

Hart, S. L. 1997. Beyond greening: Strategies for a sustainable world. *Harvard Business Review* 75 (1):66–76.

Hart, S. L., and Milstein, M. B. 1999. Global sustainability and the creative destruction of industries. *Sloan Management Review* 41 (1):23–33.

Hitt, M. A., Bierman, L., Shimizu, K., and Kochhar, R. 2001. Direct and moderating effects of human capital on strategy and performance in professional service firms: A resource-based perspective. *Academy of Management Journal* 44 (1):13–28.

Jenson, M. C., and Meckling, W. F. 1976. Theory of the firm: Managerial behavior, agency costs, and ownership structure. *Journal of Financial Economics* 3:305–60.

Johnson, G. 1992. Managing strategic change: Strategy, culture and action. *Long Range Planning* 26 (1):28–36.

Johnson, G., and Scholes, K. 1999. *Exploring Corporate Strategy*. London: Prentice Hall.

Jones, D. R. 2000. Leadership strategies for sustainable development. *Business Strategy and the Environment* 9 (6):378–89.

Kaplan, R. S., and Norton, D. P. 1996. *The Balanced Scorecard: Translating Strategy into Action*. Boston: Harvard Business School Press.

Kaplan, R. S., and Norton, D. P. 2001. *The Strategy-Focused Organization: How Balanced Scorecard Companies Thrive in the New Business Environment*. Boston: Harvard Business School Press.

Kay, J. 1995. *Foundations of Corporate Success: How Business Strategies Add Value*. Oxford: Oxford University Press.

Kay, J., and Silberston, A. 1995. Corporate governance. *National Institute Economic Review* 153: 84–96.

Kilduff, M., and Dougherty, D. 2000. Editorial team essay – change and development in a pluralistic world: The view from the classics. *Academy of Management Review* 25 (4):777–82.

Klare, M. T. 2001. *Resource Wars: The New Landscape of Global Conflict*. New York: Metropolitan/ Owl.

Klein, N. 2000. *No Logo*. London: Flamingo/HarperCollins.

Korten, D. 1995. *When Corporations Rule the World*. West Hartford, CT: Kumarian Press/Berrett-Koehler.

Kotter, J. P., and Heskett, J. L. 1992. *Corporate Culture and Performance*. New York: Free Press.

Leadbeater, C. 1999. *Living on Thin Air*. London: Viking.

Levy, D. 1994. Chaos theory and strategy: Theory, application, and managerial implications. *Strategic Management Journal* 15:167–78.

Lewis, M. A. 2000. Exploring paradox: Toward a more comprehensive guide. *Academy of Management Review* 25 (4):760–76.

Lubatkin, M. H., Lane, P. J., and Schulze, W. S. 2001. A strategic management model of agency relationships in firm governance. In M. A. Hitt, R. E. Freeman, and J. S. Harrison (eds.), *Handbook of Strategic Management*. Oxford: Blackwell.

Madsen, H., and Ulhøi, J. P. 2001. Integrating environmental and stakeholder management. *Business Strategy and the Environment* 10 (2):77–88.

Makadok, R., and Coff, R. 2002. The theory of value and the value of theory: Breaking new ground versus re-inventing the wheel. Dialogue. *Academy of Management Review* 27 (1): 10–13.

Martin, R. 2002. The virtue matrix: Calculating the return on corporate responsibility. *Harvard Business Review* (March):5–11. Reprint R0203E.

McGrath, R. G. 2001. *Academy of Management Journal* 44 (1):118–31.

Meadows, D. H., Meadows, D. L, Randers, J., and Behrens, W. W. 1972. *The Limits to Growth*. New York: Universe.

Mintzberg, H., Ahlstrand, B., and Lampel, J. 1998. *Strategy Safari*. London: Prentice Hall.

Mintzberg, H., Simons, R., and Basu, K. 2002. Beyond selfishness. Working draft paper. Available from http://www.henrymintzburg.com (accessed 19 July 2002).

Mitchell, R., Agle, B., and Wood, D. 1997. Toward a theory of stakeholder identification and salience: Defining the principle of who and what really counts. *Academy of Management Review* 22:853–86.

Morgan, G. 1986. *Images of Organization*. Thousand Oaks, CA: Sage.

Nahapiet, J., and Ghoshal, S. 1998. Social capital, intellectual capital, and the organizational advantage. *Academy of Management Review* 23 (2):242–66.

Ohmae, K. 1989. Managing in a borderless world. *Harvard Business Review* (May–June):2–9.

Oliver, C. 1991. Strategic responses to institutional processes. *Academy of Management Review* 16:145–79.

Oliver, C. 1997. Sustainable competitive advantage: Combining institutional and resource-based views. *Strategic Management Journal* 18:697–713.

O'Reilly, C. A., and Pfeffer, J. 2000. *Hidden Value: How Great Companies Achieve Extraordinary Results with Ordinary People*. Boston: Harvard Business School Press.

Parkinson, J. 1999. The socially responsible company. In M. K. Addo (ed.), *Human Rights Standards and the Responsibility of Transnational Corporations*. The Hague: Kluwer Law International.

Pettigrew, A. M., Woodman, R. W., and Cameron, K. S. 2001. *Academy of Management Journal* 44 (4):697–713.

Pfeffer, J. 1994. *Competitive Advantage through People*. Boston: Harvard Business School Press.

Pfeffer, J., and Salancik, G. 1978. *The External Control of Organizations*. New York: Harper and Row.

Porter, M. E. 1990. *The Competitive Advantage of Nations*. New York: Free Press.

Prahalad, C. K., and Hamel, G. 1990. The core competence of the corporation. *Harvard Business Review* 68 (3):79–91.

Prahalad, C. K., and Hart, S. L. 2001. The fortune at the bottom of the pyramid. *Strategy and Business* 26:2–14.

Priem, R. L., and Butler, J. E. 2001. Is the resource-based "view" a useful perspective for strategic management research. *Academy of Management Review* 26 (1):22–40.

Quinn, R. E. 1988. *Beyond Rational Management*. San Francisco: Jossey-Bass.

Reich, R. B. 2001. *The Future of Success*. New York: Knopf.

Reichheld, F. 1996. *The Loyalty Effect*. Boston: Harvard University Press.

Roman, R., Hayibor, S., and Agle, B. 1999. The relationship between social and financial performance. *Business and Society* 38 (1):109–25.

Sanders, W., and Carpenter, M. 1998. Internationalization and firm governance: The roles of CEO compensation, top team composition and board structure. *Academy of Management Journal* 41:158–78.

Sawhney, M., Gulati, R., and Paoni, A. 2001. *Tech-Venture: New Rules on Value and Profit from Silicon Valley*. New York: John Wiley.

Schein, E. 1985. *Organization, Culture and Leadership*. San Francisco: Jossey-Bass.

Scott, W. R. 1995. *Institutions and Organizations*. Thousand Oaks, CA: Sage.

Senge, P. M., and Carstedt, G. 2001. Innovating our way to the next industrial revolution. *MIT Sloan Management Review* (winter):24–38.

Senge, P. M., Kleiner, A., Roberts, C., Ross, R., Roth, R., and Smith, B. 1999. *The Dance of Change: The Challenges to Sustaining Momentum in Learning Organizations*. New York: Doubleday-Random House.

Sharma, S. 2000. Managerial interpretations and organizational context as predictors of corporate choice of environmental strategy. *Academy of Management Journal* 43 (4):681–97.

Sharma, S. 2001. Stakeholder integration and corporate sustainability strategy: A dynamic capability perspective. Paper presented to the Woodlands Conference, January. Houston Advanced Research Centre, Houston, Texas.

Sharma, S., and Vredenburg, H. 1998. Proactive corporate environmental strategy and the development of competitively valuable organizational capabilities. *Strategic Management Journal* 19:729–53.

Shiva, V. 2002. *Water Wars: Privatization, Pollution and Profit*. Toronto: Between the Lines.

Shrivastava, P. 1995. Ecocentric management for a risk society. *Academy of Management Review* 20:118–37.

Stacey, R. 1992. *Managing Chaos: Dynamic Business Strategies in an Unpredictable World*. London: Kogan Page.

Stacey, R. 1993. Strategy as order emerging from chaos. *Long Range Planning* 26 (1):10–17.

Stacey, R. 1995. The science of complexity: An alternative perspective for strategic change processes. *Strategic Management Journal* 16 (6):477–95.

Starbuck, W., and Milliken, F. 1988. Executives' perceptual filters: What they notice and how they make sense. In D. Hambrick (ed.), *The Executive Effect: Concepts and Methods for Studying Top Executives*. Greenwich, CT: JAI.

Starik, M., and Marcus, A. A. 2000. Introduction to the special research forum on the management of organizations in the natural environment: A field emerging from multiple paths, with many challenges ahead. *Academy of Management Journal* 43 (4):539–46.

Starik, M., and Rands, G. P. 1995. Weaving an integrated web: Multi-level and multi-system perspectives of ecologically sustainable organizations. *Academy of Management Review* 20:908–35.

Stewart, T. A. 1997. *Intellectual Capital: The New Wealth of Organizations*. New York: Doubleday.

Stiglitz, J. E. 2002. *Globalization and its Discontents*. New York: W. W. Norton.

Svendsen, A. C., Boutilier, R. G., Abbott, R. M., and Wheeler, D. 2001. Measuring the value of stakeholder relationships. Part 1. Vancouver: Simon Fraser University.

Tallman, S. 2001. Global strategic management. In M. A. Hitt, R. E. Freeman, and J. S. Harrison (eds.), *Handbook of Strategic Management*. Oxford: Blackwell.

Tapscott, D., Ticoll, D., and Lowy, A. 2000. *Digital Capital: Harnessing the Power of Business Webs*. Boston: Harvard Business School Press.

Teece, D. J. 2000. *Managing Intellectual Capital: Organizational, Strategic and Policy Dimensions*. Oxford: Oxford University Press.

Teece, D. J., Pisano, G., and Shuen, A. 1997. Dynamic capabilities and strategic management. *Strategic Management Journal* 18 (7):509–33.

Thompson, J. D. 1967. *Organizations in Action: Social Science Bases of Administrative Theory*. New York: McGraw-Hill.

Tidd, J., Bessant, J., and Pavitt, K. 2001. *Managing Innovation: Integrating Technological, Market and Organizational Change*. Chichester: John Wiley.

Trompenaars, F., and Hampden-Turner, C. 1998. *Riding the Waves of Culture: Understanding Cultural Diversity in Global Business*. New York: McGraw-Hill.

Waddock, S. A., and Graves, S. 1997. The corporate social performance-financial performance link. *Strategic Management Journal* 19:303–17.

Watson, Wyatt 2000. Human Capital Index. Survey Report.

Watts, P., and Holme, R. 1999. *Meeting Changing Expectations: Corporate Social Responsibility*. Geneva: World Business Council on Sustainable Development.

Weick, K. E. 1979. *The Social Psychology of Organizing*. Reading, MA: Addison-Wesley.

Welford, R. J. (ed.). 1997. *Corporate Environmental Management 2: Culture and Organizations*. London: Earthscan.

Wernerfeld, B. 1984. A resource-based view of the firm. *Strategic Management Journal* 5:171–80.

Wheatley, M. 1992. *Leadership and the New Science*. San Francisco: Berrett-Koehler.

Wheeler, D., and Sillanpää, M. 1997. *The Stakeholder Corporation*. London: Pitman.

Wheeler, D., and Sillanpää, M. 1998. Including the stakeholders: The business case. *Long Range Planning* 31 (2):201–10.

Wheeler, D., Colbert, B., and Freeman, R. E. 2002b. The creation of value in the new economy: Reconciling social responsibility, sustainability and a stakeholder approach to business. Paper presented at the Academy of Management Conference, Denver, August.

Wheeler, D., Fabig, H., and Boele, R. 2002a. Paradoxes and dilemmas for aspiring stakeholder responsive firms in the extractive sector – lessons from the case of Shell and the Ogoni. *Journal of Business Ethics* 39 (3):297–318.

Wheeler, D., Rechtman, R., Fabig, H., and Boele, R. 2001. Shell, Nigeria and the Ogoni: A study in unsustainable development. Vol. 3. Analysis and implications of Royal Dutch/Shell Group Strategy. *Sustainable Development* 9 (4):177–96.

Wheeler, D., Sutherland, N., and Kelly, B. 2000. Corporate strategy and sustainability in business: A North American review. *Proceedings ERP Environment Conference on Eco-Management and Auditing*. Manchester, July.

Williamson, O. E. 1975. *Markets and Hierarchies*. New York: Free Press.

Wind, Y., Mahajan, V., and Gunther, R. E. 2002. *Convergence Marketing: Strategies for Reaching the New Hybrid Consumer*. London: FT Prentice Hall.

World Commission on Environment and Development 1987. *Our Common Future*. Oxford: Oxford University Press.

World Resources Institute, United Nations Environment Program and World Business Council for Sustainable Development 2002. *Tomorrow's Markets: Global Trends and their Implications for Business*. Washington: WRI.

Yoshimori, M. 1995. Whose company is it? The concept of the corporation in Japan and the West. *Long Range Planning* 28 (4):33–44.

Zietsma, C., and Vertinsky, I. B. 2002. Shades of green: Cognitive framing and the dynamics of corporate environmental response. In P. N. Nemetz (ed.), *Bringing Business on Board: Sustainable Development and the B-School Curriculum*. Vancouver: JBA.

10

Integrating Work and Personal Life: Leadership Past, Present, and Future

SUZAN LEWIS

Work–family or work–personal-life issues have become hot topics in organizations in recent years. However, the question of how people can make optimum contributions to employing organizations without sacrificing personal life has evolved over more than four decades, as new social and organizational challenges have presented themselves. This has also involved evolving leadership challenges. Leadership in relation to work–personal-life integration has developed in a number of guises. They include leadership within organizations (those who lead debate, action, and practice within organizations); leadership by organizations (organizations that have been at the leading edge in terms of work–personal-life strategies); and leadership beyond organizations that impacts on the way people work (forces beyond the organization that lead to change in the workplace).

This chapter first looks back at work–family debates and developments over the past few decades, identifying the leadership by, within, and beyond organizations that has helped the field to evolve so far, as well as the barriers to further progress. It is then argued that the current context of globalization, changes in the nature of work, and increasingly blurred boundaries between work and personal life present unique new challenges to all forms of leadership in this field. There is a need for new and innovative thinking about work practices and cultures in order to sustain organizations, families, and communities in the future. While earlier initiatives have come mainly from large organizations, it is suggested that smaller organizations and teams within large corporations may be the leaders of future change.

The Evolution of Work–Personal Life Issues and Organizational Responses

Concern about the integration of work and family began in the 1960s, stimulated by the influx of women, especially mothers, into all areas of the labor market. While some women had always worked outside the home, particularly in female "niches," women were now entering workplaces designed primarily for men, without family obligations other than as providers. Men were slower to take on more family work and thus women were usually working a "double shift" of paid work (whether full or part time) and family work. Early discussion about "managing" work and family therefore focused on women, especially employed mothers, and this was initially treated as an individual or household issue rather than a workplace concern. This trend was reflected in research examining the impact of maternal employment on families and on women's own stress and well-being. However, accumulating evidence that work–family stress is a potential but not an inevitable consequence of multiple roles, that men as well as women need to integrate work and family roles, and that the outcomes can, in the right circumstances, be very positive, led to a call for organizations to change in recognition of employees' complex lives (see Lewis and Cooper 1999). This heralded the development of what became known as family friendly employment policies (or work–family, and later, work–life policies), developed ostensibly to enhance well-being and equal opportunities, but, in reality, largely driven by business concerns such as recruitment and retention.

Leadership

Leadership within Organizations

Leadership within organizations for the development of policies and practices to support work–personal-life integration came primarily from those with responsibility for human resources, equal opportunities, and/or, diversity. In the United States many large companies appointed these leaders as work–life managers, which marked the beginning of the development of a whole work–life profession – people working within organizations as work–family or work–life champions together with a growing consultancy sector offering support on these issues. Elsewhere work–life has not become so specifically delineated as a sector, though some HR or personnel professionals have come to specialize in work–life issues. Work–life or HR professionals in this field made considerable progress in putting work–life issues on company agendas, in some cases developing childcare or other family care support, especially in countries where public childcare provision is minimal. They also developed a range of flexible working arrangements; that is, organizational policies and practices that enable employees to vary, at least to some extent, when and/or where they work or to otherwise diverge from traditional working hours. They include, for example, flexitime, term-time working, part-time or reduced hours, job sharing, career breaks, family related and other leaves, compressed workweeks and teleworking. Some organizations have been highly innovative in their development of such policies and practices; others are more cautious. Champions within organizations have worked to change the agenda from one of "helping" employed mothers to addressing business issues of how to recruit, retain, and support women and men with family obligations and other nonwork involvements.

Nevertheless, it is debatable whether identifying a work–life leadership sector within organizations remains the way forward or whether this may have prevented work–personal life issues becoming a mainstream concern. Work–life tends to remain in the "HR ghetto" and as such is seen primarily as a people issue rather than as both a people and a strategic business issue. As such, family friendly policies are often marginalized (Hochschild 1997; Lewis 1997, 2001; Bond et al. 2002). Some formal HR policies are likely to be necessary, but are not sufficient to bring about more fundamental organizational change (Rapoport et al. 2002).

Leadership by Organizations: Leading Edge Organizations?

Largely as a consequence of these champions within organizations some employers saw the potential benefits of having a program of family friendly or work–life policies, not least, the PR benefits. These PR benefits, which also impact on recruitment, have been reinforced by national or high profile awards for the most family friendly companies in, for example, the UK, USA, and Japan. Those organizations, which were in the forefront of these developments, became constructed as leading edge companies which others sought to follow and learn from.

It appears to have been easier for work–life champions to succeed in terms of policy development in certain types of organizations, especially larger organizations in the public sector and in the finance and service sector. This has been explained using institutional theory. The institutional theory approach begins with the basic assumption that there is growing institutional pressure on employers to develop work–family arrangements. It is argued that changes in the demographics of the workforce have increased the salience of work–family issues, and that public attention to these issues and/or state regulations have heightened institutional pressures on employers to be responsive to the increasing need for employees to be able to integrate work and family life (Goodstein 1994). Variability in organizational responses to these normative pressures is explained by differences in visibility of companies and in the extent to which social legitimacy matters to them. Hence public sector and large private sector organizations are most likely to develop policies because of concern about their public image (Bardoel, Tharenou, and Moss 1998; Ingram and Simons 1995; Morgan and Milliken 1992; Wood 1999; Forth et al. 1997; Hogarth et al. 2000). Within the private sector, arrangements are more common in the service and financial sector compared to construction and manufacturing, which may be related to economic or demographic factors. It is usually believed that having more women in the workforce creates internal pressure for developing work–life policies. However, research findings on the influence of proportion of women in the workforce are mixed. Some studies find that proportion of women in the workforce is associated with likelihood of adopting flexible working arrangements and work–family policies such as childcare (Bardoel, Tharenou, and Moss 1998; Glass and Fujimoto 1995; Goodstein 1994); while this relationship is not found in other studies (Ingram and Simons 1995; Morgan and Milliken 1992.) This may depend on the status of women, and women's leadership role as there is evidence that organizations with a relatively large share of women managers seem to provide work–family arrangements more often than organizations where women's employment consists mainly of lower-skilled jobs (Glass and Fujimoto 1995; Ingram and Simons 1995).

Whatever the factors associated with the development of innovative work–life policies, institutional pressures are also exerted when some companies within one sector begin to introduce work–family arrangements (Goodstein 1994). Hence those organizations that are the first in their sector to introduce work–life policies or to be particularly innovative in this respect become leaders, providing models for others to follow or adapt.

Leadership beyond Organizations

Government and also international institutions can provide leadership in the evolution of work–personal-life initiatives, by regulation or encouragement and by indicating the importance of valuing family and personal life. In Europe in particular there has been much debate on the relative leadership roles and responsibilities of employers and the state in enabling employees to reconcile work and family life. Thus the focus on the need for employer family friendly, or work–family arrangements has been against a backdrop of statutory provisions. This has been much influenced by the European Union (Lewis and Smithson 2001). Similarly the International Labour Organization (ILO) has influenced work–personal-life interventions in Australia. The ILO Convention 156, on Workers with Family Responsibilities, was ratified in Australia in 1990 and came into force in 1991, resulting in a number of legislative reforms to support work and family (Squirchuk and Bourne 2000).

As a consequence of leadership at these supranational and also national levels, social policy, such as the statutory provision of childcare and legislation to support work and family integration, varies cross-nationally and this impacts on organizations. For example, where there is good public provision of childcare the need for employer provided dependent care initiatives is reduced, while parental leave regulation at the national level can reduce the need for individual organizational provisions, especially if this is paid leave, supported by the state.[1] It reduces the scope for some employers to gain competitive edge from introducing such policies, but does provide a floor of rights so that parental leave or other benefits are available to all and not just those working in "leading edge" corporations (although, as with organizational policies, there is often a low take-up rate, particularly among men). Legislation may also help to create a normative climate that gives rise to higher expectations of employer support (Lewis and Lewis 1996; Lewis and Smithson 2001). Edleman (1990) argued, "when a new law provides the public with new expectations or new bases for criticizing organizations, or when the law enjoys considerable societal support, apparent non-compliance is likely to engender loss of public approval" (Edelman 1990, 1406). Social policies such as the provision or absence of publicly provided childcare also contributes to institutional pressures on organizations to take account of work–family issues. Evidence from a five country European study of young workers' orientations to work and family suggests that supportive state policies including legislation and public childcare provision can enhance young people's sense of being entitled to expect support for integration of work and family, not just from the state but also from employers (Lewis and Smithson 2001), which may increase internal as well as external pressures on organizations.

There has been some debate about whether statutory entitlements and provisions encourage employers to implement more voluntary flexible working arrangements and other work–family policies, thus playing a leadership role, or whether these provisions absolve employers from responsibility for employees' nonwork lives (Evans 2000; Brewster et al. 1993). Cross-national research suggests that both may be true to some extent. Dependent care policies are less relevant in, for example, the Nordic countries where public provision of childcare is high and statutory leave rights are generous, although some employers still supplement public provisions (Brewster et al. 1993; Evans 2000). Elsewhere employers may introduce voluntary provisions to compensate for lack of state provision However, organizations in countries with a higher level of statutory provisions do not have to give so much consideration to providing support for childcare or parental leaves and are therefore free to focus on flexible ways of organizing work. Indeed, it has been suggested that the need to organize work to accommodate family leaves can oblige employers to develop such flexibility (Kivimaki 1998).

Drivers of Change: The Business Case

The most influential argument used by champions of work–personal-life initiatives is the business case; that is, the argument that the development of flexible working arrangements and dependent care policies is cost effective, having a positive impact on recruitment, retention, turnover, and other work related variables (Bardoel, Tharenou, and Moss 1998; Bevan et al. 1999; Prutchno, Litchfield, and Fried 2000). The evidence to support this argument is mixed (Kossek and Ozeki 1999) but it does seem that formal policies can have a positive impact on organizations as well as individual employees if they are well implemented and provide employees who do not normally have flexibility in their working hours with some control over their working time (Lewis 2003). Despite this potential business argument, formal family friendly workplace policies have developed unevenly (Forth et al. 1997; Hogarth et al. 2000). Moreover, the effectiveness of HR work–family policies depends on good implementation, the supportiveness of line managers and a supportive culture.

Barriers to Real Change

Conversely, organizational systems, practices, and cultures can constitute powerful barriers to effectiveness of formal work–personal-life initiatives and hence to their business advantages. Even when formal policies are available in workplaces, there is often an implementation gap between formal policy and informal practice, and take-up is often low, particularly among men. Opportunities for flexible working are not always well communicated (Bond et al. 2002). Often employees with most need for flexibility are unaware of the possibilities (Lewis, Kagan, and Heaton 2000). Even if policies are well communicated many employees have a low sense of entitlement to make use of policies, which are regarded as favors and as individual accommodations while standard ways of working remain the norm

(Lewis 1997; Lewis and Smithson 2001). Formal policies are also increasingly undermined by trends such as job insecurity, which creates reluctance to take up opportunities for flexible or alternative forms of work (Lewis and Cooper 1999).

Organizational culture or climate is a crucial variable contributing to the outcomes of flexible working arrangements, especially when these are formulated as "family friendly" rather than productivity measures (Lewis, 1997, 2001; Lewis et al. 2002; Bailyn 1993; Hochschild 1997; Friedman and Johnson 1996; Fried 1998). In this context aspects of culture such as the overvaluing of long working hours and undervaluing or marginalization of part-time workers and other alternative forms of work can coexist with more surface manifestations of work–life support such as work–life policies (Perlow 1998; Lewis 1997, 2001; Cooper et al. 2001; Lewis et al. 2002; Bailyn 1993; Rapoport et al. 2002). Aspects of organizational cultures that militate against work–personal-life policies are highly gendered (Rapoport et al. 2002). Assumptions such as the association of long working hours with commitment privilege a "male" definition of commitment based on the assumed separation of the public and private spheres, but serves the needs of neither women nor men and undermines possibilities for work–life integration. For example, in a study of accountants in Britain it emerged that some working hours are valued more than others (Lewis et al. 2002). Those accountants who work from nine to six, or even ten until seven, are considered committed workers, while those who work from eight until five, or seven until four, are regarded as virtually part-timers because they "go home early." Thus some nonwork activities such as taking children to school (which fathers often do) are legitimized, while others such as spending time with children after school are not. Taking children to school is viewed as something that can be done en route to paid work, by implication the primary role, while collecting children from school (more often done by women) is perceived as implying that family is the primary activity.

Supervisory support is a critical aspect of organizational climate that is essential for policies to be effective in practice (Thomas and Ganster 1995; Goff, Mount, and Jamison 1990) but it is not always forthcoming, and many employees feel that taking up opportunities for flexible working will be career limiting (Cooper et al. 2001; Perlow 1998; Bailyn 1993; Lewis et al. 2002). In many occupations, especially at professional and managerial levels "strong players" are regarded as those who do not need to modify hours of work for personal reasons; hence flexible working arrangements and those who make use of them are marginalized.

Thus despite the evolution of an increasingly wide range of formal work–personal-life initiatives and flexible working arrangements, the reality is that for many white collar workers working hours have extended rather than contracted and it remains necessary to work in ways that are difficult to integrate with personal life in order to advance in careers. For other workers, working hours may have remained constant but there is an intensification of work (Burchall et al. 1999). That is, more and more work must be completed in less and less time. In the modern economy, call centers epitomize this trend. In this context it is energy rather than time that is depleted. Thus both time and energy for family, community, and other aspects of personal life are compromised by current trends, notwithstanding the development of HR policies on work–personal-life integration.

New Challenges

It is evident that formal work–family or work–life policies are necessary but not sufficient to bring about the fundamental changes that will enable workers to integrate their
work and nonwork lives in gender equitable ways. More fundamental shifts in workplace
practices, and the values and assumptions that underpin them, are required. A major
question facing researchers and practitioners in this field, therefore, is how to move
beyond the current impasse by influencing workplace *practices*, structures, and cultures.

Furthermore, recent trends in working hours and the permeability of work–family
boundaries create new challenges for integrating employment with family life or other
activities. As time expands in the global 24-hour marketplace and space and distance are
compressed by information and communication technology, temporal and spatial boundaries between paid work and personal life have become increasingly blurred. This may
bring new opportunities and horizons for the most highly educated and skilled workers to
work when and where they choose, but it also presents new challenges. For some, work
is increasingly interesting, absorbing, and challenging, but it can also encroach into all of
workers' time and space, crowding out personal life and obligations. Flexible working
arrangements are less relevant in this context than workplace culture and practices. Perlow
(1998) has argued that work–life policies developed in the 1980s and 1990s were designed
for a different workforce. Flexible working policies and the view that work–life conflict
can be reduced by providing workers with flexibility were applicable to workers in
industrial times who were "managed by the clock" and lacked control over their working
hours. While some continue to work in this way, this is not the case among the growing
numbers of knowledge workers in postindustrial times, who are, Perlow contends, managed not by the clock, but by organizational culture. Based on a study of engineers,
Perlow demonstrates the ways in which managers use organizational culture to control
subordinates' boundaries between work and personal lives, by the various ways in which
they "cajole, encourage, coerce or otherwise influence the amount of time employees
spend visibly at the workplace" (Perlow 1998, 329).

The "use" of workplace culture in this way is based on the prevailing assumption that
only those who are working long hours are committed or productive. This obscures the
value of alternative, and often more efficient, ways of working that workers often develop
in order to meet the competing demands of work and nonwork responsibilities (Lewis
1997; Perlow 1998; Rapoport et al. 2002; Lewis et al. 2002). On the more positive side,
however, there is some evidence of a growing trend for younger workers to reject the
culture of long working hours and to focus on the need to "have a life" beyond work
(Brannen et al. 2002; Lewis et al. 2002), which can, if supported at the workplace level,
lead to more efficient working practices. For example, in a national study of British
accountants, younger accountants who challenged the traditional culture expressed a view
that having a life beyond work should be congruent with firms' objectives, as working
shorter more focused hours is more efficient (Lewis et al. 2002). This emerging new set of
beliefs can change working practices. There is an attempt to focus on the work that has to

be done rather than time taken to do it and to respect the boundaries between work and nonwork time.

The ongoing barriers to the effectiveness of work–life policies together with the changes in the nature and experiences of work and in the needs of younger workers demand new forms of leadership to help the work–personal-life field to evolve and adapt. In the past, leadership has been mainly by and within large organizations, which have the resources to develop elaborate formal policies but have not necessarily led in terms of actual practice. The new leadership could emerge from small organizations and smaller units within large corporations, which can contribute to the more transformational organizational learning needed in the current context.

The New Leadership? Smaller Organizations and Work Teams

It is often argued that small businesses do not have the resources to implement work–life policies, with an implication that they are less advanced in terms of work–personal-life strategies than large corporations. Recent research, however, suggests that this may be an oversimplification. There is some indication that smaller organizations are more likely than larger ones to develop informal practices that are often implemented in an *ad hoc* way to meet the needs of individual employees (Cooper et al. 2001; Dex and Schreibl 2001; Bond et al. 2002).

Dex and Shreibl (2001) describe a range of formal and informal arrangements that were introduced in small businesses in Britain, in response to institutional, business, and economic pressures as well as ethical concerns. They found that small organizations were more hesitant about introducing flexibility and were particularly concerned about costs, but it was also in the small businesses compared to large businesses in their study that attempts were made to introduce a culture of flexibility; for example, encouraging employees to cover for each other. Lack of formalization of policies in small businesses could be associated with inequity. On the other hand, formal policies in larger organizations are not necessarily applied in an equitable or consistent way (Lewis 1997; Cooper et al. 2001; Lewis et al. 2002; Powell and Mainiero 1999; Bond et al. 2002), and there is some evidence that employees in small organizations with informal practices can feel more supported than those in large organizations with a coherent program of policies but difficulties in practice (Cooper et al. 2001).

There remains a need for certain formal entitlements for workers in small and large organizations to integrate work and personal life. For example, rights for part-time workers, which may be provided by national legislation or organizational policies. Within this context, however, the focus on practices in small businesses or teams within larger companies may suggest new ways forward. Clearly practices adopted in small organizations cannot be directly transferred, and indeed small organizations can struggle to sustain informal practices as they grow. However, there is evidence that changes can occur at the level of workgroups within larger organizations, which then have the potential to bring about deeper change if they are more widely diffused.

Achieving Change at the Level of Work Teams

Working collaboratively with work teams to examine assumptions underpinning working practices that make it difficult to integrate work and personal life can lead to a rethinking of the ways in which everyday work is performed and have very positive organizational as well as personal consequences. This is one of the conclusions reached by Rhona Rapoport and her colleagues based on a program of action research, which they call collaborative interactive action research (CIAR) in a range of US organizations (Rapoport et al. 2002).

Based on a dual agenda approach that aims to enhance both organizational effectiveness and work–personal-life integration, the CIAR process involves identifying, examining, and challenging traditional assumptions which can support work practices that are inefficient and ineffective in the current work environment – but are often internalized as the norm and therefore not questioned. The method focuses on the way work is done. It involves surfacing and challenging entrenched organizational norms and highlighting the way those norms can undermine the work as well as the people who do it. Collaboration is crucial at every stage, leading to the collaborative identification of leverage points for change and the piloting, implementation, and monitoring of appropriate interventions. Such interventions are specific to that team context. The process, but not the solution, is transferable.

Case Study

The initial stages of this CIAR approach is being used with a group of accountants in Britain. This is a consequence of a national study indicating that although there are a range of highly developed "work–life" policies in larger accountancy firms, employees in these firms generally report low feelings of support and are often reluctant to take up policies because they are perceived as career limiting. In order to gain a better understanding of the factors undermining these policies a decision was made to work with a cross-functional work team serving one client, to examine the working practices that make it difficult to integrate work and personal life, the assumptions underpinning these practices and the consequences for organizational effectiveness. Three major sets of assumptions have been identified as perpetuating a culture of the inevitability of long and inflexible working hours. These are as follows.

Assumptions about client relations, professionalism and "super pleasing the client"

It is assumed that the clients' demands must take priority at all times. This is often discussed in terms of "super pleasing" the client. This is related to the idea of being willing to "go the extra" which is also widely discussed as an indicator of professionalism and commitment. Super pleasing could include doing more than the client asked for, or fitting in with their unrealistic timelines. Thus it is accepted that personal time is sacrificed in the interests of super pleasing the client and being "professional." Often clients are late in providing information, which means that team members may have to work all night to meet account deadlines. There is a great deal of talk about team working but the client is not constructed as an equal member of the team with responsibilities as well as rights. It is considered unprofessional to "hassle" the client for the information earlier. Hence work schedules are unpredictable and chaotic, which benefits neither the client nor the team ultimately.

Assumptions about time

There is an assumption that all working time can be, and is, accurately recorded in time sheets, which obscures a great deal of invisible working time. In theory time sheets should make it easy to schedule and account for working hours, but there are a number of informal/cultural processes whereby a norm of longer hours is sustained. There are both explicit rules and also implicit norms about how to complete time sheets. The explicit rhetoric is that all work on a particular account must be charged to that client, to ensure that this is reflected in billing. The informal norm however is that any hours that are in excess of what has been estimated in the budget will not be recorded. Thus internalization of the high standards of professionalism can result in extra hours of work, which are then regarded as a "choice" rather than a reflection of heavy workloads or unrealistic budgets.

Some of the assumptions about time are contradictory. For example, an assumption that long hours represent effort and productivity conflicts with the belief that not recording all hours worked makes people look more efficient. This reflects the contradictory assumptions underpinning visible and invisible work, which imply that people should be seen to be working long hours but should not record, and especially charge for, all hours worked.

Again the consequence is that working hours are extended. It also means that the firm is not charging for all hours worked, which the team recognizes is inefficient.

Assumptions about flexibility and trust

Despite the emphasis on professionalism in this context and the common practice of working more hours than are recorded, it is surprising to find that there is a low level of trust in the team with regard to flexible forms of work. Managers feel they have to manage by what they called "doing the wander" (walking around) in order to see that everybody is working, and there is a view that people might not be trusted to work at home or flexibly because they cannot be monitored in this way. This is exacerbated by the belief in the need for constant availability to client. This perpetuates inflexible forms of working, unnecessarily, and obscures opportunities for more innovative working practices.

This study continues at the time of writing but the interventions under consideration by the team include involving the client as part of the team to avoid unnecessary deadlines, looking at alternative ways of accounting for time, and piloting a flexibility scheme based on mutual trust.

This approach is much more labor intensive than implementing HR policies but has the potential to get to the cause of working patterns that are inimical to family life and meet a dual agenda of organizational effectiveness and work to personal-life integration. The challenge will then be to diffuse outcomes of this process more widely within and between organizations. It is the process not the outcome that must be diffused. Work teams that go through this process may thus become the new leaders in the next phase of the evolution of work to personal-life initiatives.

Diffusion of Experience and Organizational Learning

A key question for future research concerns how organizations can ensure that the learning of work teams or small units is diffused more widely. This will depend on effective processes of organizational learning. One study (Lee, McDermid, and Buck 2000) examined the organizational learning that took place in relation to responses to managerial and professional workers' requests for reduced hours of work and may be relevant to this question. They found three different paradigms of organizational learning in this situation: accommodation, elaboration, and transformation. Accommodation involves making individual adaptions to meet the needs of specific employees, usually as a retention measure but not involving any broader changes. Indeed, efforts are made to contain and limit this different way of working, rather than using this as an opportunity for developing policies or broader changes in working practices. In other organizations with formal policies on flexible working backed up by a well-articulated view of the advantages to the organization, *elaboration* takes place. This goes beyond random individual responses to a request for flexibility where full-time employees are still the most valued, as employers make efforts to contain and systematize procedures for experimenting with new ways of working. In the *transformation* paradigm of organizational learning, alternative ways of working are viewed as an opportunity to learn how to adapt managerial and professional jobs to the changing conditions of the global marketplace. The concern of employers is to experiment and learn. These emergent paradigms were considered by Lee, McDermid, and Buck (2000) to be representative of more general organizational variability in response to changes in the external environment or challenges to the status quo. A key challenge for work–personal-life leadership in the future may be to ensure that the learning that occurs in small units, whether as a result of policy implementation, everyday practice, or more interventive action research, can be used in a transformational way as a strategy for responding to key business issues.

Conclusions

New forms of organizational leadership are needed to move beyond work–personal-life policies to practice and to bring work–personal-life issues from the margins to the mainstream. Recent research suggests that collaborative styles of leadership, focusing on working practices in small organizations or work groups, aiming for systemic changes with a dual agenda of workplace effectiveness and gender equity, and providing opportunities for transformational organizational leadership offer a way forward. The challenge now is not only to work with small businesses and teams to effect change, but to diffuse these changes more broadly within larger organizations so that work–personal-life practices can really make a difference to individual employees, organizations, families, and communities. As this will take time some external leadership at the level of public and/or organizational policy is likely to continue to be necessary to provide a basic floor of rights for all employees, as a basis for more fundamental change processes to take place at the workplace level.

NOTES

1   Paid parental leave is an entitlement in many European states and in some countries, particularly in Scandinavia, fathers as well as mothers are encouraged to take up this entitlement (Brannen et al. 2002; Deven and Moss 2002). Maternity but not parental leave (for either parent) is paid in the UK and parental leave is unpaid in the USA.

REFERENCES

Bailyn, L. 1993. *Breaking the Mold: Women, Men and Time in the New Corporate World.* New York: Free Press.

Bardoel, E. A., Tharenou, P., and Moss, S. A. 1998. Organizational predictors of work–family practices. *Asia Pacific Journal of Human Resources* 36 (3):31–50.

Bevan, S., Dench, S., Tamkin, P., and Cummings, J. 1999. *Family Friendly Employment: The Business Case.* London: DfEE Research Report RR136.

Bond, S., Hyman, J., Summers, J., and Wise, S. 2002. *Family Friendly Working? Putting Policy into Practice.* York: Joseph Rowntree Foundation.

Brannen, J., Lewis, S., Nielson, A., and Smithson, J. 2002. *Young Europeans, Work and Family: Futures in Transition.* London: Routledge.

Brewster, C., Hegwisch, A., Lockhart, L., and Mayne, L. 1993. *Issues in People Management: Flexible Working Patterns in Europe* 6. London: IPD.

Burchall, B., Day, D., Hudson, M., Lapido, D., Nolan, J., Reed, H., Wichert, I., and Wilkinson, E. 1999. *Job Insecurity and Work Intensification: Flexibility and the Changing Boundaries of Work.* York: Joseph Rowntree Foundation.

Cooper, C. L., Lewis, S., Smithson, J., and Dyer, J. 2001. *Flexible Futures: Flexible Working and Work–Life Integration. Report on Phase One* London: ICAEW.

Deven, F., and Moss, P. 2002. Leave arrangements for parents. *Community, Work and Family* 5 (3):237–56.

Dex, S., and Schreibl, F. 2001. Flexible and family friendly working arrangements in SMEs: Business Case 2001. *British Journal of Industrial Relations* 38 (3):411–31.

Edelman, L. B. 1990. Legal environments and organizational governance: The expansion of due process in the American workplace. *American Journal of Sociology* 95 (6):1401–40.

Evans, J. E. 2000. Firms' contribution to the reconciliation between work and family life: Experiences in OECD countries. Paper presented at the Seminar on Family-Friendly Employment organized by the Family Policies Studies Centre, November, London.

Forth, J., Lissenburgh, S., Callender, C., and Millward, N. 1997. *Family Friendly Working Arrangements in Britain, 1996.* London: DfEE Research Report 16.

Fried, M. 1998. *Taking Time: Parental Leave Policy and Corporate Culture.* Philadelphia: Temple University Press.

Friedman, D. E., and Johnson, A. A. 1996. Moving from programs to culture change: The next stage for the corporate work–family agenda. In S. Parasuraman and J. H. Greenhaus (eds.), *Integrating Work and Family: Challenges and Choices for a Changing World*. Westport, CT: Quorum.

Glass, J., and Fujimoto, T. 1995. Employers' characteristics and the provision of family responsive policies. *Work and Occupation* 22 (4):380–411.

Goff, S. J., Mount, M. K., and Jamison, R. L. 1990. Employer supported child care, work/family conflict, and absenteeism: A field study. *Personnel Psychology* 43:793–809.

Goodstein, J. D. 1994. Institutional Pressures and Strategic Responsiveness: Employer Involvement in Work–Family Issues. *Academy of Management Journal* 37 (2):350–82.

Hochschild, A. 1997. *The Time Bind: When Work Becomes Home and Home Becomes Work*. New York: Henry Holt.

Hogarth, T., Hasluck, C., Pierre, G., Winterbotham, M., and Vivian, D. 2000. *Work–Life Balance 2000: Baseline Study of Work–Life Balance Practices in Great Britain*. London: DfEE.

Ingram, P., and Simons, T. 1995. Institutional and resource dependence determinants of responsiveness to work–family issues. *Academy of Management Journal* 38 (5):1466–82.

Kivimaki, R. 1998. How work is structured by the family? The impacts of parenthood on the work community. Paper presented at the Gender, Work and Organization Conference, Manchester.

Kossek, E. E., and Ozeki, C. 1999. Bridging the work–family policy and productivity gap: A literature review. *Community, Work and Family* 2 (1):7–32.

Lee, M. D., McDermid, S. M., and Buck, M. L., 2000. Organizational paradigms of reduced-load work: Accommodations, elaboration and transformation. *Academy of Management Journal* 43 (6): 1210–26.

Lewis, S. 1997. Family friendly organizational policies: A route to organizational change or playing about at the margins. *Gender, Work and Organization* 4:13–23.

Lewis, S. 2001. Restructuring workplace cultures: The ultimate work–family challenge? *Women in Management Review* 16 (1):21–9.

Lewis, S. 2003. Flexible working arrangements: Implementation, outcomes and management. In I. T. Robertson and C. L. Cooper (eds.), *Annual Review of Industrial and Organizational Psychology*. John Wiley, Chichester.

Lewis, S., and Cooper, C. L. 1999. The work–family research agenda in changing contexts. *Journal of Occupational Health Psychology* 4:4382–93.

Lewis, S., and Lewis, J. 1996. Work family conflict: Can the law help? *Legal and Criminological Psychology* 2:155–67.

Lewis, S., and Smithson, J. 2001. Sense of entitlement to support for the reconciliation of employment and family life. *Human Relations* 54 (11):1455–83.

Lewis, S., Kagan, C., and Heaton, P. 2000. Family diversity for parents of disabled children: Beyond policy to practice. *Personnel Review* 29 (3):417–31.

Lewis, S., Smithson, J., Cooper, C. L., and Dyer, J. 2002. *Flexible Futures: Flexible Working and Work–Life Integration. Report on Phase Two*. London: ICAEW.

Morgan, H., and Milliken, F. J. 1992. Keys to action: Understanding differences in organizations' responsiveness to work and family issues. *Human Resource Management* 31 (3):227–48.

Perlow, L. A. 1998. Boundary control: The social ordering of work and family time in a high tech organization. *Administrative Science Quarterly* 43:328–57.

Powell, G. N., and Mainiero, L. A. 1999. Managerial decision making regarding alternative work arrangements. *Journal of Occupational and Organizational Psychology* 72 (1):41–57.

Prutchno, R., Litchfield, L., and Fried, M. 2000. *Measuring the Impact of Workplace Flexibility*. Boston: Boston College Center for Work and Family.

Rapoport, R., Bailyn, L., Fletcher, J., and Pruitt, B. 2002. *Beyond Work–Family Balance: Advancing Gender Equity and Workplace Performance*. San Francisco: Jossey-Bass.

Squirchuk, R., and Bourne, J. 2000. From equal opportunity to family friendly policies and beyond: Gender equity in Australia. In L. Haas, P. Hwang, and G. Russell (eds.), *Organizational Change and Gender Equity: International Perspectives on Fathers and Mothers at the Workplace*. Thousand Oaks, CA: Sage.

Thomas, L., and Ganster, D. 1995. Impact of family supportive work variables on work family conflict and strain: A control perspective. *Journal of Applied Psychology* 80:6–15.

Wood, S. 1999. Family friendly management: Testing the various perspectives. *National Institute Economic Review* 168:990116.

11

Work Stress and Well-being: Mutual Challenge and Fuller Interaction

ALVIN L. GIBSON AND JAMES C. QUICK

Senior leaders in organizations involved in mergers, acquisitions, or downsizings in today's competitive global environment are faced with the need to make more decisions and respond to situations more rapidly (DeFrank and Ivancevich 1998). This need for enhanced performance occurs at a time when fewer employees regard their employment as secure, the pace of work is increasing faster than before, and flat organizational structures have become the rule in the workplace (Cooper 1998). The fact that a large fraction of organizational transformations are later deemed unsuccessful (Kupiec 2001) is an indicator that leaders' enabling resources are often not utilized effectively enough, even though efficiency increases often result (Swanson and Power 2001). Senior managers need to efficiently mobilize all available assets for major change to be successfully managed. This applies especially, because they are so often insufficiently utilized, to the organization's human resources.

In the meantime employees in these work settings are in critical need of resources, too. Employees need early preparation and high levels of knowledge to be most advantageous to themselves and the organization during dynamic periods (Tang and Crofford 1999). When these are lacking, employees suffer. A chief indicator of insufficient resources and decreased well-being for employees during periods of merging, acquisitions, and downsizing is high levels of work stress (Begley 1998; Swanson and Power 2001).

The purpose of this chapter is to explore conditions that involve work stress and well-being during downsizings, mergers, and acquisitions. The two sections are, first, causes of work stress and, second, positive actions and preventive management of work stress. In the first section the concept of mutual challenge will be introduced as a means for leaders to initiate the process of uncovering work stress causes. In the second section fuller interaction is mentioned as a climate within which positive actions and preventive management may prevent future work stress.

Causes of Work Stress During Turbulent Times

Cartwright and Hudson (2000) introduced categories of work stressors specifically related to mergers, acquisitions, or downsizings. These stressors are associated with the following:

1. *Survival*: fears about layoff, relocation, lower status positions, lessened pay, changes in responsibility, and less desirable career paths.
2. *Loss of identity and uncertainty*: feelings of detachment, bereavement, reactions to delayed change, information insufficiency, information overload, reduced resilience.
3. *Changed working arrangements*: increased workloads of survivors due to smaller overall worker base, departure of many of the most efficient employees, training needs of new transferees, new reward systems, and supervisors who use different work methods.
4. *Changed relationships*: adapting to new peers and supervisors, different norms, old colleagues as source of conflicting and negative rumors.
5. *Acculturation*: disruptive tension experienced by members of one culture when they are required to interact with another culture and adopt its ways; this problem is more pronounced with cross-national mergers and acquisitions.

The importance of the above categories is borne out by the observation that it has long been known that high levels of employee stress during critical periods can impair the job performance and organizational commitment of persons in a firm (Parasuraman and Alutto 1984). Some workers, de-energized because of high stress, tend to be disengaged from their tasks. Others, negatively energized, may retaliate against management (Mishra and Spreitzer 1998). They feel threatened by the organizational change, and have increased levels of absenteeism (McGarvey 1998).

The typical organizational transformation process has three periods: planning, change, and consolidation. Once the planning period begins, leaders need to be 100 percent energized toward identifying areas where employees and resources will be needed, and the nature of these resources. During the change period leaders need a rich stream of reactions and responses to important initiatives from organizational members (Lewis 1999), sometimes preferably before the initiatives are implemented. In the consolidation stage senior leaders should be able to concentrate on the return to normalcy (Klein 1996), which involves further inputs to and outputs from employees. Throughout, leaders have the need for employee inputs to evaluate the change process, while also receiving employees' evaluations of their actions. Successfully managing human resources throughout transformation can result in lessened work stress and better achievement of outcomes during mergers, acquisitions, and downsizings (Solomon 1993).

Presentation of the Mutual Challenge Concept

Mutual challenge, a process for addressing the causes of work stress and other survival issues particularly during critical periods, is a way for senior leaders to proactively support themselves and employees. It can provide a means toward later achieving purposeful and beneficial patterns of interaction throughout the organization during each of the three periods of organizational change. These fuller interaction patterns include positive actions for the preventive management of stress, which include behaviors, programs, and systems that directly or indirectly improve well-being in the workplace.

An early start for mutual challenge is strongly recommended, ideally even before, or else soon after the onset of transformational periods. An earlier start will produce more total benefit. These beneficial patterns are needed in the pre-change period after a merger, acquisition, or downsizing plan is announced (Lewis and Seibold 1993); during the change period itself, when employees' perceptions that a just process is occurring can result in minimized work stress (Rosenblatt and Schaeffer 2000); and in the post-change normalization period, when successes during the transformation may be highlighted (Klein 1996). Mutual challenge may be undertaken in addition to all formal reporting and feedback systems the organization has in place, since it is expected to add value in addition to them.

Nytro et al. (2000) highlighted the importance of process whenever efforts are made to reduce stress in organizations. They stated that, while the efforts themselves are important, the quality of the process that occurs during these efforts is equally important. One reason for this may be that a solid process affects thoughts and behaviors of leaders and employees in matters relating to fellow members of the organization and to the organization itself.

Recognizing this, mutual challenge is presented as a means to achieve strong working relationships in an organization, devoid of the immediate need to assess the benefits or value of the relationship through the use of outcome measures. That is, to allow sufficient growth the relationships outlined in mutual challenge needs to first be evaluated by using process measures such as those presented at the end of this section. Once a strong, robust, and resilient working-process-based relationship has been attained, joint projects that involve outcome measures to prevent stress may be undertaken. Some of these future efforts may succeed and some will likely fail. In the meantime, the process-based relationship, mutual challenge, is the "glue" that will sustain a setting in which both success and failure are permitted. These joint projects are the essence of fuller interaction and positive actions for preventive management, which will be presented in the second section.

While it may find its greatest profit during transformational periods, mutual challenge is intended as an enduring organizational activity. It can be a component of a larger program or include smaller initiatives having compatible process objectives. It may be used in both union and nonunion settings. Large or small organizations may benefit from it.

Leader Challenge

Mutual challenge is a process that has two components, leader challenge and employee challenge. It is based on two statements, the first to be known as the leader challenge and the second as the employee challenge. The first statement, or leader challenge, is the following: Leaders need to adopt a mindset that continually seeks more employee input. This invokes senior managers to come to a better understanding of how much employees can provide for them, and then to effectively seek to have that provided. The statement implies that managers' search for decision-making input is an open process that reaches out to employees in various ways, rather than a closed one that is limited to the top ranks (Solomon 1993). And, like the continuous improvement component of TQM, the effort to reach out never ends. Leader challenge assumes employees are a dynamic and inexhaustible source of benefit for senior managers and that therefore leaders need to keep abreast of changes in employee potential and conditions in a dynamic workplace.

In searching effectively for ways that employees can be of benefit to them, senior leaders must first find the population of possible ways that exist in their organization for employees to potentially benefit them. From this, they then select the subset of actual ways that employees would be beneficial. In some cases leaders must try out possibilities before being able to determine their degree of value. Periodically, the population of possible ways and the subset of actual ways should be updated.

Leader challenge assumes that managers' talent and decision-making prowess alone are not sufficient for steering the organization through a merger, acquisition, or downsizing. Further, it assumes that there are stress-reduction benefits to employees that may accrue to the organization as a result of a strongly performed leader challenge. Leader efforts to reach out to employees can help increase productivity and reduce stress (Solomon 1993). Overall there is an assumption of great net benefit for the organization whose leaders unreservedly reach out to employees for information and feedback.

Leader challenge ought to be answered proactively. Senior managers who currently have employee programs and practices in place are not exempt from it. Rather than having thoughts such as "We already have mechanisms that tap employee input" or "our employees are already pretty satisfied," responding to leader challenge requires senior managers to reflect and imagine "Where are we failing to utilize employees? What additional untapped resources can employees provide to help run our organization?"

In each organization the leader challenge is somewhat different. Senior leaders have different needs, employees have unique things to offer, and organizations have varying performance requirements and agendas. Every merger, acquisition, and downsizing is different. The relative needs of the organization and capabilities of senior managers and employees to meet those needs differ also (Cooper and Cartwright 1994).

As a result of these differences there are a variety of possible reasons why leaders need to hear more from employees during a merger, acquisition, or downsizing period. Employees are typically considered the organization's most important resource. The employee perspective often reflects and can sometimes generate organizational realities. Managers, then, need to be informed of the most important areas where employee perspectives do not clearly reflect the organization. Sometimes managers' perspectives themselves do not reflect organizational realities (Geber 1996), leading to a further reason why employee input is needed. In cultures where rumors abound and strongly affect organizational outcomes such as turnover and motivation, direct unfiltered employee input and feedback may become a major force related to the stability of the organization.

The need for leaders to hear from employees is usually critical during transformational periods due to increased organizational vulnerability. The range of employees' perspectives may vary widely during these periods, rather than converging. This indicates a workforce that is pulling in different directions. Senior managers need to know if this is occurring.

Leaders' decision to use more time to hear from employees can, in time, help to spawn programs and initiatives that improve employee well-being (Cartwright and Hudson 2000). There may be individual employees whose perspective or skills place them in a unique position to advise senior leaders from time to time. Additionally, empowered employees can help managers to quickly make and enact major decisions when crises arise. Energized workers can also act as "eyes and ears" to monitor the change process, rapidly reporting unexpected or undesirable trends and events.

Employee Challenge

The second component of mutual challenge, employee challenge, is based on the following statement: Employees need to adopt mindsets that provide more input for leaders. One prerequisite for effective employee challenge is that senior managers must create and provide efficient mechanisms for messages initiated by employees to reach them. Employee challenge presupposes employee access to higher-level managers and senior leaders. Workers and lower-level managers commonly experience circumstances that cannot be improved because senior managers never find out about them. The permission to initiate contacts with management, and even a list of initial steps for employees to take, may need to be provided to an underempowered workforce by senior leaders. To help the employee challenge process to start strongly, senior leaders may explain to employees that a difficult period for the organization is about to occur; show how employees will play a critical role during this period; and state that the organization needs to find out, throughout this period, how each employee can remain fully engaged in his or her changing work roles.

Employee challenge relies on the workforce body to become one that energetically and intelligently questions leaders and reaches toward entire expression of its own meaningful needs. Like senior leaders, employees must find all possible ways that senior leaders might benefit them, and then determine which to employ. Employees would be encouraged to collect their individual ideas; then, depending on the size of the organization, gather in groups to collate and discuss them. This should result in a prioritized listing of employee needs and reasons for each. Both the population scan and the process leading to the prioritized listing should be repeated periodically.

Further Mutual Challenge Aspects

It has been suggested that the success of organizational processes such as leader challenge and employee challenge largely rests on senior managers' leadership styles, two-way communication skills, and how they view organizational change (Nytro et al. 2000). Employee challenge requires senior leaders to exhibit an extra measure of faith and confidence toward workers. Doing so will enable employees to reciprocate both in attitudes and behaviors. When senior leaders withdraw from their employees during periods of transformation, they fail to provide them with proper direction and an opportunity to rise to the occasion. Employees in such a situation are likely to experience high stress.

While employees are responding to their challenge, workers likely will feel out the sincerity of management. Some employees or groups are likely to make stronger initial overtures than others. How these are handled and how that handling is perceived will have an effect on future responses. Once employees know that their upward messages, so long as these respect the employee challenge framework, will be seriously listened to and responded to and will not lead to reprisals or evaluations that affect their status with the firm, the number and variety of messages will increase.

Overall, mutual challenge is a call for leaders to develop initiatives – one to be used by themselves and one by employees – through which each more fully utilizes the resources of the other. Each challenge employs importance-weighted scans that search for ways that greater resources can be obtained. It is up to leaders to initiate both leader challenge and employee challenge. Leader challenge is based on the realization that employees have potential to help managers to make decisions and provide other important inputs. Employee challenge comes from the fact that employees can come to know that they will be listened to and be respected by senior leaders, making them the leaders of their meaningful concerns.

Mutual challenge honors process and holds that the most honorable and intelligently shepherded path during merger, acquisition, or downsizing is a joint one. It assumes a process where managers are open to managerial decision-making input from employees carries a better probability that an organization will succeed. Meanwhile, employees who meet the challenge by deciding to voice their concerns and needs fully and openly to management become part of a process that is open to unlimited growth and increased well-being. Both leader challenge and employee challenge are needed because they represent different perspectives. What leaders feel they can gain most from employees is likely to be at least moderately different from that information which employees feel their leaders need most.

Values Associated with Mutual Challenge

Mutual challenge provides that employees and senior leaders need each other. The following principles from Quick, Quick, and Nelson (1998) serve as a guide to show how leader, employee, and organization needs are tied together. They provide markers for focusing attention on work stress during mergers, acquisitions, and downsizings.

1. Individual and organizational health are interdependent.
2. Leaders have a responsibility for individual and organizational health.
3. Individual and organizational distress are not inevitable.
4. Each individual and organization reacts uniquely to stress.
5. Organizations are ever-changing, dynamic entities.

Viewed from within these values, mutual challenge is a way for leaders and workers to jointly attend to the task at hand while minimizing the pain so often suffered during mergers, acquisitions, and downsizings. It offers senior managers and employees a high standard to live up to, a way for each to justifiably help the other toward higher standards, and a means for correction and resumption of high standards when lapses occur. It can provide a framework for trying new initiatives.

Areas for Leader Challenge

The best list of possible areas where leader challenge can be beneficial is one tailored to your organization's needs. Adopting a way of thinking that continually seeks more input from employees will bring about a search for possibilities. This will lead to a wealth of ideas on how and in which areas employees can contribute potentially valuable inputs. Like improvement projects involving technology, these can be ranked in terms of value to the organization, keeping in mind that reducing employee stress is one such source of value. Unlike projects, humans need lots of feedback after their inputs are received (Perry 1999).

Improving adequacy of communication environment

Communications is one of the most potentially beneficial areas for organizational improvement (Lewis 1999) and for leader challenge. It has aspects that may be improved by employee input in a given organization. Communication can help to create an environment where most employees experience low to moderate stress in the work setting during the transformation. More than simply providing information, a goal of communication must be to gain commitment from employees (Thomson 1997). Although much or most of the total communication may occur between employees and their direct supervisors (Klein 1996), the need for leaders to receive input directly is not diminished. Employees who feel their inputs are sought and valued will experience an increase in personal power (Brott 1994).

Direct two-way communication with employees is often required when complex or difficult issues are involved. It allows leaders and employees to come to a meeting of the minds, or at least an understanding of areas where more work remains to be done. Direct communication can clarify organizational goals and help to reduce morale problems (Brott 1994). Sometimes a talk with a question-and-answer session afterward is sufficient. In other situations a roundtable forum, which affords greater opportunities for interaction, is preferable. In some settings, regular meetings can help employees to air their concerns about the work environment before they build up greatly. Simply having the chance to speak about them and knowing that leaders want to hear them can be enough to keep workers from having demoralizing thoughts and feeling the need to say negative things about the organization to co-workers (Perry 1999).

Understanding employee personal concerns

Working to achieve and maintain a high degree of comprehension of issues that are personally important to employees is important. Aloofness from employee concerns is harmful to leader challenge. Leaders who connect psychologically with their employees are able to gain credibility with employees (Goman 1997). Rather than deny that meaningful and sometimes intractable problems exist, it can be valuable to willingly receive and accept information that relates to realities of the workplace under transformation. Knowing these realities well provides an important calibration standard from which leaders can more intelligently judge the results of decisions they make and initiatives they undertake.

During change periods employees suffer many losses: company identity, close friends, previous work roles, familiar routines, and sometimes their own place in the organization. Some employees have to carry these problems back to an empty apartment. Others carry home unacceptable news of changed circumstances that later results in divorce proceedings. Some workers have to make a choice between their careers and their familiar surroundings. Others must change careers or face both career and individual failure. Many suffer a tremendous loss of self-esteem when a once-thriving organizational entity becomes barely able to support its own existence.

Part of a willing acceptance of these concerns lies in viscerally relating to them. Leaders who can "feel the pain" of the transformation will comprehend an additional dimension. Relating personally to difficulties faced by employees will enable better assessment of how the organization is faring (Solomon 1999). This hopefully will lead to purposeful decisions that manage employee pain and suffering as well as organizational performance and success. Some of the responsibility for accepting and relating to employees in this way may be borne by lower-level managers (Lewis 1999).

Listening to employees' business concerns

As part of communicating effectively with employees, leaders may need to know what employees think about how the business is doing. It can be valuable to come to know employee perceptions and beliefs regarding strengths and weaknesses of the organization, departmental units, work teams, and their own individual roles (Thomson 1997). One of the best ways to effectively assess whether this is occurring is to establish a policy of soliciting direct employee input on this issue. Some face-to-face input is likely essential for this assessment, since it is the most interactive form of communication (Klein 1996). Additionally forms of communication such as emails, letters, and telephone messages may be received from employees to elicit their viewpoints. Surveys and other systematic means of collecting employee opinions and beliefs may also be employed.

It is important for leaders to have accurate indications of the character of informal communication that is occurring in the organization. An efficient campaign to educate employees in the workplace about the transformation can be negated by misinformation and inaccurate rumors. Senior leaders who keep an ear to the ground will have an opportunity to correct these rumors (Klein 1996). In many other cases informal communication can be helpful to the organization. Understanding the underlying chaos of the workplace can aid leaders in making complex decisions (Goman 1997). For instance, an organization-wide technology initiative may be under consideration by senior leadership. If at the start, employees at different levels are placed on the committees that plan and implement this change, they can help to educate the workforce regarding it. By the time that formal communiqués about the initiative make their way to employee mailboxes the employees will have been prepared for it.

Enlisting help to establish a strong communications network

During mergers, acquisitions, and downsizings, a more extensive communications network is needed than during normalcy. This is partly because the hearts and minds of the employees need to become energized for the change to be most successful. More extensive and redundant communications are needed when it is desired that employees come to agree and identify with the change effort. The establishment of several reliable communications channels will likely be needed (Hendrickson 1989). When a message is sent over several channels in different forms, the information going through one channel should logically agree with that going through the others. The communication should be backed by congruent actions (Perry 1999).

Benefit may be derived from inquiries to find which communications channels are most used and which are most enjoyed by employees. In some cases, a letter sent to workers' homes will be perceived as formal and credible. In others it may be an intrusion. Emails do not work in some organizational settings because many individuals do not read them. In others emails are preferred means of communication.

One form of communicating that needs to be used to good effect in almost any setting is face to face. For strong credibility this is a necessary component of a communications network (Perrewe 2000). For employees, personal and meaningful contact with a senior leader can result in reduced stress (Brott 1994). With this form, the choices lie in how to best use it. One-on-one meetings with employees, auditorium meetings involving one senior leader and a large group, or meetings with a work team can be effective means of acquiring employee input.

Providing special attention to overburdened work units

Some departments or teams experience more stress then others (Geber 1996). This may occur for different reasons. For instance, a number of departments in the organization may rely on inputs or outputs from one single department in order to complete their work. This makes the single department a focal point for problems. The one department that is the bottleneck should be singled out for help. Until the process can be improved, the workers in the beleaguered unit need extra resources to keep their performance high (Geber 1996). In the meantime, for the sake of leader understanding of the organization it is important to secure and chronicle input from the work unit regarding factors causing the problem. Once the department realizes that the organization understands there is a problem and is taking action regarding it, its morale will improve (Klein 1996). Senior leaders will be able to understand the organization better when its most difficult functioning problems are documented and understood.

Providing special attention to highly stressed individuals

Some individuals experience greater amounts of stress than do others, even in similar settings. The additional stress may be attributable to a more demanding work role; different individual makeup; personal stress issues that exacerbate those at work; or other factors. While senior leaders cannot take the time to relate to the problems of individual low-level employees in a large work setting, they can anticipate these problems and delegate lower-level managers to help employees who have them. Preferably these managers should work outside the disciplinary system with these employees (Solomon 1999), so long as such employees do not break company rules and provided the employees become an active part of their own improvement. Again, it is important to document the problem for future reference.

Providing special attention to newly transferred employees

Bringing employees into a work unit during transformations, while necessary, can be disruptive to existing workers. This can be a source of organizational conflict (Brott 1994). Preexisting employees may already be in the role of survivors after a round of layoffs, quits, or early retirements. In addition, new technological implementations may be occurring in the work unit. Managing the new relationships and new responsibilities simultaneously may be more than existing employees can handle without experiencing high stress.

Leaders can help the transferees during this period by assuring they are provided with a good start (Farrant 1990). They can make sure the new persons are positively introduced into the team. It is important that the transferees feel imbued with a sense of personal power, which provides them a psychological working space to keep their stress manageable (Brott 1994). Immediately highlighting a new person's skills and how these are expected to enhance the team will provide perspective to existing team members. The work unit as a whole should be assured that it will be provided sufficient training and other resources to mitigate its other problems, allowing existing workers to have the energy to develop new relationships with the transferees. The leader should also directly introduce himself or herself to the transferees, welcoming them into the unit and assuring them that they are both needed and wanted (Solomon 1999). The new persons need to know that the organization realizes it will take time for them to reach their peak performance, and that the organization is willing to supply the resources and the time needed for this to occur (Farrant 1990). This can help get the transferees over initial jitters.

Leader challenge can enhance the benefit of transferees to the organization. Inputs from employees to leaders about the dynamics of the work unit change can be a source of leader learning. Taking time at the start to find out how employees feel and what the issues are when new transferees are involved can greatly help leaders to deal with these issues in the future. Documenting these dynamics systematically will provide the organization with data for analysis and future improvement.

Areas for Employee Challenge

The essence of employee challenge lies in the evolution of a workforce with a drive to settle for nothing less than continuous betterment of their relationship with management. Characteristics associated with this drive include a positive way of thinking, an unwillingness to hide knowledge of uncomfortable circumstances, and the belief that employees' stake in the organization's future is as great as that of leaders. When employees have a genuine interest in the organization's success, they have the potential, whether they realize it or not, to help management to make better decisions during turbulent times. When management encourages a culture of employee openness this potential can become first recognized and, over time, actualized.

For employee challenge to be successful employees must clearly convey their issues or complaints. If they are not allowed to do this, one result will be an out-of-touch management that is lowering its probability of merger, acquisition, or downsizing success. If they are repeatedly unwilling to do this, employees cannot "blame them" for failure to improve stressful working situations or to communicate effectively with the bulk of workers.

It is equally important that employees voice their satisfactions or achievements to management. They need to let the company know in detail when they like the results of decisions or when they are pleased with their work circumstances during the change. Thinking positively can be infectious. It is very important for employees to think and talk about the positive aspects of their work settings. Employees may, for example, wish to set up a bulletin board, where they can place photos and notes about the positive aspects of the workplace (Perry 1999).

Employees should also periodically convey their feelings of confidence and appreciation to management for good leadership and a strong firm. Leaving out reports of the positive aspects of their work and environment indicates an unbalanced approach to employee challenge. When good news and praise are earnestly directed toward senior leaders it is their obligation to accept them in a gracious manner, rather than dismissing the employees' sincere words as unimportant, flattery, or a means to secure future gains.

Business outlook apprehensions

When employees are afraid of how the organization will fare in the future, it can increase work stress and affect their performance (Adkins 1999). Rather than simply "live with" these fears in the face of an uncommunicative management, these fears should be conveyed upward. Management responsiveness to these fears is vital. When employees feel they are being listened to and that their input is important, they will let management know about critical problems in time to avoid damage (Perry 1999). Along with letting management know their current fears, employees should seek to know how the organization is faring during the change process. Whether the knowledge obtained seems to indicate a bright or a dismal outlook for the organization, employees in a mature workforce need accurate, complete, and current information in order to make their own decisions and draw their own conclusions.

Many issues exist that lead to employee apprehension in a turbulent framework. Some of these fears are of becoming laid off; having to become identified with a weak organization rather than a strong one; being transferred; breakup of the work unit; losing friends; and having to initiate a new career (Cartwright and Hudson 2000). A survey initiated by employees and sent upward to management can let senior leaders know there is a problem. A request for a conference between leaders and employees can serve as a means for the parties to develop respect for each other. Employees should also suggest solutions for their outlook apprehensions that are best for them.

Job control issues

Employees who experiences losses in personal control over aspects of their work should make management aware of this. Emotional distress, job dissatisfaction, and lowered self-esteem begin to appear when the amount of control over demands in the workplace starts to lessen (Sauter, Murphy, and Hurrell 1990). They should clearly inform leaders that this is occurring, explain what changes have occurred, and specifically let leaders know the effects of the changes on them. This information should also be communicated to other workers, who can help and be helped through sharing and support. Job control has been described as the greatest source of work stress during mergers, acquisitions, and downsizings (Sauter, Murphy, and Hurrell 1990). Since circumstances that threaten employees' health can be considered to threaten the health of the organization, when it is practical work should be adapted to the worker (Levi, Sater, and Shimomitsu 1999) to minimize stress. Loss in job control has been linked to depression, absenteeism, and thoughts of quitting. Even though individual employees may be able to make accommodations and adjustments to partly alleviate this problem, management should still be fully made aware that there is a problem and which adjustments have been made.

Particularly, employees should let managers know when the pace of change is too great or resources to cope with the change are inadequate. Areas of insufficiency in resources include training for new systems, quality control, time to develop new working relationships, time off work, and authority to carry out directives. During periods of rapid change employees need to inform leaders regarding what the organization needs to do to keep them physically, psychologically, and behaviorally on board and prevent them from detaching themselves from total psychological inclusion in the change effort.

The most tumultuous organizational events, such as severe downsizings, bankruptcies, and plant closings, test the health of the organization as a whole (Adkins 1999). These events are also, obviously, highly stressful to employees. However, a relationship that emphasizes quality in both upward and downward communications can minimize the harm done in even these circumstances.

Positive Actions and Preventive Management for Turbulent Times

Leading in turbulent times is one of the most challenging aspects of senior managerial work. Turbulent times may well be the most important times for senior leaders to manage work stress and enhance the well-being of all in the organization. Fuller interaction between leaders and employees during these periods is necessary both to successfully implement the change and to provide a setting for positive actions and preventive management. In this second part of the chapter we outline positive actions and preventive management strategies for senior managers. We place these in the context of the missions of psychology, as identified by the American Psychological Association's Past-President

Martin Seligman. These three missions are to build on strength, to prevent problems, and to repair damage. How can senior leaders build on strength within their organizations, prevent work stress from becoming a problem, and repair damage when it does occur? Senior managers can build on strength through positive organizational behavior (Luthans 2002). They can prevent work stress problems through preventive stress management (Quick, Quick, and Nelson 1998). Finally, they can repair damage and heal the wounded by relying on organizational heroes who metabolize the emotional toxins at work (Frost and Robinson 1999).

Positive Organizational Behavior: Strength and Support for Turbulent Times

Mutual challenge and fuller interaction are euphemisms for the two human instinctual drives for exploration and attachment. The drive for exploration leads people to seek mastery over the world in which they live, to work hard, and to achieve great things. This instinctual drive is balanced by a second and somewhat intractable drive for attachment, which leads people to seek security, safety, and reassurance. These two drives are best reflected in the two dimensions of the Job Stress Survey (JSS), recently developed and tested by Spielberger, Vagg, and Walasa (2003). The two major sources of work stress according to the JSS are job pressure and lack of organizational support. The presence of excessive job pressure combined with a lack of organizational support creates an unhealthy work stress condition that can lead to a wide range of physical, psychological, and behavioral forms of distress. However, when job pressure is combined with the presence of healthy organizational supports, this creates the potential for a vibrant, dynamic, and challenging work environment in which people can grow, become strong, and achieve their full potential. People at work must be challenged to achieve their full potential, they must be challenged to achieve their best results, and they must be challenged to develop their greatest strengths. Their experience of the right among of job pressure can help them achieve these outcomes.

While job pressure and organizational support exist within the work environment, Luthans (2002) emphasizes developing and managing psychological strength in his positive organizational behavior (POB). In his framing article for POB, Luthans explores five psychological strengths: confidence, hope, optimism, happiness, and emotional intelligence. As a senior human resource executive from the Men's Wearhouse put it: "We don't look for people with specific levels of education and experience. We look for one criterion for hiring: optimism. We look for passion, excitement, energy. We want people who enjoy life" (Luthans 2002, 57). Hence, a positive approach to organizational behavior is not a soft approach but is rather a strong approach that emphasizes strength, performance, achievement, and self-respect. Positive organizational behavior is a form of adult management; that is, treating people like adults and expecting them to act like adults (Forward et al. 1991).

In the first part of the chapter, we have outlined and discussed the challenges that senior managers and employees face during turbulent times. Hence, there is little need for senior managers to create or enhance the amount of job pressure and challenge experienced in the workplace. The changes and pressures of these turbulent times are doing rather enough in this regard. Rather, from a positive perspective, a key task for senior managers is to provide the organizational support and encouragement individuals need to meet the natural and inevitable challenges of these times. This entails senior managers encouraging employees to feel confidence in their own abilities, to work with hope rather than in desperation, to perceive events optimistically, to be happy without being complacent, and to work out of their positive emotions as well as their intelligence. Senior managers and employees are mutually challenged by these times, and senior managers can be highly helpful to employees through positive and supportive interactions.

Preventive Stress Management: Executive Coaching, Character, and Integrity

Stress and job pressure can be healthy and productive forces at work when managed in positive ways that prevent distress and damage. Elsewhere (Quick, Quick, and Nelson 1998) we have set forth a comprehensive theory of preventive stress management in organizations with an accompanying, though not exhaustive, set of primary, secondary, and tertiary prevention strategies. What we explore here are the concepts of executive coaching and character development as preventive stress management strategies for senior managers in organizations (Kilburg 2000; Gavin 2002). There is great value for senior managers to have an executive coach who is politically independent of the organization and there is also great strength in a senior manager of character and integrity in turbulent times.

Executive coaches must be individuals with a deep understanding of psychology and people coupled with an understanding of work (Kilburg 2000). Moss (1981) did pioneering work in executive coaching with his psychoanalytic consultations with senior Mobil Oil executives and other senior managers. While Moss's work with Mobil's senior managers might well fall into the category of tertiary prevention or therapeutic treatment, we argue that this kind of psychological consultation with senior managers is a form of primary prevention for tens, hundreds, and even thousands of employees in the workplace. Good executive coaching leads to executive health (Quick et al. 2002). In the same way that one unhealthy senior manager can cause emotional turmoil, pain, and suffering throughout an organization, conversely one emotionally healthy senior manager can lift the spirits, hopes, and aspirations of his or her entire division while becoming an inspiration to peers and others throughout the company. Executive coaches become independent consultants to senior managers who are able to provide direct, frank, and honest feedback that others in the organization are not easily in a position to do. This was modeled in NBC's *The West Wing* television show by US President Josiah Bartlett's psychiatrist.

A second strategy for primary prevention at the senior manager level during turbulent times is character and integrity (Gavin 2002). We have seen the devastating consequences of the lack of integrity and character on the part of senior managers in the collapse of Enron in the US energy industry (Nelson and Quick 2003). As senior managers walked out of Enron with tens of millions of dollars they locked in their employees to a stock collapse that wiped out life savings and retirement security. These failures in integrity and character were surely contributing factors to the suicide of J. Clifford Baxter, former senior manager in Enron (Quick et al. 2002). Gavin (2002) argues that senior managers can become "good" managers and help their organizations by developing strength of character, by seeking the virtues that consider the best interests of all (not just self-interest), and by looking to the long term as opposed to the short term. Gavin found that CEOs are significantly better able to delay gratification than other managers but are also much more concerned with their own needs than those of others. While the former attribute is a strength for acting in the best interests of the organization, the latter is a clear vulnerability. A counterpoint example of the best in senior managers is the case of Dr. Joseph M. Grant, the Chairman and CEO of Texas American Bancshares in the mid-1980s (Grant 1996). Rather than place his needs first and abandon his bank and employees during the great Texas banking crash of the 1980s, Dr. Grant worked in cooperation and teamwork during this difficult period. His character and integrity are to be emulated by other senior managers during turbulent times.

Organizational Heroes: Healing Emotional Turmoil and Toxins

Emotional turmoil and psychological toxins are endemic to organizational life (Frost and Robinson 1999). Major organizational changes and restructuring are inevitable characteristics of the new organizational reality and they are dictated by environmental events and changing industrial circumstances (Gowing, Kraft, and Quick 1998). One of the unintended side effects of these environmental changes is that employees often feel threatened, which results in a tendency toward rigid, well-learned responses that may in fact be dysfunctional and counterproductive (Staw, Sandelands, and Dutton 1981). All this macro-level change in organizations creates deep-seated emotional turmoil that frequently manifests itself in defensive behavior, either aggressively defensive or passively defensive. The emotional turmoil, psychological toxins, and defensive behavior require therapeutic attention on the part of senior managers. We are clearly not suggesting these senior managers take on the therapeutic and treatment activities themselves. However, as Frost and Robinson (1999) suggest, there is a need for organizational heroes who serve as therapeutic, or even homeopathic, agents in this process (Quick and Gavin 2000).

This emphasis on treatment and clinical intervention to heal the organization is nicely illustrated in the case of ICI-Zeneca during the late 1980s and early 1990s (Teasdale and McKeown 1994). During this period the pharmaceutical business was growing rapidly, with the associated stress that accompanies dramatic organizational change. The company found a significant increase in psychological and psychiatric referrals over a ten-year period. In formulating a six-level stress management strategy, the company placed the treatment of casualties and the identification of other cases as the first two levels of action to be taken.

The positive effects of therapeutic intervention and of clinical treatment are to enhance emotional and psychological life within the organization. As emotional toxins are metabolized, neutralized, and cleansed from the system, the quality of life at work improves. However, there is a risk in this work for those who act as organizational heroes. The risk is that they internalize these toxins and place their own health and well-being at risk. So, there is a need for senior managers to have their organizational heroes debriefed and psychologically cared for on a periodic basis so that they too maintain their health and well-being. This entire process falls within the emergent realm of what Edgar Schein labels organizational therapy (Quick and Gavin 2000).

Alumni Networks: Keeping in Touch with Ex-Employees

In a world where change is a constant, keeping in touch with the familiar can be a prime asset. But sometimes the familiar, once departed, is considered taboo. This has been true in the case of employees who depart organizations. Historically, most organizations have had an unwritten policy against rehiring or dealing with former employees (Canabou 2002). Leaders have felt that workers leaving an organization was like severing a rope in that, once cut, the elements could never successfully be rejoined. But by doing this managers cut themselves off from one of their greatest potential assets; their own former employees (Kirsner 2002).

The major purpose of alumni networks is to recognize that loyalties and ties to the organization can last beyond the employment period (Klingbeil 2001). The recognition of this possibility leads to several premises. First, in a competitive world, former employment relationships should be retained whenever possible. They represent a valuable investment that may still bring a return. Second, it pays to keep good relationships with employees. Former employees become consultants, customers, competitors, boosters who praise, or naysayers who decry their former organizations, regulatory overseers in the organization's industry, and every other conceivable type of organizational stakeholder. Sometimes past employees even refer new business to their former employers (Kirsner 2002). Third, recognizing past employment relationships rather than disregarding them is a way to reduce innate habits of arrogance among leaders in the organization. Recognizing former employees as continuing stakeholders implies that, rather than castoffs from an all-powerful organization, former employees are potentially valuable assets of an entity whose perpetual survival remains uncertain. In this way former workers retain a meaningful status (Klingbeil 2001).

Alumni networks can be viewed as a means of reducing stress in existing employees during change. Employees who truly care about the organization, and there are many, feel relieved by knowing that regardless of the firm's business outlook, they can still legitimately stay in touch with their friends and with the firm's unfolding history. In cyclical industries some laid-off workers will take advantage of the option to reapply when the economy improves (Canabou 2002). This may result in valuable employees rejoining the organization on a repeated basis. Survivors of downsizing will appreciate the fact that they can still keep in contact with and observe the career reboundings of their former associates and friends. This may, in fact, lessen the intensity of the "survivor syndrome" and improve the wellness of the organization during change. And, due to the addition of a new stakeholder group, leaders themselves will have an opportunity to reformulate their own concept of the organization.

Forrester Research in Cambridge, Massachusetts, is a firm that uses an alumni network. Its company alumni website allows former and current employees to exchange messages. A profile section is included so former employees can keep the site updated on their current whereabouts and employment circumstances. This network has helped Forrester to recruit and rehire both former Forrester employees and their colleagues, who are referred to Forrester by them. The cost of the network is more than offset by recruitment value. These and other benefits are available to organizations that use alumni networks (Canabou 2002). When organizations do not create networks employees sometimes do so on their own (Britt 2002). In addition, there are service firms, such as Boston-based Corporate Alumni Inc., that create alumni networks for organizations or groups of employees (Klingbeil 2001).

NOTES

The authors can be contacted at the addresses below:

Alvin L. Gibson
Assistant Professor of Business Administration
School of Business
Mount Ida College
Newton Centre, Massachusetts 02459
Phone: 617-928-7336 Fax: 617-928-7378 Email: agibson2@attbi.com

James Campbell Quick
Professor of Organizational Behavior
Center for Research on Organizational and Managerial Excellence (CROME)
The University of Texas at Arlington
UTA Box 19467
Arlington, Texas 76019-0467
Phone: 817-272-3869 Fax: 817-272-3122 Email: jquick@uta.edu

REFERENCES

Adkins, J. 1999. Promoting organizational health: The evolving practice of occupational Health Psychology. *Professional Psychology: Research and Practice* 30 (2):129–37.
Alterman, T., et al. *Stress at Work.* 1999. NIOSH Publication 99–101. National Institute for Occupational Safety and Health: Columbus, OH.
Begley, T. 1998. Coping strategies as predictors of employee distress and turnover after an organizational consolidation: A longitudinal analysis. *Journal of Occupational and Organizational Psychology* 71 (4):305–6.
Britt, J. 2002. Alumni networks can cut recruiting costs, boost employer's image. *HRMagazine* 47 (2):25–6.
Brott, A. 1994. New approaches to job stress. *Nation's Business* 82 (5):810–82.
Bryan, J. 1994. Glue for the re-engineered corporation. *Communication World* 11 (7):20–3.
Canabou, C. 2002. Gone, but not forgotten. *Fast Company* 58:28–30.

Cartwright, S., and Hudson, S. 2000. Coping with mergers and acquisitions. In R. J. Burke, and C. L. Cooper, *The Organization in Crisis: Restructuring, Downsizing, and Privatization*. Blackwell: Oxford.

Cooper, C. 1998. The 1998 Crystal Lecture: The future of work – a strategy for managing the pressures. *Journal of Applied Management Studies* 7 (2):275–81.

Cooper, C., and Cartwright, S. 1994. Healthy mind, healthy organization – a proactive approach to occupational stress. *Human Relations* 47 (4):455–69.

Cooper, C., Dewe, P., and O'Driscoll, M. 2001. *Organizational Stress: A Review and Critique of Theory, Research, and Applications*. Thousand Oaks, CA: Sage.

DeFrank, R., and Ivancevich, J. 1998. Stress on the job: An executive update. *Academy of Management Executive* 12 (3):55–66.

DeLima, F. 1998. Don't let technology stress you out. *Computing Canada* 24 (37):42.

Farrant, A. (1990). Your goal should be less stress and anxiety. *Supervision* 51 (9):17–19.

Forward, G., Beach, D., Gray, D., and Quick, J. C. 1991. Mentofacturing: A vision for American industrial excellence. *Academy of Management Executive* 5 (3):32–44.

Frost, P., and Robinson, S. 1999. The toxic handler. *Harvard Business Review* 77:97–106.

Gavin, J. 2002. Transformational decision-making: Defining the role of virtue-based character in the decision-making process. Unpublished doctoral dissertation, The University of Texas at Arlington.

Geber, S. 1996. Pulling the plug on stress. *HR Focus* 73 (4):12.

Goman, C. 1997. Energizing a restructured work force. *Communication World* 14 (3):55–8.

Gowing, M., Kraft, J., and Quick, J. C. 1998. *The New Organizational Reality: Downsizing, Restructuring, and Revitalization*. Washington, DC: American Psychological Association.

Grant, J. M. 1996. *The Great Texas Banking Crash: An Insider's Account*. Austin, TX: University of Texas Press.

Hendrickson, R. 1989. Proactive approach to minimize stress on the job. *Professional Safety* 34 (11):29–33.

Kilburg, R. R. 2000. *Executive Coaching: Developing Managerial Wisdom in a World of Chaos*. Washington, DC: American Psychological Association.

Kirsner, S. 2002. Alumni relations. *Darwin* 2 (3):20–2.

Klein, S. 1996. A management communication strategy for change. *Journal of Organizational Change Management* 9 (2):32–46.

Klingbeil, A. 2001. Corporations build networks for former employees. *New York Journal News*, July 22.

Krell, T. 2000. Organizational longevity and technological change. *Journal of Organizational Change Management* 13 (1):8–14.

Kupiec, E. 2001. Workforce reduction. *CMA Management* 75 (9):14–17.

Lennart, L. 1990. Occupational stress: Spice of life or kiss of death? *American Psychologist* 45 (10): 1142–5.

Levi, L., Sauter, S., and Shimomitsu, T. 1999. Work-related stress – it's time to act. *Journal of Occupational Health Psychology* 4 (4):394–6.

Levine, C. 1979. More on cutback management: Hard questions for hard times. *Public Administration Review* (March–April):179–83.

Lewis, L. 1999. Disseminating information and soliciting input during planned organizational change: Implementers' targets, sources, and channels for communicating. *Management Communication Quarterly* 13 (1):43–75.

Lewis, L. K., and Seibold, D. R. 1993. Reconceptualizing organizational change implementation as a communication problem: A review of literature and research agenda. In M. E. Roloff (ed.), *Communication Yearbook* 21. Newbury Park, CA: Sage.

Luthans, F. 2002. Positive organizational behavior: Developing and managing psychological strengths. *Academy of Management Executive* 16:57–72.

McGarvey, R. 1998. Stress case. *Entrepreneur* 26 (11):85–7.

Mishra, A., and Spreitzer, G. 1998. Explaining how survivors respond to downsizing: The roles of trust, empowerment, justice, and work redesign. *Academy of Management Review* 29 (3):567–88.

Moore, S., Kuhrik, M., Kuhrik, N., and Katz, B. 1996. Coping with downsizing: Stress, self-esteem and social intimacy. *Nursing Management* 27 (3):28–9.

Moss, L. 1981. *Management Stress.* Reading, MA: Addison-Wesley.

Nelson, D., and Quick, J. C. 2003. *Organizational Behavior: Foundations, Realities, and Challenges.* Mason, OH: South-Western.

Nytro, K., Saksvik, O., Mikkelsen, A., Bohle, P., and Quinlan, M. 2000. An appraisal of key factors in the implementation of occupational stress interventions. *Work and Stress* 14 (3):213–25.

Offerman, L., and Gowing, M. 1990. Organizations of the future: Changes and challenges. *Journal of Personality and Social Psychology* 46:655–68.

Parasuraman, S., and Alutto, J. 1984. Sources and outcomes of stress in organizational settings: Toward the development of a structural model. *Academy of Management Journal* 27 (2):330–50.

Perrewe, P. 2000. Political skill: An antidote for workplace stressors. *Academy of Management Executive* 14 (3):115–23.

Perry, P. 1999. Stressed out. *American Nurseryman* 190 (2):90–4.

Quick, J. C., and Gavin, J. 2000. The new frontier: Edgar Schein on organizational therapy [interview]. *Academy of Management Executive* 14:31–44.

Quick, J. D., Cooper, C., Gavin, J., and Quick, J. C. 2002. Executive health: Building self-reliance for challenging times. In C. L. Cooper and I. T. Robertson (eds.), *International Review of Industrial and Organizational Psychology* 17. Chichester: John Wiley.

Quick, J. D., Quick, J. C., and Nelson, D. L. 1998. The theory of preventive stress management in organizations. In C. L. Cooper, ed., *Theories of Organizational Stress.* New York: Oxford University Press.

Rosenblatt, Z., and Schaeffer, Z. 2000. Ethical problems in downsizing. In R. J. Burke and C. L. Cooper, *The Organization in Crisis.* Blackwell: Oxford.

Sauter, S., Murphy, L., and Hurrell, J. 1990. Prevention of work-related psychological disorders: A national strategy. *American Psychologist* 45 (10):1146–58.

Solomon, C. 1993. Working smarter: How HR can help. *Personnel Journal* 72 (6):54–61.

Solomon, C. 1999. Stressed to the limit. *Workforce* 78 (9):48.

Spielberger, C., Vagg, P., and Wasala, C. 2003. Occupational stress: Job pressures and lack of support. In J. C. Quick and L. E. Tetrick (eds.), *Handbook of Occupational Health Psychology.* Washington, DC: American Psychological Association.

Staw, B., Sandelands, L., and Dutton, J. 1981. Threat-rigidity effects in organizational behavior: A multilevel analysis. *Administrative Science Quarterly* 26:501–24.

Swanson, V., and Power, K. 2001. Employees' perceptions of organizational restructuring: The role of social support. *Work and Stress* 15 (2):161–78.

Sykes, C. 2000. Say "yes" to less stress. *Tea and Coffee Trade Journal* 172 (5):113.

Tang, T., and Crofford, A. 1999. The anticipation of plant closing: Employee reactions. *Journal of Social Psychology* 139 (1):44–8.

Teasdale, E., and McKeown, S. 1994. Managing stress at work: The ICI-Zeneca pharmaceutical experience 1986–1993. In C. L. Cooper and S. Williams (eds.), *Creating Healthy Work Organizations.* Chichester: John Wiley.

Thomson, K. 1997. Market for employee buy-in: Organizational communication of change programs. *Communication World* 14 (5):14–15.

Part IV

Leading Change

12

Realizing Vision through Envisioning Reality: Strategic Leadership in Building Knowledge Spheres

PHILIPPE BYOSIERE AND DENISE J. LUETHGE

The research presented in this chapter addresses the primary key issue of strategic organizational change and development expressed in the duality, how executives lead organizations to new levels of flexibility, and how CEOs and senior management provide the necessary intensity of strategic thinking required by an environment of continuous innovation.

CEOs and senior management are constantly pursuing higher speed in research and development, manufacturing, and the marketing of their products and services given the mere fact that these products and services become very quickly obsolete and outdated once brought to market. Walking this tightrope gives executives not only the jitters, but in cases of even minor mishaps, executives are often penalized with dismissal or resignation.

In this new millennium, what options, in addition to conventional strategic business models, are available to CEOs and executives in order to realize their, often vulnerable, visions and maintain competitive advantage in specific desired domains? Given the turbulent, uncertain characteristics of the external environments in practically all major industries, executive management teams often reformulate their strategic intent and exercise impromptu adjustments.

Knowledge is a strategic resource of any organization. The organization that can obtain, integrate, transfer, and apply knowledge has perhaps the most important resource for sustaining a competitive advantage (Grant 1996a, 1996b; Zack 1999). In addition, tacit knowledge tends to be very unique, difficult to copy and context-specific (Zack 1999). As a result, it takes firms that do not have this knowledge years of experience, or a huge investment, to acquire this knowledge. It follows, then, that those firms that master the knowledge conversion process have the ability to develop a strategic advantage.

The research reported here is theoretical, empirical, and experiential in nature and serves as a testimonial of how a large multinational organization is coping with the duality of ever-increasing external environmental business changes with equally increasing internal organizational flexibility. The common denominator in this balancing act is based on the utilization and creation of knowledge residing in individuals, groups, and departments throughout the organization in a historical, actual, and prospective context. The overall objective of this strategic effort is to realize the company's vision through envisioning the reality, which is realized by focusing on the causal relationship between knowledge creating behavior and competitive advantage. Cognitive representations about this relationship held by the firm's constituents (top management, middle management, and frontline management) serve as the guiding principles for creating and implementing strategic initiatives and efforts.

Two Types of Knowledge

Starting from the fact that human beings know more than they can tell, Polanyi (1966) developed the dichotomous distinction between tacit and explicit knowledge. Tacit knowledge is knowledge that is hard to formalize and extremely personal. Encompassing intuition, hunches, gut feelings, and subjective insights, tacit knowledge is knowing more than can be related in words (Polanyi 1966). It is entrenched in values, ideals, customs, routines, and emotions (Cohen and Bacdayan 1994; Schon 1983). Hence, tacit knowledge relates to the "right now," requiring the simultaneous processing that makes it difficult to communicate (Hayek 1945). Explicit knowledge, on the other hand, is knowledge that can be expressed in verbal and written language, and therefore be shared relatively easily. It can be formally presented in data, scientific equations, instruction manuals, and other documents. As such, explicit knowledge is easily transferred from individual to individual, group to group, spanning periods of time as well as context (Nonaka, Byosiere, and Toyama 2001).

Although tacit knowledge is more subjective and difficult to transfer, it is not without cognitive and technical components. The cognitive elements focus on "mental models," where individuals create working models or views of the world (Johnson-Laird 1983). These views, such as paradigms, perspectives, or schemata, help individuals organize and define their world. Thus, cognitive elements reflect the perceptions of individuals' current view of their world as well as the normative view of their world; what is versus what should be (Nonaka, Byosiere, and Toyama 2001). The technical components of tacit knowledge relate to the informal, difficult to explain, skills of an individual, much like those of the artisan, who through years and years of experience has developed a wealth of expertise. If one were to ask this individual to write or explain the technical details of this expertise or knowledge, it likely would be impossible.

The focus an individual or organization places on knowledge varies by culture. For example, Eastern cultures tend to regard knowledge as primarily tacit, while Western cultures tend to consider knowledge as primarily explicit. Since both types of knowledge are essential for knowledge creation within an organization, it is dangerous to center on one type of knowledge over the other. A focus on explicit knowledge over tacit knowledge can lead to the condition of "paralysis by analysis," while a focus on tacit knowledge over explicit knowledge may cause one to rely too much on past success with limited attention to the future (Nonaka, Byosiere, and Toyama 2001). Instead, it may be more helpful to look at both tacit knowledge and explicit knowledge as a key and a lock, complementary in the process of knowledge creation. If we do not examine what has happened in the past, we are destined to make similar mistakes in the future, or at best, not increase the knowledge we have attained in the past. In addition, we must be able to reflect upon and integrate the analytical information in order to understand meaning for future experiences.

The Process of Organizational Knowledge Creation

Tacit and explicit knowledge interact with each other in a complementary fashion. It is this interaction that is called "knowledge conversion." Knowledge conversion is a social process between individuals whereby knowledge is created through the interactions among individuals who possess different types of knowledge. As this conversion process occurs, both tacit and explicit knowledge grow in quality and quantity (Nonaka 1990, 1991, 1994; Nonaka and Takeuchi 1995; Nonaka, Byosiere, and Toyama 2001).

The interaction between tacit and explicit knowledge is expressed in four distinct modes of knowledge, introduced to the management sciences as the SECI Process (Socialization-Externalization-Combination-Internalization) (Nonaka 1991, 1994). Our model further develops the SECI Process by refining the terminology in a manner that is not only more descriptive of the actual processes, but also is more useful to managers in understanding and communicating these processes (see figure 12.1). To that extent in our model we distinguish four conversion modes. Two stem from changes in tacit knowledge

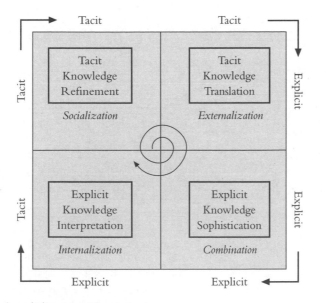

Figure 12.1: The knowledge conversion process
Note: Nonaka and Takeuchi (1995) terminology in italics.

and two stem from changes in explicit knowledge. Hence, we identify tacit knowledge refinement (socialization), tacit knowledge translation (externalization), explicit knowledge sophistication (combination) and explicit knowledge interpretation (internalization).

Tacit Knowledge Refinement (Socialization)

Tacit Knowledge Refinement (socialization in Nonaka terminology) is the process of learning tacit knowledge from tacit knowledge through sharing experiences. It is an informal, context-specific acquisition of knowledge by spending time with an individual, living in the same environment, and participating in joint activities. The apprentice learns a skill or craft by practicing under the watchful eye of the master, who transfers his knowledge or expertise to the apprentice who then tries to imitate and emulate the actions of the master. An organizational view of tacit knowledge refinement would be the use of informal meetings, parties, trips to museums or football games, and dinners to create an atmosphere of trust and appreciation by Brazilian companies. Participants get to know each other, developing a common view of the world as well as mutual trust and common tacit knowledge, which can be transferred via socialization to suppliers or customers.

Since the tacit knowledge refinement process involves the conversion of tacit knowledge to tacit knowledge, it tends to be informal, and thus is very difficult to manage. To encourage tacit knowledge refinement within an organization, an atmosphere of trust, caring, and consideration needs to be established. Tacit knowledge is very rich and can be a motivating force for additional high-quality knowledge creation when the atmosphere fosters individual trust and creativity.

Tacit Knowledge Translation (Externalization)

The process of converting tacit knowledge into explicit knowledge features characteristics of a translation process. Tacit knowledge needs to be expressed and is hence externalized through the use of semantics, as well as recorded audio and/or video images. The creation of explicit knowledge from tacit knowledge is critical in organizations, allowing the informal, individually held tacit knowledge concepts to be crystallized and shared with other members, creating new knowledge. A sequence of specific necessary steps to perform surgery expressed in documents as a result of the accumulation of tacit knowledge by members of a medical association over the years is an example of tacit knowledge translation.

In addition to continuous dialogue, one way that tacit knowledge can be successfully translated into explicit knowledge is through the sequential application of metaphor, analogy, and model (Nonaka, Byosiere, and Toyama 2001). Metaphor is a way of understanding one thing by applying a term that is not necessarily related, but forms a link symbolically. Thus, metaphor allows one to use symbols or terms to connect concepts or ideas that may be far apart or unrelated in our minds. This connection enables one to make abstract concepts more concrete, or to discover new meaning from previous knowledge.

Analogy then allows the differences to be reduced through the identification of commonalities, using the known to understand the unknown. Models can then be developed once the explicit concepts have been created through the use of metaphor and analogy.

Explicit Knowledge Sophistication (Combination)

Explicit Knowledge Sophistication is the reconfiguration of explicit knowledge into more complex explicit knowledge (combination in Nonaka terminology). Explicit knowledge can be exchanged among individuals and groups in a variety of ways, such as through documents, meetings, media, telephone conversations, and email. Thus, new knowledge can be created by sorting, combining, reorganizing, and categorizing explicit knowledge that existed previously, making this knowledge more sophisticated. It is the process of synthesizing existing knowledge from a variety of sources in order to create new knowledge.

In reality, three sequential processes are at work in explicit knowledge sophistication. First, explicit knowledge is collected from a variety of sources that could be external to the organization, internal to the organization or both. Second, the explicit knowledge is reconfigured forming new explicit knowledge that is then disseminated throughout the organization. Finally, the new explicit knowledge is processed within the organization, with the knowledge processed or edited to make it more usable.

Explicit Knowledge Interpretation (Internalization)

Interpretation is the process of converting explicit knowledge into tacit knowledge, or learning by practicing. As individuals use explicit knowledge to develop skills and tacit knowledge, this explicit knowledge needs to become part of the individual and hence become internalized. For example, an individual may improve his or her golf swing by studying a number of books, videos, and other tangible resources accessible to any golfer. Based upon the interpretation of this explicit knowledge the person can start to practice diligently. Through practice, experimentation, and simulation, the movements to create that improved swing become part of muscle memory and become so ingrained within the individual that he or she completes the correct movements without thinking about them – the explicit knowledge has been transferred to tacit knowledge. This individual could now use the process of tacit knowledge refinement to tailor his or her golf swing. In an organization setting, skills developed and transferred into an individual's tacit knowledge base become valuable assets that can be shared with others in the organization through the tacit knowledge refinement process, spiraling a new wave of knowledge creation.

Nonaka (1994) described this as a "knowledge spiral," where organizational knowledge increases as a result of the interaction between explicit knowledge and tacit knowledge increasing in scale while moving through the department to the divisional to the organizational levels. This amplification of organizational knowledge occurs through the four modes of knowledge conversion as the process moves upward through the organization. New knowledge can trigger a new spiral of knowledge creation, both horizontally and vertically within an organization, triggering even more knowledge creation. This process is not limited only to single organizations. Different knowledge bases among different organizations that interact with each other can create additional wells of new knowledge (Badaracco 1991; Inkpen 1996; Nonaka, Byosiere, and Toyama 2001; Nonaka and Takeuchi 1995; Wikstrom and Normann 1994) that can further amass knowledge in external constituencies, such as consumers, distributors, competitors, universities, or government agencies. This interaction with the external environment acts as a trigger for further development of knowledge creation, as the tacit knowledge of customers, competitors, or distributors are conveyed to the organization, generating a new cycle of organizational knowledge creation.

Managing the Knowledge Creation Process

Traditional models for managing information flows within organizations focus on either "top-down" or "bottom-up" methods of management. "Top-down" models are the classic hierarchical or bureaucratic models where information is passed up the organization to top managers, who create plans and procedures that are then passed back down the hierarchy. In essence, top managers create concepts that become operational conditions for middle managers who must determine how to realize the concepts. Middle managers then provide operational conditions for lower managers charged with implementation of the decisions. In this structure, middle and lower levels are more concerned and involved with information processing than with knowledge creation. Knowledge creation is considered to be the domain of top managers in this model. "Bottom-up" models tend to be autonomous, where information is created by middle and lower managers, and top managers give limited direction or instruction to lower level members of the organization. Top managers function primarily as sponsors of individual, autonomous entrepreneurs (Nonaka and Kiyosawa 1987; Pinchot 1985); thus, knowledge creation occurs at lower levels of the organization.

In both of these models, the focus is on individuals as the creators of knowledge. This can be problematic as organizations place too much reliance on any one top manager or creative entrepreneur. In addition, the locus of knowledge creation is at the ends of the continuum for both models: at the top management level in top-down models and at the front line in bottom-up models. Neither of these two models considers the important role of middle managers in the process of knowledge creation. An alternative model that has been suggested is the middle-up-down model for managing knowledge creation (Nonaka, Byosiere, and Toyama 2001).

In the middle-up-down model, all members of the organization who work together both vertically or horizontally are important participants in knowledge creation activities. Members of the organization interact at all levels, forming cooperative relationships and interacting in ways that facilitate the development of knowledge creation. In this particular model, middle managers play a vital role as bridgers in the knowledge creation process.

In the middle-up-down model, top management provides direction for the organization by creating and articulating a vision that provides guidance to its members in the type of knowledge acquisition desired, as well as commitment to the process of knowledge creation. This vision defines not only the type of knowledge the company should create in the future, but also defines the value system within the organization that evaluates knowledge and judges the quality of that knowledge. Thus, these values dictate what knowledge will be needed and what will be created and retained within the organization (Leonard-Barton 1995). Hence, top management's primary role is to provide a knowledge vision and communicate that vision throughout the organization (Nonaka, Byosiere, and Toyama 2001). Frontline employees and managers, on the other hand, have the primary role of implementing the concepts to fulfill top management's vision. Their main focus is on reality, characterized by an often chaotic environment. Middle managers act as bridgers, who translate top management's vision into concepts recognized at the implementation level by "envisioning reality." They provide the linkage in knowledge creation that allows organizations to build vast knowledge assets. Their task is to break down the vision and values of the organization into concepts and images that guide the knowledge creation process.

Fluctuation and Creative Chaos

As an organization interacts with its environment, the process of fluctuation often occurs. This is the situation where disorder occurs that is difficult to predict, at least initially. It is not total and complete disorder, but consists of disorder with difficult to determine patterns, such as changes in market needs or changes in competitive growth rates (Gleick 1987). Organizations that face environments with a great deal of fluctuation face a situation that causes an interruption of habits and routines. This interruption may change the perspective of the members, such that individuals must reconsider their original thinking and ways of doing things, essentially unlearning old ways and relearning new ways. This process of reevaluating old ways and considering new possibilities advances organizational knowledge creation. In a similar manner, when an organization faces a crisis situation, members of the organization are encouraged to challenge old ways of thinking and "stretch" the organization to reach new levels of performance. This sense of crisis, when intentionally created to get organization member to "think outside of the box," is called "creative chaos." The focus of the organization is on defining the problem and resolving the crises in order to reduce tension within the organization.

Advocating the Knowledge Creation Process

The promotion of the knowledge creation process is vital to an organization. Just as it is essential for top management to communicate and live the vision of an organization, it is also crucial for top management and knowledge producers to facilitate the process of knowledge creation throughout the organization. In order to facilitate knowledge creation, all four modes of knowledge conversion – tacit knowledge refinement, translation, explicit knowledge sophistication, and interpretation – must be facilitated as well. This is particularly important for translation, where knowledge producers may synthesize tacit knowledge from both frontline employees and top management, and make it explicit, thus allowing its incorporation into new products or processes.

Another part of the promotion process is the cross-leveling of knowledge to other departments. In order to do this, knowledge producers may need to improvise. This is particularly important when working with tacit knowledge. These knowledge producers should be able to use language effectively, including the use of analogy and metaphor. This is particularly important in the translation process, and producers try to create concepts from tacit knowledge. Nonverbal expression is vital when promoting the tacit knowledge refinement process, while clear, articulated language that must be disseminated widely would be crucial in the explicit knowledge sophistication process (Nonaka, Byosiere, and Toyama 2001).

In sum, articulating the knowledge vision of the organization facilitates knowledge creation within an organization. Managers must carefully manage the knowledge spiral, with particular attention focused on the facilitation of the roles of the middle managers. These are the knowledge producers who act as bridgers between levels of the organization. While the bridgers perform a crucial role, organizations should acknowledge that knowledge creation at all levels will accrue invaluable knowledge assets that can create a competitive advantage for the organization. Any actions that can facilitate this knowledge creation, such as promotion of the four modes of knowledge conversion, will only serve to increase that advantage.

The Company

Until now, the major focus in the research on knowledge and cognitive representations has been theoretical and empirical in nature. Limited attention has been paid to the practical application of the theoretical propositions. In this section we attempt to fill this void by focusing on how theoretical development and empirical research in knowledge creation and cognitive representations have led to real-life strategic initiatives and implementation in organizations.

The results reported here stem from a four-year-long strategic effort in a large multinational corporation which builds next generation networks and delivers integrated end-to-end voice and data communications solutions to carriers. The company employs over 100,000 people and has an annual turnover of US$25 billion. The company is operating in more than 130 countries, invests more than US$3 billion per year in research and development and adds more than 800 innovations to its patent portfolio each year. Its worldwide research and development organization employs about 23,500 people. This strategic exercise of linking knowledge creation and competitive advantage took place in the largest R&D division of the parent company. This corporate research center employs 9,000 engineers, scientists, and support staff. The center is specialized in advanced research into network architecture, network access, and software. More specifically, this research center plays a key role in developing Internet product strategy, multimedia mobile communications, VDSL (Very high bit-rate Digital Subscriber Line), optical access networks,

TINA (Telecommunications Information Networking Architecture), and Wavelength Division Multiplexing-technology.

Given these product and service specifications, one might be of the opinion that this organization is a new high tech company that grew exponentially the last two decades. Nothing could be less true. Although the growth has been enormous in the last 20 years at the same physical location, this corporate research center saw its first activity in 1882 and went through 120 years of transformation from manufacturing hardware through today's development of software.

Envisioning Reality

A combination of three major factors prompted the CEO and his executive team to envision reality and investigate how existing knowledge could be combined with newly created knowledge in order to increase competitive advantage in several domains. First, there was 120 years of accumulated experience and unique knowledge residing in the company. Second, in the last three years more than 1,000 new engineers had joined the company. Third, the volatile and complex telecommunication market was more and more characterized by cut-throat competition.

The major explanation for the CEO and his executive team to embark on this strategic effort was not to be found in nostalgic motives but in the hard everyday reality of competitive advantage. The CEO's performance was not limited to the attainment of financial objectives of double digit growth and profit, but largely based on improved customer satisfaction that all stemmed from better existing business processes. The CEO was convinced that such could only be realized through boosting the knowledge capital of the engineers and all other employees in the organization. As such the company attempted to realize its vision through the optimal utilization of its knowledge based on envisioning the realities of today. This meant that a strategic role was to be performed not only by top management but, primarily, by other constituents of the firm, middle management, and frontline management.

Because of its wide recognition as the technology leader in its field, the company had few problems recruiting the top young engineers and researchers from the most reputable universities. In the last decade, however, a shift took place and involuntary external turnover became a thorn in the side of many senior executives. It was even more frustrating to be confronted with the reality that young engineers and researchers were not leaving the company for increased financial benefits, but rather for increased freedom and flexibility in pursuit of their ideas at smaller software houses, often risky startup companies. Given increased shortages in the IT labor market as well as the long and expensive training at the early career stages, the company saw a lot of its investments in primarily young people fly out the door.

This apparently innocent problem at the outset became acute and serious when units developing software reported problems of succession and transfer of crucial knowledge in many products and services due to thinner cohorts of engineers and researchers. On the one hand, this problem found its origins in the dilemma that the technologies developed over the years had become so complex and difficult that it took an average of two years of initial training in order to become familiar with these technologies. On the other hand, the knowledge deemed necessary for developing new products became obsolete much faster. It did not take long for young engineers and scientists to realize that after five years of university and two years of initial training in the technology, at most they would be able to work another five years successfully in developing new technologies. After seven years with the company, a substantial portion of the knowledge they had acquired would be obsolete. Many worried about extinction and dead-end career tracks and opted to bail out, much to the dismay of senior executives who realized that a major transformation in the roles, responsibilities, and contributions of these engineers and scientists should be more strategic and managerial than technological. A key concern at this point was how to envision the transition of key personnel from the technical side to the business side of the company. How was this process to be developed, and what were the key issues involved?

The Strategic Leadership Process

As a result of these developments, the CEO and his executive committee decided to embark on a rather vague task: to find out how this 120-year-old corporate house could endure and survive these turbulent times. After several investigative sessions with different generations of engineers and researchers, it became apparent that the success of the company, whether during times of hardware production or in times of software development, was solely based on the unique knowledge residing in the individuals and different departments of the company. Thus, it became essential for the company to identify and to make this knowledge fluid to flow throughout the complex and rigid structure of the organization.

"What is the meaning of knowledge for this organization?" was the main question that needed to be addressed. First, an inventory was made to identify the mechanisms that were currently utilized in efficiently disseminating generated knowledge in the company. The underlying philosophy for knowledge identification was based on determining which mechanisms were present and available, rather than using a "clear the deck" approach and starting from scratch. This identification process led to the discovery that there were an abundance of IT-supported mechanisms that each served their specific purposes but that were underutilized. In examining the existing situation the suggestion was made to "create a mega-database capturing all the underutilized databases". This prompted top management to engage in an entrepreneurial mode of action to determine how existing knowledge and new knowledge could be better utilized and integrated.

The next step involved an assessment phase in which the causal relationship between current knowledge-creating behavior and actual competitive advantage was established. The result of this assessment phase was expressed in two cognitive representations that we define as "knowledge spheres." The existing situation was compared with the desired situation, and this led to the start of several initiatives throughout the company. In addition, more than 1,500 people became familiar, through several training sessions, with communicating and sharing knowledge. More than two dozen strategic initiatives began focusing on how knowledge creating behavior could increase specific domains of competitive advantage. Most initiatives had a positive outcome; however, not all. We are reporting on two major initiatives that exceeded the expectations. As a footnote we also report the failure of what many experts in knowledge management consider the starting point, namely the setup of the so-called "Yellow Pages" identifying the skills, abilities, and knowledge of each individual in the organization.

Realizing the Vision

Four years after the first strategic planning meetings in the executive committee the organization had constructed its "Knowledge Sphere" and developed a good understanding on what specific knowledge creating behaviors influenced specific domains of competitive advantage. As such the realization of the vision is based largely upon the envisioning of reality.

Although there is a myriad of relationships between all of these strategic initiatives, it is difficult to report in much detail on each one of them. As stated above, we have opted to select three strategic implementations. Two of these initiatives, "Chip design" and "Vision-café," demonstrate how the executive management team in close interaction with middle and frontline management provided the organization with the necessary degrees of flexibility so they could anticipate and handle external environmental changes more efficiently. Only one initiative fell short of accomplishing the expected results; namely, the "Corporate Yellow Pages."

Generation-capturing knowledge creation in "chip design"

In order to maintain and sustain competitive advantage in the chip design market, there is a continuous influx of new human resources in the organization. The newest knowledge brought in by young engineers ought to be integrated with the existing knowledge of the experienced chip design engineer. This would not be a major hurdle were it not for the fact that the knowledge of previous generations of engineers becomes almost obsolete after five years, and were it not for the fact that it takes about two years to integrate a new engineer into the organization. Furthermore, it is a major challenge for any organization to keep up with the pace, given the fact that the chip market is moving so rapidly technologically. This department, which employs about 300 top engineers, found little time for a proper hand-over or transfer of the knowledge acquired over the last couple of generations of engineers, primarily as a result of increased pressure to develop new products and bring them to market quickly. This led to the common practice that new products were developed and the same mistakes were made by different generations of engineers. In addition, young engineers were taking valuable time away from their experienced colleagues by asking questions that were considered basic or elementary, resulting in both decreased motivation of the new engineers as well as the experienced colleagues. However, all firm constituents – management, new engineers, and experienced engineers – realized that this knowledge that was no longer transferred was the key to the successful continuation of technological competitive advantage. As a result, a strategic plan was constructed to determine how this knowledge, or at least parts of it, could be transferred.

A multistep procedure was developed that was dynamic in nature. Engineers whose knowledge was no longer up to date with new chip design worked in groups to identify the knowledge they had acquired based upon the years of designing and developing chips. This knowledge was not present in the new generation of engineers but could help them vastly. Using existing IT chip design, practices were placed into active windows concurrently accessible as the new engineers were programming. At the same time knowledge-capturing meetings were held. Several overlapping generations of engineers, spanning the last 20 years of product development, were represented in these meetings. In order to disseminate the captured knowledge, knowledge descriptions within standard models were constructed. The final step was a dedicated website that allowed substantial parts of the knowledge to be transferred.

The development and implementation of this transfer process took about 44 man-weeks. The results far exceeded the expectations set out by both the management team and the Knowledge Creation Team. Two results were remarkable, though difficult to express in monetary value. However, it became clear that the competitive advantage in terms of technology has now been secured for the future. First, the integration time for a new engineer to work autonomously was reduced from 24 months to 6 months. This resulted in a flexible continuous flow of unique knowledge both explicit and tacit in nature that now can be transferred from generation to generation of engineers. In addition, the generation gap was not that severe, and the social interactions between the different generations can be seen as one continuum. In short, new explicit knowledge held by the rookie engineers was blended with acquired tacit knowledge of the experienced engineers. A side effect of this reduction in time for autonomous work, which was not part of the primary focus of the knowledge creation project, was the reduction from three years to 18 months in the time to lead a major project. This resulted in an increase of the internal voluntary turnover from 4 percent to 25 percent. Today, four years after the start, similar procedures are being implemented in all other research sites worldwide, through the voluntary movement of engineers and scientists.

"Vision-café": fluidity in tacit and explicit knowledge transfer

Another strategic initiative was to overcome duplication of new product development. Because of extreme security measures, more and more departments shielded the most innovative ideas on which they were working. The result of this was that each year the organization had several booths at commercial fairs where the respective departments presented the newest technological breakthroughs. Thus, the first time these departments found out from one another what each had been pursuing occurred each year at the fairs. Oftentimes it was the case that new products with the same purpose were presented by different departments of the same organization, resulting in internal competition. This led not only to mutual embarrassment, but it was also an obvious signal to the external environment that the organization's executive team was not aware of the different avenues pursued by each department. In order to prevent this from happening in the future, the company established what was called "Vision-café." "Vision-café" is essentially set up as a poster session at scientific conferences. The company holds these cafés once every two months.

In a typical session, a maximum of six slides are allowed in order convey the innovative ideas, yet still ensuring security. Engineers and researchers walk through the posters, garnering information. The sessions are not dry, as the company provides a small snack and serves a glass of wine and beer, in effect ensuring that the sessions are well attended. These sessions serve as a first personal contact opportunity that is followed by exchanging email and sharing information. When two departments determine that they are pursuing the same idea, they sometimes merge, or at least share, specific human resources. They also often redirect their focus in order to avoid duplication. Over the past three years, this has led to the formation of more consolidated, flexible, cross-functional research and has resulted in the pursuit of more complex, more groundbreaking and more complete efforts. No duplication at commercial fairs has taken place since the implementation of this initiative. Again, it is a rather straightforward platform that was developed in order to make the knowledge residing in the organization flow more easily.

"Corporate Yellow Pages": storing static explicit knowledge

Experts in knowledge management posit that oftentimes a first important step is to create an inventory of all the skills, abilities, and knowledge the different individuals within the organization possess. In this company a similar initiative was started in which the corporate pages were named after the company color. Rather early on in the process of building the "Corporate Yellow Pages," issues of privacy and security, as well as the amount of information to be placed in a standardized format, resulted in major difficulties and compromises that would defeat the purpose of the project. In addition, it became apparent that the completion of a standardized homepage by the 9,000 individuals would result in yet another database for which it was very difficult to develop useful queries. Hence, the construction of these corporate "Yellow Pages" was abandoned because it was not considered an effective platform to share and disseminate knowledge throughout the organization. However, this effort resulted in several offshoot initiatives more focused in scope and resulted in moderate success.

Conclusion

In this chapter, we have attempted to provide a concise overview of a major strategic change initiative in order to increase competitive advantage through the more efficient utilization and transfer of knowledge in large multinational organizations. The theory of knowledge creation served as an effective basis for this effort through the construction of cognitive "knowledge spheres." It is further suggested that the theory of knowledge creation can provide a viable alternative to today's management in order to stand up to the challenge of handling the duality of more rapid external changes and organizational flexibility.

The management of knowledge within an organization is vital to support the mission of the firm, to articulate its vision, to fortify its competitive advantage and to increase shareholder value (Zack 1999). In order to sustain competitive advantage, and thus increase the value of the organization, existing knowledge must be assimilated with new knowledge. Several points can be taken from this chapter. First, creation of new knowledge in combination with existing knowledge can improve business processes and thereby increase competitive advantage. Second, insufficient management of knowledge conversion as part of knowledge creation can lead to a competitive *disadvantage*. Third, the development of knowledge spheres, and comparing the current knowledge situation with the desired knowledge situation, can increase the domains of competitive advantage. Finally, in a turbulent or high-growth environment, knowledge conversion and creation is not only an advantage; it is essential.

NOTES

The authors can be contacted at the addresses below:

Philippe Byosiere, PhD
Associate Professor of Organization Management and International Business
School of Management
University of Michigan at Flint
Flint, MI 48502
Phone: 810-762-3288 Fax: 810-762-3282

Denise J. Luethge, PhD
Associate Professor of Corporate Strategy and International Business
School of Management
University of Michigan at Flint
Flint, MI 48502
Phone: 810-762-3270 Fax: 810-762-3282

REFERENCES

Badaracco, J. L., Jr. 1991. *The Knowledge Link: How Firms Compete through Strategic Alliances.* Boston: Harvard Business School.

Byosiere, P., and Nonaka, I. 1999. Decomposition of competitive advantage through tacit knowledge creation in a European MNC. Paper presented at the Nineteenth Annual International Conference of the Strategic Management Society, Berlin.

Byosiere, P., Nonaka, I., and Konno, N. 1996. Effects of methods for promoting organizational knowledge creation on competitive advantage in Japanese multinationals. Paper presented at the Strategic Management Society, Arizona.

Byosiere, P., Nonaka, I., and Konno, N. 1997. Organizational knowledge creation and competitive advantage through the eye of the strategist. Paper presented at the Strategic Management Society, Barcelona.

Byosiere, P., Nonaka, I., and Konno, N. 1998. Relay, sashimi or rugby: How strategic planning managers balance the relationship between organizational knowledge creation and competitive advantage for R&D, manufacturing and marketing managers. Paper presented at the Strategic Management Society Conference, Orlando.

Cohen, M., and Bacdayan, P. 1994. Organizational routines are stored as procedural memory: Evidence from a laboratory study. *Organization Science* 5 (4):554–68.

Ginsburg, A. 1994. Minding the competition: From mapping to mastery. *Strategic Management Journal* 15 (special issue):153–74.

Gioia, D. 1986. The state of the art in organizational and social cognition: A personal view. In H. Sims and D. Gioia (eds.), *The Thinking Organization*. San Francisco: Jossey-Bass.

Gleick, J. 1987. *Chaos*. New York: Viking.

Grant, R. M. 1996a. Prospering in dynamically competitive environments: Organizational capability as knowledge integration. *Organization Science* 7 (4):375–87.

Grant, R. M. 1996b. Toward a knowledge-based theory of the firm. *Strategic Management Journal* 17 (winter special):109–22.

Hall, R. 1992. The strategic analysis of intangible resources. *Strategic Management Journal* 13 (2): 135–44.

Hall, R. 1993. A framework linking intangible resources and capabilities to sustainable competitive advantage. *Strategic Management Journal* 14 (8):607–18.

Hamel, G. 1991. Competition for competence and inter-partner learning within international strategic alliances. *Strategic Management Journal* 12 (summer):83–103.

Hayek, F. A. 1945. The use of knowledge in society. *American Economic Review* 35:519–30.

Inkpen, A. C. 1996. Creating knowledge through collaboration. *California Management Review* 39 (1):123–40.

Johnson-Laird, P. N. 1983. *Mental Models*. Cambridge: Cambridge University Press.

Leonard-Barton, D. 1992. Core capabilities and core rigidities: A paradox in managing new product development. *Strategic Management Journal* 13 (5):363–80.

Leonard-Barton, D. 1998. *Wellsprings of Knowledge: Building and Sustaining the Sources of Innovation*. Boston: Harvard Business School Press.

Miller, C., Burke, L., and Glick, W. 1993. Cognitive diversity among upper-echelon executives: Implications for strategic decision processes. *Strategic Management Journal* 19 (1):39–58.

Nonaka, I. 1990. *Chishiki-souzouno Keiei (A Theory of Organizational Knowledge Creation)*. Tokyo: Nihon Keizai Shinbun-Sha (in Japanese).

Nonaka, I. 1991. The knowledge-creating company. *Harvard Business Review* (November–December):96–104.

Nonaka, I. 1994. A dynamic theory of organizational knowledge creation. *Organization Science* 5 (1):14–37.

Nonaka, I., Byosiere, P., Borucki, C. C. and Konno, N. 1994. Organizational knowledge creation theory: A first comprehensive test. *International Business Review* 3 (4):337–51.

Nonaka, I., Byosiere, P., and Toyama, R. 2001. A theory of organizational knowledge creation: Understanding the dynamic process of creating knowledge. In M. Dierkes, J. Child, I. Nonaka, and A. Antal (eds.), *Handbook of Organizational Learning and Knowledge*. Oxford: Oxford University Press.

Nonaka, I., and Kiyosawa, T. 1987. *3M no Chousen (The Challenge of 3M)*. Tokyo: Nihon Keizai Shinbun-Sha (in Japanese).

Nonaka, I., and Takeuchi, H. 1995. *The Knowledge-Creating Company*. New York: Oxford University Press.

Pinchot, G., III. 1985. *Intrapreneuring: Why you Don't Have to Leave the Corporation to Become an Entrepreneur.* New York: Harper and Row.

Polanyi, M. 1966. *The Tacit Dimension.* London: Routledge and Kegan Paul.

Schon, D. A. 1983. *The Reflective Practitioner.* New York: Basic.

Spender, J. C. 1996. Making knowledge the basis of a dynamic theory of the firm. *Strategic Management Journal* 17 (winter special issue):45–62.

Wikstrom, S., and Normann, R. 1994. *Knowledge and Value: A New Perspective on Corporate Transformation.* London: Routledge.

Zack, M. 1999. Developing a knowledge strategy. *California Management Review* 41 (3):125–46.

13

The Competitive Dynamics of Workforce Heterogeneity: A New Paradigm for Diversity

MARY A. HAMILTON

Building a sustainable competitive advantage in today's business environment depends on the integration of heterogeneous knowledge resources into multiple and varied business operations (Barney 1991). Competing in a volatile, global business environment has led to the inclusion of workforce heterogeneity as an essential component of business strategies (Cox 1993; Prahalad and Bettis 1986) necessary for the development of dynamic organizational capabilities (Teece 2000) such as knowledge absorption (Grant 1996), technological expertise (Ghoshal 1987), group process skills (Jackson 1992), and market expansion strategies (Zahra, Ireland, and Hitt 2000). As such, the development of high quality, talented employees (Pfeffer 1994) with diverse demographic characteristics (Dutton and Brown 1997) is an important component of a firm's strategy.

Workforce heterogeneity as a strategic resource has received little theoretical and empirical attention even though human capital has grown in importance to firm performance along with the critical role of knowledge. There are two conflicting hypotheses about the relationship between workforce heterogeneity and firm performance. Research supports the view originally espoused by Hoffman and Maier (1961) that workforce heterogeneity improves firm performance by creating higher problem solving capabilities (Cox 1993; McLeod, Lobel, and Cox 1996) and the view that these aggregate differences inhibit firm performance by creating problems with social integration and informal communication (Jackson, Stone, and Alvarez 1993; Smith et al. 1994). These inconsistencies have led to the conclusion that workforce heterogeneity will not be found to improve firm performance until researchers gain an understanding of the relevant contextual factors (Williams and O'Reilly 1998).

To address this challenge, this chapter examines the role that organizational attitudes about sharing diverse streams of knowledge obtained from workforce heterogeneity have in processing knowledge making strategic decisions. I start with the assumption that competitive instability is one of the conditions in which workforce heterogeneity may lead to improved strategic performance and restrict my discussion to hypercompetition as one of the growth conditions in which this instability manifests itself. A hypercompetitive environment is one in which "the frequency, boldness and aggressiveness of dynamic movement by the players accelerates to create a condition of constant disequilibrium" with increasing levels of complexity, uncertainty, and change (D'Aveni 1994, 2). I argue that when heterogeneous identity groups are included in the strategic decision making process, it increases the diversity of problem solving abilities, perspectives and cognitive resources available for strategic purposes and, therefore, the knowledge obtained from workforce heterogeneity is likely to lead to positive performance outcomes especially in volatile growth contexts. Further, this translation process depends not only on the existence of heterogeneity among the firm's strategic decision makers but also on the attitudes that the firm has toward identity group participation in strategic decision making that enables or disables the use of this knowledge in shaping strategic performance.

Since the type of knowledge that is relevant to firm performance is likely to be context dependent, performance criteria for different growth conditions may lend themselves to different types of workforce heterogeneity. In this light, workforce heterogeneity herein refers to a systems representation of people with physical and cultural distinctions such as racioethnicity (Cox 1993; Nkomo 1992), gender, and age (Jackson 1992). I restrict my focus to these identity group characteristics to reflect the dynamics of categorical human differences that permeate today's hypercompetitive organizations and recognize that these socially constructed categories reflect historical differences in access to opportunities and experiences based on factors of skin color, national origin and gender (Betancourt and Lopez 1993; Lorber 1991). These experiential differences create identity group knowledge differences as well as determine the ability to participate in strategic decision making; therefore, an investigation of strategic decision making as a translator of heterogeneous knowledge into firm performance may explain why research has consistently endorsed two conflicting hypotheses.

Hypercompetition

Rapid technological development, low cost information flow, diversity in markets, disintegrating national trade boundaries, and liberalization of international financial flows has changed the basis of a firm's competitive advantage (Teece 2000). Intra- and inter-industry boundaries have been blurred by the creation of intermediary products and services as firms attempt to keep pace with the rapid technological development and market growth around the world. Competitive superiority attained by differentiating oneself within a specific industry is being stripped away and replaced by hypercompetitiveness (D'Aveni 1994) with rapid change that requires quick responses and flexible organizational knowhow to be quickly acquired and applied to many different business opportunities simultaneously. A firm's competitive focus in this context shifts from engaging in traditional strategies that keep industry competitors off balance to strategies that facilitate the mobility of resources and capabilities across industries as opportunities are created and exploited (Teece, Pisano, and Shuen 1997).

Hypercompetition is a "condition of constant disequilibrium" in which there is continuous volatility in competitive markets (D'Aveni 1994, 2). The concept follows the views espoused by the Chicago and Austrian (Jacobson 1992) schools of economics. These schools of thought maintain that self-correcting market forces rather than government intervention monitor competitive conditions over time. Hypercompetition, however, departs from these schools on the concept of stable equilibrium. D'Aveni (1994) argues that in hypercompetitive environments there are no perfectly competitive business conditions, only movements toward equilibrium that are continuously disrupted by dynamic market and competitive movements. This disequilibruim manifests itself in market dynamics such as accelerated technological development, shorter product life cycles, blurring of industry boundaries, unexpected competitive entry and mobility, and radical shifts in market conditions.

Hypercompetition creates a situation of rapid, continuous change such that every strategy has temporal limitations and the best firms can hope for is a series of temporary advantages. It requires firms to be organized flexibly so they can react quickly to unexpected systemic disruptions and reshape their role in the industry. This flexibility rests on a process of building, integrating, configuring, and deploying knowledge and processes into distinctive competencies and strategies that lead to a series of advantages. In this context, firms are required to have flexible processes and diverse resources so they can adapt to the changing operating realities as opportunities and problems emerge. Strategic performance, in this process, rests on the flow of knowledge when making strategic decisions that have a limited competitive life.

These operating realities make it difficult for firms to rely on traditional generic strategies to sustain competitive performance in this environment. Traditionally, firms compete in four ways: (1) cost quality advantages, (2) entry and mobility barriers, (3) deep pocket advantages, and (4) timing advantages based on organizational know-how. In this section, I will review these generic strategies and their applicability to decision making in hypercompetitive environments.

Cost Quality Advantages

Cost quality advantages are the heart of competitive performance in stable industries and involve some kind of a tradeoff between cost and quality. There are three generic strategies – cost leadership, differentiation, and focus (Porter 1980) – that provide firms with cost quality advantages. Cost leadership is a mass-market strategy that rests on building efficiencies through economies of scale and experience. This enables firms to keep costs low and charge a price lower than the competition with the same profit margin so as to attain a higher market share and experience in a specific industry. Differentiation strategies involve focusing on quality that allows firms to differentiate their product or service from the competition so they can charge a premium price for a bundle of products and services that meet the needs of a number of market segments. Focus strategies involve positioning a product or service to meet the needs of one or a few market niches. Focus strategies can either involve cost leadership or product differentiation depending on the cost quality mix of the firm.

These advantages focus on developing strategies for stable industries where market forces and competitive movements are fairly predictable and can be assessed for their risk. They do not work well when forces such as new technology disrupt the flow of industry and lead to situations that shake the industry and force the existing competitors to change. Hypercompetition is one of these conditions because competitive movement is more important than competitive position in an industry. Porter (1980) argues that competitive movement is always more important than competitive position. When these movements are slow, they can give the impression of industry stasis that enables firms to determine their competitive position and take time to plan their moves. He further argues that generic positioning strategies do not consider the natural progressive movement of industries and markets, and therefore are difficult to sustain in the long run. Hypercompetition is supported by Porter's position and goes further in saying that the movement is so rapidly changing that it makes it difficult for firms to determine how they can position themselves in an industry. They are aiming for a moving target so that just when they have everything figured, it changes. Therefore, under conditions of hypercompetition, generic positioning strategies along with the nature of cost quality advantages are tenuous. This accelerated pace has intensified industry movement so that firms are now relying more on timing and know-how strategies that allow them to make quick and easy competitive movements that follow the change.

Entry and Mobility Barriers

Another way that firms compete is to limit competition to a small number of firms with entry and mobility barriers. These barriers are a source of advantage in that they allow firms to earn excess profits in an internally protected industry by making it less competitive. Limiting the number of industry players improves profits by reducing the aggressiveness of buyers and suppliers, circumventing competitive rivalry, and limiting similar or substitute product entry by potential competitors (Porter 1980). Protecting industry boundaries through tacit cooperation of existing competitors allows them to gain the oligopoly power that slows down competitive movement and leads to higher prices, lower-quality products, and fewer innovative industry advances.

These advantages usually arise after an industry shakeout when strong competitors outperform the weak ones and stabilize into a mature industry. The very nature of the hypercompetition suggests that it would be difficult for firms today to maintain stronghold industry positions with entry and mobility barriers. Technological advances, global communication networks, and ready access to investment dollars have led to the opening of industry and market boundaries and to the creation of intra-industry strategic alliances that involve focusing on specific competencies and forming partnerships with firms that have complementary competencies to configure them into an overall product/service package. Strategies involving component competencies allow firms to continuously reconfigure their resources so they can pursue opportunities in a number of industries at the same time. The emphasis of strategy in this context has shifted from gaining and protecting one's positional industry advantage to strengthening one's capabilities and resources within a larger network of industries so they can be configured for quick movement within and across a network of industries.

Deep Pocket Advantages

Deep pocket advantages are substantial financial, human, and organizational resources that provide firms with a greater ability to create and exploit opportunities, attract and acquire additional resources, and sustain significant error and change so that firms remain viable entities over time. Traditional growth strategies rest on four principles: (1) the existence of excess or underutilized resources creates opportunities for growth (Penrose 1959), (2) environmental conditions act as a signal for growth (Porter 1980), (3) competitive maneuvering determines the firm growth possible in an industry (Chen 1988), and (4) idiosyncratic resources differentiate the growth of one firm from another (Barney 1991; Peteraf 1993). Under stable conditions, the assumption is that the industry movement is slow enough that it remains relatively static over a long period of time. Firms within the same industry have widely known strategically relevant resources and can pursue similar sets of strategies in the industry based on the relationship between the competitive environment and firm resources. A sustainable competitive advantage under these conditions rests on the existence of a significant volume of resources that are used to ward off or acquire existing and potential competitors.

Even in hypercompetitive environments, deep pocket advantages can give firms a competitive edge because the uncertainty requires firms to take more risks and leads to more failed movements. Deep pockets, therefore, allow firms to sustain themselves longer than their competitors through periods of rapid change. The cumulative total of firm resources, however, do not necessarily improve the ability to maneuver through hypercompetitive environments. The type of resource available and how it is utilized by the firm must be relevant to the task at hand to be translated into value.

It is important to note that superior resources can just as easily be an obstacle as they are a facilitator of firm advantage. Superior resources when limited to creating a known advantage can turn into core rigidities and create opportunity costs that prevent firms from deploying these resources to new and diverse opportunities that can create a number of future advantages for the firm. D'Aveni (1994) points out that small firms have the opportunity to outperform large firms in hypercompetitive contexts and create their own deep pocket advantages because they do not have the ties to a given industry, competency, or strategy. Without these strings, they usually maneuver their way more quickly and easily across industries than do larger firms. Therefore, deep pocket advantages are only sustainable when they are coupled with strategic maneuverability that enables large firms to disrupt their own advantages before their competitors have the opportunity to do so.

Timing Advantages from Organizational Know-How

Creating timing advantages from organizational know-how involves two strategies: (1) first mover and (2) close follower. First mover strategies are those strategies that provide timing advantages based on being first to market and then building economies of scale and experience that enable them to build a reputation around a new or changing technology.

These brand equity effects create a unique set of intangible resources or organizational know-how that can be used to earn above normal profits (D'Aveni 1994). First mover strategies are almost always risky because the outcome is difficult to determine. This makes it difficult to create the intended imitation barriers, especially when knowledge is diffused through the industry rapidly. Close follower strategies provide similar timing advantages but without the risk because follower firms have the opportunity to learn from the first mover, to reduce development costs through reverse engineering, and to focus attention on process rather than product know-how (Drucker 1985).

Following the resource-based view (Barney 1991; Dierickx and Cool 1989; Peteraf 1993), organizational know-how is the unique configuration of intangible resources at the heart of timing advantages that provides firms with the strategic maneuverability to take advantage of opportunities not open to other firms. The main premise of the resource-based view of the firm is resource asymmetry. The resource-based view of the firm states that firms differ from one another in strategic performance because they possess a unique bundle of resources that simultaneously create and constrain each firm's strategic options for growth. Without this resource asymmetry and the resulting opportunities for and constraints on growth, firms could quickly and easily imitate any successful strategy. The existence of this resource asymmetry creates imperfections in the market and, therefore, is the substance of strategy and the source of competitive performance.

Asymmetric resources can include physical resources such as technology, plant, equipment, location, supply access (Williamson 1975), human capital such as experience, judgment, insight, and perspectives of individuals in the firm (Becker 1962), and organizational capital such as formal and informal processes, practices, and relationships (Williamson 1985). Not all of these resources are strategic. Only resources enabling firms to implement value-creating strategies that are not being simultaneously implemented or in which their benefits cannot be replicated by any current or potential competitor (Barney 1991) are strategic resources. Given that physical resources can be more easily replicated, they usually are not as valuable to firms as intangible resources. Firm value, therefore, rarely lies in the actual product/service or in its component parts but rather in the asymmetry of intangible resources that creates the unique bundles of organizational know-how necessary to develop and deploy a wide range of products and services to diverse opportunities as market conditions evolve over time.

Peteraf (1993) points to four conditions that must simultaneously exist for a firm resource to lead to a sustainable competitive advantage. The first condition, resource heterogeneity, implies that any number or combination of resources can be strategic when the existence of these resources creates earnings potential in excess of normal rates of returns. The second condition, resource inimitability, allows these excess earnings to be sustained over time through the creation of efficiency differences between firms that thwart the imitation and substitution process and preserve the resource's strategic significance. The third condition, resource immobility, means that the value of these resources is tied to firm-specific needs or entangled with other organizational resources and processes (Williamson 1985), creating a unique connection to the firm and making them more valuable to the firm possessing them than to any other firm. The fourth condition, resource uncertainty, means that competitive imperfections in strategic factor markets

(Barney 1986) and knowledge gaps between firms sustain the disparity in expected value of resources across firms that can result in suboptimal returns when they are transferred or replicated. Therefore, a sustainable competitive advantage, from the resource-based view, is an equilibrium condition of above normal returns (Hirshleifer 1982) that depends on the continued existence of the benefits of the asymmetry after duplication efforts have ceased.

From the resource-based view, timing advantages from organizational know-how can be sustained as long as they are not able to be imitated and are adaptable to changing market conditions. This view highlights the role of the firm's historical path in shaping strategy and competitive sustainability. Given the volatility of a hypercompetitive environment, however, every timing advantage also has temporal limitations. The best firms can hope for is a series of temporary advantages that are shaped by their previous position and their maneuverability within a network of industries. The focus of competitive dynamics then shifts from protecting existing resources advantages to disrupting them before an existing or potential competitor has an opportunity to do so.

The foundation of competitive strategy in a hypercompetitive environment, therefore, lies in dynamic organizational capabilities (Teece 2000), meaning the development of difficult to replicate, intangible resources (Barney 1991; Dierickx and Cool 1989), the ability to configure them strategically (Hammel and Prahalad 1994), and with it the movement away from diminishing returns and toward increasing returns on assets (Teece 2000). Cost quality advantages, entry and mobility barriers, deep pockets, and organizational know-how continue to be strong sources of a firm's competitive advantage, but the tenuous nature of an advantage from these traditional sources forces a firm to continuously reinvent itself by developing new competencies and re-appropriating existing resource value to simultaneously diverse business opportunities. This means that rather than extending the life of products and markets by renewing tangible resources as they diminish in value, a firm's advantage lies in extending the life and value of its intangible resources by reallocating them to shorter product and market life cycles.

Heterogeneous Knowledge Absorption

Hypercompetition places an even greater emphasis on the role of dynamic organizational capabilities (Teece 2000) that foster knowledge absorption (Grant 1996). The very essence of a dynamic organizational capability is that the unique combination of organizational resources cannot be readily easily replicated or reassembled through factor markets (Barney 1986). The emphasis of strategy, therefore, shifts from technological know-how to the firm's ability to the process through which knowledge flows through the organization into strategies. And the emphasis of competitive movement rests on the distinctive process of coordinating and combining diverse knowledge streams that are acquired over time and shaped into difficult-to-replicate firm-specific resources (Teece, Pisano, and Shuen 1997). This suggests that sources of heterogeneous knowledge, such as different types of workforce heterogeneity, can be strategic resources that, when combined with organizational processes, such as strategic decision making, facilitate the flow of knowledge to strategies.

Workforce diversity may be a competitive advantage in hypercompetitive environments because maneuverability through a diverse network of industries and markets requires the combination of diverse perspectives, problem solving abilities and ways of thinking to enhance the firm's base of available knowledge and its ability to deploy it in rapidly changing and diverse conditions.

These diverse perspectives, problem solving abilities, and cognitive abilities can be obtained from workforce heterogeneity. Workforce heterogeneity may be a means of processing new ways of doing things and developing a diverse set of strategies that enables firms to be flexible enough to address hypercompetitive conditions. Knowledge cannot be absorbed independently of the person in possession of the knowledge. The flow of knowledge is a process in which individual cognition is utilized to shape organizational strategies. Access to unique streams of knowledge obtained from workforce heterogeneity is an essential component of the process; however, it isn't enough. For this knowledge to be critical in building effective strategies, it must be related to and yet different from that already possessed by the network. This knowledge must then be absorbed through face-to-face communication with individuals who have experience with the context in which it is embedded and who understand its relevance to the strategic issues of the firm. This suggests that workforce heterogeneity may be positively related to firm performance when the knowledge possessed provides the firm with exposure to information about the diverse operating realities. And the organization must have processes in place that facilitate the sharing and combining of this knowledge when making strategic decisions. This requires firms to value difference; in other words to value workforce heterogeneity.

Given the interrelationship between strategy and process (Czarniawska 1997), when there is a shift in strategic focus from product and markets to knowledge flow, it requires flexibility in strategic decision making. Strategic decision making in a hypercompetitive context involves attempts to be knowledgeable of a network of diverse markets and industries so that sets of organizational resources can be simultaneously deployed to opportunities as they emerge. Hypercompetition requires a strategic decision-making process with the ability not only to identify and assess new opportunities, to gather and disseminate information, and organize flexibly and efficiently to embrace them, but also to deploy resources quickly and easily among strategic opportunities. This suggests that the process of strategic decision making can be a source of competitive advantage when it facilitates the flow of diverse streams of knowledge into strategic initiatives that are flexible and responsive to volatile business circumstances.

The Role of Strategic Decision Making

Strategy has been argued to be a decision-making process (Bourgeois 1981; Mintzberg 1979). The strategic significance of decisions can be measured by the relative use of strategic versus tactical initiatives. Strategy theory defines strategic decisions as having long time horizons, large expenditures, and significant departures from the status quo that are difficult to undo (Chen, Smith, and Grimm 1992), whereas tactical initiatives such as price changes tend to be incremental and have limited implications.

Strategic decision making in a hypercompetitive context focuses on the effects of the interrelationship of systemic changes and competitive movements on the performance of the firm. System thinking (Senge 1990) takes into account the effects of all network stakeholder actions, attempts to bring as many of these component actions as possible into consideration during strategic decision making, and shifts the firm's strategic attention to understanding systemic interrelationships of the networks, of which firm actions are only one of many contributors to its dynamic competitive movement. This doesn't mean the firm has the ability to understand and control all systemic factors, but rather it is an understanding that issues outside of and unknown to the firm can have a significant impact on firm performance within the network. Strategic decision making, therefore, also involves the flow of knowledge about systemic interrelations and requires the use of decision criteria based on network plausibility rather than on the accuracy of a given strategic decision in leading the firm to an intended future state.

Since hypercompetitive networks operate through stakeholder interrelations rather than through exerting competitive power to control network actions, firms only have the ability to use their knowledge resources to enact and respond to change. These interrelational forces are the same forces originally espoused by Porter (1980) when describing the competitive dynamics of industries. Strategic decisions based on revolutionary first-mover strategies create disruptions in the network that are likely to elicit strong competitive responses. Evolutionary first-mover strategies are less disruptive in that they allow change to unfold over time through smaller continuous network reconfigurations that are less likely to be noticed by competitors or elicit a response. Therefore, a strategic decision focus on smaller, continuous, incremental adaptations that have the largest perceived value to the firm creates strategic maneuverability advantages by giving the network time to reconfigure itself in light of the change before its strategic significance is recognized by other firms in the network. Close follower strategies, therefore, require knowledge not only of radical network reconfigurations but also of less noticeable incremental adaptations in order to lead to strategic maneuverability advantages.

Strategic decision making in hypercompetitive environments also requires that heterogeneous knowledge be readily available to the firm, since performance depends on the distinct process of combining knowledge and shaping it into sets of resources that are deployed simultaneously to many different opportunities. This suggests that the degree of heterogeneous knowledge available to the firm will be determined by the degree of identity group heterogeneity among its decision makers.

Workforce Heterogeneity

Much of the workforce heterogeneity literature has focused on group dynamics (O'Reilly, Caldwell, and Barnett 1989; Milliken and Martins 1996). Ethnically diverse work groups have been shown to make higher-quality decisions (Cox 1993; McLeod, Lobel, and Cox 1996) by possessing nontraditional perspectives that lead to the generation of new strategic alternatives (Watson, Kumar, and Michaelsen 1993) and a more thorough identification and analysis of critical business issues (Jackson 1992). Identity group heterogeneity, however, fails to reach its potential because dysfunctional group processes compromise productivity (Wagner, Pfeffer, and O'Reilly 1984) and introduce problems of motivation, coordination, and conflict (Jehn 1995). Studies of group processes (Jackson 1992), conflict (Jehn 1995), and social integration (Jackson, Stone, and Alvarez 1993) found identity group differences to have a negative impact on group functioning and performance. Research on cooperative norm development (Chatman and Flynn 2001) points to the role of organizational factors in these negative outcomes.

Call for a New Paradigm

Workforce heterogeneity is a concept loaded with preconceived notions, many of which are negative, that can affect how heterogeneous identity groups are perceived and interact when making strategic decisions. Perceptions about workforce heterogeneity are often confused by the rhetoric about and past experience with affirmative action issues. The emphasis of workforce heterogeneity on overcoming past wrongs or on managing its resulting tension rather than on creating an atmosphere in which a heterogeneous workforce can participate in knowledge sharing activities shifts the focus to short-term performance measures and limits the ability to utilize identity group knowledge differences when making strategic decisions.

Workforce heterogeneity grows out of a disadvantaged paradigm in which minority identity groups needed protection from unfair and unequal treatment in the workplace through legislative, regulatory, and judicial actions. Title VII of the Civil Rights Act of 1964 gave legal protection against job discrimination. The Civil Rights Act of 1991 was enacted to remedy enforcement limitations. Since then, lawsuits, estimated in billions of dollars, have led organizations to be more conscious of their business practices and to the development of intervention policies that shape discourse about and actions toward protective classes. This has led to a "political construction of diversity" that is usually met with confusion, disorder, and hostility (Thomas 1993) and is seen by employees as sensitivity overload and a waste of time (Lunt 1994). Further, organizational fear of the legal implications of inappropriate behavior and policy decisions about protected classes tends to be masked behind political correctness which, in turn, leads to further escalation of the negative perceptions of workforce heterogeneity.

This initial phase of workforce heterogeneity enactment in firms continues to play a critical role in improving the conditions of those disadvantaged and should not be disregarded or discontinued. However, it is equally important to note that this initial phase has led to perceptions of workforce heterogeneity as a required operating cost with limited benefit to the firm beyond the prevention of legal consequences. From an organizational perspective, interventionist strategies that focus on minimizing the negative effects of diversity (Nkomo and Cox 1996) rather than on proactively uniting a heterogeneous workforce around strategic issues limits the ability to link it to firm performance in a meaningful way.

Without a paradigm shift, adverse organizational attitudes toward workforce heterogeneity may continue to manifest themselves in negative performance outcomes. When workforce heterogeneity is viewed solely from a disadvantaged perspective, firms have a tendency to develop policies and practices that eliminate all forms of difference, meaning that disadvantages are eliminated and advantages are ignored. Firms that are able to accomplish this are in full compliance with EEOC requirements and may even be furthering the advancement of these protected classes in the labor market. However, this approach does not lead to valuing difference, meaning respecting the uniqueness of positive outlier tendencies (i.e., knowledge, perspectives, social skills, problem solving abilities, etc.) and their contribution to the performance of the firm. When workforce heterogeneity is viewed from a resource advantage perspective, it involves an organizational attitude of valuing difference that is essential to the sharing of positive outlier tendencies (i.e., knowledge, perspectives, social skills, problem solving abilities, etc.). The process of sharing these advantages when making strategic decisions enables firms to build collective decision-making competencies that facilitate the absorption of heterogeneous knowledge that can lead to positive performance outcomes in volatile growth contexts.

Firm Attitudes as Translation Mediators

There is a paucity of literature on organizational processes that translate workforce heterogeneity into firm performance. A seminal study by Hitt et al. (2001) demonstrates that this process is complex with both direct and indirect effects. The focus of the discussion in this section is on one such indirect effect: the way in which identity group differences are perceived in the organization. These perceptions are shaped by organizational attitudes toward difference that manifest themselves in espoused policies and organizational practices. I propose that the degree to which workforce heterogeneity affects firm performance, positively or negatively, is dependent not only on espoused attitudes that shape policy decisions but also on organizational practices affecting strategic decision making. These organizational practices, when biased, affect the degree of power that is dispersed to identity groups and the degree of motivation to share knowledge that in turn affects the degree of participation in strategic decisions.

Attitude Bias

The influence of situational and personality factors (see Bowers 1973) on individual and collective decisions has long been debated. Classic social psychology studies demonstrate that context has a strong influence on individual behavior (Milgram 1963; Asch 1955) and collaborative action (Darley and Latane 1968) and can, therefore, affect the attitudes of persons and collectives. Since most actions, whether individual or collective, are determined by mental processes, operate outside of conscious awareness (Wilson, Lindsey and Schooler 2000), and are guided by prevailing attitudes (Dovidio et al. 1997) and environmental circumstances (Bargh and Chartrand 1999) that coexist in a state of tension (Festinger and Carlsmith 1955), reliance on well-established heuristics to make strategic decisions is prevalent even if it leads to predictive and estimation errors (Tversky and Kahneman

1974). Further, the elaboration likelihood model (Petty and Wegener 1999) indicates that it is efficient to do so.

Petty and Wegener (1999) argue that although people are motivated to maintain unique attitudes, the amount and nature of environmental phenomena and the time involved in processing information make it necessary for people to seek out and rely on the opinion of others to assess a situation. These opinions serve as peripheral cues to form attitudes about certain events and groups of people. When elaboration likelihood is high, people tend to use argument scrutiny; however, when low, they are more likely to rely on peripheral cues. Further, the use of argument scrutiny as an assessment tool is dependent on the motivation and ability of people to process messages in a relatively objective and timely manner that is affected by the volume and impact of relevant issues and by the degree of distraction from these issues. As motivation and/or ability decreases, peripheral cues become more important determinants of judgments, not by affecting the operation of central and peripheral processes but by determining which set of heuristic process will be retrieved. This suggests that as the multiplicity of strategic alternatives increase along with hypercompetitive forces, all other things being equal, strategic decision making will be influenced to a greater degree by organizational attitudes than by rational judgments.

Attitudes are summary statements reflecting a psychological tendency to evaluate a particular object with favor or disfavor (Eagly and Chaiken 1993) and signal the worth of objects. They perform an essential approach-avoidance function (Fazio 1986; Katz 1960; Smith, Bruner, and White 1956) by operating as a "predisposition or readiness for response" (Allport 1935). Recent theories acknowledge the existence of dual attitudes – explicit and implicit – that operate as stereotypes (Devine 1995) and lead to racial ambivalence (Katz, Wackenhut, and Hass 1986), racial aversion (Gaertner and Dovidio 1986), and valence differences (Wilson, Lindsey, and Schooler 2000). Explicit attitudes, conscious reflective evaluations, and implicit attitudes, nonconscious automatic evaluations made without connection to its cause, operate simultaneously. These attitudes can conflict with each other and, therefore, can be manifested simultaneously through different behavioral expressions that are overlooked by conscious processes so that they are not seen as conflicting attitudes (Wilson et al. 2000).

This suggests that dual attitudes toward workforce heterogeneity can exist at the organization level and be manifested in differences between what is espoused and what is practiced. Policies toward workforce heterogeneity are conscious reflective evaluations and tend to reflect the way in which firms believe they ought to behave toward particular identity groups. Organizational practices, on the other hand, are automatic routines that evolve from historical precedent, are embedded in day-to-day operations, and are performed without conscious thought of their antecedents or outcomes. Conflicting explicit and implicit attitudes are usually reflected in disparity within and between organizational policies and practices. Whether the disparity exists within or between policy and practice depends on the specific circumstance.

For example, an organization can espouse valuing difference and, at the same time, have organizational practices that are biased toward one identity group. This disparity can lead to differences in attitudes between identity groups that are not necessarily related to difference in general. In this case, the conflict is likely to arise between policy and practice.

Another situation may exist in which formal organizational practices are aligned with the policy of inclusion and informal practices, such as invitations to professional social events that are exclusive. In this example, the disparity exists between formal and informal organizational practices; in other words what is being espoused in formal practices has not been implicitly accepted by the organization as a new routine.

When disparity occurs, organizations have a tendency to reevaluate their policies or re-espouse their beliefs about workforce heterogeneity. As the examples above indicate, even when the firm openly espouses workforce heterogeneity, biases toward identity group differences may continue to prevail because these routines tend to be shaped by past organizational experiences with and perspectives about difference. Therefore, focusing on policy issues when disparities arise, even when paved by good intentions, can lead to perceptions of organizational hypocrisy and even more disparity between policy and procedure that further disrupts relations with and between identity groups. A comprehensive understanding of the existence of these dual attitudes as manifested in actual organizational practices and their relationship to espoused policies is essential to uncovering and addressing firm attitudes toward identity group differences that may be automatically activated through biased routines. This suggests that organizational practices are an equally important focal point of workforce heterogeneity initiatives, especially when identity group conflict arises and/or the performance of heterogeneous workgroups declines.

The way in which the firm understands its implicit attitude toward workforce heterogeneity and reshapes its organizational practices to embrace it will determine the degree and way in which heterogeneous knowledge is absorbed by the organization when making strategic decisions. Therefore, focusing on organizational practices that strengthen the ability of identity groups to make strategic decisions and the motivation to share knowledge is likely to lead to a greater degree of heterogeneous identity group participation in strategic decision making. Three questions arise that will be addressed in this section. First, what does it mean to participate in strategic decision making? Second, if heterogeneous identity groups do participate, do they have the ability to make strategic decisions? Lastly, if they have the skills and knowledge to make strategic decisions, do they have the motivation to share their identity group knowledge?

Participation Bias

Participation of diverse identity groups in strategic decision making is determined by the interaction configurations of economic and social exchanges. Interaction configurations influence the degree of involvement of a diverse workforce in strategic decisions that shapes the voice of identity group members during these exchanges and the opportunity to shape future decisions. Voice (Hirschman 1970) takes many forms in organizations, from whistle blowing (Miceli and Near 1992), selling an important issue to management (Ashford, Saks, and Lee 1998), as well as expressions of dissatisfaction and difference. Mobility is the degree to which participation in strategic decision making leads to the ability to create opportunities to shape future strategic decisions. The degree of voice and mobility afforded to members of any identity group confirms or disconfirms both their instrumental value and intrinsic worth that shapes organizational attitudes about identity group differences, their future knowledge contributions, type of decision-making participation afforded to them, and their expected productivity levels. Full participation of heterogeneous identity groups in strategic decision making is defined as access to and involvement in economic and social exchanges based on the same degree of identity group representation as is in the workforce.

Organizational stressors on participation can impede performance levels and the absorption of heterogeneous knowledge arising from workforce diversity. Two major stressors are organizational silence (Morrison and Milliken 2000) and social traps (Barry and Bateman 1996; Platt 1973). Organizational silence is a collective level phenomenon whereby employees are unwilling to share perspectives, concerns, and knowledge. It arises from forces within the firm, stemming from management practices such as a strategic focus on cost control, top management homogeneity, and a high level of dissimilarity between top management and employees that systematically reinforce silence (Morrison and Milliken 2000). Social traps are situations in which individuals or groups of individuals adopt seemingly beneficial behaviors that have negative personal consequences over time or for the organization as a whole (Platt 1973). Subordinated identity groups can lack explicit knowledge of these conflicts due to perspective differences that when voiced or acted upon can adversely affect their reputation and access to future opportunities for involvement that are theoretically open to everyone (Barry and Bateman 1996). Both of these phenomena can act as significant obstacles to identity group participation in economic and social exchanges.

Participation in economic and social exchanges involves reciprocal trust that is a reflection of organizational attitudes and relational value systems. Agency theory (see Eisenhardt 1989) portrays economic exchanges as formal relationship structures with contractual interactions in which one party has an obligation to perform a task that provides an extrinsic benefit to the principle in exchange for compensation. Economic exchanges emphasize utility maximization and risk minimization (Coase 1988) as inputs are monitored (Alchian and Demsetz 1972) and agent actions are directed toward the interests of the principle (Jensen and Meckling 1976). Due to the contractual nature of these transactions, legal mechanisms act as enforcement and remedy guarantees and, therefore, they do not necessarily engender reciprocal trust.

Social exchanges (Blau 1964), on the other hand, are voluntary reciprocal relationships where mutual value is given without any obligation and received without knowledge of the value or with any guarantee of its expected value. Social exchanges of a diverse workforce can provide participants with instrumental value such as heterogeneous knowledge absorption, intrinsic value such as organizational support and friendship, or both. Given the value and reciprocation uncertainty, these interactions require reciprocal trust (Whitener et al. 1998). Trust is an attitude ensuing from perceptions and attributions based on previous observations and/or experiences (Robinson 1996). As the degree of trust increases over time, social exchanges tend to evolve from low- into high-value interactions with more and more knowledge relevant to the parties' professional roles and personal relationships being exchanged.

Participation in strategic decision making involves inclusion of heterogeneous identity groups in economic and social exchanges. The degree of participation in formal strategic decision making is shaped by the social interaction between heterogeneous identity groups that develops into a firm-wide relational value system. High-quality social exchanges, comprised of behavioral consistency and integrity, sharing control over and communication in the exchange, and mutual concern and consideration (Butler 1991) and representative of an organization characterized by "risk taking, inclusiveness, open communication and valuing people," engender reciprocal trust (Whitener et al. 1998). Accordingly, developing trusting interrelationships with and between heterogeneous identity groups involves including heterogeneous identity groups not only in the formal strategic decision network but also in the firm's social network. These social interactions can reduce relationship uncertainty and lead to heterogeneous knowledge sharing that shapes both decisions about competitive movements and future interactions between heterogeneous identity groups when making strategic decisions.

Ability Bias

In order for identity groups to participate in making strategic decisions, they have to have the ability to do so. Ability encompasses having the knowledge and skills necessary to generate, analyze, and implement strategic decisions and the power to put these skills and knowledge into action. Knowledge and skills without the power to act on them have no impact on firm performance. Therefore, ability bias arises from improper training, lack of knowledge, and/or lack of power. Since most identity groups have the knowledge and skills to make strategic decisions, ability bias related to workforce heterogeneity is for the most part related to the lack of organizational power to use their skills and knowledge to create value for the firm.

First, identity groups throughout the firm have been trained to make decisions at the group level. Most firms have embraced group decision-making processes at all levels of the organization in an attempt to be more responsive and flexible to changing market conditions (Donnellon 1996) and to identify and develop better solutions to business issues as they unfold (Dumaine 1991). These skills facilitate the sharing of knowledge, experience, and value differences (Jackson 1992) and synchronous intergroup communication (Nohria 1991) that leads to the consolidation of these differences into an overall decision.

Second, identity groups have the knowledge that is essential to making strategic decisions. Individual learning perspectives are representative of the idea that individual knowledge is the essential component of organizational knowledge (Attewell 1992; Crossan, Lane, and White 1999). Weick (1991) argues that individual learning reflects different responses to the same stimuli; in other words it is a process of replacing a habit/routine with a new response. However, the opposite is true for organizational learning. It is the creation of an organizational practice that enables individuals to respond similarly in different circumstances. Organizational knowledge absorption then can only occur when individual responses vary from the standard practice. Therefore, the presence of identity group heterogeneity among strategic decision makers can lead to the variation from standard practice that is a prime source of diffusing heterogeneous knowledge throughout the firm and is essential to positive performance outcomes in volatile contexts.

The question that remains is, why don't heterogeneous identity groups have the power to make strategic decisions? Power is "at once the most necessary and the most distrusted element exigent of human progress" (Pfeffer 1994, 32). It is a necessary component of organizational action and the way in which it is expressed in an organization can determine the degree to which heterogeneous knowledge is solicited and shared. Power (1) provides decision makers with the means to scan the business environment for opportunities, formulate strategies, and allocate resources (Porter 1980), (2) determines the degree of individual versus collective, and directive versus consensual, decision making (Peng and Heath 1996), and (3) is demonstrated in the extent of proactive versus reactive behavior in decision processes. More importantly, it determines the people or groups of people involved in making strategic and tactical decisions for the firm.

The degree of strategic decision-making power of identity groups is dependent on its organizational status. According to intergroup theory (Alderfer 1986), two types of groups exist in organizations: (1) identity groups where roles and interactions are enacted based on demographic characteristics (race, ethnicity, gender, age, class) and (2) work groups where roles are defined by common work tasks (product team), experience (functional), and position (hierarchical) in the organization. When there is a dominant identity or work group in organizations, strategic and tactical decisions tend to favor that particular group, increase their organizational power, strengthen the saliency of group identities within the firm, and lead to in-group and out-group distinctions based on personal-related or task-related attributes. Consequently, strong intergroup identities can create organizational faultlines (Lau and Murnighan 1998) as each group seeks to maintain or increase its power by promoting organizational practices that give the group preferential treatment over another that is justified by its role in the organization.

In work groups, this dominance usually manifests itself by preferential treatment based on positional importance. For example, when a product or service is elevated or subordinated relative to others, organizational attitudes develop that lead to the categorization of business groups as critical or noncritical to the growth and profitability of the firm, which, in turn, tends to impact the allocation of firm resources across business units. When this occurs, firms are likely to have business unit taxonomies such as rising stars, cash cows, niche players, and dogs where the cash cows feed the rising stars, the niche players are ignored, and the dogs are divested. There can also be experiential dominance, such as technology companies elevating the status of engineers and consumer products companies elevating the status of the marketing department, and positional dominance, such as hierarchical distinctions that determine the degree of access to resources and the type of decision-making involvement throughout the organizational hierarchy. Some of this categorization is necessary, especially in stable environments where industry conditions tend to be relatively static. However, in hypercompetitive environments where strategic performance is dependent on continuous market and competitive disruptions, the salience of categorizations, irrespective of their strategic significance at a given point in time, has a tendency to limit the firm to what is known and practiced and has led to lost advantages and opportunities.

The same logic applies to organizational practices toward identity groups. Exclusive practices based on demographic characteristics such as promoting based on the number of deals that are made while excluding certain identity groups from professional social interactions that preclude them from attempts to make deals is likely to lead to not only conflict but also to a loss of organizational power. This loss of power prevents subordinated identity groups from utilizing their skills and knowledge to create value for the firm. Therefore, there is also an opportunity cost associated with exclusive organizational practices that prevents identity groups from participating in strategic decision making. The cost is difficult to measure, but it involves the loss of heterogeneous knowledge that can be used to shape decisions related to timely and flexible responses to dynamic competitive movements.

Further, these practices tend to lead to dominance and subordination bias that further solidifies the degree of organizational power available to members of identity groups. A subordination bias is likely to lead to limited interactions between identity groups and to the further development of identity group faultlines. It also prevents the solicitation and sharing of heterogeneous knowledge that can lead to innovative approaches to business, pursuit of new opportunities, and development of new advantages. On the other hand, an identity group dominance bias can lead to familiar perspectives and business approaches and, in turn, to the inability to create first mover advantages or develop timely follower strategies essential to successful competition based on organizational know-how.

Motivation Bias

Motivation plays a critical role in the absorption of heterogeneous knowledge that arises from identity group differences. Since knowledge sharing occurs in both formal and informal professional settings, understanding the relationship of these interactions to goal commitment and motivation is essential. The way in which intergroup relational patterns manifest themselves affects the degree of commitment to organizational goals (Latham and Erez 1988) and the motivation to share identity group knowledge with other organizational members in economic and social exchanges.

Knowledge sharing between identity groups during social exchanges can impact the value attached to identity group membership (Tajfel 1982) and the construction of social reality (Alderfer 1986) that in turn affects intergroup motivation to participate in economic exchanges. Social identity provides a sense of belonging (Ashforth and Mael 1989) along with a categorical valuation (Turner and Oakes 1989) of a particular group. Social identity has been argued to be comprised of personal (individual traits) and group (affiliation type) components (Tajfel 1982). Recent theories have expanded the definition to encompass individual, collective, and relational orientations each with their own knowledge (traits, group type, relationship roles), motivations (self, group, and relational wellbeing) and worth frames (self to other, group to nongroup, role performance to relational standards) (Brewer and Gardner 1996; Brickson 2000).

This view of social identity links social identity not only to existence of knowledge differences but also to the motivation to share it with others. Identity group motivation, therefore, is dependent not only on the value that firms attach to their knowledge, but also on the value that they attach to their identities. Therefore, the motivation to share identity group knowledge is determined not only on intrinsic motivational factors, defined as the three identity orientations of a person (Brickson 2000), but also on extrinsic motivational factors, defined as the organization's ability to value these intrinsic differences (Peters, O'Connor, and Eulberg 1985). This suggests that exclusive and subordination practices in network exchanges prevent the valuing of the intrinsic worth of identity group differences and are likely to lead to a reduction in heterogeneous knowledge sharing between identity groups.

First, social networks can act as an enabler and/or constraint of these motivations (Peters, O'Connor, and Eulberg 1985). Gaining significant instrumental (Burt 1992) and psychosocial (Ibarra 1995) support is important for effective functioning of members of identity groups in an organization. The instrumental value of social exchanges arises from access to resources and opportunities and is dependent on the network range (Burt 1992) and the coalition status of network contacts (Kram 1988). Since the instrumental value lies in gaining a sense of control over one's professional activities, the motivation to share identity group knowledge depends on the degree to which sharing it will provide access to a wider network of contacts and those with the power to influence professional activities. The psychosocial value is obtained as the relational power of the contact strengthens one's identification and effectiveness in a professional role that provides exposure to and advocacy from top management (Ibarra 1995). Since psychosocial value resides in providing a sense of personal competence and belongingness to the organization, heterogeneous knowledge sharing is also dependent on the degree to which identity groups are included in the formal and social networks of strategic decision making and their knowledge contributions during these interactions are appreciated and valued by the firm.

Second, exclusive and subordination practices of firms can frustrate the knowledge sharing process even when members of identity groups are aware of its value to the firm and want to participate in strategic decision making. When identity groups are subordinated or excluded, network range, predictive of career mobility in white males (Burt 1992), may have greater breadth reflecting the desire for sufficient advocates and less depth due to signaling concerns about belonging to a subordinated identity group (Ibarra 1995). Consequently, subordinated groups may lack the relational motivation to develop professional networks with their identity groups that strengthens their knowledge of that group and may be unwilling to share identity group knowledge for fear that this affiliation will prevent them from advancing in the firm.

Third, since certain identity groups are considered to be less adept at dominant organizational practices and norms (Nkomo 1992) and are not yet included in primary circles (Cox and Nkomo 1990), leader member exchanges, positively related to commitment to organizational goals (Klein and Kim 1998), is constrained. Without access to top management, subordinated groups may also lack the opportunity and motivation to share heterogeneous knowledge critical to the strategic performance of the firm.

The link between identity group knowledge sharing and motivation suggests that the emphasis on heterogeneous knowledge needs to include not only its instrumental value but also its psychosocial value. Firms may be able to enhance knowledge sharing if the motivation to do so is activated by organizational sanctions for valuing not only the knowledge differences but also the identity groups associated with the knowledge advantage. This suggests that organizational practices need to emphasize the psychosocial value of identity group heterogeneity by creating (1) a sense of professional competence associated with a given identity group membership and (2) a unique sense of belongingness in the firm. Further, the psychosocial value of network ties suggests that the extrinsic motivation to share identity group knowledge may be tied to access to and acceptance in social exchanges rather than from the monetary reward of economic exchanges. Therefore, the firm's implicit attitude toward workforce heterogeneity found in its social practices may be an equally important indicator of the degree to which heterogeneous knowledge sharing is likely to occur as is the degree of heterogeneous identity group representation in the strategic decision-making team.

Where Is the Value?

This chapter supports the value in diversity hypothesis. From this perspective, hypercompetition introduces a level of volatility and complexity into strategic decision making that necessitates the continuous acquisition and integration of heterogeneous knowledge into the firm's strategic initiatives. In this context, unique knowledge and perspectives about business practices (Hitt, Hoskisson, and Kim 1997) and consumption patterns (Prahalad and Hammel 1990), when understood in their context of an interrelational network, can facilitate the accumulation of knowledge resources and the development of value creating organizational capabilities (Ghoshal 1987) essential for positive performance outcomes.

The diverse operating conditions that exist in a global economy highlight the paradoxical nature of growth through instability. Growth opportunities in these contexts drive the uncertainty and volatility found in hypercompetitive environments and can also provide access to the type of knowledge that enables firms to manage this instability. In this light, a multicultural perspective, dependent on effect utilization of heterogeneous knowledge obtained from workforce heterogeneity, can enable firms to obtain positive performance outcomes in volatile operating contexts.

Richard (2000) demonstrates that racial heterogeneity is positively related to firm performance in growth contexts by providing the firm with the heterogeneity knowledge and experience (Cox 1993; Priem, Harrison, and Muir 1995) and the flexibility to manage change (Iles and Hayers 1997). Literature on top management team decision making supports these findings by demonstrating that heterogeneity in top management characteristics is positively related to innovativeness (Bantel and Jackson 1989), change (Finkelstein and Hambrick 1990), competitive moves (Hambrick, Cho, and Chen 1996), and growth rates (Eisenhart and Schoonhoven 1990). Even though these studies do not focus on identity group heterogeneity, they do highlight the role of diverse experiences in facilitating the translation of heterogeneous knowledge into firm performance through strategic decision making and to positive performance outcomes that are related to volatile growth contexts.

The strategic value of workforce heterogeneity in hypercompetitive environments, therefore, lies in the full participation of heterogeneous identity groups in strategic decision making. Full participation requires the inclusion of heterogeneous identity groups in both the decision makers' formal and social networks and the ability and motivation to share heterogeneous knowledge during these economic and social exchanges. This sharing is a process of knowledge absorption that provides firms with the ability to configure and deploy sets of intangible resources to a number of different business opportunities simultaneously and to enact and respond to evolutionary and revolutionary competitive movements. Organizational practices, as implicit firm attitudes toward workforce heterogeneity, can act as biased mediators that inhibit the ability and motivation of identity groups to share knowledge with other identity groups. They are, therefore, an important focal point of diversity initiatives.

The focus of this chapter has been on the translation of heterogeneous knowledge obtained from workforce heterogeneity into firm performance through the firm's strategic decision making and on organizational practices as mediating attitudes that facilitate/inhibit this translation process. In a response to calls for identification of firm level constructs (Pfeffer 1994; Williams and O'Reilly 1998), I have explored the intricacies of this relationship in a particular growth context, hypercompetition. Futhermore, investigation of organizational attitudes as mediators may also reveal indirect effects on the translation process in order to explain why previous empirical research has consistently arrived at two conflicting hypotheses.

NOTES

I gratefully acknowledge the financial support of the Batten Institute and the Olsson Center at the University of Virginia, Darden School of Business in carrying out this research.

Please do not cite this chapter, in whole or in part, without my written permission. I can be contacted at the address below:

Mary A. Hamilton
University of Virginia
PO Box 6550
Charlottesville, Virginia 22906-6550
1225 S Lake Park Boulevard
Carolina Beach, North Carolina 22901
Phone: 910-458-3654 Email: HamiltonM@darden.virginia.edu

REFERENCES

Alchain, A. and Demsetz, H. 1972. Production, information costs, and economic organization. *American Economic Review* 62:777–95.

Alderfer, C. P. 1986. An intergroup perspective on group dynamics. In Lorsch (ed.), *Handbook of Organizational behavior*. Englewood Cliffs, NC: Prentice-Hall.

Allport, G. W. 1935. Attitudes. In C. Murchison (ed.), *A Handbook of Social Psychology*. Worcester, MA: Clark University Press.

Asch, S. E. 1955. Opinions and social pressure. *Scientific American* 193:31–5.

Ashforth, B. E., and Mael, F. 1989. Social identity theory and the organization. *Academy of Management Review* 14:20–39.

Ashforth, B. E., Saks, A. M., and Lee, R. T. 1998. Socialization and newcomer adjustment: The role of organizational context. *Human Relations* 51:897–926.

Attewell, P. 1992. Technology diffusion and organizational learning: The case of business computing. *Organization Science* 3:1–19.

Bantel, K., and Jackson, S. E. 1989. Top management and innovations in banking: Does the composition of the top management team make a difference? *Strategic Management Journal* 10: 107–24.

Bargh, J. A., and Chartrand, T. L. 1999. The unbearable automaticity of being. *American Psychologist* 54:462–79.

Barkema, H. G. 1997. Working abroad, working with others: How firms learn to operate international joint ventures. *Academy of Management Journal* 40 (2):426–42.

Barkema, H. G., and Vermeulen, F. 1998. International expansion through start-up or acquisition: A learning perspective. *Academy of Management Journal* 41:7–26.

Barney, J. B. 1986. Strategic factor markets: Expectations, luck and business strategy. *Management Science* 32:1231–41.

Barney, J. B. 1991. Firm resources and sustained competitive advantage. *Journal of Management* 17:99–120.

Barry, B., and Bateman, T. 1996. A social trap analysis of the management of diversity. *Academy of Management Review* 21:757–74.

Becker, G. S. 1962. Investment in human capital: Effects on earnings. *Journal of Political Economy* 70:9–49.

Betancourt H., and Lopez, S. R. 1993. The study of culture, ethnicity and race in American Psychology. *American Psychologist* 48:629–37.

Blau, P. M. 1964. *Exchange and Power in Social Life*. New York: Wiley.

Bourgeois, J. L. 1981. On the measurement of organization slack. *Academy of Management Review* 8:29–39.

Bowers, K. S. 1973. Situationism in psychology: An analysis and a critique. *Psychological Review* 80:307–36.

Brewer M. B., and Gardner, W. 1996. Who is this "we"? Levels of collective identity and self-representations. *Journal of Personality and Social Psychology* 71:83–93.

Brickson, S. 2000. The impact of identity orientation individual and organizational outcomes in demographically diverse settings. *Academy of Management Review* 25:82–101.

Brown, J. S., and Duguid, P. 1991. Organizational learning and communities-of-practice: Toward a unified view of working, learning, and innovation. *Organization Science* 2:40–57.

Burt, R. S. 1992. *Structural holes: The Social Structure of Competition*. Cambridge, MA: Harvard University Press.

Butler, J. K., Jr. 1991. Towards understanding and measuring conditions of trust: Evolution of a conditions of trust inventory. *Journal of Management* 17:643–63.

Chatman, J. A., and Flynn, F. J. 2001. The influence of demographic heterogeneity on the emergence and consequences of cooperative norms in work teams. *Academy of Management Journal* 44:956–74.

Chen, M. J. 1988. Competitive strategic interaction: A study of competitive actions and responses. PhD diss., University of Maryland, 1988.

Chen, M.-J., Smith, K. G., and Grimm, C. M. 1992. Action characteristics as predictors of competitive responses. *Management Science* 38:439–55.

Coase, R. H. 1988. *The Firm, the Market and the Law*. Chicago: University of Chicago Press.

Cox, T. 1993. *Cultural Diversity in Organizations: Theory, Research and Practice*. San Francisco: Berrett-Koehler.

Cox, T., Jr., and Nkomo, S. M. 1990. Invisible men and women: A status report on race as a variable in organization behavior research. *Journal of Organizational Behavior* 11:413–25.

Crossan, M. M., Lane, H. W., and White, R. E. 1999. An organizational learning framework: From intuition to institution. *Academy of Management Review* 24:522–37.

Czarniawska, B. 1997. *Narrating the Organization*. Chicago: Chicago University Press.

Darley, J. M., and Latane, B. 1968. Bystander intervention in emergengies: Diffusion of responsibility. *Journal of Personality and Social Psychology* 8:377–83.

D'Aveni, R. A. 1994. *Hyper-Competitive Rivalries*. New York: Free Press.

Devine, P. G. 1995. Prejudice and out-group perception. In A. Tesser (ed.), *Advanced Social Psychology*. New York: McGraw-Hill.

Dierickx, I., and Cool, K. 1989. Asset stock accumulation and sustainability of competitive advantage. *Management Science* 35:1504–11.

Donnellon, A. 1996. *Team Talk: The Power of Language in Team Dynamics*. Cambridge, MA: Harvard Business School Press.

Dovidio J. F., Kawakami, K., Johnson, C., Johnson, B., and Howard, A. 1997. On the nature of prejudice: Automatic and controlled processes. *Journal of Experimental Social Psychology* 33:510–40.

Drucker, P. F. 1985. Entrepreneurial strategies. *California Management Review* 27 (2): 9–25.

Dumaine, B. 1991. The bureaucracy busters. *Fortune*, 36–50.

Dutton, K. A., and Brown, J. 1997. Global self-esteem and specific self-views as determinants of people's reactions to success and failure. *Journal of Personality and Social Psychology* 73:139–48.

Eagly, A. H., and Chaiken, S. 1993. *The Psychology of Attitudes*. Fort Worth: Harcourt Brace Jovanovich.

Eisenhardt, K. M. 1989. Agency theory: An assessment and review. *Academy of Management Review* 14:57–74.

Eisenhardt, K. M., and Schoonhoven, C. B. 1990. Organizational growth: Linking founding team, strategy, environment, and growth among semiconductor ventures, 1978–1988. *Administrative Science Quarterly* 35:504–29.

Fazio, R. H. 1986. How do attitudes guide behavior? In R. M. Sorrentino and E. T. Higgins (eds.), *The Handbook of Motivation and Cognition: Formulations of Social Behavior*. New York: Guilford.

Festinger, L., and Carlsmith, J. M. 1955. Cognitive consequences of forced compliance. *Scientific American* 194:203–10.

Finkelstein, S., and Hambrick, D. 1996. *Strategic Leadership*. St. Paul: West.

Fiske, S. T., and Taylor, S. E. 1991. *Social Cognition*. 2nd ed. New York: McGraw-Hill.

Gaertner, S. L., and Dovidio, J. F. 1986. The aversive form of racism. In J. F. Dovidio and S. L. Gaertner (eds.), *Prejudice, Discrimination, and Racism*. Orlando, FL: Academic.

Gailbrath, J. 1973. *Designing Complex Organizations*. Reading, MA: Addison-Wesley.

Ghoshal, S. 1987. Global strategy: An organizing framework. *Strategic Management Journal* 8:425–40.

Ghoshal, S., and Bartlett, C. 1990. The multinational corporation as an interorganizational network. *Academy of Management Review* 31:9–41.

Grant, R. M. 1996. Prospering in dynamically-competitive environments: Organizational capability as knowledge integration. *Organization Science* 7:375–87.

Hambrick, D. C., Cho, T. S., and Chen, M. 1996. The influence of top management team heterogeneity on firms' competitive moves. *Administrative Science Quarterly* 41:659–84.

Hammel G., and Prahalad, C. K. 1994. *Competing for the Future*. Boston: Harvard Business School Press.

Hayek, F. A. 1948. *Individualism and Economic Order*. Chicago: University of Chicago Press.

Hirschman, A. O. 1970. *Exit, Voice, and Loyalty.* Cambridge, MA: Harvard University Press.

Hirshleifer, J. 1980. *Price Theory and Applications.* 2nd ed. Englewood Cliffs, NJ: Prentice-Hall.

Hitt, M. A., Hoskisson, R. E., and Kim, H. 1997. International diversification: Effects on innovation and firm performance in product-diversified firms. *Academy of Management Journal* 40: 767–98.

Hitt., M. A., Bierman, L., Shimizu, K., and Kochhar, R. 2001. Direct and moderating effects of human capital on strategy and performance in professional service firms: A resource-based perspective. *Academy of Management Journal* 44:13–28.

Hoffman, L. R., and Maier, R. F. 1961. Quality and acceptance of problem solutions by members of homogeneous and heterogeneous groups. *Journal of Abnormal and Social Psychology* 62:401–7.

Ibarra, H. 1995. Race, opportunity, and diversity of social circles in managerial networks. *Academy of Management Journal* 38:673–703.

Iles, P., and Hayers, P. K. 1997. Managing diversity in transnational project teams: A tentative model and case study. *Journal of Managerial Psychology* 12 (2):95–117.

Jackson, S. E. 1991. Team composition in organizational settings: Issues in managing an increasingly diverse workforce. In S. Worchel, W. Wood, and J. A. Simpson (eds.), *Group Process and Productivity.* Newbury Park, CA: Sage.

Jackson, S. E. 1992. Consequences of group composition for the interpersonal dynamics of strategic issue processing. In P. Shrivastava, A. Huff, and J. Dutton (eds.), *Advances in Strategic Management* 8. Greenwich, CT: JAI.

Jackson, S. E., and Alvarez, E. B. 1992. Working through diversity as a strategic imperative. In S. E. Jackson (ed.), *Diversity in the Workplace: Human Resources Initiatives.* New York: Guilford.

Jackson, S. E., Stone, V., and Alvarez, E. 1993. Socialization amidst diversity: The impact of demographics on work team oldtimers and newcomers. In L. L. Cummings and B. M. Staw (eds.), *Research in Organizational Behavior* 15. Greenwich, CT: JAI.

Jacobson, R. 1992. The "Austrian" school of strategy. *Academy of Management Review* 17 (4): 782–805.

Jehn, K. 1995. A multimethod examination of the benefits and detriments of intragroup conflict. *Administrative Science Quarterly* 40:256–82.

Jensen, M. C., and Meckling, W. H. 1976. Theory of the firm: Managerial behavior, agency costs, and ownership structure. *Journal of Financial Economics* 3:305–60.

Katz, D. 1960. The functional approach to the study of attitudes. *Public Opinion Quarterly* 24:163–204.

Katz, D., Wackenhut, J., and Hass, R. G. 1986. Racial ambivalence, value duality, and behavior. In J. F. Dovidio and S. L. Gaertner (eds.), *Prejudice, Discrimination, and Racism.* Orlando, FL: Academic.

Klein, H. J., and Kim, J. S. 1998. A field study of the influence of situational constraints, leader-member exchange, and goal commitment of performance. *Academy of Management Journal* 41:88–95.

Kram, K. E. 1988. *Mentoring at Work, Developmental Relationships in Organizational Life.* New York: University Press of America.

Latham, G. P., and Erez, M. 1988. The determinants of goal acceptance and commitment. *Academy of Management Review* 13:23–39.

Lau, D. C., and Murnighan, J. K. 1998. Demographic diversity and faultlines: The compositional dynamics of organizational groups. *Academy of Management Review* 23:325–40.

Lorber, 1991. Job Queues, gender queues: Explaining women's inroads into male occupations. *Contemporary Sociology* 20 (6): 882–4.

Lunt, P. 1994. American Bankers Association. *ABA Banking Journal* 86:53.

McLeod, P. L., Lobel, S. A., and Cox, T. H., Jr. 1996. Ethnic diversity and creativity in small groups. *Small Group Research* 27:246–64.

Miceli, M. P., and Near, J. P. 1992. *Blowing the Whistle*. New York: Lexington Books.

Milgram, S. 1963. Behavioral study of obedience. *Journal of Abnormal and Social Psychology* 67:371–8.

Milliken, F., and Martins, L. 1996. Searching for common threads: Understanding the multiple effects of diversity in organizational groups. *Academy of Management Review* 21:402–33.

Mintzberg, H. 1979. *The Structuring of Organizations*. Englewood Cliffs, NJ: Prentice-Hall.

Mischel, W., and Shoda, Y. 1995. A cognitive-affective system theory of personality. *Psychological Review* 102:246–68.

Morrison, E. W., and Milliken, F. J., 2000. Organizational silence: A barrier to change and development in a pluralistic world. *Academy of Management Review* 25:706–25.

Nkomo, S. M. 1992. The emperor has no clothes: Rewriting race in organizations. *Academy of Management Review* 17:487–513.

Nkomo, S. M., and Cox, T. 1996. Diverse identities in organizations. In S. R. Clegg, C. Hardy, and W. R. Nord (eds.), *Handbook of Organization Studies*. London: Sage.

Nohria, N., and Garcia-Pont, C. 1991. Global strategic linkages and industry structure. *Strategic Management Journal* 12:105–24.

O'Reilly, C., Caldwell, D., and Barnett, W. 1989. Work group demography, social integration, and turnover. *Administrative Science Quarterly* 34:21–37.

Pederaf, M. A. 1993. The cornerstones of competitive advantage: A resource-based view. *Strategic Management Journal* 14:179–91.

Peng, M. W., and Heath, P. S. 1996. The growth of the firm in planned economies in transition: Institutions, organizations, and strategic choice. *Academy of Management Review* 21:492–528.

Penrose, E. T. 1959. *A Theory of the Growth of the Firm*. New York: Wiley.

Peteraf, M. A. 1993. The cornerstones of competitive advantage: A resource-based view. *Strategic Management Journal* 14:179–91.

Peters, L. H., O'Connor, E. J., and Eulberg, J. R. 1985. Situational constraints: Sources, consequences, and future considerations. In K. Rowland and G. Ferris (eds.), *Research in Personnel and Human Resources Management* 3. Greenwich, CT: JAI.

Petty, R. E., and Wegener, D. T. 1999. The elaboration likelihood model: Current status and controversies. In S. Chaiken and Y. Trope (eds.), *Dual Process Theories in Social Psychology*. New York: Guilford.

Pfeffer, L. 1994. Competitive advantage through people. *California Management Review* 36:9–28.

Platt, J. 1973. Social traps. *American Psychologist* 28:641–51.

Porter, M. E. 1980. *Competitive Strategy*. New York: Free Press.

Prahalad, C. K., and Bettis, R. A. 1986. The dominant logic: A new linkage between diversity and performance. *Strategic Manaement Journal* 7:485–501.

Prahalad, C. K., and Hammel, G. 1990. The core competence of the corporation. *Harvard Business Review* 68 (3):79–91.

Priem, R., Harrison, D., and Muir, N. 1995. Structured conflict and consensus outcomes in group decision making. *Journal of Management* 21:691–710.

Richard, O. C. 2000. Racial diversity, business strategy, and firm performance: A resource-based view. *Academy of Management Journal* 43:164–77.

Robinson, G. 1996. Don't hijack the stakeholder. *British Journal of Administrative Management* 21.

Robinson, G., and Dechant, K. 1997. Building a business case for diversity. *Academy of Management Executive* 11:21–31.

Schumpeter, J. A. 1950. *Capitalism, Socialism and Democracy*. New York: Harper Perennial.

Senge, P. M. 1990. *The Fifth Discipline*. New York: Currency Doubleday.

Smith, K. G., Smith K. A., Olian, J. D., Sims, H. P., O'Bannon, D. P., and Scully, J. A. 1994. Top management team demography and process: The role of social integration and communication. *Administrative Science Quarterly* 39:412–38.

Smith, M. B., Bruner, J., and White, R. W. 1956. *Opinions and Personality*. New York: John Wiley.

Tajfel, H. 1982. Social psychology of intergroup relations. *Annual Review of Psychology* 33:1–30.

Teece, D. J. 2000. *Managing Intellectual Capital: Organizational, Strategic and Policy Dimensions*. Oxford: Oxford University Press.

Teece, D. J., Pisano, G., and Shuen, A. 1997. Dynamic capabilities and strategic management. *Strategic Management Journal* 18:509–33.

Thomas, A. S., Litchert, R. J., and Ramaswarmy, K. 1991. The performance impact of strategy-manager coalignment: An empirical examination. *Strategic Management Journal* 12:509–22.

Thomas, R. R., Jr. 1993. Racial dynamics in cross-race developmental relationships. *Administrative Science Quarterly* 38:169–94.

Turner, J. C., and Oakes, P. J. 1989. Self-categorization theory and social influence. In P. B. Paulus (ed.), *Psychology of Group Influence*. Hillsdale, NJ: Lawrence Erlbaum.

Tversky, A., and Kahneman, D. 1974. Judgment under uncertainty: Heuristics and biases. *Science*, New Series, 185 (4157):1124–31.

Wagner, W. G., Pfeffer, J., and O'Reilly, C. A., III. 1984. Organizational demography and turnover in top-management groups. *Administrative Science Quarterly* 29:74–92.

Watson, W. E., Kumar, K., and Michaelsen, L. K. 1993. Cultural diversity's impact on interaction process and performance: Comparing homogeneous and diverse task groups. *Academy of Managment Journal* 36:590–602.

Weick, K. E. 1991. The nontraditional quality of organizational learning. *Organization Science* 2: 116–24.

Weick, K. E. 1995. *Sensemaking in Organizations*. Thousand Oaks, CA: Sage.

Whitener, E. M., Brodt, S. E., Korsgaard, M. A., and Werner, J. M. 1998. Managers as initiators of trust: An exchange relationship framework for understanding managerial trustworthy behavior. *Academy of Management Review* 23:513–30.

Williams, K., and O'Reilly, C. 1998. The complexity of diversity: A review of forty years of research. In D. Gruenfeld and M. Neale (eds.), *Research on Managing in Groups and Teams* 20. Greenwich, CT: JAI.

Williamson, O. E. 1975. *Markets and Hierarchies: Analysis and Antitrust Implications*. New York: Free Press.

Williamson, O. E. 1985. *The Economic Institutions of Capitalism*. New York: Free Press.

Wilson, T. D., Lindsey, S., and Schooler, T. Y. 2000. A model of dual attitudes. *Psychological Review* 107:101–26.

Zahra, S. S., Ireland, R. D., and Hitt, M. A. 2000. International expansion by new venture firms: International diversity, mode of market entry, technological learning, and performance. *Academy of Management Journal* 43:925–50.

14

Culture in Corporate Combinations

PHILIP H. MIRVIS AND MITCHELL LEE MARKS

The clash between cultures in a corporate merger, acquisition, or alliance absorbs executives' time, creates misunderstandings and conflicts, and can prevent a combination from achieving touted synergies. Yet, in the typical deal, attention to culture is an afterthought. Few firms take account of culture compatibility in selecting a partner and even fewer have a clear and cogent acculturation strategy in mind when they combine. On the contrary, executives downplay the likelihood of a culture clash with comments like "we're in the same industry," "we're the same kind of people" or "the more I know about them, the more I see how similar we are."

With 20/20 hindsight, however, these same executives lament not paying attention to differences in style, work habits, time frames, and values about customers, products, and profits. In study after study, chief executives in North America and Europe report, after the fact, that cultural compatibility is a more important factor than price paid, product mix, and even market strategy in determining the success of their deals (cf. Cartwright and Cooper 1996).

When Time merged with Warner in the late 1980s, for example, industry watchers and company execs touted the "creative synergies" that would come from joining words, song, and film (Read the book! Listen to the disk! See the movie!) and from cross-marketing and selling these wares through multiple delivery systems. The culture clash featured in magazines, books, and on television, concerned the fortunes and fates of Time's patrician east coast executives versus Warner's deal makers from Hollywood. Eventually that headline story went away with the departure of Nick Nicholas from Time, the death of Steve Ross from Warner, and the elevation of Gerald Levin, a seemingly bicultural guy, to CEO. What never went away was a deeper culture clash between the two firms.

Top management's style aside, there were differences in structure, norms, and values between Time and Warner that would hamper co-creation of content and limit cooperation across business units. The "old" Time, for instance, was organized in vertical lines, operated via agreed-to budgets and predictable cycles, and maintained a professional and collegial environment through consensual decision making. It could count on its people to set aside personal stakes and work together for the sake of pride in final products.

The "old" Warner, by comparison, was more of a "brotherhood" where individual entrepreneurs were loyal to the studio head (the "godfather") and honored deals with one another – but only up to a point and always with an eye to self-interest. People worked in project groups, regularly bartered with other groups over budgets and priorities, and operated on their own idiosyncratic rhythms and schedules – generally late and over budget.

Conflicts between these different structures, modes of operating, and norms of behaving were kept in check – initially – by decisions to operate Time and Warner as more or less independent businesses, albeit with some corporate integration. Then came the acquisition of Turner Broadcasting, development of a corporate superstructure, attempts to integrate business lines, and the emergence of what many described as "internecine warfare." Time Warner cable, for instance, refused to carry CNN's financial news network on many of its systems, and Warner Bros., in turn, tried to extort a billion dollars licensing fee from the cable division for use of its trademark Road Runner image on cable modems. Commenting on the combined company culture, one executive described it as a "complex, divided, and divisive animal" (Rose 2000).

The merger with AOL in 2000 injected yet another corporate culture into the mix. This culture clash would be between old and new economy companies. At first, symbolizing their seeming compatibility, the two company CEOs arrived at the merger announcement dressed as their counterpart: Levin in an open collared shirt and Steve Case, AOL CEO, in a button-down shirt with coat and tie. Less than a year later, however, Levin was shoved out the door, AOL's top management was turned over, revenue and the stock price were in free-fall, and the idea of integrating cross-company business lines in various "content hubs" via "traffic aggregators" was in utter shambles. The result was described as a corporate version of the Holy Roman Empire – a confederation of fiefdoms just as likely to be at war with each other as with outsiders.

A Perspective on Culture in Combinations

For the past 15 or so years, we have studied and written about the role of culture in corporate combinations and worked with executives to manage acculturation processes and their impact (summarized in Mirvis and Marks 1991; Marks and Mirvis 1998).[1] To date, our research and practice concerning culture in combinations has addressed the "fit" of company cultures (Mirvis and Marks 1992; Marks and Mirvis 1993), how pre–merger mindsets affect perceptions of one's own and the other company's culture (Marks and Mirvis 2001), types and levels of cultural integration (Sales and Mirvis 1984; Mirvis and Sales 1990), and how to manage these things – as best possible. Here we want to address, with some fresh thinking and data, five aspects of managing culture(s) in business combinations:

1. Surfacing perceptions of company cultures in a merge.
2. Examining similarities and differences in respective company cultures.

3. Identifying a desired cultural end state.
4. Mapping cultural integration.
5. Designing rites and rituals needed to bring the desired culture to life.

Layers of Culture

Culture encompasses the way things get done in a company. One useful way to think about it is as an iceberg: Some aspects of culture are obvious – figuratively above the surface; others are deeper down and hidden from view. These include norms, values, and, at the base, understandings about human nature and how the world works. These subsurface elements form the larger mass of the iceberg and have been shaped by a firm's founding and history, as well as its national origins, the ethnic and demographic composition of its leaders and workforce, and industry characteristics. Passed on via socialization, they become taken-for-granted assumptions about how you do business (Schein 1992).

To see the layers of culture in a merge, start with public business-related behavior – the design and decor of headquarters and facilities, the appearance of annual reports, websites, product packaging, advertisements, and the like, and of course the makeup of staff, and their dress and demeanor. Then look deeper into people's private thoughts and dealings. When "formal" IBM execs first visited acquired Lotus, for example, they dressed in sports clothes to meet their historically "informal" counterparts who, in the spirit of camaraderie, had donned blue sports jackets and rep ties (the old IBM uniform). This cross-dressing evoked a good laugh (and preceded the same trick by Time-Warner and AOL). But the tone changed quickly when it was found that IBMers had brought along overhead transparencies of proposed policies while Lotus leaders had put theirs on Notes software and had no "hard copies" available for distribution. Japes about the surface culture clash between "hardware" and "software" companies took on deeper meaning when "Big Blue" execs were lampooned as "backward" by "Lotans" who were comparably ridiculed as "college pranksters" who would have to be supervised by "grown ups." True to form, the pranksters never did locate an overhead projector for their new owners.

Structure is another area of high visibility that conceals deeper meaning. There was, for instance, no way to reconcile the state-driven regulatory structure of SBC with the centralized corporate model in Ameritech. On paper, a hybrid structure held out promise. But beneath these two structures were layers of lawyers on one side versus business managers on the other – with their different backgrounds, work orientations, and political networks. A comparable problem vexed the merger of Milwaukee's Mt. Sinai and Samaritan hospitals that had similar functional organization structures but very different work processes. Work flowed up and down the former through independent, functional fiefdoms, while in the latter it progressed laterally via cross-functional teams. Here was a case, one physician opined, where the "anatomy" of the two sides matched but not the "physiology."

The search for an agreeable structure and compatible business behavior is complicated by differences in interpersonal norms (Weber and Schweiger 1992). Acquired executives in a telecommunications firm described their lead company counterparts as "crisp and decisive" whenever they advanced their own ideas or took a decision on their terms. At the same time, they kept things "close to the vest" when asked for supportive data and were unable (or else unwilling) to engage in give-and-take or respond creatively to ideas proposed by the acquiree. All of this seemed strange to acquired management who were very "process-oriented" and put "everything on the table" in discussions. Such differences in behavior led to deeper inferences about the values of the two organizations. Acquired executives came to believe that their new owners were "political animals." And buying company executives referred to acquired management as "naïve" and "a bunch of kooks!"

Bringing the Depths to the Surface

There are many methods for assessing corporate culture prior to and during a combination (Marks and Mirvis 1992). Small-group discussions, one-on-one and group interviews, and questionnaires all enable people to talk about their company cultures, and the implications of a combination for their culture, in more and less structured ways. The advantage of a discussion or interview is that it is more freewheeling and more apt to bring deeper thoughts and feelings about culture to the surface. The advantage of the more structured survey, of course, is that it can cover a broader sample of people economically and address a standard set of issues. None of these methods, however, is designed to reveal the more tacit elements of culture by tapping into the nonconscious attitudes and feelings that people have about their company and its prospects in a merge.

Psychologists typically turn to free-association and projective tests to find out "what's really going in" in people's minds. Using these techniques, Mirvis (1994) has had employees draw "pictures" of themselves and of their company prior to a merge. Asking people to prepare songs, act out skits, and write narrative stories are other expressive ways of capturing deep-seated thoughts and feelings about culture and the implications of a combination. In an interesting variation, Campell-Ewald, a marketing firm in the US, made innovative use of "toys" to surface feelings about culture in the merger of two large Midwestern firms (labeled Companies X and Y).

In an innovative "pick a toy" exercise, employees from each of the two merging companies were asked to choose from a variety of toys the one that represented best their company's culture. Among the items available were plastic figures of lions, sharks, monkeys, a tornado, and an egg plus a viewfinder, etch-a-sketch, and so on. Consider the toys selected as emblematic of Company X's culture:

- Triangular puzzle – represents technical excellence.
- Horse – embodies solidity and strength
- Lion-on-the-prowl – aggressive in the marketplace.

The technical strength and market muscle of Company X is apparent in these selections. Subsequent conversation stressed the importance to employees of the company's long history and its "nuts-and-bolts" way of doing things.

Employees in Company Y selected some of the same toys but used them to represent different aspects of their company culture:

- Horse – independent, runs to new places.
- Lion – fierce teeth, operates at the "cutting edge."
- Egg – hard shell, soft inside, speaks to family feeling within the company.

More emphasis in this group was given to innovativeness and to their company's strong people orientation. In the impending "merger of equals," Company Y was seen as the "lead" partner that would have more say about integration and more impact on the combined company culture. Interestingly, some of the toys selected by employees in Company X also symbolized the anxiety of the moment. One employee, for instance, chose the "etch-a-sketch" to represent the current corporate culture because "everything is a blank screen." Long-standing traditions and familiar work routines would likely be "rewritten" in the merger. Other toys evoked more harrowing circumstances:

- Tornado – an "upheaval" – "Where we're at, you don't want to be."
- Egg – our company is "scrambled."
- Shark – "We're up to our . . . in deep water."

These selections, freighted with uncertainty and anxiety, reveal a depth of feeling that is missing in many "cultural audits" and prepackaged culture assessments.

However one tunes into people engaged in a combination, one would find evidence of both the surface and depth layers of culture (Buono et al. 1985). Although these layers can be differentiated, cultures are unified and internally consistent: Values are evident in behaviors, and behaviors, in turn, give form and meaning to underlying values. This means that changes in seemingly superficial aspects of organizational behavior also can, over time, impinge on fundamental values and beliefs in a firm. This is what makes it so important that executives affecting a combination become aware of how and why company cultures clash.

Why Company Cultures Clash

Companies have unique histories, folklore, and personalities, as well as products, markets, and ways of running the business. Typically, people are proud of their company cultures or, at minimum, have learned how to operate effectively within them. A combination brings together companies with different cultures. What people notice first are differences between the two company cultures and what makes their own unique. Think, for example, of traveling abroad. What gets noticed is how a foreign land is different than one's homeland. The same is true of a combination: People notice how their own company is different than a partner's and begin to focus on what makes their company unique.

Indeed, the culture clash begins as people pay attention to their own culture. It then unfolds in several steps:

- *Perceiving differences.* At this first stage, people notice differences between the two companies in terms of the style of their leaders, their products and reputation, the ways they make decisions, the kinds of people that work in the two firms, and so on.
- *Magnifying differences.* Next people begin to magnify differences that they observe. Instead of being merely different, the partner's ways become *very* different. Distinctions become sharper and more polarized. This is the start of "we" versus "they" when talking about cultures.
- *Stereotyping.* Then people start to typecast others in a partner company as embodiments of the other culture. Every contact in a parent company is characterized as a "bean counter," every engineer in an acquired software house is a "whirlybird," and all corporate staff are "storm troopers."
- *Put-downs.* The culture clash reaches full height as the partner company is put-down as inferior. "We" becomes the superior culture and "they" are denigrated. The "innovators" in an acquired firm put down their parent company managers as "pants pressers" who are more concerned with neatness than running a fast-moving business. In turn, the "seasoned hands" at the parent company feel obliged to teach the "greenhorns" in the entrepreneurial shop a thing-or-two about running a profitable and lasting business.

When individuals in a combination turn inward, they typically come to revalue key aspects of their organization and company culture. Implicit knowledge of how their company works, and how policies and systems sustain the firm, come to be explicit as employees reflect on what might be lost in a combination. Culture clash is especially a threat to people who see their company as a "loser" in a combination. They not only see differences between the two company cultures; they also feel a sense of vulnerability and fear losing their culture. As in any situation in which people experience loss, they go through predictable phases of disbelief and denial, and then anger, and then rejection – in many cases rejecting what might otherwise be seen as valuable and worthy of emulation in a partner company.

The difficulty here is that in accepting another culture's way of life people believe that they run the risk of failing – as an individual and as a member of a successful company. Employees in a decentralized firm, for instance, believe that this gives their operation the "market focus," and themselves the "running room," to get "close to the customer" and affect change "on a dime." At least these were the themes reported by managers and engineers from a Rockwell business unit acquired by Boeing. These themes fit together into a recipe for success in the marketplace. Take any one ingredient out or, worse, centralize operations, and the recipe is no longer reliable. Rockwell employees fretted that they would not be successful working in the hands of the more centralized Boeing's "tight fist." Furthermore, they feared that the combined company would move like a "snail" and lose out on peripheral business.

On the other side, culture clash affects self-ascribed "winners" in a combination as well. They also notice and magnify differences in company cultures and feel a strong sense of cultural superiority. Affiliation with the dominant side in a deal is received as vindication that one's own ways are superior to the other side's. Headiness develops and reinforces the winner's recipe for success. Hence Boeing managers, while sensitive to the merits of decentralization in theory, were nevertheless insistent that the economies of scale and scope afforded by centralization, as well as its expertise in cross-functional coordination and project management, were the keys to competitive advantage in the marketplace.

Examining Cultural Similarities and Differences

Easing a culture clash begins with acknowledging its presence, educating employees as to its dynamics, and preparing people to be culture-sensitive (Siehl et al. 1988). The idea of conducting cultural "due diligence" dates from the 1970s. Nowadays, many corporate mergers and acquisitions departments and all the national consulting firms undertake them when sizing up candidates and sometimes when actually planning integration (Marks 1999). As useful as the kind of third-party due diligence can be, there is no substitute for in-depth cross-talk between the two sides. To understand a culture, you need to appreciate the "why's" behind the "what's" that you observe. Many misunderstandings and communication breakdowns result from managers lacking the means to decode, translate, and contextualize the overt messages and publicly available information about their partners. Unless key players from the combining organizations learn to read these deeper roots of the other side's culture, then mutual working relations will always be under threat.

We use a hands-on "cultural clarification" activity to help teams joining forces in a merger, acquisition, or alliance to learn about one another. Its objectives are, first, to bring to the surface cultural perceptions and stereotypes between the partners and, second, to initiate dialogue on the desired cultural end state for the combination. The activity is built around each partner group making three lists: (1) how we view our organization's culture, (2) how we view the other side's culture, and (3) how we think the other side views our culture. The rosters include business practices, interpersonal behaviors, and values. Participants are instructed to include characteristics that either have been experienced first hand or heard about second hand.

Figure 14.1 shows a sample of output from this activity with the senior executives from an energy industry alliance. The two groups had been working together for about two months, so they had plenty of time to develop initial impressions of each other. Look at the lists and you'll see how both sides tend to describe their own culture positively and be more critical of the other side's culture. For example, company A viewed itself as having a balanced business and technical approach, but regarded company B as being financially driven – the implication here was that company A regarded B's technological expertise as inferior to its own. Note that, in its self-description, B recognized it put a priority on financial performance but nowhere did it indicate any technical inferiority. Yet executives from company B knew how A felt about their technological capabilities. This was a sore point for them and it surfaced in the ensuing discussion.

Frequently, the two sides agreed on their differences. Company B had a norm of confronting people head-on over disagreements. They cited this as "push back required." Executives from A described it as "in your face" and "decisions don't hold – always argue

How Company A views its own culture	How Company B views its own culture
Balances commercial and technical	Financially Driven
Collegial decision making	Push back required
Respectful of people	Empowered people
Ethics and integrity	Setting the bar high
Structured management	Delayered organization
Program management program	Speed and simplicity
Civil	Sense of humor

How B views A's culture	How A thinks that Co. B views A's culture	How A views B's culture	How B thinks that Co. A views B's culture
Bureaucratic	Bureaucratic	In your face	Rude
Consensus decisions	Consensus decisions	Financially driven	Technological neophyte
Too polite	Gentlemen's club	Darwinian	Stubborn
1950s organization	Respected competitor	Line-of-business model	Nontraditional company
Too serious	Willing to take risks	Decisions don't hold	Undisciplined
Unwilling to change	Over-facilitated	No clear processes	High risk takers

Figure 14.1: How two companies view each other's cultures

and revisit." Interestingly, executives from B knew this behavior irritated the "too polite" A group. In their list of how they thought A viewed them, the B executives unambiguously reported "rude, in your face." The airing of this cultural distinction led to a discussion between the two groups regarding the desired norms for their combined culture. Both sides agreed that A's style was too reserved and polite – a faster paced style of decision making and more head-on debate of the issues were required. But, A's executives felt that B's style went too far in the other direction. Together, the two groups settled on a desired end state of "polite confrontation" – speak up and challenge, but not in a rude manner.

This example shows two of the benefits of the culture clarification process. First, it brings the language being used behind closed doors – when one side discusses the other – out in the open between the two partners. What company B valued as "push back," company A distastefully regarded as "rude." Second, this activity engages the two sides in mutually discussing which aspects of the existing cultures should be retained in the combination and which should not be carried forward. Sometimes, as in the "polite / push back" example, the end result is a hybrid born from the two precombination cultures. Other times, the partners agree that one side's norms are preferable. In this case, both sides admired B's efforts at pushing decision making down the hierarchy through "empowerment" and identified this as a component of the desired postcombination culture. Still other times, the partners agree that a characteristic shared by the two sides should not be carried forward. When this culture clarification exercise was used in a large bank merger, both sides characterized their cultures as "bureaucratic" and neither wanted to retain so many layers of staff and decisions approvals. Perhaps as testimony to why culture change takes so long, their follow-up action step was to establish a "Committee on Eliminating Bureaucracy"!

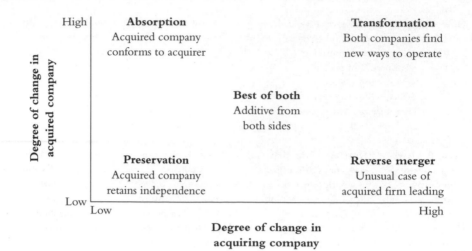

Figure 14.2: Combination end states

Defining the Desired Culture

Leaders in successful combinations understand that the work of building a new organization also means building a new culture (Shrivastava 1986). Beyond surfacing the issue, how should they factor it into combination decisions? A prime consideration is their desired "cultural end state." Employees involved in a combination want clarity – they want to know where their firm is headed, what matters in getting there, and how they can contribute. People's psychological need for direction increases during the insecure and uncertain days and months following a combination announcement. In the short run, a well-crafted statement of the desired cultural end state – backed up by executive actions that reinforce the desired ways of doing things – satisfies this need and reassures employees that the combination is being well managed. In the long run, it is essential for aligning employee behaviors and attitudes in pursuit of the strategic and financial objectives of the combined entity.

Consider five different types of postcombination (see figure 14.2) end states:

- *Preservation*. This is the case where the acquired company faces a modest degree of integration and retains its ways of doing business. This end state is typically found in diversified companies that promote cultural pluralism among business units. To succeed, corporate management has to protect the boundary of the subsidiary or alliance partner, limiting intrusions by its corporate staff and minimizing conformance to its rules and systems. Strategic synergies generated in a preservative combination come from the cross-pollination of people and work on joint programs.
- *Absorption*. Here the acquired company is absorbed by a parent and assimilated into its culture. Lead companies generally bring in new management in these cases and conform the target to corporate reporting relationships and regimens. Acquisitions

in the airline industry, such as American's absorption of Air California and Reno Air, USAir's of PSA and Piedmont, and Delta's of Western, are classic examples.

• *Reverse takeover.* This is the mirror image of the absorption combination. Here the acquired company dictates the terms of the combination and effects cultural change in the lead company. When this unusual type of combination occurs, it typically involves an acquired business unit or division absorbing the operations of a parallel unit in an acquirer. For example, Marriott Corporation acquired Saga and folded its own contract food services business into it.

• *The best of both.* This is the case of achieving synergy between companies through their partial to full integration. Studies find this additive kind of combination to be more successful than others – and most fraught with risk. It can also be the bloodiest. Financial and operational synergies are achieved by consolidation. This means crunching functions together and often leads to reductions in force. The optimal result is full cultural integration – the blending of the policies and practices of both companies. The "merger of equals" between Chemical Bank and Manufacturers Hanover and the combination of Canada's Molson Breweries with Australia's Carling O'Keefe are examples.

• *Transformation.* Here both companies undergo fundamental change following their combination. Synergies come not simply from reorganizing the businesses, but from reinventing the company. This is the trickiest of all the combination types and requires a significant investment and inventive management. Transformation poses a sharp break from the past. Existing practices and routines must be abandoned and new ones discovered and developed. In the integration of Pfizer Incorporated's Animal Health Group and Smith Kline Beecham's animal pharmaceutical business in Europe, president Pedro Lichtinger took two orthodox operations and transformed them into a new organization geared toward the emerging realities of the European Community. In doing so, he broke down traditional country-specific structures and cultures and forged a pan-European strategy, structure, team, and identity as the precombination parties merged.

As the combination unfolds, executives on both sides gain a better understanding of each other's culture. And it may be prudent to revisit and revise definitions of desirable levels of acculturation. For instance, the cultural assimilation that would follow from a parent company "absorbing" an acquiree might not be appropriate if, say, technical talent threatens to depart or brand identity would suffer. IBM, for example, moved from an expectation of assimilating Lotus to a more pluralistic stance as its networking strategy developed through conversation with its partner. While Lotus is not a stand-alone business, it has nevertheless retained much of its cultural distinctiveness.

Obviously a best-of-both combination looks toward cultural integration. But will the market reward it? And is it the best model for staff? In a merger between two hospitals with different religious affiliations, for instance, attempts to create distinct medical specialties in each generated resistance from both patients and staff. Furthermore, cross-hospital meetings and dialogue were met by a collective "blah" from nonmedical staff and nurses. And physicians did not even bother to attend. Thus, executives focused integration on consolidating the two back offices, purchasing, transport, and a variety of administrative functions. In essence, a holding company was created and the two hospitals retained their unique identities in the market and for the majority of employees.

This is not to recommend cultural pluralism or coexistence between firms. In most cases that would result in modest integration that is unlikely to create much synergy or produce anything more than one plus one equals two. In many instances, cultural pluralism results in portfolio management. In other cases, it breeds bad blood, as seen in the KLM and Northwest alliance in which both partners thought they knew best how to run an airline, regularly put down each other's cultures in the business press, and took their differences to court. When people guided by differing values or conflicting behaviors attempt to work together and must share common systems and practices, the result can only be antagonism and in-fighting. These people put their energy into fighting internal battles rather than fighting off competitors. Let's also be clear that cultural assimilation – one side absorbing the other – can contribute to a common culture and a productive combination.

The point here is not to a priori favor one form of acculturation over another (c.f., Nahavandi and Malekzadeh 1988). Rather, our counsel is that the two sides talk things through to develop an agreeable view of the desired cultural end state and then align their actions accordingly. The dialogue begins in the precombination phase when an integration strategy is set and synergies are defined (Bower 2001). In a merger or acquisition, the lead company, with its partner, needs to clarify to what degree absorbing a target versus preserving its autonomy serves its intentions and creates value. That discussion sets the framework for determining whether cultural assimilation, integration, or pluralism will follow. In an alliance, ideally, the two parent companies' senior managements come to some shared understanding of the desired cultural end state and quickly bring into the discussions the management who will be running the combined entity.

Mapping Cultural Integration

Although, at the broadest level, senior executives need to decide how much to integrate two firms in their combination, when it comes to putting together, say, manufacturing or marketing, the synergies therein may dictate different levels of integration. For instance, in many high tech acquisitions, marketing and sales in a subsidiary are absorbed into the parent company – which often has more competence and better distribution channels. But the acquiree's engineering and manufacturing are given high levels of autonomy to "do their thing." In healthcare combinations, back office functions may be consolidated, and systems and procedures standardized, but the delivery of care is left to each of the providers. In alliances in the oil industry, in turn, refining and distribution are often consolidated yet each company's dealerships and brand kept separate. In all of these cases, decisions about integration hinge on the business case behind the combination.

In the same way, there needs to be a "case" for combining cultures – function by function. It is very likely, for example, that senior executives will see a need for a common and unified culture in some areas of the combination and for more pluralism in

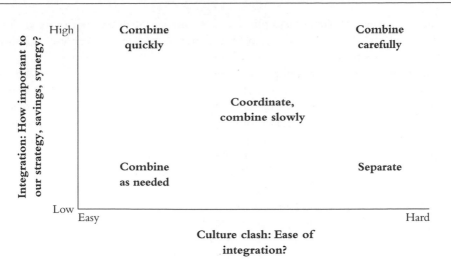

Figure 14.3: Importance versus ease of integration

others – as in high tech engineering, frontline healthcare, and gas stations. As a result, the desired cultural end state will feature a mix of these options. In such cases, the senior executive needs to assert up front

1. which components of the lead or parent company's culture will prevail,
2. where the partner's cultural autonomy will be honored,
3. where the two intend to blend cultures, and
4. where new cultural themes need to be developed through a transformational process.

When building a combined culture, partners need to declare which beliefs and values are sacrosanct and which are "in play" for discussion and development as combination planning and implementation move forward. Furthermore, executives need not have an intricate or fully worked out cultural end state from the get go. To the contrary, combination partners learn a lot about each other and their cultures only after they work together and the two sides get to know each other. Nor does culture change require a complete overhaul to current values and norms. In fact, successful culture change builds on the strengths of the precombination cultures. Even when one side's culture is going to predominate over the other's in the postcombination organization, the process of changing the target still requires considerable time to break down the old and introduce the new.

How do you factor in timing and the potential for a culture clash when planning integration? We worked on a study of over 100 banking mergers with the Management Analysis Center of Cambridge, Massachusetts, to develop a framework for this purpose (see figure 14.3). The north–south axis considers the business case for how much to integrate companies function by function. The key question is "How important is it to integrate this function for purposes of strategy, savings, or synergy?" The east–west axis posits the cultural case for integration. The key question is "How easy will it be to put the two functions together?" Answers to this question consider the degree of culture clash that will erupt and attendant consequences of staff turnover, customer defections, operational hassles, and managerial headaches.

From the matrix emerge several options. For instance, in the case of a high technology combination, involving software and hardware component manufacturers, senior management chose to "combine quickly" in the areas of marketing and product development. The two sides were familiar with each other's product lines and had worked together in several large customer accounts. As for the sales force, the case for rapid consolidation was compelling. However, the two sides had different sales approaches and there were considerable risks that sales people would leave for competitors unless their needs were addressed. Thus management went on a campaign with the combined sales forces that involved seminars on how the product lines fit together and attractive incentives for selling package deals combining products from the two partners. In addition, there were off site sessions held at resorts around the US where the two sales forces could mingle and socialize together – featuring hats, t-shirts, watches, and other corporate identity material and lots of drinks! At these events, senior sales management did plenty of "ego massaging." In short, their aim was to "combine carefully."

In turn, it was decided to combine as needed several human resource programs and various policies and procedures where savings would be modest as would the payoff. Importantly, it was decided to keep the basic research-and-development functions of the companies more or less separate. The same conclusion applied to manufacturing. Here, it was reasoned, there were no short-term benefits and some risks that either side, or both, would miss on schedules if caught up in a combination. At the same time, the company formed an internal technology council that brought together researchers and manufacturers to build camaraderie and inform strategy. This council held regular brown-bag lunches where technicians and professionals from the two sides could mingle and compare notes. What emerged was a kind of cultural coexistence between hardware and software types – under an overarching company culture of technical excellence.

Finally, it was decided to run several corporate systems – such as sales order/entry, scheduling, and the like – in parallel at least through the first year of the combination. That way sales personnel could focus on customers, and manufacturing on deadlines, without the hassles and hang-ups entailed when integrating systems. In most instances, the lead company, with generally superior systems, took things over, though, in several cases, new systems were developed and "eased" into place. The combined company today has a clear and shared culture overall, but also has distinctive subcultures that vary by function and, for those who remember, by precombination cultures.

Rites and Rituals

When a firm is to be absorbed, its people have to deal with the loss of their "old ways" and need some time to disengage from their past identities. We find that a "grieving meeting" can help them to move through stages of denial, anger, and loss. In such sessions, acquired executives mourn together the end of what one group called the end of their "glory days" and can speak to the impending breakup of their team and organization. This ritual prepares them to adopt "new ways" and to establish new identities, whether or not they remain in the combined firm. That said, grieving is not necessarily the right choice when you are building something new. After its merger with McDonnell-Douglas, seminars on "dealing with loss" at Boeing were quickly abandoned when course leaders learned that most people were raring to go into the merger and not hung up at all on where they had been.

The problem is that most executives underestimate and underresource the tasks of managing the human and cultural aspects of the combination process. After months of plotting a deal, identifying candidates, selecting a target, negotiating the terms, and waiting for legal approval, most senior executives have psychologically moved on and are more inclined to look ahead to their next combination rather than carefully lead and manage the current merger, acquisition, or alliance. As one senior manufacturing executive told us, "acquiring is fun; integrating is hell." So, senior executives hand off the work of combination management to their reports, who have neither the vision nor the budget to do an adequate job of culture building.

In cases where the two companies aspire to integrate based on the "best of both," it helps to have both sides identify values and practices of which they are most proud. The top teams at Chemical Bank and Manufacturers Hanover, as an example, separately listed cultural elements that they wanted to carry forward into their combined entity. The "new" Chemical that emerged emphasized reliable work processes and speedy delivery – strengths that the respective partners brought to the deal. This activity also highlighted "undesirable" cultural characteristics, such as bureaucracy, which were present in the pre-merger partners but weakened or eliminated in the process of combining the banks. Interestingly, this exercise was not repeated when Chemical subsequently combined with Chase Manhattan. More than a few veteran bankers have noted that neither Chemical nor Manny Hanny has been integrated into the "new" Chase.

When the desired end state is cultural transformation, we favor quite a different approach. Here, rather than value pre-merger strengths, it is useful for people to find fault with their "old" cultures. Research has shown that self-criticism is an important element in attitude change. As the task here is to invent new ways of doing things, self-criticism aims at freeing people up from prior commitments and bring to light sacred cows. One CEO met these requirements superbly when he said to his newly combined top team, "We have a half-ass approach to serving customers and you have a half-ass way of doing it. If we put our two ways together, we'll make a complete ass of ourselves!" His challenge stimulated transition managers to benchmark customer service outside their company, and their industry, and ultimately develop an entirely new approach.

Transformation: A Case Study

John Lee, a venture capitalist and turnaround artist, took over the reins of Hexcel Corporation in the early 1990s and brought the firm out of bankruptcy with new financing and disciplined management. As the global chemicals business began to shake-out, Lee purchased the composites business of Ciba-Geigy through a complex stock exchange and additional cash and securities. No sooner was the ink dried on this deal than Lee bought a division of Hercules. In just a few years, a company on the brink of collapse had through two acquisitions achieved a "global presence" in the market of structural materials used in aerospace and other select industries. The question facing Lee and his management team was, what kind of culture would the firm need?

At a series of meetings, Lee and his team first had to grapple with "Who are we"? According to extant organizational charts, Hexcel was a mix of strategic business units (SBUs) that manufactured lightweight materials used in airplane interiors, boats, and skis, plus structured honeycomb products used in building, transport, and some consumer products goods. The boom in aerospace, modernization of railroads, and opportunities abroad put a gleam in the eye of attendees when they contemplated the prospects for growth in each of their SBUs. As these several SBUs were vertically integrated, from weaving to fabrication to the creation of structures, its was agreed by the executives that they would work cooperatively to deliver high-performance products on a global scale at a reasonable price.

Through a series of highly interactive dialogues among the executive team members – reviewing the "theory of the case" underlying their combinations, sizing up the competition and market trends, and sharing their personal visions of where each would take the company as a whole – a new idea was born. Hexcel would become the "franchise player" in the still emerging "engineered components industry." This opened up new markets: automobiles, the wings and engines of airplanes, and a whole swath of industrial and durable goods that were currently constructed from steel or aluminum. "My God," one SBU head concluded, "we are creating an industry!"

At the same time, the pre-merger cultures of the three combining companies were decidedly oriented to old lines of business. Executives from each entity joined in a culture clarification exercise in which they described their own prior company cultures and perceptions of one another. Then, to stimulate thinking about what kind of culture was needed in going forward, groups were formed, joining executives from each of the pre-merger firms. They participated in a variety of activities to understand more fully the pre-merger cultures, and to identify how they could work together as part of Hexcel. One activity, a take-off on the TV show *Jeopardy*, had "contestants" guess – for $10 – which of the three pre-merger firms was most bureaucratic, least customer oriented, or slowest to innovate. Together, the executives could laugh at some of their prior ways of operating and build a shared perspective on their desired new culture. And the process of going through these activities created some bonding time to contribute to a "one team going forward" mindset.

There were strategic and operational challenges in the integration. The post-merger Hexcel had to lower the life cycle costs of products, provide environmentally superior product alternatives, and structure the business to operate globally and with a maximum of fiscal responsibility. To achieve these aims, the combined company had to develop and solidify norms of transparency and open communication across hitherto independent SBUs and establish a workable transfer pricing system. In line with aspirations to become more market oriented, the business heads had performance measures correlated with shareholder value and compensation tied to stock performance. And, in a most unexpected fashion, the heads of business in France and the United Kingdom began to exchange production information and communicate regularly with each other's staffs. Here is a case where a merger was managed in a manner in which the "old way" was abandoned and a new one is taking shape – a true cultural transformation.

Culture Building Ceremonies

Finally, there is a need to develop symbols of the new culture. One firm's acquisition brought together sides with a history of bitter competition and a strong dislike for one another. Executives at the top of the combined organization forged good working relationships, but middle managers continued to hold onto their precombination attitudes and behaviors. To counter this, each of the 80 middle managers in the business unit took part in either individual or group interviews to express their views on impediments to building a unified culture. At a follow-up offsite meeting, small groups reviewed the data, described the issues and identified actions that they and their leaders could take to minimize their negative impact. A presentation on common issues and success factors in combining organizations broadened managers' awareness of actions that could be taken to build better working relationships.

While the problem identification process and presentation succeeded at raising awareness on an intellectual level, the managers needed to be moved at a deeper, more emotional level if they were going to let go of their old ways. The highlight of the meeting, then, was a "graduation" ceremony. After the presentation, managers discussed their ideas for successful combination in small groups. They came back together as a large group, and each one was asked to write down "the three worst ways in which the combination could affect me personally." Each also received a sheet of stationery with his or her former company's letterhead and an old business card. Managers then were asked to stand up and were led outside where a wooden coffin awaited. Off to the side, a marching band sounded a somber funeral march.

One by one, each of the 80 managers stepped up to the coffin, crumpled his or her worst-case list, letterhead, and business card and tossed them in. As the last managers stepped back from the coffin, the group heard a low, grumbling noise. Slowly, a 100-ton paver rolled around the corner and headed straight at the group. At first the managers stood paralyzed, unsure of what was to transpire. The band broke into a rousing rendition of "On, Wisconsin," and the paver veered toward the wooden casket, flattening it and its contents. Spontaneous cheering broke out among the managers as the paver rolled back and forth on top of the coffin.

Abuzz with excitement, the managers returned inside. As they entered the building, they received academic caps and gowns and instructions to put them on. Ushers assembled the managers into two orderly lines and marched them into an auditorium where banners proclaiming "Congratulations, Graduates!" awaited them. Once all were seated, their senior executive welcomed them and embarked on the classic graduation speech: "The day has come for which we have all worked so hard to prepare you. It is now your turn:

Our destiny lies in your generation's hands." The managers sat quietly, absorbed in the speech, appreciating the meaning of these words for them. Then the ushers brought one row of "graduates" at a time to their feet and marched them up to the stage. There, the senior executive presented each on with a diploma, a "Masters of Merger Management," and a graduation gift – a share of company stock. After all proceeded across the stage and back to their seats, the group turned the tassels on their caps from left to right and proclaimed that they had graduated into their positions as contributors in the postcombination organization.

This effort did not eliminate the culture clash. But it did minimize unintended consequences, prepare all involved to join forces, and serve as a visible symbol of a new company culture.

NOTES

1   We have also worked with many of the companies featured in this article. Material on Time-Warner, IBM-Lotus, Hexcel's transformation, SBC and Ameritech, Mt. Sinai and Samaritan Hospitals, Boeing's deals, Chemical Bank and Manufacturer's Hanover, Molson, and Carling O'Keefe, companies A and B, X, and Y, and from Campbell-Ewald, come from our files.

REFERENCES

Bower, J. L. 2001. Not all M&As are alike – and that matters. *Harvard Business Review* 79 (3):92–101.

Buono, A. F., Bowditch, J. L., and Lewis, J. W., III. 1985. When cultures collide: The anatomy of a merger. *Human Relations* 38 (5):477–500.

Cartwright, S., and Cooper, C. L. 1996. *Managing Mergers, Acquisitions, and Strategic Alliances: Integrating People and Cultures*. Woburn, MA: Butterworth-Heinemann.

Marks, M. L. 1999. Adding cultural fit to your diligence checklist. *Mergers and Acquisitions* 34 (3): 14–20.

Marks, M. L., and Mirvis, P. H. 1992. Tracking the impact of mergers and acquisitions. *Personnel Journal* (April):70–9.

Marks, M. L., and Mirvis, P. H. 1993. The stiff challenge in integrating cross-border mergers. *Mergers and Acquisitions* 70 (4):37–41.

Marks, M. L., and Mirvis, P. H. 1997. *Joining Forces: Making One Plus One Equal Three in Mergers, Acquisitions, and Alliances*. San Francisco: Jossey-Bass.

Marks, M. L., and Mirvis, P. H. 2001. Making mergers and acquisitions work: Strategic and psychological preparation. *Academy of Management Executive* 15 (2):80–94.

Mirvis, P. H. 1994. Merged teams. In R. L. Elledge and S. L. Phillips (eds.), *Team Building for the Future*. San Diego: University Associates.

Mirvis, P. H., and Marks, M. L. 1991. *Managing the Merger*. Englewood Cliffs, NJ: Prentice Hall.

Mirvis, P. H., and Marks, M. L. 1992. The human side of merger planning: Assessing and analyzing "fit." *Human Resource Planning* 15 (3):69–92.

Mirvis, P. H., and Sales, A. S. 1990. Feeling the elephant: Culture change following a corporate acquisition and buyback. In B. Schneider (ed.), *Organizational Climate and Culture*. San Francisco: Jossey-Bass.

Nahavandi, A., and Malekzadeh, A. R. 1988. Acculturation in mergers and acquisitions. *Academy of Management Review* 13 (1):79–90.

Rose, F. 2000. Reminder to Steve Case: Confiscate the long knives. *Wired* (September):156–74.

Sales, A. S., and Mirvis, P. H. 1984. When cultures collide: Issues in acquisition. In J. R. Kimberly and R. E. Quinn (eds.), *Managing Organizational Transitions*. Homewood, IL: Irwin.

Schein, E. 1992. *Organizational Culture and Leadership*. 2nd ed. San Francisco: Jossey-Bass.

Shrivastava, P. 1986. Postmerger integration. *Journal of Business Strategy* 7 (1):65–76.

Siehl, C., Ledford, G., Silverman, R., and Fay, P. 1988. Preventing culture clashes from botching a merger. *Mergers and Acquisitions* 22 (5):51–7.

Weber, Y., and Schweiger, D. M. 1992. Top management culture conflict in mergers and acquisitions: A lesson from anthropology. *International Journal of Conflict Management* 3 (4):285–302.

15

Shaping History: Global Leadership in the Twenty-First Century

NANCY J. ADLER

> *We have a responsibility in our time, as others have had in theirs, not to be prisoners of history, but to shape history . . .*
> **Former US Secretary of State Madeleine K. Albright, 1997**

Shaping history; that is the challenge of global leadership – creating a twenty-first century in which our organizations and the societies in which they operate enhance, rather than diminish, civilization. For global leaders, economic viability is necessary, but no longer sufficient for organizational, let alone societal, success.

Success; none of us can claim that the twentieth century exited at the level of success we aspire to, a success defined by peace, prosperity, compassion, and sustainability. As we ask ourselves which of the twentieth century's legacies we wish to pass on to the children of the twenty-first century, we are humbled into shameful silence. Yes, we have advanced science and technology, but at the price of a world torn asunder by a polluted environment, cities infested with social chaos and physical decay, an increasingly skewed income distribution that condemns large portions of the population to poverty (including people living in the world's most affluent societies), and rampant physical violence continuing to kill people in titularly limited wars and seemingly random acts of aggression. No, we did not exit the twentieth century with pride. Unless we collectively learn to treat each other and our planet in a more civilized way, it may soon become blasphemy to even consider ourselves a civilization (Rechtschaffen 1996).

Entering the Twenty-First Century

As the twentieth century becomes history, do the events of the opening years of the twenty-first century encourage us? Unfortunately, no. If anything, many economic and societal trends appear to be heading in the wrong direction. We need look no further than the events of September 2001 to be humbled into silence, if not despair. Review just a few of the facts from that tragic month.

September 2001 opened with the UN-sponsored World Conference Against Racism in Durban, South Africa.[1] As the world watched with high expectations, the conference drowned in a cacophony of intolerance, expressed by official delegates from more than 160 countries as well as by thousands of representatives of nongovernmental organizations. "The meeting, which was intended to celebrate tolerance and diversity, became an international symbol of divisiveness" (Swarns 2001, A1). According to the world press, the results reflected "less a new international unity than a collective exhaustion" (Slackman 2001, A1).

One week later, on September 11, terrorists destroyed the World Trade Center and parts of the Pentagon, killing over 3,000 people. In the immediate aftermath, while stock markets plummeted, public rhetoric and behavior became increasingly susceptible to simplistic definitions of good and evil and calls for large-scale military retaliation. The escalation of ignorance-based hatred attempting to pit the Western world against Islamic communities and nations became palpable. Perhaps the danger, absurdity, and pain can be best symbolized by the fate of a woman living far from both Durban and the World Trade Center. As the woman, a Montreal doctor, made her usual hospital rounds the week after the terrorist attacks, she was strangled. Why? Strictly because she is Muslim. Her status as a physician and good citizen, working daily to save the lives of her fellow human beings, was obliterated in the eyes of her attacker solely because she practices a religion he fails to understand.

Hate and intolerance, optimism reduced to hopelessness, compassion eclipsed by anger, ignorance motivating senseless action: Is this the scenario that will define the twenty-first century; that will define our children's future? Possibly, but hopefully not. Hope for a better outcome rests largely with the quality of business, political, and societal leadership offered by women and men worldwide.

Although from the perspective of September 2001 it seems otherwise, the twenty-first century need not become just a time of terrorism, intolerance, fear, and deteriorating economic conditions. It also could herald an era of unprecedented global communication, global contact, and global commerce; led in large part by global companies and organizations (Friedman 2000). The ability of global companies to work successfully across cultures, however, while better than the track record of participants at UN-racism conferences, remains humbling. Historically, three-quarters of all international joint ventures fail.[2] One wonders, at times, why societies choose to continue to become more globally interconnected and companies choose to continue to expand beyond their borders, when the track record of global cross-cultural relations remains so dismal.[3] Weaving the peoples of the world together, whether in companies or in the society at large, is clearly not easy. Our current approaches beg for new – or perhaps ancient-but-forgotten – perspectives. Is it not possible to imagine a world defined by peace and prosperity in the twenty-first century, to imagine a global civilization that we could bequeath with pride to our children and our children's children? Would not our wisest global leaders know how to guide us in creating such a world. Naïvely idealistic? Perhaps, but not historically. Such visionary leadership only appears naïve from the parochial perspective of the last 9,000 years.

As archaeologists and other scholars have observed, there have always been legends and writings about an earlier, more harmonious and peaceful age (Eisler 1987).[4] The Bible, for example, tells us of the Garden of Eden. But many, if not most people assume that these are only idyllic fantasies, expressing universal yearnings for seemingly impossible goals. Only now, thanks to new scientific dating methods and specific findings, are archaeologists exposing the facts, rather than the myths and fantasies, of our distant past (Gimbutas 1991).

New excavations reveal that these supposed legends derive not from idealistic fantasies, but from folk memories about real flesh and blood people who organized their societies along very different lines from our own. At Chatal Huyuk and Hajilar, for example, both located in modern day Turkey, archaeologists date communities to 7,000 BCE, 90 centuries ago. These communities were located in the middle of fertile plains, not in defensible positions against stone cliffs or atop mountains, nor surrounded by moats, walls, or other defense systems. Their art, moreover, shows no sign of either individual or community level violence. Excavations reveal only minimal indications of hierarchy.

Just as Columbus's discovery that the world was not flat made it possible for our ancestors to "find" a world that, in fact, had been here all along, the archaeologists' new findings allow us to rediscover prosperous communities that were organized peacefully and cooperatively with their neighbors (Eisler 1987). Their recent findings allow us to ground supposedly naïve, unattainable idealism in the reality of history. Perhaps not coincidentally, women led most of these communities.

Is Such a World Possible Again?

What would it take to remarry such idealism with contemporary global realities? First, we would need to again believe that prosperity and a civilized way of living together on this planet are possible, that twenty-first century humanity is capable of success, broadly defined. To that end, the archaeologists' findings are crucial. We know that we achieved such success once; the only question is if we can achieve it again in this century. Second, we would need to believe that change is possible, that society is capable of moving from a world organized around war and violence, the extremes of poverty and wealth, and an overall mentality of scarcity to one organized around peace, prosperity, compassion, and abundance. And third, we would need to move from discrete local perspectives to broadly encompassing global perspectives. We would need to move away from divisiveness and return to more unifying images and strategies. For humanity to embrace each of the beliefs needed to create a healthy, economically vibrant, and sustainable global society, we would need approaches to leadership that differ quite markedly from those offered by most leaders in recent history.

Where are we to find leaders to guide us toward such beliefs that differ so distinctly from those of the recent past? While most societal commentators continue to review men's historic patterns of leadership in search of models for twenty-first century success, few have begun to recognize, let alone appreciate, the equivalent patterns of historic and potential future contributions of women leaders. What could the world's women leaders

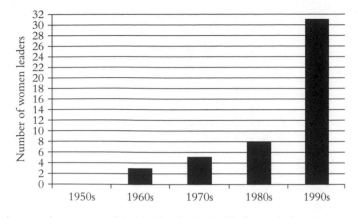

Figure 15.1: Increase in women political leaders in last half of twentieth century

bring to society? Have we begun to enter an era in which both male and female leaders – rather than just men alone – will literally and symbolically "shape history"?

Women Leading Countries and Companies: No Longer Men Alone

While rarely recognized or reported in the media, the trend toward women joining men in senior leadership began in the twentieth century and now, in the twenty-first century, has become inescapable. The pattern is easiest to see when observing leaders of countries. Whereas in the past almost all political leaders were men, the number of women selected to serve as president or prime minister of their country in the last half century has increased markedly, albeit from a negligible starting point. As highlighted in figure 15.1, no women presidents or prime ministers came into office in the 1950s, just 3 came into office in the 1960s, 5 in the 1970s, 8 in the 1980s, and 31 in the 1990s. The number of women serving their country at the highest level of political leadership increased by almost 100 percent in just the last decade. As listed in table 15.1, countries as dissimilar as France, India, and Rwanda have all selected women to lead them. While the increase is impressive, the total is not. Given that there are more than 185 countries in the world, many with both a president and a prime minister, and each with multiple leaders over the past 50 years, a total of 47 women in a half century is neither a large nor an impressive number.

Are the increasing numbers a new trend? Yes. Among the 47 women leaders, 85 percent are "firsts," the first woman whom their particular country has ever selected to lead them. Take Ruth Dreifuss, for example, who became President of Switzerland in 1999 after a 700-year history of male-led democracy. Among the women who are not "firsts" – those who followed another woman into office – all seven took office in just the last decade. As can be gathered from table 15.1, the countries that have selected a second woman to lead them (and, to date, no country has ever selected more than two women)

Table 15.1 A chronology of women political leaders

Country	Name	Office	Date
Sri Lanka	Sirimavo Bandaranaike	Prime Minister	1960–5; 1970–7; 1994–2000
India	(Indira Gandhi)	Prime Minister	1966–77; 1980–4
Israel	(Golda Meir)	Prime Minister	1969–75
Argentina	(Maria Estela [Isabel] Martínez de Perón)	President	1974–6
Central African Rep.	Elizabeth Domitien	Prime Minister	1975–6
Netherlands Antilles	Lucinda da Costa Gomez-Matheeuws	Prime Minister	1977
Portugal	Maria de Lourdes Pintasilgo	Prime Minister	1979
Bolivia	Lidia Gueiler Tejada	Interim President	1979–80
Great Britain	Margaret Thatcher	Prime Minister	1979–90
Dominica	Mary Eugenia Charles	Prime Minister	1980–95
Iceland	Vigdís Finnbógadottir	President	1980–96
Norway	Gro Harlem Brundtland	Prime Minister	1981; 1986–9; 1990–6
Yugoslavia	Milka Planinc	Prime Minister	1982–6
Malta	Agatha Barbara	President	1982–7
Netherlands Antilles	Maria Liberia-Peters	Prime Minister	1984; 1989–94
The Philippines	Corazon Aquino	President	1986–92
Pakistan	Benazir Bhutto	Prime Minister	1988–90; 1993–6
Lithuania	Kazimiera-Danute Prunskiene	Prime Minister	1990–1
Haiti	Ertha Pascal-Trouillot	President	1990–1
Burma (Myanmar)	Aung San Suu Kyi	Opposition Leader★★	1990–★★
East Germany	Sabine Bergmann-Pohl	President of the Parliament	1990
Ireland	Mary Robinson	President	1990–7
Nicaragua	Violeta Barrios de Chamorro	President	1990–6
Bangladesh	Khaleda Zia	Prime Minister	1991–6
France	Edith Cresson	Prime Minister	1991–2
Poland	Hanna Suchocka	Prime Minister	1992–3
Canada	Kim Campbell	Prime Minister	1993
Burundi	Sylvia Kinigi	Prime Minister	1993–4

Country	Name	Title	Date
Rwanda	(Agatha Uwilingiyimana)	Prime Minister	1993–4
Turkey	Tansu Çiller	Prime Minister	1993–6
Netherlands Antilles	Susanne Camelia-Romer	Prime Minister	1993; 1998–9
Bulgaria	Reneta Indzhova	Interim Prime Minister	1994–5
Sri Lanka	★Chandrika Bandaranaike Kumaratunga	Executive President & Former Prime Minister	1994–★
Haiti	Claudette Werleigh	Prime Minister	1995–6
Bangladesh	★Hasina Wajed	Prime Minister	1996–★
Liberia	★Ruth Perry	Chair, Ruling Council	1996–★
Ecuador	Rosalia Artega	President	1997
Bermuda	Pamela Gordon	Premier	1997–8
Ireland	★Mary McAleese	President	1997–★
New Zealand	Jenny Shipley	Prime Minister	1997–9
Guyana	Janet Jagan	Prime Minister, President	1997–9
Bermuda	★Jennifer Smith	Premier	1998–★
Lithuania	Irene Degutienė	Acting Prime Minister	4–18 May 1999
Mongolia	Nyam-Osorily Tuyaa	Acting Prime Minister	22–30 July 1999
Switzerland	Ruth Dreifuss	President	1999
Latvia	★Vaira Vike-Freiberga	President	1999–★
Panama	★Mireya Moscoso	President	1999–★
New Zealand	★Helen Clark	Prime Minister	1999–★
Finland	★Tarja Halonen	President	2000–★
Philippines	★Gloria Macapagal Arroyo	President	2001–★
Senegal	★Madior Boye	Prime Minister	2001–★
Indonesia	★Megawati Sukarnoputri	President	2001–★

( ) = No longer living

★ = In office as of December 2001

★★ = Party won 1990 election but prevented by military from taking office; Nobel Prize laureate.

Source: Adapted and updated from Nancy J. Adler. 1996. Global women political leaders, an invisible history, an increasingly important future. Leadership Quarterly 7 (1):136.
© Nancy J. Adler, 2001

represent a culturally, geographically, and economically very diverse group of nations; including Bangladesh, Bermuda, Haiti, Ireland, New Zealand, and Sri Lanka.[5]

Given these trends, there is no question that more women will be leading countries in the twenty-first century than have ever done so before. Already in the opening years of this century, four additional women have been selected to lead their country: Tarja Holonen in Finland, Gloria Macapagal Arroyo in the Philippines, Madior Boye in Sengal, and Megawati Sukarnoputri in Indonesia. Arroyo is the second woman to assume the presidency in the Philippines.

Women Leading Companies

Are there similar increases in the number of women leading major corporations? (See, among others, Adler 1997a, 1997b, 1999b, 2002; Adler and Izraeli 1994.) Whereas the patterns among business leaders are not as clear as those among political leaders, surveys suggest an increasing number of women leading global companies. The initial numbers, however, are very small. Even including executives who had held positions below the number one position in their company, women still held less than five percent of the most senior management positions in the United States and less than two percent of all senior management positions in Europe at the end of the twentieth century.[6] Moreover, not until the late 1990s did either the *Fortune* top 30 or the *Financial Times* FTSE 100 include a woman among their lists of leading CEOs.[7]

Contrary to popular belief, however, women's scarcity in leading major corporations does not reflect their absence as leaders of global companies. Unlike their male counterparts, most women chief executives either create their own entrepreneurial enterprises or assume the leadership of a family business (for a discussion of women who are global entrepreneurs, see Adler 1999a, 1999c).

Women Leading: A Global Trend, Not a Local Oddity

As table 15.2 highlights, similar to women-led countries, women-led businesses are distributed worldwide. They are not clustered in the few countries considered to be female-friendly – those countries providing women with equal property rights, equal access to education, healthcare, and employment, and equal protection under law. The women leaders come from some of the world's largest and smallest countries, some of the world's richest and poorest countries, and some of the world's most socially and economically advantaged and disadvantaged countries. They come, moreover, from every geographical region, represent all six of the world's major religions, and lead companies in a wide range of industries. The changing trend toward women's leadership is a broad-based, worldwide phenomenon, not a trend limited to a few particularly pro-women countries, a few particularly pro-women industries, or one particular region of the globe.

Moreover, most major corporations that select women as senior business leaders are not those that have implemented the most advanced female-friendly policies (such as those

Table 15.2 Global women business leaders

How many of us recognize the names of the world's women business leaders? All of the women included on the following list lead or have led companies with current revenues over US$1 billion, or for banks, with assets over US$1 billion:

Ernestina Herrera de Noble, Argentina, $1.2 billion; President and editorial director of Grupo Clarin, the largest-circulation Spanish newspaper in the world.

Francine Wachsstock, Belgium, $2.25 billion; President of the board of administrators, La Poste, Belgium's state-owned post office and largest employer.

Beatriz Larragoiti, Brazil, $2.9 billion; Vice president (and owner) of Brazil's largest insurance company, Sul America SA.

Maureen Kempston Darkes, Canada, $18.3 billion; President and General Manager of General Motors of Canada.

Ellen R. Schneider-Lenne, Germany, $458 billion in assets; Member of the Board of Managing Directors, Deutsch Bank AG, responsible for operations in the UK (deceased).

Nina Wang, Hong Kong, $1–2 billion in assets; Chairlady of Chinachem Group, property development.

Tarjani Vakil, India, $1.1 billion in assets; Chairperson and managing director, Export-Import Bank of India, highest ranking female banking official in Asia.

Margaret Heffernan, Ireland, $1.6 billion; Chairman, Dunnes Stores Holding Company, largest retailing company in Ireland.

Galia Maor, Israel, $35.6 billion in assets; CEO of Bank Leumi le-Israel.

Gloria Delores Knight, Jamaica, $l.86 billion in assets; President and managing director, The Jamaica Mutual Life Assurance Society, largest financial conglomerate in English-speaking Caribbean (deceased).

Sawako Noma, Japan, $2 billion; President of Kodansha Ltd, largest publishing house in Japan.

Harumi Sakamoto, Japan, $13 billion; Senior managing director, The Seiyu, Ltd, a supermarket and shopping center operator expanding throughout Asia.

Khatijah Ahmad, Malaysia, $5 billion; Chairman and managing director, KAF Group of Companies, financial services group.

Merce Sala i Schnorkowski, Spain, $1.1 billion; CEO of Renfe, Spain's national railway system, currently helping to privatize Colombian and Bolivian rail and selling trains to Germany.

Antonia Ax:son Johnson, Sweden, $6 billion; Chair, The Axel Johnson Group, retailing and distribution, more than 200 companies.

Elisabeth Salina Amorini, Switzerland, $2.8 billion; Chairman of the board, managing director, and chairman of the group executive board, Société Generale de Surveillance Holding

Table 15.2   (cont'd)

SA, the world's largest inspection and quality control organization, testing imports and exports in more than 140 countries.

Emilia Roxas, Taiwan, $5 billion; CEO, Asiaworld Internationale Groupe, multinational conglomerate.

Ellen Hancock, USA, $2.4 billion; Executive vice president and co-chief operating officer, National Semiconductor Corp.

The list includes most other countries of the world when companies are included with revenues over $250 million, including such women business leaders as:

Donatella Zingone Dini, Costa Rica, $300 million; Zeta Group, fifth largest business in Central America, conglomerate.

Nawal Abdel Moneim El Tatawy, Egypt, $357 million in assets; Chairman, Arab Investment Bank.

Colette Lewiner, France, $800 million; Chairman and CEO, SGN-Eurisys Group, world's largest nuclear fuels reprocessing company.

Jannie Tay, Singapore, $289 million; Managing director, The Hour Glass Ltd, high-end retailer of watches.

Aida Geffen, South Africa, $355 million; Chairman and managing director, Aida Holdings Ltd, residential commercial real estate firm.

Ann Gloag, United Kingdom, $520 million; Stagecoach Holdings Plc; Europe's largest bus company.

Linda Joy Wachner, United States, $1.1 billion (combined); Chairman of The Warnaco Group ($789 million) and Authentic Fitness Corporation ($266 million).

Liz Chitiga, Zimbabwe, $400 million; General manager and CEO, Minerals Marketing Corporation of Zimbabwe; in foreign-currency terms, the biggest business in Zimbabwe.

Source: Caitlin Kelly. 1996. 50 world-class executives. Worldbusiness 2 (2):20–31.

providing day-care centers and flextime). Among the 61 American *Fortune 500* companies employing women as chairmen, CEOs, board members, or one of the top 5 earners, for example, only 3 are the same companies that *Working Woman* identified as the most favorable for women employees.

As can be seen, the trends among political and business leaders appear similar. More women are leading global firms than has ever been true in the past, with the vast majority being the first woman that their particular firm has ever selected to hold such a position. Based on such increases, we can easily predict that women's voices will become a more common, and therefore more important, addition to the world's global leadership dialogue in the twenty-first century. Change is not only possible; it has already begun to happen.

Global Leadership: Numbers Are Not Enough

Increasing the number of women in leadership positions is certainly a necessary condition for equity, but it is not a sufficient condition for shaping history. The fundamental challenge is not simply to get more women into senior leadership. Rather, it is to get the type of leadership in the world that will foster global society's survival and prosperity.

Based on research observing women managers, many people have predicted that women leaders would exhibit the new sought-after twenty-first century leadership style, including incorporating new, more inclusive, trustworthy, and humanistic approaches. They base their predictions on the many researchers crediting a disproportionate number of women with many, if not all, of the following qualities:

> empathy, helpfulness, caring, and nurturance; interpersonal sensitivity, attentiveness to and acceptance of others, responsiveness to their needs and motivations; an orientation toward the collective interest and toward integrative goals such as group cohesiveness and stability; a preference for open, egalitarian, and cooperative relationships, rather than hierarchical ones; and an interest in actualizing values and relationships of great importance to community (see, among others, summary of traits in Fondas 1997, 260).

By contrast, traits that have been culturally ascribed to men include

> an ability to be impersonal, self-interested, efficient, hierarchical, tough minded, and assertive; an interest in taking charge, control, and domination; a capacity to ignore personal, emotional considerations in order to succeed; a proclivity to rely on standardized or "objective" codes for judgment and evaluation of others; and a heroic orientation toward task accomplishment and a continual effort to act on the world and become something new or [different] (Fondas 1997, 260).

To date, however, no research focused on senior leaders (rather than employees or managers) exists to support or refute claims that women would make more effective twenty-first century leaders than men. Not surprisingly, similar to men, women exhibit a wide range of leadership visions, approaches, and levels of effectiveness (Adler 2003). One need look no further than the ouster on corruption charges of Turkey's former prime minister, Tansu Çiller, or the demise of Sotheby's former CEO Diana Brooks (indicted, along with Sotheby's former chairman, Alfred Taubman, on criminal conspiracy and price fixing charges) to know that women leaders, like their male counterparts are neither perfect nor a universal solution to the world's or any particular company's problems.[8]

Do some women exhibit exemplary styles of leadership? Yes; not all women, but certainly many give us reason for hope, especially those not mimicking the style of leadership of most twentieth-century male leaders. Ireland's first woman president, Mary Robinson, for example, brilliantly took her commitment to human rights into the presidency of Ireland, transforming the position from one of ceremony to one of substance. She then let go of the presidency – a typically feminine use of power, "letting go" – in order to continue her human rights agenda on a broader, worldwide scale at the United

Nations. Aung San Suu Kyi, the legally elected leader of Burma (Myanmar), was incarcerated in her own home by the military for more than six years. While under house arrest, the military dictatorship even denied her the right to see her husband one last time before he died of cancer. Given her situation, does Suu Kyi advocate annihilating the military dictatorship that has imprisoned her and her people for so long? No, to this day, she fearlessly advocates dialogue – words, not guns – a unity strategy typically attributed to what many consider to be a more feminine approach to leadership.

Agatha Uwilingiyimana, the former prime minister of Rwanda, similarly exemplifies the courage it takes to break with traditional leadership approaches and use unifying strategies – strategies many attribute to a more feminine approach. By 1993, the level of violence in Rwanda had forced the Hutus and Tutsis to seriously consider signing a peace agreement. But who would have the courage to sign such a paper with the sworn enemy? No one relished the risk, as extremists on both sides considered those who would sign as traitors. At that crucial moment in Rwanda's history, no man accepted the risk of becoming a peace-making prime minister. In July 1993, it was Uwilingiyimana, in the name of peace and unity, who agreed to serve her country as prime minister. Less than a month later, the peace agreement was signed. Less than a year later, extremist Hutus began hunting down and killing Tutsis and moderate members of the Hutu government. Agatha Uwilingiyimana, a moderate Hutu, was one of the first murdered. Although reported as a Tutsi murder in the Western press, Agatha was killed by her own people, by extremist Hutus who rejected her attempts at unity and peace.

Is the situation in Rwanda so extreme that it would be inappropriate for the rest of the world to attempt to learn anything from Uwilingiyimana's story? The answer is a resounding no. Think for a moment of some of the other women leaders with whom we are perhaps more familiar. Former President of the Philippines, Corazon Aquino, like Uwilingiyimana, also believed in building coalitions with the opposition. She invited members of both her own and the opposition party to join her presidential cabinet. The world press, viewing her leadership through the obsolete lens of divisive twentieth century perspectives, labeled her invitation to the opposition as the naïve act of a housewife who doesn't know what it means to be president. In response, Aquino explained that she never again wanted political differences resolved by murder. She wanted to preclude the possibility that any persons would have to watch the political assassination of their spouse as she had to witness when her husband, Benigno Aquino, the then opposition leader, was murdered upon his return to the Philippines. In her cabinet, animated discussion replaced murder as the accepted form of political discourse.

Aquino, similar to Robinson in Ireland, refused to run for a second term because she believed that democracy, not her longevity as president, was more important. Having lived through years of Marcos's dictatorship, she believed that Filipinos deserved to choose a new president after she had served her initial six year term. Each of these leaders went outside of the patterns of history and said "Enough! There has to be a better way."

Are the stories of more inclusive leadership all stories of political leaders? Of course not. Rebecca Mark, for example, as CEO of Enron Development Corporation, negotiated the first major commercial agreement among the Arabs and Israelis following the Oslo Peace Accords.[9] Rebecca Mark saw coalition building – including across groups that the world had always viewed as enemies – as a smart business practice. Did people question her judgment? Of course. Did she do what hadn't been done before? Yes. As Rebecca Mark's decisions show, true leadership, by definition, is not the act of the usual.

As both business and political leaders, women regularly challenge conventional wisdom and practice in their leadership approaches. Britain's Anita Roddick, founder and former CEO of The Body Shop, for example, challenged conventional practice in the beauty and healthcare industry in her product design (e.g., by not allowing animal testing), in her marketing (by not promising unattainable beauty), in her organization design, and in her strategic intent (e.g., by tying societal commitments to product strategies). Sweden's Antonia Ax:son Johnson, CEO of the fourth-generation, 200-company family business, The Ax:son Johnson Group, eliminated all war- and violence-related toys from the company's department stores. Although the toys would have increased revenues, they were not consistent with her concept of "the good company."

People's Aspirations: Hope, Change, and Unity

To understand the dynamics of the twenty-first century, we must go beyond strictly attempting to assess if, or how, women's approaches to leadership differ from those of their male counterparts. We know that they differ in some cases, but certainly not in all, or maybe most, cases. Given the absence of consistently substantiated differences and, at the same time, the rapid increase in the number of women leaders (especially in the last decade), we must ask why countries and companies worldwide – for the first time in modern history and after so many years of male-dominated leadership – are choosing (often for the first time) women to lead them. It appears that people worldwide may want what all women symbolize, but what only some women leaders exhibit.

Leadership Symbolism: The Possibility of Change

Perhaps the most powerful and attractive symbolism of women leaders is the possibility of significant change. When a woman is chosen to become president, prime minister, or CEO – when no other woman has ever held such an office and when few people thought she would be selected, people begin to believe that other, more substantive and less symbolic changes are also possible. The combination of a woman being an outsider at senior leadership levels previously controlled by men and of her beating the odds provides powerful public imagery supporting the possibility of broad-based societal and organizational change. The fact that most women, to date, are the first women to assume senior leadership positions underscores the beginning not just of symbolic change, but of real change. Mary Robinson's presidential acceptance speech captures the unique event of Ireland electing its first woman president coupled with the possibility of national change: "I was elected by men and women of all parties and none, by many with great moral courage who stepped out from the faded flags of Civil War and voted for a new Ireland. And above all by the women of Ireland . . . who instead of rocking the cradle rocked the system, and who came out massively to make their mark on the ballot paper, and on a new Ireland."[10]

The fact that the women who become leaders are perceived to differ from their male counterparts (whether or not they actually do) fosters the sense that change is possible. In Kenya, for example, when Charity Ngilu became the first woman to run for the presidency, many Kenyans saw her as representing "a complete break with [the] divisive tribal politics of the past" (McKinley 1997, section 1, 3). As one Kenyan observed, "Charity is talking about unity, and this unity will unite both men and women . . . If we vote for a man, there will be no change. With a woman, there will have to be a big change" (McKinley 1997, section 1, 3).

The symbolism supporting the possibility of change is almost identical in the business world, where most women CEOs are "firsts"; not only the first woman, but also often the first outsider that the company has selected to lead them. Notable examples include Marjorie Scardino, the first woman, first outsider, and first American to become CEO of Britain's Pearson Plc, as well as the first woman to lead a *Financial Times* FTSE 100 firm; Carly Fiorina, the first woman and first outsider to lead Hewlett-Packard and a *Fortune* top-30 firm; and Charlotte Beers, the first woman and the first outsider that Ogilvy and Mather Worldwide had ever brought in to lead their worldwide advertising business.

Leadership Symbolism: The Possibility of Unity

In addition to the possibility of change, women also symbolize unity – and women leaders are no exception. Nicaragua's former president Violetta Chamorro, for example, became a symbol of national unity following her husband's assassination. Chamorro even claimed "to have no ideology beyond national 'reconciliation'" (Benn 1995). Chamorro's ability to bring her four adult children (two of whom were prominent Sandanistas while the other two equally prominently opposed the Sandanistas) together every week for Sunday dinner achieved near legendary status in war-torn Nicaragua (Saint-Germain 1993, 80). Chamorro gave symbolic hope to the nation that it too could find peace based on a unity that would bring all Nicaraguans together. That the behavior of a woman leader led to family unity becoming a symbol for national unity is neither surprising nor coincidental.

On the basis of similar dynamics, Pakistan's former prime minister Benazir Bhutto and the Philippines former president Corazon Aquino each came to symbolize unity for their strife-torn countries. As the scope of governments' influence and companies' operations expand to encompass the world, the desire and need for unifying strategies increase. Currently, women symbolize the hope for unity within multinational and multicultural constituencies.

The hope that women leaders will foster unity and inclusiveness is heightened by the ways in which women gain access to power. In contrast to many of their male counterparts, most women leaders develop and use broad-based popular support, rather than relying primarily on traditional, hierarchical political party or corporate structural support.

This broad-based inclusiveness, often seen as a precursor of other hoped-for unifying strategies, has been particularly apparent among the aspiring women political leaders who often are not seriously considered as potential candidates by their country's main political parties. They are consequently forced to gain support directly from the people (which, of course, is a profoundly democratic process).

Mary Robinson, for example, campaigned in more small communities in Ireland than any previous presidential candidate before either her party or the opposition took her seriously. The opposition later admitted that they did not seriously consider Robinson's candidacy until it was too late to stop her (Finlay 1990). Similarly, Corazon Aquino, whose campaign and victory were labeled the People's Revolution, held more than 1,000 rallies during her campaign, while incumbent Ferdinand Marcos held only 34 (Col 1993). Likewise, Benazir Bhutto, who succeeded in becoming Pakistan's first woman and youngest prime minister, campaigned in more communities than any politician before her. Only later did her own party take her seriously (Anderson 1993; Weisman 1986).

In business, the disproportionate number of women who choose to start their own companies echoes the same pattern of broad-based support. Rather than attempting to climb the corporate ladder and to break through the glass ceiling into senior leadership positions in established corporations, these entrepreneurial women build their success directly in the marketplace. The types of broad-based support developed by women political leaders and entrepreneurs differ only in their source, with the former enjoying support directly from the electorate whereas the latter gains support directly from the marketplace. In both cases, the base of support is outside of the traditional power structure and therefore more representative of new and more diverse opinions and ideas. Their sources of support, and therefore of power, more closely reflect the flattened network of emerging twenty-first century organizations and society than they do the more centralized and limited power structures of most twentieth century organizations.

Shaping History

As President of the Czech Republic Vaclav Havel (1994, A27) has said, the world is "going through a transitional period, when something is on the way out and something else is painfully being born," it is not surprising that people worldwide are attracted to women leaders' symbolic message of bringing change, hope, and the possibility for unity. The interplay of women's and men's styles of leadership will define the contours and potential success of twenty-first century society. The risk is in encapsulating leaders, both women and men, in approaches that worked well in the twentieth century but foretell disaster for the twenty-first century. The challenge is in the urgency and complexity. As poet David Whyte (1994) enjoins us:

> *The journey begins right here, in the middle of the road,*
> *right beneath your feet.*
> *This is the place.*
> *There is no other place, there is no other time.*

NOTES

Please do not cite this chapter, in whole or in part, without my written permission. I can be contacted at the address below:

Nancy J. Adler
McGill University
Faculty of Management
1001 rue Sherbrooke ouest
Montreal, Quebec, Canada H3A 1G5
Phone: 514-398-4031 Fax: 514-398-3876 Email: nancy.adler@mcgill.ca

1   The official title of the UN Conference was the United Nations' World Conference Against Racism, Racial Discrimination, Xenophobia and Related Intolerance.

2   A. T. Kearney study reported in Haebeck et al. (2000) and in Schuler and Jackson (2001). The same study, as cited by Schuler and Jackson, concludes that "only 15 percent of mergers and acquisitions in the US achieve their objectives, as measured by share value, return on investment and post-combination profitability." For research on the instability of international joint ventures, see summary by Yan (1999). Although the definitions (complete termination versus significant change of ownership) and overall results vary, numerous studies have reported substantial international joint venture instability, including 55 percent termination reported by Harrigan (1988), 49 percent termination reported by Barkema and Vermeulen (1997), and 68 percent instability through termination or acquisition reported by Park and Russo (1996). Also see Gary Hammel's classic 1991 article.

3   For a notable exception, see the description of the Norway-based global company Norske Skog, in Adler (2003).

4   This section is excerpted and adapted from Riane Eisler's insightful 1987 book (see book jacket).

5   Countries with two women presidents and prime ministers include Bangladesh with Khaleda Zia (1991–6) and Hasina Wajed (1996–), Bermuda with Pamela Gordon (1997–8) and Jennifer Smith (1998–), Haiti with Ertha Pascal-Trouillot (1990–1) and Claudette Werleigh (1995–6), Ireland with Mary Robinson (1990–7) and Mary McAleese (1997–), New Zealand with Jenny Shipley (1997–) and Helen Clark (1999–), and Sri Lanka with Sirimavo Bandaranaike (1960–5; 1970–7; 1994–2000) and Chandrika Bandaranaike Kumaratunga (1994–).

6   United States statistics based on the research of Catalyst as originally published by Wellington (1996). European statistics reported in Dwyer et al. (1996).

7   Carly Fiorina, CEO of Hewlett-Packard and Marjorie Scardino, CEO of Pearson Plc.

8   For a description of the case against Sotheby's former chairman, A. Alfred Taubman, on criminal conspiracy charges for a price-fixing scheme with archrival auction house Christie's, see the business press in November–December 2001, including the *New York Times* reporting (see, e.g., Blumenthal and Vogel 2001).

9   Note that this was long before the demise in 2001 of Enron, under the leadership of chairman Kenneth L. Lay. Among many other business articles covering Enron's downfall, see Oppel and Atlas (2001).

10   Speech in the RDS, Dublin, November 9, 1990, as reported in Finlay (1990, 1).

REFERENCES

Adler, Nancy J. 1997a. Global leaders: A dialogue with future history. *International Management* 1 (2):21–33.

Adler, Nancy J. 1997b. Global leadership, women leaders. *Management International Review* 37 (1):171–96.

Adler, Nancy J. 1999a. Global entrepreneurs: Women, myths, and history. *Global Focus* 11 (4):125–34.

Adler, Nancy J. 1999b. Global leaders: Women of influence. In Gary Powell (ed.), *Handbook of Gender and Work*. Thousand Oaks, CA: Sage.

Adler, Nancy J. 1999c. Twenty-first-century leadership: Reality beyond the myths. In Alan M. Rugman (series ed.) and Richard Wright (vol. ed.), *Research in Global Strategic Management*. Vol. 7 in series *International Entrepreneurship: Globalization of Emerging Business*. Greenwich, CT: JAI.

Adler, Nancy J. 2002. Women joining men as global leaders in the new economy. In Martin Gannon and Karen Newman (eds.), *Handbook of Cross-Cultural Management*. Oxford: Blackwell.

Adler, Nancy J. 2003. Global companies, global society: There is a better way. In Marshall Goldsmith, James Belasco, and Larraine Segil (eds.), *The Leader as Partner*. New York: AMACOM.

Adler, Nancy J., and Izraeli, Dafna (eds.). 1994. *Competitive Frontiers: Women Managers in a Global Economy*. Cambridge, MA: Blackwell.

Albright, Maleleine K. 1997. Harvard commencement address as reported in the *New York Times*, June 6, A8.

Anderson, Nancy Fix. 1993. Benazir Bhutto and dynastic politics: Her father's daughter, her people's sister. In Michael A. Genovese (ed.), *Women as National Leaders*. Newbury Park, CA: Sage.

Barkema, Harry, and Vermeulen, Freek. 1997. What differences in the cultural backgrounds of partners are detrimental for international joint ventures? *Journal of International Business Studies* 28 (4):845–64.

Benn, Melissa. 1995. Women who rule the world. *Cosmopolitan*, February.

Blumenthal, Ralph, and Vogel, Carol. 2001. Trial prosecutor depicts ex-chief of Sotheby's as price fixer. *New York Times*, December 4, A20.

Col, Jeanne Marie. 1993. Managing softly in turbulent times: Corazon C. Aquino, President of the Philippines. In Michael A. Genovese (ed.), *Women as National Leaders*. Newbury Park, CA: Sage.

Dwyer, P., Johnston, M., and Lowry, L. 1996. Europe's corporate women. *Business Week*, April 15, 40–2.

Eisler, Riane. 1987. *The Chalice and the Blade: Our History, our Future*. San Francisco: Harper and Row (book jacket).

Finlay, Fergus. 1990. *Mary Robinson: A President with a Purpose*. Dublin: O'Brien.

Fondas, Nanette. 1997. The origins of feminization. *Academy of Management Review* 22 (1):257–82.

Friedman, Thomas L. 2000. *The Lexus and the Olive Tree: Understanding Globalization*. New York: Anchor.

Gimbutas, Marija. 1991. *The Civilization of the Goddess: The World of Old Europe*. San Francisco: HarperSanFrancisco.

Haebeck, M. H., Kroger, F., and Trum, M. R. 2000. *After the Mergers: Seven Rules for Successful Post-Merger Integration*. New York: Prentice Hall/FT.

Hammel, Gary. 1991. Competition for competence and inter-partner learning within international strategic alliances. *Strategic Management Journal* 12 (1):83–103.

Harrigan, Kathryn R. 1988. Strategic alliances and partner asymmetries. In F. Contractor and P. Lorange (eds.), *Cooperative Strategies in International Business*. Lexington, MA: Lexington Books.

Havel, Vaclav. 1994. The new measure of man. *New York Times*, July 8, A27.

McKinley, J. C., Jr. 1997. A woman to run Kenya? One says, "Why not?" *New York Times* (world late edition), August 3, section 1, 3.

Oppel, Richard, A., Jr., and Atlas, Riva D. 2001. Hobbled Enron tries to stay on its feet. *New York Times*, December 4, C1, C8.

Park, Seung H., and Russo, Michael V. 1996. When competition eclipses cooperation: An event history analysis of joint venture failure. *Management Science* 42 (6):875–90.

Rechtschaffen, Stephan. 1996. *Timeshifting*. New York: Bantam Doubleday Dell Audio, 1996.

Saint-Germain, Michelle A. 1993. Women in power in Nicaragua: Myth and reality. In Michael A. Genovese (ed.), *Women as National Leaders*. Newbury Park, CA: Sage.

Schuler, Randall S., and Jackson, Susan E. 2001. Seeking an edge in mergers and acquisitions. *Financial Times*, October 22, special section, part 2: People Management.

Slackman, Michael. 2001. Divisive UN race talks end in accord. *Los Angeles Times*, September 9, A1.

Swarns, Rachel L. 2001. Race talks finally reach accord on slavery and Palestinian plight. *New York Times*, September 9, A1.

Weisman, S. R. 1986. A Daughter returns to Pakistan to cry for victory. *New York Times*, April 11, 12.

Wellington, Shelia W. 1996. *Women in Corporate Leadership: Progress and Prospects*. New York: Catalyst.

Whyte, David. 1994. *The Heart Aroused*. New York: Currency Doubleday.

Yan, Aimin, and Zeng, Ming. 1999. International joint venture instability: A critique of previous research, a reconceptualization, and directions for future research. *Journal of International Business Studies* 30 (2):397–414.

Index